MAIL CALL

MAIL CALL

*The Wartime Correspondence
of an American Couple
1943–1945*

Terri Halbreich David

*Full Court Press
Englewood Cliffs, New Jersey*

Brian AsackFirst Edition

Copyright © 2013 by Terri Halbreich David

Published in the United States of America
by Full Court Press, 601 Palisade Avenue
Englewood Cliffs, NJ 07632
www.fullcourtpressnj.com

ISBN 978-1-938812-07-1
Library of Congress Control No. 2012955150

*Editing and Book Design by Barry Sheinkopf for Bookshapers
(www.bookshapers.com)*

*Cover art from the author's collection
Author photo by Jay Feeley*

Colophon by Liz Sedlack

ACKNOWLEDGMENTS

I would like to thank my friend and mentor, Carol Grant Gould, for her expert editorial guidance in preparing this manuscript. Without her generous help, the book would be only a shadow of what it is now.

Carol's husband, James Gould, also deserves my deepest appreciation for his research into the naval war in the Pacific.

I would like to thank Barry Sheinkopf as well for his professional assistance and suggestions that expedited the book's publication.

And most important, I would like to thank my husband, Michael, for his constant support and encouragement throughout the entire process.

AUTHOR'S NOTE

This book is drawn from a collection of about six hundred letters that were exchanged between my parents during their wartime separation. To preserve the very human quality of this correspondence, I chose to arrange the text of this book by topic, setting aside the strict chronology of the letters. Organized in this way, the reader is given an opportunity to see how each theme evolves, and it permits some author commentary at appropriate moments. This format, which does not adhere to traditional timelines, may initially confuse the reader when a new chapter begins or when transitioning from one parent's letters to the other's. Noting the dates of the letters should help as a guide in placing the narrative within the eighteen-month period.

I hope that this editorial choice adds to the enjoyment of reading these lovely and often fascinating letters, and that the reader is left with a richer understanding of Lester and Shirley Halbreich's experiences of wartime separation.

FOREWORD

The USS Oxford

THE *USS OXFORD* (APA189), OR THE "BLUE OX," as she was often called by the men serving on board, was a Haskell-class attack ship 450 feet long and 62 feet wide, displacing 12,450 tons. The ship carried 480 enlisted men and 56 officers, including one lonely dentist from Brooklyn. While it was not a destroyer, it still had some weaponry on it, such as one 5 3/8-inch gun, and twelve 40-mm and ten 20-mm guns. The main purpose of the *Oxford* was to transport troops to and around combat zones. When she was assigned this duty, the number of personnel on board greatly exceeded the size of the permanent crew.

The *Oxford* was launched on July 12, 1944, which helps to explain Lester's call to active naval duty in Washington State at just that time, and she was officially commissioned on September 11, 1944. After test runs, she left the West Coast carrying 1,478 men on October 26, 1944, and reached New Guinea about two weeks later, on November 12.

Once in the Pacific, the *Oxford* served in the vicinity of New Caledonia and Florida and Mantis Islands. Between January 11 and 13, 1945, she participated in the landing at Lingayen Gulf, Luzon, in the Philippines, as part of a task group troop transport (TG 77.9).

The next stop was Guam, on her way to Pearl Harbor and her home port of San Francisco, where she arrived on May 11, 1945, in order to take on replacement troops. The European war had just ended, so those servicemen, no longer necessary there, were hurriedly transferred to the still-raging Pacific War, and the *Oxford* was probably ferrying some of these men from one theatre of war to the other. But the vessel's stay in port was too short to allow Lester and Shirley time to see each other, which was a strong disappointment to them both.

The Blue Ox left California after only a week, heading for the Southwest Pacific, to the Carolinas, the Philippines, New Guinea, and Eniwetok, where she arrived on July 22, 1945. A few days later she again headed for California, leaving on July 29 and arriving in early August, this time permitting the delighted couple a welcome reunion.

After repairs to the ship were completed, the *Oxford* left San Pedro, only to dock at San Diego and then San Francisco, finally heading back to Eniwetok on August 23 with more replacement troops. Once back in the Pacific, she made stops at Ulithi, Manila, Subic Bay, and Japanese ports, and finally returned to San Francisco in late November 1945, whereupon Lester was able to return to his family.

The *Oxford* was released from service in January 1946, sent to Norfolk, Virginia, and finally decommissioned that April. Her end came in 1974, when she was scrapped.

The War In The Pacific

JAPAN HAD INVADED PEARL HARBOR on December 7, 1941, the immediate cause of the United States entering World War II. This date was also just three weeks before Lester and Shirley's wedding. Initially, Japan was successful in numerous Pacific battles, as the United States had been unprepared for the war. By April 1942, the Japanese had conquered all of Southeast Asia, the Philippines, and Singapore, and then invaded New Guinea.

However, that was the high point of Japanese wartime success, as events began to turn for the Allied forces. In May 1942, the Battle of the Coral Sea stopped Japan from invading Australia, and in the next month, June 1942, the Battle of Midway prevented Japanese expansion into the North Pacific.

From then on, the Japanese regrouped and focused on the South Pacific. In August 1942, the United States invaded Guadalcanal, which began the huge war of attrition fought over many months through February 1943, when the Japanese finally gave up and evacuated. A naval stalemate then held for the following six months in the Pacific, while the United States rapidly accelerated war production. That stalemate began to change by September 1943 when the United States launched a campaign to retake New Guinea, which lasted through December.

The new year of 1944 saw the beginning of the effort to recapture Southeast Asia, as various islands were taken throughout that spring. In June 1944, the United States began to bomb Japan itself, largely destroying its air power, while also continuing to recover other Pacific islands. By October, just as the *USS Oxford* left the West Coast for the Pacific Theatre, the United States Navy began the task of liberating the Philippines. The Battle of Leyte Gulf, part of that larger effort, succeeded in destroying most of the Japanese navy.

The battles for the Philippines and for other islands continued into 1945. In March of that year Tokyo was firebombed; then Okinawa was invaded in April. In Europe, Germany surrendered in May, while the activity in the Pacific consisted largely of mopping-up actions (in Southeast Asia, the Philippines, and the islands), along with preparations for the invasion of Japan. These all continued through early August, until the dropping of the atomic bombs on Hiroshima and Nagasaki, on August 6 and 9, brought the Pacific War to a sudden end on August 14. However, as had been true in Europe, soldiers were not immediately discharged and sent home. There were on-going military needs in the recently conquered territories, and there were also requirements that had to be met in order to earn that trip home.

TABLE OF CONTENTS

INTRODUCTION

CHILDREN ARE NOT BORN to be historians of their little world. They do not interview their parents about events that happened earlier in their parents' lives. Children live in the moment, caring only about their own lives and about their friends.

I was fortunate to be a child in the 1950s, that decade of idealized happy family life that, for me, was a reality. My parents' love for each other and for their children allowed me to become a reasonably well-adjusted and productive adult, capable of having a professional life and lucky enough to find a husband very similar to my father.

Now I want to return the favor, albeit posthumously. After my mother's death my father handed me a plastic bag filled with the letters that they had written to each other during World War II. But it took another decade or more before I could overcome my ambivalence about violating their emotional privacy, so their letters remained unread. Eventually, some years after my father, too, had died, I finally decided to venture into their world of the 1940's.

I could not have imagined the wonderful surprise that awaited me. There, in black and white, I found the richly-textured and detailed account of my parents as a newlywed couple, very much in love but separated for month after month by the demands of war. Through these letters I was able to step back in time and come to know them years before I was born, to see them when they were very young, quite unlike the middle-aged or older couple I had known, and learn about their daily lives, their concerns, their friends, and their aspirations. I also had glimpses of my grandparents when they, too, were much younger, of my older brother as an infant, of my two aunts as teenagers, and of our other relatives.

Shirley and Lester, as special as they are to me, were not unique or in any way famous. Rather, they were emblematic of their time and place; and so their personal story becomes everyone's story and therefore, I believe, a story worth telling.

1

PROLOGUE

COUPLES MEET IN ALL sorts of ways—some prosaically, at work or on a blind date, perhaps electronically arranged today. Others, though, manage to become acquainted in a more uncommon manner. My parents fall right in the middle, just as they did throughout their lives.

It is the summer of 1941, those last idyllic months prior to our entrance into World War II, and eighteen-year-old Shirley Scheller was on an extended vacation, along with her parents, Sam and Rose, and her younger sister, Elaine, who was thirteen, at the Stevensville Hotel in the Catskills region of New York State. As was then the custom, the family was there for several weeks while Sam commuted to his work selling insurance in New York City, coming up for weekends. Shirley had just graduated from Erasmus Hall High School, in Brooklyn, and was about to enter New York University in the fall; the vacation was a carefree interlude between those two educational venues.

Lester Halbreich, twenty-four, was also at Stevensville that summer of 1941, but as a waiter, not a guest. He came from a poorer, working-class background, having grown up the son of a disabled shoe salesman. He was raised mostly in Brooklyn, not far from Shirley, but they had never met, and his family had eventually migrated to the Bronx. He was a January 1933 graduate of Boys High School—at age fifteen, having skipped a few grades earlier in school due to higher intellectual and test-taking skills.

Upon graduation, Lester entered Cornell University's School of Agriculture, and again graduated early, in three and a half years. He went on to earn his master of science degree, also at Cornell. His thesis, "On the Growth of the Tuber," was the source of many family jokes.

Lester, or Les, as he was commonly known, was about to start a career as a science teacher when serious illness prevented it. Mastoiditis had previously claimed the life of Les's older brother, Ralph, at seventeen, but the invention of sulfa drugs in the intervening years saved Les's life. However, while recuperating at home, the direction of his life changed; he was accepted by the New York University Dental School, and entered in the autumn of 1938.

Lester would have preferred to attend medical school but there was still a quota limiting the number of slots available in any class for Jews and other minorities. Les, who was Jewish, assumed that he would not have been accepted, despite having an older cousin who had managed to become a physician and who urged him to follow in his footsteps. Lester had already followed this cousin to Cornell.

These years of education, first at Cornell and then at NYU, put a severe economic strain upon Lester's family, who could not really afford the expense. Most of his age-mates were attending a branch of the City University system, which was then free. Family lore is replete with stories of the sacrifices made to keep him in these expensive schools, particularly in the recollection of his younger sister, Roslyn, eight years his junior. She was born in 1925 and was only eight when Lester left for college, and he would not graduate from dental school for nine more years, when Roslyn was seventeen. Those nine years, which spanned the Depression, were years of relative privation for the family, of doing without, so Lester could succeed.

Lester's parents, Charles and Esther Halbreich, led lives fairly typical of urban immigrants of the era. Charlie had been born and raised in Tsarist Russia, in 1884, in the Jewish Pale of Settlement, to a relatively prosperous innkeeper father. But Charlie's mother had died during his adolescence and his father had remarried, which Charlie could never accept. He and his older siblings had all adored their mother. At about that time, he became eligible for the draft into the Russian army. Each Russian family had to supply a son to the draft, and this draft was no mere two-year stint, but extended for a lifetime of service—about twenty-five years. For Jews, despised almost universally in Russia, it was a fate to be avoided if at all possible.

However, as all of Charlie's older brothers had already passed the duty of the draft down to the youngest brother, it fell to him to serve. He, though, had other ideas on the subject and fled the country, making it to England before he ran out of money. From there he wired his father, who responded that he had arranged with the army to take Charlie back without any punishment if he would report for duty and agree to serve. If he agreed, he would get the money for the return trip.

Charlie had no intention of returning to the army or to the new stepmother, but he did tell his father that he was agreeing to the terms and would return when he received the money. Instead, he used that money to come to America.

During the anti-war years of the 1960s Charlie's tale of avoiding the draft was a popular one with the younger generation. Roslyn, his daughter, has his immigration papers which list him, not as a citizen of Russia, but as a personal subject of the Tsar. Eventually, Charlie was able to bring one younger sibling, his sister, Becky, from Russia to the United States; except for her, he never saw the rest of his family again.

As most Jewish immigrants did in those days, Charlie began his new life on the Lower East Side of Manhattan, where he eventually met and married Esther Golden.

Esther, or Essie, had also emigrated from Russia, but she had arrived as an infant, with her family—both parents, her brother, Abraham, and her sister, Dorothy. For all of them—Halbreichs and Goldens—Yiddish had been the native tongue, and though Charlie and Essie learned to speak, read and write English to one degree or another over the years, Yiddish remained their first language for communication.

Essie and Charlie were married on April 1, 1911, and, as was common for Jewish women, Essie went to the *mikvah*, the ritual cleansing bath, before the ceremony. However, having a rebellious streak similar to that of her husband-to-be, she decided that, instead of merely dipping herself into the water, she would instead swim laps, horrifying and scandalizing all onlookers. Essie was a strong swimmer who would routinely swim in the East River and saw no reason for sudden meekness. She created this scandal a hundred years ago, as a bride of twenty-one, having been born in 1890.

She and Charlie had their first child, Ralph, the following year, in 1912. It was he who died in 1929 from mastoiditis. Lester arrived in 1917, and Roslyn was born in 1925.

Early in their marriage Charlie and Essie bought a candy store on Hamilton Avenue in Trenton, New Jersey, and they ran it successfully until 1920, when they sold it and returned to New York City because Essie missed her own family. Les was actually born in Trenton and lived there for his first three years.

Charlie was not to prosper once back in Brooklyn. He worked in Essie's brother-in-law's shoe store, but he fell and severely injured his back, which precluded further full-time work. In later years, Charlie worked bringing towels to the patrons of Raven Hall, the part of Coney Island that housed the bath house and pool. Regardless of their financial condition, Charlie remained the Papa and, in his quiet way, ruled the home, which definitely revolved around him. The children were always told, "*Sha*, your papa is talking." Materially, however, they never had much, living in small apartments with few possessions and never buying a car. Instead, they moved around the city by subway and bus, even when traveling took a few hours.

Shirley's parents, Sam and Rose Scheller, came from very similar backgrounds, Russian-Jewish immigrant stock, although they were both born in this country. In their case, the immigration to this country had occurred a generation earlier. They were somewhat younger than Charlie and Essie, as well. Sam was born on the Lower East Side in 1896, into a family that included two other sons and two daughters. Economic necessity prevented Sam from attending school beyond the elementary grades, yet he wound up becoming a highly successful businessman, entering the insurance business and eventually acquiring his own company. He used to boast about having sold the first million-dollar insurance policy in the country, and this was during the Depression. He also owned a pizza parlor on Forty Second Street and Eighth Avenue in the Times Square area, which was not considered a safe part of town at that time. His children were forbidden to go there, but that never stopped them from going and getting some free pizza. That property was sold at some point, but Sam had also purchased a block of stores in Garden City, in Nassau County on Long Island, around 1950, that remained in the family until recently. He meant for it to assist his grandchildren financially later in their lives.

Besides these stories, Sam used to love to tell about his early friendship with George Burns, and how he had loaned George five dollars for dancing lessons, which Burns had never repaid. His children and grandchildren urged him to contact Burns to collect that long-owed money, but he never did.

Sam loved his work and the business world in general, but he was told to retire after a heart attack. He did so reluctantly, but it was easier to do than he otherwise might have thought possible, because he had earlier taken in his younger daughter's husband as his business partner. So he was free to continue to maintain his interest in the business and to visit whenever he wanted.

Rose Rosenberg, Shirley's mother, was born in 1901, the eldest of five children and the only girl. There were several years between her birth and that of her next oldest brother. She was alternately proud of and very jealous of her four younger brothers, Sammy, Leo, Milton and Sidney. They were all, including Rose, quite intelligent, but Rose, being both female and the eldest, had to quit school early to help raise the family. The brothers all went on to college and law school; Rose was not allowed to pursue an education, which she resented all her life. In later years she enrolled in the New School and took various classes but, as she would often point out, it was no substitute for college. Rose's mother ran a boarding house and Rose was needed to assist with the myriad daily chores. Each of her brothers helped the next younger ones to complete college, but there was no sibling to help her, nor did she live in an age that even considered gender equality. It caused her ongoing sorrow.

While all of her brothers became attorneys, none wound up actually practicing law. Sammy passed away while still a relatively young man, from a heart attack, leaving Martha a widow. Leo volunteered for the Lincoln Brigade during the Spanish Civil War in the 1930s to fight against fascism, eventually joining the Communist Party. As a result, he was banned from many professional pursuits and was called before the House Un-American Activities Committee. Consequently, he and his wife, Mildred, struggled financially for the rest of their lives. He and Sammy, who had both come of age during the Depression, had to make ends meet as best they could while continuing to help their younger brothers.

Milton served in World War II and met his future wife, Frances, while stationed at an army base in New Jersey. He later moved to live in her home town, Burlington, New Jersey, and joined her father in his plumbing business.

Sidney, the baby of the family, became an educator in New York City, rising through the ranks of the Board of Education. His wife, Vita, became a university professor.

This emphasis on education continued through the next generation, which was typical of Jewish immigrants to America at the time. The grandchildren became physicians, attorneys, teachers and psychologists, and all went to college and beyond. Thus we have the Schellers, the Rosenbergs, the Halbreichs and the Goldens, four families who had emigrated from Russia —though so many others could tell very similar stories.

2

THE FIRST YEARS

THIS BRINGS US BACK to that idyllic summer of 1941, at the Stevensville Hotel, Shirley Scheller and her family on vacation and Lester Halbreich working as a waiter. As it happened, Les was assigned to the Scheller's table, but he did not initially notice Shirley, as there is a huge difference between a high school girl and a twenty-four-year-old, fourth year dental student. Things must have moved along pretty quickly, though, because they were engaged within six weeks and married four months later.

What was it that brought these two together? Actually, it was milk—which Shirley was refusing to drink, and her mother would not let her leave the table until she did. Lester, in a rush, did not have time to waste while some child acted out, so he took matters into his own hands and proposed that, if Shirley would drink that milk, he would meet her later for a game of tennis.

The rest, as they say, is history. The stars, sun, moon and several planets began to explode from that first tennis game. Shirley did not actually know how to play and Lester had to teach her—but he did not seem to mind, and the fact that she could barely hit a ball over the net hardly seemed to matter. They were in love and remained in love for the rest of their lives.

This unlikely pairing was aided by Lester's innocence. Having started college so young, he had remained shy and ill at ease around most women and even had trouble making friends among the other college men, who were much older than he was. Lester was also naturally shy and bookish. While the other boys read comics over their lunchtime sandwiches, Lester read more serious books and the dictionary, which did not help him in his love life.

The wedding date was set for December 24, 1941, permitting both of them to complete the full year of their educations. Shirley got to finish her freshman year of college; Lester graduated from dental school in the spring of 1942. The caption under his dental yearbook picture became part of family lore: "A blond Adonis off the streets of Oslo. Too late, girls, he's married." That was indeed an apt description of Lester in his youth, for he was something rather unusual for a Jewish boy from Brooklyn—blond and blue-eyed. Shirley was more typical, a brown-eyed brunette, but soon after their marriage she made her hair match his, and she remained a blonde for the rest of her life.

Three weeks before the wedding something happened to force a change in their life plans: the bombing of Pearl Harbor and the consequent entrance of the United States into World War II. When they set the date and planned the details of their wedding they had had no inkling of the coming invasion by Japan and the start of the U.S. involvement in the war. However, the wedding went on as scheduled. It began at 8:00 PM on Christmas Eve, although the actual ceremony was not until midnight—to allow anyone in business sufficient time to arrive, after keeping their stores open late for the holiday. An unanticipated consequence of that, however, was the inebriated state of many of the guests by the time the wedding ceremony finally began. Legend has it that spitballs were thrown, along with other lamentable behavior.

But none of this detracted from the essential solemnity of the moment. Shirley, looking beautiful, walked down the aisle, smiling and waving at her friends, who, like her, were still teenagers. Lester, stiff and formal in his tuxedo, was escorted down the aisle by his parents, who were still whispering to him, "It's not too late to change your mind." They liked their future daughter-in-law, but they thought their son was too young to marry.

For their honeymoon they went, by bus, to Lakewood, New Jersey, then a popular vacation and honeymoon destination. Several hotels surrounded the lake in the middle of town. And then they began their married life, which included the final semester of school for each of them.

The onset of war had altered the plans of thousands of couples, this one included. Instead of establishing a dental practice and a family upon graduation, Lester volunteered to join the service. He had been in the naval ROTC at Cornell and therefore entered the navy as an officer. It took awhile, however, before he received his orders, and he had to go through training in Brooklyn, so that the rest of 1942 and early 1943 slid easily by. In fact, the summer of 1943 found the couple working as counselors at Camp Brookwood, a sleep-away camp in upstate New York. They worked with the youngest campers, the three- and four-year-olds, and they used to tell funny stories of their adventures with these pint-sized campers. One child almost jumped out of a third story window, with a yellow towel tied to his neck, thinking he was Superman. Only Shirley's timely arrival saved him from take-off and tragedy.

The bucolic idyll was unexpectedly interrupted — not by war, but by a recurrence of Lester's mastoiditis, which landed him in the hospital in New York City. Shirley remained in camp for the rest of the summer, about a week, writing her first letters to him, not as a war bride, only as a camp counselor to her sick and hospitalized spouse.

> *Brookwood Camps*
> *August, 1943*
>   *Darling,*
>   *I have only three minutes in which to write this. Lillian is getting a weak heart just yelling for me to come down and watch the children, but I don't give a damn!*
>   *I've missed you so. I told Haas that he's a very lucky man that I've stayed here so far instead of going home. Please darling, please hurry up and get well. These days are crawling—I wonder if the angels are spiteful.*
>   *I packed your trunk and it's going off this morning. I think one of your bathing suits is missing. How many did you have? Tell me also how many instruments you left at the clinic so that I can check them. I'm enclosing a $25 check which I can't get cashed here as it needs your endorsement. Sign it dear, and cash it in the city. Daddy is sending me up $7, which I need until I can get the check money.*
>   *I speak to my parents every morning, and they let me know how you are. But they don't seem to know exactly what is wrong with you! What is it? I wish someone would tell me.*
>   *Oh nuts! Ruthie just told me the mail has left. That means*

this won't go off until tomorrow. I was so anxious that you should receive a letter from me quickly.

I gave the nurses $5. The canteen bill was close to $9—so I'm pretty short on cash. I haven't enough to pay the waiters as yet— until I get the check from Daddy.

I hear your parents know. I hope they haven't been worrying.

I finally did meet the crowd in Monticello—I got a ride with a fruit truck. The picture was excellent—I don't know, however, why I was crying, for the picture or for you. Everyone in camp has been asking for you and sending you their best wishes.

Darling, I can't write anymore now. Lil has come up and is threatening me with dire results if I'm not down immediately.

I'll write more later!

August, 1943

I just received your letter. I was so happy and relieved to hear from you. I stood there and laughed with tears running down my face—a prize idiot...

I am sending you the application for the A.D.A. in the same mail. Sign it and send it in. They ask for $6 in dues.

I'm glad that there is nothing seriously wrong with you darling, but I will worry. Stubborn, ain't I?

I have spoken to Dr. Stitch about your instruments and I will get them today.

August 28, 1943

...I felt so utterly alone last night, darling. It was the night of the Senior Prom and I watched these kids go out—so young and so alive—and I felt like such an A.K. [Note—A.K. is an abbreviation for the Yiddish term "alte kaker," which translates as "old person."] Please don't laugh at me—you know how I feel. I never tell anyone else these inner feelings and longings. I know I was dramatizing again – it probably wouldn't have occurred if you were here with me. The girls stayed out until 4:00 in the morning—at a hot necking session—and did I miss you, brother!

...This is probably the last letter that I will write to you as you will get this on Monday. From then on, big boy, I shall carry

*on our conversations with no more than six inches distance between
us. You understand? I've been away from you much too much.*

*...I will try to see you as soon as I possibly can, and if the hospital won't let me in after visiting hours, I shall climb up the fire
escape, so there!*

At this point, and as Shirley said, she was only twenty years old, even
though she already felt so old (like an *alte kaker*), and Lester was all of twenty-
six. He had been taken ill with a recurrence of a mastoid infection, but more
modern medications permitted him to recover, again. Shirley did not even
know what was wrong with him, but remained in camp to finish out the season. She was also discovering that she was no longer the high school girl
who dressed up to go to proms, but a married woman, and while she pined
for those carefree days, she was impatient to get back home to see her
beloved husband once again.

Shirley came home to see Lester when camp finally ended. He had
by then recovered, and was soon assigned his first military duty, as a dentist
on a naval base in Texas.

3

TEXAS

L ESTER REPORTED TO CORPUS Christi, Texas, to assume his formal
naval duty. He came alone, living a bachelor life, although Shirley
came to visit him there in October. His earliest letters to her were
written as she was on the train back to Brooklyn. She was accompanied on
the return trip by their cocker spaniel, Skipper, who was treated almost as
their first child, and who had entered their life there in Texas.

Les always addressed his letters to Churl, a favorite pet name for Shirley,
which arose very early in their relationship. Part a play on her name and part
because she was the exact opposite of "churlish." For some private reason,
that nickname stuck.

> *October 6, 1943*
> *Wed. Morn.*
> *Churl Darling,*
>
> *This is being written from the office between patients, so that
> it may arrive in New York and be waiting for you, a token that even
> though thousands of miles are between us, we are really not far
> apart.*
>
> *After the train left last night, I drove slowly home (averaging
> 35–40). Picked up a rider at Sinton; but even with him the trip
> was a lonely one. No Churl alongside of me; no sad-eyed Skipper.*
>
> *But the hardest part of all was going to bed. The pillow is only
> a poor substitute for you, my darling. It was cold and lonesome last*

night. And now sweet, I want this to get the early mail out. So long, take care of yourself and Skipper. My love to all, but to you, "even more than that."

Love,

Lester

October 7, 1943

By now you are walking the streets of St. Louis, with Skipper in tow and mighty glad to be together again, I know...Man, was it cold last night. I froze. And was it lonesome. There was no place to put my feet to get them warm. I miss you, darling. Without you to go home to, there seems no point in doing anything at all...Have a good time, darling. Don't forget, you must replenish your wardrobe. That's an order.

So long for the moment, darling wife. Keep well and think of me.

Love,

Lester

October 8, 1943

Churl darling,

It is 0815 now. You must have finished breakfast, gone to your roomette, and started to play with Skipper. In about another hour and a half, if the train is on time, you will be in New York.

You will step out of the train and there will be Dad S. and Mom S. Dad will be a little gruff, but mom will have unfeigned and undisguised tears in her eyes. You'll be home, my darling, and what a tonic to your parents. Remember that even though we miss you here, we want you to have the best time.

...Now that I'm driving in by myself I can sleep till 0730. Then I dress in a hurry, grab a glass of juice and a cup of coffee at home and get out to the base.

Churl, my love, my sweet, my darling, my wife, please miss me lots! But don't be unhappy. I'll join you as soon as I can.

Darling, do me a favor and call my folks whenever you hear from me. Please don't put it off.

Now, love to all; and to you, "even more than that."

Love

And Shirley wrote to Lester as well:

October 12, 1943

…Darling, As glad as I am to get home, and as thrilled as I am to see mom and dad, I'm desperately lonely for you. I really prefer Beeville to New York without you.

…Skippy is barking to say that he misses his "daddy" too. So you better not stay away too long.

Please, honey, try to get home as soon as possible. I promise to be a good girl from now on, if you only will.

Do you miss your family?

Darling,

I'm writing this on the train—my last night of travel—so don't mind the drunken writing.

The trip has been pretty pleasant so far; everything has come along smoothly – connections, tickets, and Skipper.

I've had company with young Navy and Army wives all the way. Even 2 Jewish girls from Brooklyn.

…Traveling by Pullman is wonderful! I actually slept, and very well. However, I was always worried about Skipper. I wasn't able to see him at all, while he was on the baggage car, I didn't even know if he was on the same train. And at Houston, they charged me $3 for traveling from Houston to St. Louis and said that I should have been charged at Corpus for him too. I never heard of such a thing. I guess he must have been excess baggage weight.

Love,

Shirley

The train trip took a few days, each of which is marked by a letter to Shirley, and Lester kept up his almost-daily correspondence through October. He was anticipating a leave of sufficient duration to allow a trip home to Brooklyn, which was to happen by early November, and he was writing about his attempts to get himself home by airplane, although that appeared unlikely. Les's letters end on October 25 with the final "only nine more days to go."

So either he got a sudden chance at a flight, or the letters from those nine days were lost, which seems unlikely, as all the others have been pre-served. Most likely, he was able to somehow get home early.

At this time, October, 1943, Shirley and Les were twenty and twenty-six and had been married for just under two years. Every letter from Lester began with his private nickname for Shirley, "Churl," given to her early in their relationship and retained throughout their married lives. In their let-ters, other nicknames would also be used, but this one was his favorite and usually began his letters.

Certain topics were recurring in those first letters, from their earliest war-induced separation. The most common themes were Lester's loneliness, the extent of his missing Shirley, and his consequent sleep problems. Issues relating to their dog, Skipper, also cropped up frequently, as did references to friends and relatives, along with everyday concerns, such as paying bills and making purchases. How they spent their days apart was a major topic for writing. And very quickly, Lester began to write to Shirley about the lack of letters from her, which would continue as a major complaint throughout their time apart.

Here, right at the very beginning, Lester is already bemoaning the lack of mail, which builds in intensity as the days without mail continue. What becomes apparent are the various and confused emotions this elicits and which are not easily put to rest, due to the absence of personal interaction.

Instead, Les coped by forcing himself to be patient and to have a sense of humor, but when that patience waned he began to get angry, but finally apologized.

When Lester returned to Texas a few weeks later, Shirley was with him, and she remained there for the duration of his assignment, including his trans-fer to Beeville, Texas. There are several oral stories of this interlude, but no letters, as two people living happily together have no need of them.

But Shirley was concerned about her possible infertility. During her train trip home to Brooklyn, Les tried to reassure her.

> *October 21, 1943*
> *...Now look, darling, it's a good idea about not consulting Es-ther's dad. And what's more, don't go worrying about yourself. The important thing is that you be comfortable. We're in no urgent rush about a baby now. So don't think that what must be done, must be done at once.*

October 23, 1943

...After all, we only tried to have you conceive for a few days and not the most favorable days at that. So it is scarcely surprising that you are not as yet pregnant. Give yourself a chance. Someday, when you least expect it, bang, there will be the baby. And remember, we've got plenty of time to try for a baby yet. After all, neither of us wanted a child yet, or for some time to come. So come on now, don't be foolish and waste your time in useless worry. Forget about the whole thing. Concentrate on missing me.

October 25, 1943

... Your description of Rosie K. (Korchin—one of Lester's cousins) is typical. Don't worry about her comments. Remarks like that get me good and sore. And if it comes down to it she might be gently but firmly reminded that of her three daughters and one son, only one grandchild had been produced, and that one when the daughter was 28. Don't worry about kids. Those people are going ahead and having babies because the war has scared them. For the same reason that most of them have married. The situation is analogous to what it was when even we married. Everyone thought we were crazy. Then, a few months later the whole world went mad and trouped [sic] to the altar. Don't worry about it! We'll have our child when we are ready for it; and no amount of mental pushing around is going to make me spoil our lives by changing our plans and rushing in immature haste for a baby because Tom, Dick and Harry are having them. I've always said that 50 million Frenchmen not only can be, but usually are wrong. And when I see a tremendous push by the entire populous [sic] to propagate, my first impulse is to say, "Whoa, take it easy. Something's wrong there."

Around that time, however, Shirley did become pregnant and her worry subsided. The ensuing months in Texas were recalled vividly in later years. Shirley gained a great deal of weight during an uncharacteristically hot Texas winter. The Brooklyn girl was unprepared for the intense heat when she discovered Dr. Pepper soda, which was then only a regional product and unfamiliar to her. It was love at first swallow, and since diet soda had not yet been invented, she ultimately gained sixty pounds during the pregnancy. Riding a mule on a visit to Mexico almost killed the mule, she would later joke.

Shirley also delighted in telling other stories in later years about the time in Beeville. Insects were a fact of life, and they would drip out of the faucet when she turned on the tap at the sink. Mosquitoes were everywhere. Fleas were ubiquitous, and they sometimes cropped up in unexpected places. At a dinner party, someone, in making an emphatic point during a discussion, hit the sofa. Suddenly, thousands of fleas flew out of it. They were living in inexpensive furnished rental quarters, which didn't help. Shirley and Les eventually learned to keep everything in containers to prevent infestations and, judging from the tone of their stories, they took it all in stride.

Another favorite tale occurred while Shirley was driving across a bridge near Corpus Christi. Since the war began, the country had been fearful of aerial attacks and had developed a series of warning sirens to give people some chance to reach cover. Various signs were also posted, instructing people what to do or where to go if an attack were to happen. One such sign on a local bridge, which she routinely had to cross, stated in bold letters, *In Case Of Air Raid Drive Off Bridge*. Shirley took the instruction too literally, living in fear of having to comply with the directive and drive straight into the river, sacrificing herself for the war effort.

Lester and Shirley otherwise lived a relatively quiet and peaceful life in Texas. Each day, Les would have breakfast at home with his wife, then go to work at the dental clinic on base, working with several other dental officers. As an officer, he was able to go to the officers club after work with his friends, mostly other dentists and doctors, for a drink or to play some game. And each evening, he went home to his wife for dinner. Often, they socialized with other young couples who were in similar situations. On occasion, they went into Mexico, which was nearby. They made several friends in Texas, which they kept for years afterwards.

All the naval personnel on base, officers and enlisted men alike, were awaiting their orders for overseas duties on board ship. They all knew it would happen, but none knew exactly when. It was just there, hanging over them, an unacknowledged threat to their marital comfort and personal safety. However, either individually or in small groups, they were eventually called.

Les and Shirley's time in Texas came to an end in the spring of 1944, but Lester was not directly ordered to a ship. Instead, he was sent back to New York, to the Brooklyn Navy Yard, to continue his dental work there while awaiting his orders for overseas duty. The benefit of this transfer was that it brought Les and Shirley home, near both families, their friends, and everything familiar; yet their imminent separation, and the threats attendant with war, had crept that much closer. Shirley's pregnancy was also well advanced by then, which increased their anxiety. They hoped, but could not be certain, that Lester would still be home for the birth.

In his months at Beeville, Lester's good dental work had been welcomed by the civilians in town, and he had been asked to return there after the war to open a practice. He and Shirley considered the possibility for awhile, having by then adapted to Texas life, but they decided that they did not want to live that far from their family and friends. This represented a fairly significant professional choice, as the New York City area had a good deal of competition but if he had returned to Beeville, he would have been the only dentist for miles.

One other incident happened in Beeville which may have influenced their decision. An older gentleman had walked up to Shirley one day, put his hand on her head, and felt her skull. Confused by this, she asked him what he was doing. He replied, "I heard that you were Jewish, but I don't feel any horns."

While it was already much less common by then, many people still believed several myths about Jews, including the belief that they had horns hidden under their hair. Lester and Shirley had found this incident more amusing than frightening, yet it highlights one important reason why people live where they do, and certainly why Lester and Shirley opted for Brooklyn over Beeville – one's level of personal comfort of living with culturally-similar people versus standing out as a lone representative of a different cultural group. Even in the absence of laws requiring segregation, people often tend to segregate themselves.

So Shirley and Les returned to Brooklyn, but daily life for them did not change very much. There was still the routine of work at the dental clinic and then home for dinner. They lived in a small apartment near the Naval Yard for the duration of Lester's assignment.

Soon enough, though, Les finally received his orders to ship out, and they came at an incredibly inconvenient time. He was ordered to appear in Washington State by the end of July, and to do so he had to leave Brooklyn by the middle of the month. Any leave-taking for war is difficult, but by then Shirley was in her ninth month and due at the end of July. Les would have to leave just prior to the birth of his first child, and to leave his heavily-pregnant young wife alone while she faced labor and delivery without him. Neither knew how long the separation would be, although it would last at least a year. And the threat of dying under fire was ever-present, turning a long separation into a potentially permanent parting. He now faced the added burden of not meeting and getting to know his first-born.

4

BIRTH OF THE BABY

BABIES ARE BORN THOUSANDS of times a day; it's an ordinary event —unless it happens to you. Then it seems as if the world stops in its orbit, fireworks explode, and banner headlines shout the news. For each couple living through the birth of their first child, there is much excitement, awe and wonder. One of the few variations on this theme occurs during wartime, when expectant parents are separated and unable to experience the highly emotional event together. It happens far too frequently, and World War II was no exception. Shirley conceived shortly after their first exchange of letters, in October of 1943. While she was describing her fear that she would never get pregnant, she either already was or was soon to be, though she did not know it.

In mid-July of 1944, the navy ordered Lester to leave Brooklyn for the West Coast and the start of his Pacific tour – just thirteen days before his son was born. The tale of the birth itself, its aftermath, and Lester's discovery of it are available in letter form. That so many women have given birth alone in wartime does nothing to lessen each woman's individual and unique suffering over having been deprived of her partner at such a moment. As is true of so much of their story, they had this in common with many, many others.

And their attempts to cope in the face of it were hardly new. Whatever each of them may have inwardly felt, little of the negative emotions were ever expressed in writing, as they tried to shield the other from feelings of helpless worry and to protect themselves with a small dose of momentary denial. For those few moments, while writing to each other, both revel in the joy of the new life, in their new roles as parents, and in descriptions of everyone else's reactions. Typically unmentioned is his frustration or anger at being torn away just before she gave birth, her fear and pain during the delivery, and her anxiety about facing motherhood without him. Shirley was luckier than most other women in that she was living with her parents, who were there to provide love and support, avoiding true isolation in parenthood. Yet they were no substitute for her husband, a belief that they both must have shared.

Many happy moments are described in their letters of this period—when Lester boasted to his new shipmates about the birth of his son and handed out cigars, when friends and family sent congratulatory cards (many of which were saved, along with the letters), and when both their teen-aged sisters wrote to describe their own reactions.

Neither, however, ever discussed this parting. No references of any kind about it, or of their feelings as it occurred, exist. We can only assume that some experiences remain too painful for words, even years later.

They did part in mid-July. Lester's first letter to Shirley is dated July 15, 1944, just after his departure. Jeffrey Neal was born on July 28—but Lester was among the last to learn of it.

> *July 22, 1944*
> *Well, baby darling, soon we'll have another baby darling. I'm so nervous and excited. I can't wait. How do you feel? How much love I have for you and my baby? My two love-childs. God bless you and take care of you. Have you decided on a girl's name yet?*

> *July 26, 1944*
> *I don't think I go for Jill as a name for a girl. I rather like Cheryl Sue or Bonnie Gail*
> *. . .As soon as I drop this in the box, I'm going to buy myself a drink and drink my daily toast to you and to an easy time for you. Good night for now.*

Lester's sister, Roslyn, also wrote to him on the day that Jeff was born.

> *July 28, 1944*
> *Dearest Les,*
> *You already know the good news and you know how happy we*

all are. I don't think that anything more beautiful could have happened to us than your son.

My deepest congratulations to you.

I'm so happy, my sweet brother. God bless you both.

All my love,

Roslyn

So did Shirley's sister, Elaine, who was away at camp.

Dear Mommy,

I'm so happy that I've been walking around in a daze since I received the news that Skipper has a brother, and, oh yes, you're a mommy. The girls tell me that the moment that daddy told me I threw down the receiver and fell out of the booth. They had to push me back in and hold up the receiver to my ear for I was too happy to think straight. I really wish I could hide inside this letter and get in to see you and Jeffrey, but I'm a little too heavy. I wanted to go in immediately, but I guess there's excitement enough without any extra added to it.

How does Jeffrey look and who does he look like? Have you heard from Lester? I bet he was more excited than you ever could be. He'll probably get home before I do, but hold him for me, won't you, so I can congratulate him.

Who has been up to see you, or rather should I say who hasn't been up? Did you receive the telegram that I sent? You know you're not allowed to send congratulations in them so I worded it the best I could.

Write soon and tell an anxious aunt about it all.

Always,

Elaine

Lester's mother, Esther, also wrote to him upon the occasion of Jeffrey's birth.

July 30, 1944

To my dear son,

Darling, first let me say Mazel Tov to you and then I want to tell you that I have seen your son three times. The third time was Sunday. Roslyn, Dad, and I came in the room when Shirley was nursing and we all gave them the once-over and the moment dad looked at your son he said he looked like him. Now I know he is going to be beautiful. I am also glad to inform you that Shirley looks grand and feels fine. Thank God you have a lovely baby and we hope and pray that the war will be over very soon and we all will be together again.

Love,
Mother and Dad

Les didn't find out about his son's birth until three days later.

July 31, 1944

   Well, now that I can write, I don't know what to say. I'm thrilled, of course, and overjoyed at the birth of our son, but mostly I'm concerned about you. Was it hard, darling? Were you hurt? I've been with you every moment, mentally. I've had no word since the telegram. I assume, of course, that no news is good news, in that case.

   Remember I told you Friday night that we had a party for the ship's officers? . . .We all started drinking. . .I was talking to one of the group who has a son at home. He was very proud of that son. "Would you like to know the secret of getting a son?" he asked me.

   At that moment there was a phone call for me. It was the dispensary. There was a telegram for me. I knew at once what it was. "I bet I'm now a father," I yelled. I dashed over to the dispensary and was handed a yellow envelope. My hands trembled as I opened it and my heart leaped a great leap as I read it.

   It's a boy. 7 lbs, 9 ozs. Arrived this morning. Both doing fine. Oh, how good it felt. First to know that you were all right, next that we were at last parents. The medical O.D. and the nurse congratulated me and off I stumbled. I went back to the party, stopping off on the way to get some cigars, but none could be found. When I got back everyone was seated at the table and eating. When asked where I had been, I merely showed the telegram. Naturally, everyone gave me profuse congratulations. I was taken over and introduced to the skipper, and people bought me drinks and I drank them. Everyone had a good time. Everyone got a little tight.

We had community singing, led by a certain Hilo Hatt, a rather well-known Hawaiian hula dancer. I requested "La Cucuracha" and much to my chagrin, she made me sing it. So I sang both dirty verses I know in Spanish. Of course, no one understood me. And so it went. When the party broke up I drove the commander home.

Saturday morning I got up at 5:00 to put through a call to you. I had hoped that there would be a phone near your bed, unfortunately there was none, so I couldn't speak to you; but the nurse must have told you I called so that is some compensation, at least.

August 2, 1944
My Darling Wife,

I hope by this time you are over the strain of your recent ordeal and have recovered, in some measure at least, the strength our child must have cost you.

I had no word from home since the telegram announcing Jeff's arrival. Naturally, I was some worried, so last night I called home and spoke to your folks. Doll baby, stay at the hospital for as long as they let you. Don't hurry home. Remember they can give you much better care there than they can at home.

I was surprised when they told me you were nursing the baby. Listen, honey, don't change your mind out of a mistaken idea that that's what I would want you to do, because it is not. Yes, nurse our child for a while, a week or two, then after that, wean him from the breast. Don't lose that hour glass figure that cost you so much anguish. Tell me, do you now look like that lovely creature that knocked me flat at Stevensville not so long ago?

From the telegram your father sent me, and from your last letter, which I received after the birth of Jeff, I know that you had quite a long labor. I only hope that it wasn't too bad. I am relieved to know that you have such excellent care, at least if your folks are telling the truth it is excellent care.
August 19, 1944

. . .Are you feeling all right now, my sweet?. . .I know that yes-

terday was to have been Jeff's first day outside. . .I want you to get outside a good deal from now on. It would be nice if you could find a place to go sun bathing and get back some of that Texas tan. And be sure to take at least a medium long walk every day.

5

WAITING TO SHIP OUT

THE UNITED STATES NAVY *officially orders Lester Halbreich to Bremerton Naval Base in Washington State, to be attached to the USS Oxford.* With these words, or others to that effect, Lester was transferred from Brooklyn, from his pregnant wife and from his soon-to-be-born son, to finally begin his overseas duty. Or not. It turned out that the need to leave Shirley just before she gave birth, to appear at the base by that particular date, had nothing to do with an immediate departure. That departure did not, in fact, occur for three additional months. The ship had to be fitted out for sea duty; then there were several trial runs, during which it sailed between Washington, Oregon and California. One is left to wonder what the rush was all about, why Lester could not have remained in Brooklyn two more weeks to see his wife through her labor and delivery. But one knows not to question military orders.

However, the activities of the coming months were unknown to Lester as he first reported for duty that summer of 1944. He participated in the many trial runs and the various training exercises, but the three months in dry dock, apart from being separated from Shirley and the newborn Jeffrey, were in the end undemanding for Lester. He settled into his assigned bunk, met his bunkmates and the other medical and dental personnel, but generally had little to do. There were hardly any patients to see and only some regular naval drills to participate in. Even when underway to another West Coast port or on a trial run out to sea, duties remained very light. He compensated by setting up his dental office, starting his daily reading, bridge and chess playing, and in general, having extended periods of free time.

Shirley was experiencing just the opposite as she tried to adjust to motherhood and her newborn, which was anything but undemanding. She was extremely busy with this immense change in her life, and all of the attendant responsibilities and chores that come with an infant.

July 22, 1944

This morning I must have turned the alarm off while I slept. . . but I managed to get here only five minutes late and. . .unobserved. Why I had to rush, I don't know. No patients have shown up yet, so I spent the morning reading a textbook, and now I'm writing to you.

I've got the afternoon off, but I'm not sure what to do. I've got some laundry to bring (three-day service, I understand). . .Then there's some dry cleaning to do, and a few small purchases at ship's services and I want to see the executive officer of my ship to say hello. Maybe I can find out the home port of the ship, but I don't think so. After that, I've got to call for a ration book (gasoline) and grease the car, and if it's still nice out, I'll wash the car.

. . .The region hereabout is very hilly, almost mountainous. The club is smack on top of the steepest of the hills. I've got to put the car in second to make it.

And it is in this setting (the club) that your debonair, blonde, and slightly bald husband will sit in a corner. . .nursing his drink and his lonesomeness and envying the other men the company of their wives. And it is here that you must picture me tonight, thinking, as when do I not, of my own sweet darling, my love-child, my curly-bump, my Aurora, my vonce [literally "bedbug" in Yiddish], whom I love to distraction, and who, thank God, for some unknown reason, loves me too. Goodnight for now, my darling.

July 24, 1944

Today is my last day of taking it easy. Tomorrow the men of the ship's company will start to come aboard and I'll start to examine them and work on them.

July 25, 1944
Churl Darling,

After work yesterday I walked over to where one of our large aircraft carriers is in dry dock. I thought I'd go on board and look around, but after strolling around it, I found it was too late. The ship was so gosh-blamed big. It is a majestic thing to see a ship that size sitting on its blocks, in dry dock.

. . .Scuttlebutt is still rife about the ship and different dates keep passing back and forth, but I guess we will know nothing until the last moment, and I think it is safer that way.

July 28, 1944

Remember, darling, how easy-going I used to be with corps-men? Well, I've changed so much you wouldn't recognize me. I've become very strict and G.I., but at the same time very fair and good-natured. I realized that the entire pattern of my relations with my corpsman could be determined by the way I treated him now. [The problem was complicated by the fact that, for the previous six months, he had been working in the record office, practically his own boss.] What I did was just mention things I'd want done, with no question of whether or not it suited him. And he did it. A few times he started to question what I wanted, or just some other way to do something. I would listen to him; say it was a good idea; but things were done my way. Today we are to have an inspection, so yesterday, before leaving, I said I wanted a 4.0 inspection tomorrow. He said something to the effect that the captain was an old fuss budget, and he would do what he usually did for an inspection and get away with it. I immediately took the opportunity to say very levelly that I didn't give a hoot-in-hell for the captain or anyone else but I wanted the office shiny and ship-shape tomorrow for my own sake; and that it would be that way tomorrow. I wasn't mean about it. I just kept my voice very matter-of-fact, as if I was passing out information. He looked at me as if seeing how far he could try, but said nothing. I left for the day, after that.

This morning I walked in and the office glowed. My point had been made.

...This morning was uneventful except for an air raid drill...
Since I am on temporary duty here they did not assign me a battle
station, so I was able to watch from my office window. It was nicely
done. They had two squadrons of Wildcats practice strafing the
station

August 2, 1944
All that I can get about the ship is still mostly scuttlebutt.
The crew will go on a training cruise sometime in the near future, not on our ship, but on one like it. At first I was told I
would go along, then I was told I wouldn't. Then I was told I
would move to Seattle with the crew even if I don't go on the
cruise. Then I was told I might go to Seattle, or I might not.
Now I don't know.

August 15, 1944 [After a two-week leave]
...When I checked in at the base this morning, the first person
I saw, the personnel officer, told me that I was detached. Soooo, I
went through the usual hustle and bustle of getting detached, and
finally find that I was ordered to Seattle for temporary duty. Sooo,
I got over here about 7 o'clock tonight and checked in. How long
I am to stay here I don't know. I may be sent to Astoria tomorrow,
or I may be sent there after a few days.
The latest scuttlebutt, and I repeat, scuttlebutt, is that the commissioning date of the ship has been pushed back further.

August 16, 1944
Churl Darling,
Well, your husband is still in a fog concerning his future...as
I keep telling you, no one knows nothing; but it seems as if I will be
here for awhile.
I checked in at the base today and evidently the duty will be
very light. Dentistry will occupy me only one day in five. The rest
of the time will be spent in classes on damage control, navigation,
etc.
It seems that there are only two dental offices here, and they
are run by officers regularly attached to the station, so we take the

watch from 4-9 on our duty night, which only comes about once every five days.

. . .It seems that I am very lucky to have been given quarters here at B.O.Q. The others, all of them, have been forced to take rooms at a navy-run hotel in town. They pay what I do, but they have a long bus ride to and from work and their linen charge is $14.00 a month, where mine is $3.00 a month. Quite a savings in money and convenience.

The station is very new and is bustling with activity. Evidently, they are going into this program in a very big way.

August 17, 1944

I walked over to the dispensary to see the Senior Medical Officer regarding my disposition. He didn't know what to do with me, so he called some other ranking officer to find out. It seems that my crew is in Tacoma, and it seems that the question is whether to remain here or to go down there and await the commissioning of the ship with the rest of the crew. Finally, he got this officer on the phone and it was decided that I should stay here and take certain courses.

In the afternoon we had some lectures. One on strictly medical details; the other on compartmentation. At this last we were shown a model of our ship made of Lucite. It was really beautiful, and our ship is really a honey.

It seems I may yet be moved to the navy hotel in town. I've been informed that this B.O.Q. is only for junior officers of A.P.A. ships, but I haven't been invited to leave yet.

Before supper I walked over to the neighboring pier to check on my sea chest which should have been here yesterday.

While I was there I walked over to the dispensary and, lo and behold, the schedule had been changed. I am to work tomorrow night. No one had notified me. It was a good thing I'd dropped over, otherwise, I might have been hanged for a traitor.

August 28, 1944

. . .This morning I attended the last of a series of indoctrination lectures, and this evening I am standing the last duty I shall stand while I am at this base. So as you can see, the rest of the time will *be strictly vacation-like. If I get permission, I'm going to try to take a boat trip to Victoria. It is a beautiful trip, I'm told, and as long as I'm so close, I'd like to get there.*

Two days later in the week I have been assigned to attend fire-fighting school. . . The only drawback is that I have to wear dungarees. And that means buying a set.

September 1, 1944
My Darling Wife,

. . . This morning I climbed out of bed at 8 o'clock and sauntered over to the dispensary. There I passed some time with the rest of the medical officers aboard until finally I was able to see Commander Morrow the senior man. He told me that on Monday or Tuesday I'd be ordered to Astoria. The rest of the crew is there already. The ship will fit out there and take on stores for its shakedown cruise. So write your next letters to me at:

Lt. L. Halbreich, D.C. USMA
c/o Oxford Detail, APA 189
Astoria, Oregon

I don't know what the schedule will be my sweetest darling whom I love with all my heart; but I can tell you what scuttlebutt is (don't pass even this scuttlebutt on, though).

We will probably take three weeks to fit out and take on stores. After that (figure the last week in September) we will set out on our shakedown cruise, standing out to sea and down the coast to San Pedro, California. This will involve training the crew and checking the ship. At San Pedro some additional members of the crew will come aboard. If any kinks do come up during our trip down the coast I don't know where we will go to fix them up, but we may come back to Seattle or Bremerton, or we may stay there. Then after that I don't know what the score will be. But as I told you a long time ago, it will be months and months before we see any action areas.

September 5, 1944
Churl Darling,

Well here is your husband at still another base. I really have been doing some traveling, haven't I. This time I am at the Astoria naval Station, but I am temporarily quartered out here at the Tongue Point naval Air Station.

September 6, 1944

. . . This morning I was awakened by one of the dental officers I told you about at 7 o'clock, in time to dress and have a breakfast of juice, eggs and coffee. There was supposed to be a bus leaving the station here at 0745, but somehow or other the thing was so fouled up that we didn't get away until 0845. It was no great loss however, for there was really nothing to do. We met the senior officer of the station and he told us how little we would have to do. After that I saw my own senior medical officer. He was very cordial. I was so taken aback that it was difficult to return his cordiality, but I did. Together we went over to see the executive officer, and he told me how the situation stood as of the moment. I'm not quite sure how he stands. Perhaps he's only a bastard in his cups, or perhaps he is still an anti-Semite, but smart enough to conceal it. Most likely, I think he wants a favor of me. What it can be, I don't know, however, but if he continues to act this nicely everything will be all right.

The next item on my agenda was to try to locate my dental operating stool. I cornered the supply officer. He knew nothing about it, but referred me to another person. This person referred me to another, and so on and on. I didn't get anywhere, however, for I have learned by this time that this is the navy way and there is nothing to do about it, but "take your time, take your time, and easy, please." Finally I located a man who said that he had given it to another man. The other man said that he had never seen it. The first man said that he had signed for it, but he couldn't find the receipt, so I went with some seaman into a huge bin to inspect the crates. Way up near the roof I spied a crate that I thought would be it, why I don't know. I climbed up on the boxes and sure enough, there it was. What fun.

. . . This morning I went aboard another one of these APA's and I am more and more impressed with their completeness. So far as I am concerned there is only one drawback which already we are trying to remedy; there is no dental instrument cabinet. Instead of that they have given us an eye, ear, nose cabinet to use. Don't believe that situation will last long, however. I note too that no rubber

floor mats are provided, which makes me doubly glad to have that stool along with me.

And that is all for now darling. . . I just got a new roommate. I want to talk to him.

September 11, 1944

What a full day this has been from the beginning to the present moment. I am not sure that I can tell you all about it in this letter, but I will try.

It started out in the usual manner by my awakening at 6:45, washing and going down to breakfast. Breakfast was unusual in that the service for some unknown reason was very bad. I did finally get my juice, eggs and coffee in time to catch the 8 o'clock bus to the naval Station. I wanted to be a little early for the commissioning. I was. About an hour early. I spent the time looking for a letter from home. There was none. And talking to some of the ship's officers. Finally I went aboard ship and was directed to the after portion where I lined up with the rest of the officers well up toward the senior end of the line. We stood around and talked for awhile. Promptly at 9:30 the ceremony began. The director of the port handed over the ship to Captain Crandell, who accepted and read his orders. Colors were sounded. The national anthem was played and the flag rose slowly to the jackstaff while the entire assemblage stood at the salute. Immediately after that coffee was served in the wardroom for the officers and their guests. The ladies present were all given a corsage. I stood where they had to pass to be seated for the ceremony and not one of the darlings came even close to looking as lovely as you do. I know that that is a foolish thing to say, but being human I cannot help making comparisons

The cake incidentally was cut with a sword and a very ceremonious affair it was too. As soon as I could I went to look at my quarters. I had been hoping for one of the two staterooms for two, but I didn't get one. Our quarters are small but adequate, the more so since it is designed for four, and we have but three in them. I room with a Lieutenant McNeil, and a JG, the beach-party medical officer. Both seem to be quite pleasant fellows.

September 14, 1944

It really is interesting to listen to the various commands come over the loudspeaker. And how salty I am getting! The first thing you hear is a hum as the loudspeakers warm up. Then comes the boatswain's whistle, loud and shrill for attention, then, "Now hear this. Anderson, A. J., Seaman 1st, report to the quarter deck. On the double."Or some other similar message. Or for example at 11:30. "Knock off all work. Sweepers man your brooms. Clean sweep fore and aft." And so forth throughout the day. What I like though, is the prefatory phrase, "Now hear this!"

. . .Incidentally, if I haven't mentioned it before he (the skipper) is a very swell guy. He knows just what the score is at all times, and conducts himself just like a 100% human being.

. . .I have the medical department watch tonight. Somewhere I read that the dental officer was not supposed to stand medical duties, but it makes it much easier for everybody (duty only one night in six) and I have no place to go anyhow, so we give in.

September 18

. . .that voting officer assignment may turn out to be quite a job. It evidently carries quite a lot of responsibility. I went over to the station voting office this afternoon and he gave me the lowdown on it. If we get to use those federal ballots, I'll have a lot of work; if not. . .not.

The appointment to the various courts and boards came out today. Besides my other duties I am now a member of the auditing board of the mess, and a member of the promotion board for the hospital corpsmen.

Tonight we had the skipper as a guest of the mess. The meal as usual was really delicious. We really had a nice time, the more so since the skipper just heard this evening that he had been promoted from commander to captain. He is now a full-fledged four-striper.

September 23, 1944

As I anticipated, this voting officer job is turning into a lot of detail, and a lot of work. I just received a new batch of forms to fill out, reports to make, and letters to read. On top of all this I received a new shock when I was kindly, but sympathetically, told that at sea Sunday is not a holiday. I was so shocked. How could such things be, but alas, such things are.

September 25, 1944

Today was an interesting day indeed, from a number of viewpoints. So far as the strict perspective is concerned, we started the morning off with an inspection of the entire ship's company, and of the ship. Supposedly, this was an admiral's inspection, but it was actually accomplished by a Lt. Cmdr. All told, the ship and the men came off rather well in the inspection. The afternoon was concerned strictly with compensation of the ship's compass.

September 26, 1944

Tonight again I have the duty. Thank goodness there is nothing doing so far. I like a nice quiet duty. Don't you?

...I thought that I had explained about the voting officer. Well, in brief, it is simply that there is a very widespread plan in the navy to see that the men in service are given every opportunity to vote in this and subsequent elections. The deal is considered to be very important, and I am responsible for the whole thing on board the ship. At the moment I will gladly trade the whole job for one three-cent chocolate soda. This morning the entire crew formed at quarters, and the officers and men of the ship were presented with a commemorative plaque by the citizens of the town of Oxford, in the foothills of the Catskills. No foolin'. It started out by being foggy, and ended by pouring. After the plaque, one of the warrant officers on board was presented with the navy and Marine Corps Medal for outstanding heroism in the rescue of his shipmates on December 7, 1941. Throughout it all, we stood at attention in the pouring rain.

September 29, 1944

Today was a fairly, I might even say, very, uneventful day. The ship ran the measured mile most of the day testing its engines and finally put out to sea. As for me, I was told to secure my office as rough weather was to be expected, so of course I was unable to do *any work. When we secure for rough weather, we tie down everything movable, and lots that isn't. It pays. So for most of the day I sat around, read a little, played a little chess, schmoozed, etc. We held an abandon ship drill (I hope they continue to be drills only).*

September 27, 1944

. . .Here's the story of today in brief. A few patients in the morning, followed by lunch. A few patients in the afternoon, followed by dinner. After dinner I played chess with Ralph awhile. . . I'm going to bed now.

October 1, 1944

Time at sea is so evanescent. It seems to drag, yet lo and behold another day is suddenly gone. Where gone, and what accomplished, it is difficult to say; but undeniably those few hours are no longer yours to do with as you please. So it was yesterday. Little done, the day gone, and no letter written.

Most of the men seem to have become accustomed to the motion of the sea by now. There are a few yet who are definitely greenish, but most of us are old sea dogs by now. For my own part, outside of the first few moments of discomfort I wrote you about, I have never even been slightly bothered by sickness. As a matter of fact I find this slow rolling motion of the ship rather soothing.

There was but little to do during the day yesterday. A few patients came in, but for the most part the men are too busy getting used to the routine of the ship to bother with me. My day will come soon however. I did do a little work. Spent a little time reading, and now and again I played a game of chess with Ralph. Of course in between times there were one or two drills. The drills are introduced by a long blast of the bosun's whistle over the loudspeaker system, and then the word is passed, "General quarters, general quarters. All hands man your battle stations. All hands man your battle stations." Immediately following that a bell starts clanging over the loudspeaker system. Immediately after receipt of the "Word" we drop what we are doing, and dash for our battle stations, in my case the after battle dressing station. Down there the first thing we do is let down a few bunks so that we may have some place to sprawl in comfort, for the drill may last for a few moments to a few hours. Sometimes we have just barely settled ourselves comfortably, when there is a shrill of the bosun's pipe, and the words, "Secure from General quarters." Whereupon we pick ourselves up and pick up where we left off. On the other hand, the shrill of the pipe may be followed by the word, "Fire in the paint locker, main deck." That may mean we stay at our stations quite a long while.

October 2, 1944

. . . Things are moving along about as usual. The days with nothing getting done for one reason or another. This time the deck of my office is being painted and no one dare come in or out. So I've spent the day out on the weather decks, talking, wandering about the ship, reading, playing chess, etc., etc.

October 4, 1944

Churl Darling,

Today was the big day, the long-awaited moment, the day of the big inspection. We were wakened at 0645 for early breakfast; uniform dress blue baker (or blues with white shirt). After breakfast the word was passed to fall in at quarters. Each division lined up at its accustomed spot, and after a while the articles for the government and the navy were read page by interminable page. As quarters were dismissed the announcement was made that inspection would be at 1300. Everyone scattered and started to do some last minute cleaning up. A few minutes later the word was passed that the inspection party was aboard. Someone had evidently made a mistake. There were the boatswains whistles piping a captain over the side, and then everybody went to their station (myself to the dental office). As the inspection party passed from one station to another a bugler preceded them and blew attention. The inspection was brief and satisfactory.

. . . To paraphrase some letters I have been censoring. I can't tell you where we are, but if I should run into Lana Turner or Betty Grable do you want an autograph? Ralph was able to get ashore to see his wife tonight. I had the duty so I stayed on board tonight.

I don't mind. I told Ralph and another fellow whose family is near here that I'd take their watches while we were near bye [sic]. After all, I'd like for them to do the same for me under similar circumstances.

October 5, 1944

. . . It seems that no matter how anxious I am to get things done in the interests of the dental health of the crew, it will be quite a while before any great amount of work can be done. I schedule appointments all right, but there is usually some drill or other that causes a cancellation on the part of the men or on mine. I presume that when we get to be somewhat better organized work will present more satisfactory returns.

My battle station has been changed from the after to the forward dressing stations, along with Ralph's. Someone drew up an "abandon ship" bill under which the medical officers from the after battle dressing station had to run way forward to their abandon ship station, and the medical officers from the forward battle dressing station had to run all the way aft to theirs, both groups crossing approximately at midships. This was rather foolish, so it was remedied merely by changing the posts of the officers at the forward and after battle dressing stations. It is now a great deal more satisfactory.

Today at General Quarters, hereinafter referred to as G.Q. we went to our new station for the first time. There isn't anything to say about it, so I say nothing. G.Q. lasted quite awhile, and while we were at G.Q. several drills were held, collision, fire, man overboard, strafing attack, etc. then a little gunnery practice was held. By the end of G.Q. it was time for lunch (can you see how much dental work can be accomplished under such conditions?). After lunch I had time to lie down for awhile and relax. Then again G.Q.; but this time instead of going to the forward battle dressing station I had to report to the communications room with Ralph for we have been appointed members of the coding board. The coding board is a group of men who code and decode incoming and outgoing messages. It is supposed to be something of a nuisance, and officially we cannot be forced to stand for it; but if we kick at it we will undoubtedly get some other lousy detail thrown at us. Today we were

*given instruction in the use of an ingenious machine. The whole
job is very complicated, and I couldn't explain it even if I were permitted to, but it was rather interesting.*

*After about an hour of two of that G.Q. was over for the after-
noon. The rest of the time I spent in my dental office until 14:30,
treating a couple of cases of trench mouth and doing some reading.
After that time I went out on the fan tail and looked over the calm
blue sea. Ralph came out for a little while and we hung over the
rail talking for a while, and watching a flying fish that was jumping
alongside of the boat.*

October 9, 1944

*. . . The day was quite uneventful. We had several drills, in-
cluding some gunnery practice (what a noise our big one makes!
WHOOM!). I had to decode a test message this morning, which I
did quite satisfactorily. In the afternoon, G.Q. lasted for quite a
while so I sat me down on a little box out of the way of the busy
communications officer and put my head down, and closed my eyes,
and rested.*

October 11, 1944

*. . .Yesterday was a routine day at sea, as was the day preceding.
We indulged in quite a few drills and exercises. The most impressive
of the bunch are the gunnery exercises. To lend realism, and serve as
a target, the local air station supplied a navy plane to tow a sleeve.
The plane flies at different courses in relation to the ship, and at direction the various batteries of different caliber open fire on her. What
a racket, and how comforting it is. Of course all these drills and exercises leave very little time for dentistry, but I am managing to get
some work in between times, including a few extractions.*

October 14, 1944

*. . .Today has been another day of feverish preparation for in-
spection. The way it works in our department is that Dickey gets
the fever. The corpsmen do the work and the rest of us crap out and
stay out of the way as well as we can. For the umpteenth time my
dental office was painted and roped off. Thus being cut off from*

all possibilities of working, I walked over the ship and watched the men work, stood on the fantail for a while in the balmy breeze, and bright sunshine, and at about four o'clock took a bit of a nap. It's interesting to watch these men work. Here a group is touching up the boats. Another group is touching up rust spots about the deck. Another few are at work with the oxy-acetylene cutting torch, or else welding something to the bulkhead. This type of activity goes on all over the ship from the double bottoms to the tops of the masts. And leaning over the side are the ever present group of men who are doing nothing but shooting the breeze.

October 18, 1944
Churl Darling,

Today has been rather quiet. Dr. Dickey hasn't been on board all day. I took the watch for Dr. Davie so that he could go to a nearby town with Butch (in Butch's car) where he had interned. They left early and Goldman left soon after. Sure enough there was a possible fracture came in this evening. I sent him over to the dispensary ashore, for diagnosis. The diagnosis was merely bruised. Then a fellow came in with a slight temperature, and a peculiar rash. I ordered a smear taken and got him to bed. It was another case of malaria. What fun I don't think.

. . . The ship still sounds like a boiler factory. There is lots of work going on, and all the department heads are busy, and distracted.

October 21, 1944
My Darling Wife,

Again there will be an interruption in the continuity of our letters. We have put to sea again. I for one am glad. As long as I am aboard ship I don't feel right in the port. There is always the feeling of constraint of the urge to do something ashore, whereas at sea that feeling of tension vanishes. After all, in port it is usually difficult to get to town, and there is really very little to do once you get there, except drink, whereas on board ship, at sea, the routine, once established, is easily followed. There is no hurry to get anything done so as to get off the ship. You're there to stay. Of course it tends to get boring, but there are some books on board. There is a little chess to study or play, and there are the occasional bridge games.

There was the usual hustle and bustle about getting underway today, and as usual I stayed on the weather deck to watch the process. It is always interesting to watch a ship leave its pier. The loudspeaker blares its commands, the routine is accomplished, the tug takes hold, and suddenly we roll a bit in the ground swell. We are at sea. Everyone suddenly relaxes, an air of tension disappears. There is now time for everyone, and everything. Tom can catch up on his correspondence. Dick can now read to his heart's content. And Harry had plenty of time to relax in his bunk and be perfectly miserable . . . and sick.

By the time that the ship finally sailed, Lester had already been on active duty, albeit in Texas and New York and the West Coast, for over a year. This became important a year later, when discharges loomed, but for the moment, Shirley and Lester became just one more couple facing separation, loneliness, and fear as he left for the war. Some fought directly on land, some flew air missions, some came on ships, and some were dentists aboard them. Yet those dentists faced the same threats of torpedoes, kamikaze pilots, and other bombs that everyone else did. Lester later related that his dental office was in a part of the ship that would be closed off and sacrificed to save the rest of the ship, should it be hit, making his position among the more dangerous.

6

CROSSING THE EQUATOR

"TRADITION!" CRIES TEVYE, IN *Fiddler on the Roof*, as he tries to hold back the first cracks in his village's unchanging ways. Rituals become the stuff of study for anthropologists as they try to understand the traditions that cement other cultures.

Americans are also subject to rituals and traditions, whether we recognize it or not. When there is a birth, a wedding, or especially a death, we fall back on time-honored rituals to see us through.

Unsurprisingly, our armed forces are havens of ritual and tradition. New recruits always face a hazing, sergeants are always tough during basic training, medal or induction ceremonies always reflect the same values and follow the same order. Each branch of the military has its own traditions and the navy is no exception. It has a long and revered history, having been established over centuries of exploration at sea.

For those of us unfamiliar with those traditions who then happen upon one of the more esoteric examples—one we may not at all expect—it can come as a considerable surprise. Lester's letters to Shirley in November 1944 fall into that category of the unexpected.

Soon after finally getting underway, Lester's ship approached the Equator, an occasion for the observance of a maritime custom. It dates back to the days of sailing vessels and long months at sea, when sailors sorely needed a diversion, yet, during wartime in the middle of the Pacific, in the middle of the twentieth century, another instance of marking the crossing provided an excuse for practices that would have been familiar to sailors of centuries past.

The *USS Oxford* crossed the Equator twice, once on its way toward the war, and once on its way home.

October 28, 1944

At present, darling, your husband is only a lowly polliwog, and the venerable shellbacks are getting ready to initiate him into their order. In other words, I haven't yet crossed the equator, and those who have are making preparations to initiate me, with the rest of the polliwogs, into their society. What fun!

November 5, 1944

Churl Darling,

There is so much to tell you about in this letter that I don't know where to begin. At the same time there is so much detail that I know I shall flub miserably the telling of it all. Let me start off by boasting that I am no longer a polliwog; but a full-fledged shellback with all the rights and privileges and immunities thereunto appertaining. It is the story of the conversion of myself, and the rest of ship's company and passengers, with which I will deal for the most part.

Some few letters ago, if you have been reading my letters according to the dates on them, I told you of our impending crossing of the equator. As you have doubtless heard, the crossing of the equator is an event of great importance, and one which is celebrated with much ceremony. The ship's company and passengers are divided into two groups: those who have crossed the equator before, and can produce evidence that they have done so; the shellbacks (or trusty shellbacks)—and those who have not crossed the equator previously, or having done so do not have the proof of their passage with them. These last named of course are the lowly polliwogs, the scum of the earth, the crawling beetles. A few days before the ship was due to cross the equator a meeting of the trusty shellbacks was held and plans were laid for the initiation and conversion of the polliwogs. At this meeting, the various crew members were assigned their parts, the order of the ceremonies was arranged, and costumes were devised. Thereafter, at irregular intervals, the ship's loudspeaker would boom with a voice sounding like The Shadow. At various times he would *announce meetings of the shellbacks or put into effect new rules which the polliwogs were to observe, e.g., all polliwogs were noted down; and they were very busy writing mysterious entries in their little black books.*

Yesterday was the day scheduled to start the ceremonies. The night before the plan of the day for the succeeding day was announced, as grays or khakis were to be put on backwards. The same plan of the day contained an officer's watch list, in which all polliwog officers were assigned a place. After G.Q. yesterday the festivities started mildly enough. Some of the trusty shell backs had containers of a purple dye which they used to swab the face and arms of all polliwogs. I lay below in the sick bay for a while but was soon summoned to #2 hatch for my makeup job, and the presentation of the symbol of office. This last was a huge carpenter's shoulder drill, which I had to carry around all day. Shortly after that, the loudspeaker set the first polliwog lookout watch for the day, the eight-to-ten job. The lookouts had to wear helmets, carry a rifle, and had on wading or hip boots filled to the top with water. Two of them were stationed on the #2 hatch, one to port and one to starboard; one was sent to the crow's nest; and one or two, as necessary, were sent to the fo'castle. Their job was to scan the portion of the horizon appointed to them and yell to the officer of the deck, stationed way up on the navigation bridge, their findings. Thus, one would stand with his hand at the visor of his helmet scanning the empty sea. One of the shell backs would demand a report (emphasizing same with a lusty thump on the rump with the home-made paddle— these paddles were made of three feet length of fire hose filled with rags and sown at both ends, and then soaked in water. Were they efficient!) The lookout would turn and yell, "Officer of the Lookout (in a despairing tone but shrill and loud), Officer of the Deck (getting a response this time). Water on the port bow. Relative bearing 286."

At this juncture the shellbacks threw a pail of greasy water over his left shoulder and thump on the rump. The report of water on the starboard bow was greeted similarly. At the report of white caps the 1 ½-inch fire hose was turned full on him. All this while a group of men would be going through a part of the initiation on the hatch, said initiation consisting mainly of getting your rump thumped (but good) having various amounts of hair cut off by a tremendous shears, and axle grease rubbed on the denuded areas, then being forced to lie down on the hatch and pretend to be swimming while some shellbacks blasted away at you with this 1½-inch hose and others beat your rump with the aforementioned hoses and with vigor. I was in one of the first groups of officers to go through this ceremony and my behind still bears the marks. Withal, I was comparatively leniently treated. Some of the men really caught hell. This little affair went on throughout the day. Every two hours the polliwog officers' watch would change and the costume of the lookouts would have new and strange additions: a long chain was wound around the neck of one of them, another was given a pair of hose nozzles fastened together to use as binoculars.

Mr. Warmington, whom I've already told you about, claimed to be a shellback but could not produce proof. In addition to the rest of the initiation, he had to carry flowers with him all day.

Mr. Adams, our boat officer, and I've mentioned him to you before, had to yell "boats" through a tremendous megaphone all day long at five-minute intervals. When it wasn't loud enough, "thump on the rump."

Throughout the day a new group of seamen or soldiers would occupy the center of the stage and go through a certain amount of torture. Frankly, it was fairly funny at first, but it soon got out of hand. A group of old sadistic shellbacks somehow or other got control and some of the men got terrible beatings. When these shillelaghs are swung by 190-pound men with all their might, they cause damage. But a good time was being had, so it went on.

I was supposed to have the 1600 to sunset watch, and welcome Davey Jones on board. Davey Jones is the Ruler of the Deep and he comes on board the night before King Neptune comes on to act as his emissary. I went on watch at the regulation time, donned the prescribed costume and with Ensign Davies was assigned to a fo'-castle watch. The first thing we had to do was to face the open center hatch and practice prostrating ourselves and yelling Allah at the top of our lungs. This was to be our welcome to Davey Jones when he came on board through the eyes of the ship. At the end of 15 minutes, Ensign Davies went back to report, "Water on port and starboard bows." When he didn't come back for fifteen minutes, I thought that they were thumping his rump, and went back to make my report. I found that the captain had secured all activities for the day because one of the soldiers had been seriously hurt by a kick in the groin(that's another story). The rest of the day yesterday was anti-climactic. There was evening chow, a couple of successful chess games with Bob Bastian before turning in.

   ...This morning we had reveille at 0430 and routine G.Q. at 0445. Tired? I'll say we were. Part of the morning was spent in getting the stage ready for the day's festivities. The stage of course was the number two hatch located on the forward part of the boat deck. Facing aft on the forward part of the hatch was a gaily decorated throne, with about four chairs on each side of it. The throne was to be for King Neptune, ruler of the raging main and his court and entourage including: Davey Jones, Ruler of the Deep, the Royal Baby (a 220-pound stripling), the royal wife, the royal chaplain, the recorder, and sundry others. To the right of this group of chairs, on the starboard side of the hatch, was a chair wired for electricity, and about fifteen feet in front of that was a tank on which were located two tilt-back chairs, and which was filled with slimy water. In a little while King Neptune and his entourage filed on board to the blaring of trumpets, and cries of "clear the port passage, make way, all polliwogs, scum and scalawags." The King was briefly welcomed on board by the skipper, after which he and his following were seated.

   The court clerk, with his documents arranged on a wooden stand in front of him, called the first victim. The accused man stepped forward and stood beside a swab (mop) with loose bedraggled hair and a cap atop it and labeled "counsel for the defense." The clerk then passed the accused on to King Neptune, who read the previously prepared summons, which invariably accused the prisoner of every crime under the sun and some besides, and of course accused him of being a worthless polliwog. The King then pronounced sentence. This might consist of any one of a number of tortures. The first offender was fairly typical. He was an officer who had escaped taking part in yesterday's festivities, so they gave him the book. He was first escorted, with the usual thump on the rump, to the chair I mentioned before. Then, simultaneously, he was given a shock in the seat of his pants and had his picture taken. Taking his picture consisted of shooting a thin, powerful stream of water right in his eye. He was then escorted to the tilting chairs on the edge of this pool, his walk being made more interesting by the king's jester, who kept jabbing him in the butt with an electrified trident. Finally he stumbled into the chair, seated with his back to the pool. While waiting the next routine, the King's Baby forced a drink out of his bottle down the victim's throat. The bottle contained some particularly foul-tasting liquid. As soon as this was down, he was set upon by the Royal Barber, who trimmed his hair artistically. His chair was given the old heave-ho, and backwards he fell into the pool, where two stalwart Sons of Neptune dunked him vigorously a few times. Up he came, gasping for breath, only to find himself catapulted belly down on a slippery slide from the pool to the deck lined on each side with stalwart shillelagh wielders who proceeded to pound his butt vigorously during his journey from pool to the deck. He was helped from the deck by the few trusty shellbacks and congratulated. He was through. He was in. He was a shellback himself. Oh, happy day.

And so it went throughout the day. Those of us who had gone through the mill were let off very lightly today. The others had to make up for missing yesterday's festivities. One part of the ordeal that the officers were spared was the "tunnel of ap-cray." A piece of canvas about 15 feet long had been sown into a tunnel through which a man could crawl on hands and knees. This tunnel was filled with garbage and refuse, and lined along the sides with trusty shellbacks armed with the usual lengths of hose. The men were forced to crawl through here, and again the universal tune played "Give a Thump on the Rump and then a Bump."

And now all of the ship's company are tired, ugly, hairless, sleepy shellbacks, and tomorrow is another day. Good night for now, my sweet. Sleep well, and God bless you.

November 6 & 7, 1944
Churl Darling,

No doubt you are puzzled at the peculiar date line above. The explanation of course is that at 2:30 this afternoon we passed the International Date Line, thus having the day suddenly change from the sixth to the seventh. Incidentally, we are now members of the Society of the Golden Dragon. This is somewhat similar to the Organization of Shellbacks, and is usually accompanied by the same type of initiation. Today, however, we were merely told over the P.A. system that we might now consider ourselves members of the society of the Golden Dragon. At the same time there was some weird Chinese music and one of the Hawaiian steward's mates addressed in sing song Chinese and we were in.

And on the way back, new recruits were subjected to the same treatment, but this time Lester was a shellback.

June 25, 1945

. . . Not the least of the signs of the approaching crossing is the increasing number of dire threats made against the loathsome polliwogs, the swine, the scum, the barnacle-encrusted waste products of humanity which have yet to be initiated into the society of Davey Jones and the Emperor Neptune.

7

MILITARY TRAINING

INCE LESTER WAS A dentist on board ship, he was not directly involved in things military. He was also by nature not a violent man, one easily aroused to fighting. By temperament, he relied on verbal rather than physical skills, and repeatedly described himself as a scientist who employed the scientific methods of argument and discovery. He worked hard to understand all sides of any disagreement, and used his verbal reasoning skills to bring each side closer to solutions. He relied upon known facts or set about to discover the pertinent ones, to prove or disprove hypotheses, almost always containing his temper. He would lecture or talk about an issue, sometimes for hours, but not display anger.

In light of this, it was a shock to discover the Lester who, through necessity, became involved in various wartime drills. He did not discuss such matters in later years, so this had remained an unknown side of his life.

The most unexpected part of this was Lester's familiarity with guns. He refers periodically to cleaning his weapon, assembling, disassembling and then re-assembling it under timed conditions, and his pride when he performed well. At other times, he refers casually to having or retrieving his gun, as though it was quite a natural part of his day. His should not be as surprising as it is, given that he was part of the military during wartime, when every soldier is required to carry and maintain his weapon. Yet the mental image of an armed Lester is almost oxymoronic.

The same can be applied to his references to learning how to use a knife for combat. In later years, he was known to use a knife for cleaning fish that he had caught, and he used scalpels in his dental work, but never once did he refer to having had any prior experience with knives as combat weapons. This fact alone personalizes the vast transition that servicemen have to undergo upon their return to civilian life. They must put away forever their store of memories of so many implements of war—let alone their actual use in battle.

Less surprising, perhaps, are the references to daily drills and periodic inspections. Very early each morning the entire ship was called to battle stations—and everyone had his assigned location to report to, even a dentist. So every morning for Lester began with this call. There was a rush to get up and to get to his post on time. Once he was there, though, there was little to do—a fortunate sign that there was no actual battle, but they had to remain prepared, just in case. During these drills, he often spent the time talking to the men nearby, or reading.

Inspections, that bane of military life, only occurred when called by senior officers, but when one was imminent, a heightened level of tension was evident. Everything had to be in perfect order and perfectly clean, and there was a rush to ensure that this was indeed so. In the end, Lester's office always passed these inspections, though not always without drama.

The *Oxford*'s function was to transport troops. Lester sometimes makes reference to periods when thousands of troops were temporarily added to the regular crew, and the impact that this created. Frequently, however, this information was censored.

Censorship of letters during the war had long been in effect. It was evident that Lester's letters were censored before they were read by their intended recipients, by a round stamp on the front of the envelope, indicating that the letter had been officially opened, read, and approved by a naval censor, whose initials appeared in the center of the stamp. Lester and Shirley always knew that someone else was reading their letters to each other. The job of the censor was to black out forbidden topics, which, if the letter ever fell into enemy hands, could unintentionally disclose vital information. Each correspondent knew what could not be mentioned. This fell particularly hard on Lester, who could not tell Shirley where he was or where he was about to go. He could not describe battles that were about to happen or that had just been waged. It deprived Shirley of the information that she most wanted to know, and it proved intensely frustrating. It also was a major reason why the letters were often limited to recounting the day's more trivial events.

To make matters worse, many of their letters bore the initials of Lester's friend and bunkmate, Ralph Golden, who was also one of the official censors on the ship, so they could not even pretend that a stranger was reading them. Lester was also a censor, so that he often read the letters that Ralph wrote home to his wife, along with those of many other men.

August 17, 1944

In the morning I attended a class on chemical warfare. This was very interesting...Each of us was issued a gas mask, and the instructor showed us...how to put it on and take it off. First we watched him. Then we did it by the numbers. Then we practiced two surprise drills. After that, he had us put on the masks, and we went into a room that had some tear gas in it.... We had to remove them just before we stepped outside. Even that moment's exposure was terrific. We had to stand outside, facing into the wind for ten minutes, before our eyes stopped tearing.

After that we were given a speed test. This consisted of stepping into a gas-filled room and removing the mask from its case and putting it on. That wasn't at all bad.

September 29, 1944

...Later in the day we were issued .45's (automatics), so it's a good thing I didn't buy my own. Later on we will be issued knives, so that is all well and good.

...You should see me as I sit here. We have to wear our rubber life belts at all times, and we have to take our pistols with us to general quarters (hereinafter referred to as GQ). So I am here at the table in my khakis, typing while my ship pitches quite pronouncedly, and around my all-too-big midriff are strapped:

My belt holding up my pants.

My life belt.

My web belt holding pistol holder with its pistol contained and my clip carrier with two clips (I must weigh about 300 pounds).

Wait until they issue that knife.

October 1, 1944

... *I spent some time this morning with Ralph assembling and disassembling the .45. For such a lethal weapon, it really is quite simply constructed.*

October 11, 1944

... *I guess that I've passed my test as a coding board expert. There were several test messages sent in for me to decipher (decode) and encode, and I understand the results were satisfactory.*

December 3, 1944

... *I spent most of the afternoon in the coding room, breaking a series of messages. That gets to be a bit tiring after a while, but it is very necessary work.*

December 4, 1944

... *We have been having exercises at General Quarters lately, and practicing the handling of casualties. As I've told you, my station has comparatively little activity, so all the morning GQ exercises do is to shorten my working day by an hour or so.*

8

LETTERS TO EACH OTHER

BSENCE MAKES THE HEART grow fonder, as the saying goes, but whoever coined this phrase never went off to war. Lovers are separated for months or years, living with the ever-present fear that injury or death will claim a cherished life. And the rhythm of life as it once was is halted, placed in suspended animation, while memories and the hope of a fresh letter buoy the spirit. During World War II, letters were the life line to the world left behind, with a brief phone call available only as a rare luxury. Yet even the mail was uncertain, as Lester soon discovered. Being at sea routinely affected pick-up and delivery, but the apparent randomness of missed mail could drive couples beyond endurance.

The lack of regular mail from Shirley disturbed Lester's peace of mind for the entirety of his Pacific service. Everyone else seemed to be getting tons of mail, but, day after day, delivery after delivery, there would be nothing from Shirley. Each day, as the time for mail delivery neared, Lester's hopes would rise, even when he valiantly tried to keep himself from expecting anything, only to be cruelly dashed when, once again, there was nothing for him.

Actually, Lester did receive some mail. He got letters from his parents, his sister, his in-laws, and other relatives and friends. He received his dental journals, the Sunday New York Times and care packages from Aunt Frances. He even received dental instruments and a new dental chair, but there were often no letters from the one person from whom he wanted them most. He compared himself to Job, who "bore up under his afflictions," and complained that the lack of communication would try the patience of an angel.

Lester had developed a theory about the lack of mail from Shirley, blaming it entirely and squarely on the Brooklyn Post Office, which he came to believe was derelict in its duty. He tracked postmarks of letters received from Shirley's parents, with whom she was living, and the paltry few he had gotten from her. Lester's father-in-law, Sam, generally mailed his and Rose's letters to Lester from Manhattan, and they reached Lester in a normal amount of time, while Shirley's letters, mailed from the local Brooklyn post office, always came much later, if at all. He also asked her to stop using her pretty stationary, picked out specifically to please him, and to switch to regulation air mail letters, but there was still no difference. This created periodic emotional upheavals in their relationship, as a lonely, depressed and letterless Lester would either ask Shirley to write more often or snap at her for failing to, as she had promised. He would then be tortured by guilt, and pen long, apologetic, love-filled letters, followed by sleepless nights and days of worry. He could not just talk to her and explain what he was going through but had to rely on letters, which seemed to take so long. Shirley, on her end, was indeed writing almost daily, or she would apologize and explain why she had skipped a day. She was taken aback and hurt when he lashed out at her in his loneliness.

Often, however, they dealt with their pain by not writing about it, to avoid troubling the other and to attempt not to think too deeply themselves about the issue. They would vow to each other not to bring it up, only to have it explode out of one of them, arising from a need more primal than prudent.

Lester's first letter is dated July 15, 1944, and eight days later he is already lonely, missing Shirley and writing about it.

> *July 23, 1944*
> *Darling, one thing I want you to know. I am always lonesome for you. But you know that and I am going to try to keep my letters as cheerful as possible, and I'm not going to whine about how awful it is so far away. It is awful, but worrying about it makes it worse. So let's both be as happy as we can during this period of enforced separation.*

July 25, 1944

. . . I expect that by tomorrow I should hear from both you and the Bronx. There has not been a letter since I left; and while I know it has been unavoidable, it still is somewhat lonely.

In the following letter Lester articulates a plan to avoid more emotion-laden topics while simultaneously breaking it:

August 21, 1944

Usually, as I told you in the city, I try to keep my letters placid and calm—why rub salt in an open wound; but every once in a while it does me good to let down the bars of my self-restraint and tell you exactly, or as near exactly as I can, how I feel. And if I'm not wrong, it makes you feel better to know how much you are missed.

August 26, 1944

My Darling Wife,

Evidently, the mail system is very fouled up, for except for that one letter of yours I told you about, I've had no word from you, this despite the fact that I know that you've written to me. What it might be is that they look me up, see my crew is in Tacoma, and just send my mail out there. I am the only member of the ship's company left here.

August 27, 1944

. . . At least it seems that your letters have started to come through, at least I've got one forwarded to Bremerton (dated the 17th) and another sent here, and the descriptive booklet of the Café Chambord, also sent here. It was so good to hear from you at last. I've read and re-read your letters. I knew they would catch up with me eventually, but I couldn't help missing them when they weren't here.

This next excerpt actually mentions the hovering presence of the censor, who read each letter that left the military post or ship. It bears Ralph Goldman's initials. Whether Lester was ever aware Goldman was censoring his letters is unknown.

. . .That's about all for now my sweetheart. Please understand the stiltedness of my last few letters. I am still not used to the idea of someone else reading the things that are meant for your eyes alone. I know how silly that is, because the censors are very impersonal about their job. In a little while, I'm sure, it will make no difference.

September 21, 1944
No letter again. It starts to fall into a familiar pattern. No mail for two or three days, and on the fourth day, five or six letters. The only thing to do is grin and bear it.

This particular letter was written as a result of Lester's censoring duties. He had come across one letter which had really struck him in its simplicity yet directness in expressing its point.

September 23, 1944
My Darling Wife,
The other day, while censoring mail, I ran across a letter from a man to his wife. Obviously, the man had had but little schooling. The spelling was bad, the grammar was horrible, etc., etc., but that man wrote one of the best letters I have ever seen. All that he could do was repeat and repeat words to the effect of "Honey, I love you. Do you know that? Darling, do you know I love you, honey? Honey, I love you, do you know that?" There were about two pages that ran on and on like that. In a sense it was reminiscent of Gertrude Stein. And in a poetic quality of its repetition, it reminded me of the Biblical psalms; but that it was effective could not be doubted. So I'm sitting here and wondering how to tell you again, and again how much I miss you, and how much I love you. I cannot but think that, despite the difference in schooling between myself and the writer of the letter I described above, I can do no better than he did. All I can say, darling, is "honey, I love you. Do you know that? I miss you so much, honey, and I love you. Do you know that? Darling, when I get back, I will never leave your side. I love you, honey. Do you know that?" And Churl, my sweetest darling, even if that doesn't sound as I do usually, it says everything I mean to. Does-

n't it, darling?

It is a little rough. There is much that has been happening that I know you would like to hear about, and much that I would like to tell you about. Unfortunately, as you know, it wouldn't be right, and couldn't be done. In a way, though, it isn't bad. We'll have a lot to talk about on those cold winter nights. I'll thrill you, perhaps, with the stories of what goes on. In the meantime, I think it is all right if I tell you that I haven't been sea sick.

September 26, 1944

At last your letters are catching up to me. I am getting them in batches of three now. And I believe that I like it that way.

. . . No, Churl, your letters to me are not censored. So don't worry about that.

October 7, 1944

. . . Then I really did sort my laundry, brought it below; and on my way down stopped to thumb through a stack of incoming mail, not that I expected any, but who knows, I shouldn't have done that, because although there were no letters for me there were three for Ralph, and of course that made me feel worse. Churl, darling, you'll really have to write every day, even if your letter only consists of nonsense syllables. If you don't, you'll just ruin my morale. I'm not kidding, incidentally. Letters are very important. When we are at sea and can't receive them it isn't very bad, but in port or at sea when the mail comes in and there is none for yours truly it is bad, very bad. So you can see what I mean when I say that your letters to me are amongst your very most important tasks of the day, and I must have them regularly. After all, you don't want me to lose weight because of worry do you? And perhaps have me come home a sylph of 200 pounds.

October 9, 1944
Churl Darling,

Another mail delivery with only a membership card in the ADA for me, not very satisfying is it? I don't mean to complain, dear, for I know that you didn't write for some time, but I do mean to em-

phasize how important it is that I hear from you at every opportunity, for even knowing that I won't be hearing from you I feel bad when I don't receive your letters.

October 11, 1944
My Darling Wife,

It is a mighty tough job to write a newsy letter and still stay within the boundaries of censorship security.

...They should bring the mail on board. I hope there is something from you. It must be at least two weeks now since I've had a letter, and believe me I miss it.

Good night for now, my darling. Take care of yourself and write soon.

October 13, 1944
Churl Darling,

In the very best navy style, "Receipt is acknowledged of three very lovely letters from the addressee," and thank you very much. And excuse me very much for bitching so very much at not receiving very much mail in the past week or so...

October 14, 1944
My Darling Wife,

It is relaxing and refreshing to sit down to write my daily stint to you. Aside from the genuine pleasure I derive from writing to you, for after all when can I be closer than when I am so doing, it is one of the few means of escaping from the dreadful lethargy that so easily takes possession of one on board ship.

November 9, 1944

...And that is the chronicle of the activities. With luck I should have some letter from you shortly. Unfortunately, these will take longer to get to you. You must not worry over any delay in hearing from me. You know how the movements of a naval vessel are unpredictable, and we may not touch at a port for weeks at a time; but I am trying to write every day anyhow, so that you may follow me when the letters do come.

In this next letter, a rather lengthy one for the topic, Lester just vents his pent up frustrations over not receiving mail from Shirley, and describes for her the three-day depression that it put him into.

November 16, 1944
Churl Darling,

> *By this time I am over it; but for the last three days I've really given myself a hell of a time. "Given myself" is the right expression, because I know there is no real reason for it, but I can't help it. You see, we were told on the way over that our air mail letters would probably be waiting for us when we got to our destination, so I passed the time as best as I could on board: working, playing cards, chess, reading, or doing my correspondence course, and of course writing my daily letter to you. And all of the time I was looking forward to receiving a nice thick batch of letters from you. Often I would comment to Ralph that I felt bad because I knew it would be quite a time before you could receive my letters, but I felt good knowing that soon I would hear from you. And then we arrived and we had a mail call, and I told you of the letters I received (none from you) and the excuses I made. To cut it short we had three other mail calls, and not one letter did I get in any one of them. At the same time every other officer, including those from New York and Philadelphia, had three or four letters, some of them dated November 4th, which was remarkably quick time. I didn't know what to do. I know there must be a good reason for it (I just heard, for example, that a part of our mail was sent back to San Francisco by mistake); but, darling, after being at sea for weeks on end and doing nothing but think of you and home, and missing nothing but you and home all the time, I couldn't help but work myself into an irritable and mean state. I'm just getting over it now. For the last three days I've been a rough person to live with. I am looking forward to getting some mail this afternoon—we are making some port, and if there is none there I know that I'll go through the same cycle again, even though, as I say, I am confident that you have been writing to me every day. I can take everything that is handed out to me; tough assignments, bad weather, even Dr. Dickey at his worst, if only I keep hearing from you and reach out to you across the thousands of miles of oceans and continents that separate us through the*

letters. When they do not come when they should I just can't take it. I haven't got the resistance or the morale to get along without hearing from you. It is not that bad while we are at sea and no one expects mail anyhow, but when we make a port and we have been looking forward to receive a large accumulation of letters, and none comes for you while your bunk mates and others get a stack it makes you feel terrible. That is why I haven't written at all the last few days, because I felt badly even somewhat in a temper, and didn't want to write while in that mood.

And that is about all, my darling wife. Forgive me if I've made you feel bad by the rather churlish first page of this letter, but I had to get a little of it off my chest. I know in advance that when I do hear why you haven't written I'll feel like a heel for taxing you with it. Until the next time, then.

All my love.

At about this time, Lester seems to have figured out, at least to his satisfaction, that the reason for his lack of mail, even when everyone around him is receiving theirs, is directly due to errors made at the Brooklyn Post Office. He will repeatedly explain this to Shirley, as well as requesting her to follow his solution to the problem. Plus, he takes pen to paper and writes of his complaints directly to the post office itself.

December 7, 1944
Churl Darling,

Last night I became one of the happiest men in the entire area. In other words I finally received the letters you have been writing to me. After opening the letters and comparing the dates you had written them with the old dates postmarked on the envelopes I became one of the angriest men in the area. Every single one of your letters was postmarked November 25th. Your letters were dated October 21, 22, 23, 28, 29, 31, November 9, and 13. What has happened obviously is one of two things: either the letters were allowed to lie in the mailbox or in the post office for several weeks, in some cases for over a month before they were sent out. You remember I complained that I had no mail from you on our first mail delivery. Well, if these letters had not been grossly mishandled, I would have received mail *both then, and on the more recent mail delivery when I went without. Roslyn's letters from Manhattan seem to get through all right, so I request that from now on you give your letters to your father to mail from his office for you. Possibly in that case the mail will come through. You can't know because I haven't told you that we received our first mail delivery in about three days, and again, as at our last port I had no letters from you, just from Roslyn. Then last night when I came into the room after returning from liberty Ralph told me I had a tremendous stack of mail. You can imagine how bad I felt on the first occasion, and how glad on the second . . . and how angry when I discovered the postmark situation. Needless to say I have been walking on clouds the whole day. In the words of Bemelman, the copy cat, "I love you, I love you, I love you."*

. . . As I sat in the boat on the way to the ship I said to myself, "Now if only I have a stack of letters that are waiting for me when I get back it will be the end of a comparatively perfect day." I asked the coxswain if we had had mail brought aboard, and he said yes, but only a small amount. When I got on board I ran into the wardroom to see if there was anything in my mailbox. Nothing. So I disappointedly went above to turn in. Ralph was up reading. Les, he said, you've got enough letters on the desk to keep you up all night reading them. My mood changed like lightning. I was happy again. Of course, I sat down and read, and reread, them several times. I was so excited I couldn't sleep, but it was good to stay awake and think of the things I had just read from you. It was very good.

December 17, 1944

. . . We have an early mail delivery, but again I had no mail from you, or anyone else. I didn't expect any though, not after having noted how the letters were held up by the Brooklyn Post Office. I wish that I could someday get my hands on the s.o.b. responsible for that. I'd break his damned neck.

January 2, 1945

Churl Darling,

Today your husband is both very happy and very angry. I am happy because at long last I received two letters from you. I am angry for two reasons. First at the goddamned Brooklyn Post-office or whoever is responsible for holding your mail for such long periods before sending the letters on out. The two letters I received today, for instance, were written by you on the 21 and 23 of November. Both of them were postmarked December 22, 1944, at 10 P.M. This has gotten beyond the stage of being funny or even a little careless, even though by this time I expect such an unreasonable thing to happen. It doesn't make it any easier for me to see the rest of the ship get as many as 20 to thirty letters at a time while I stand by with none. And even if there is no cause for it I can't help but worry. I have already written to the Brooklyn Postmaster to complain. You ought to do the same thing, and besides that make sure that you give your letters to Dad to mail from Manhattan. I'm sure that will help a lot. I am so angry at that that I can't describe it to you, and if I ever meet the individual responsible for the many days of worry and sleepless nights I've had as a result of not receiving letters from you that were long overdue, it will go ill indeed with him.

In January, Lester was delighted to hear that the censors would be permitted a bit of leeway on the restrictions, which he immediately communicated to Shirley.

January 15, 1945
South Pacific
Churl Darling,

It seems to be a new day, and frankly I am not yet used to it. Our chief censor, in an impassioned pre-dinner speech this afternoon, told us that we had been censoring mail much too severely, and loosened the restrictions a startling amount. We still cannot discuss the present movements or future plans of the ship, but we can tell you where we were, up till about thirty days ago. At this stage of the game that is a rather doubtful privilege, since so much time has passed that it is difficult to discuss the things and places. Nevertheless I know that you have been consulting maps and atlases trying to guess where I have been, so perhaps this little summary will help you ascertain how good a guesser you are.

January 20, 1945
*   . . . Time drags on. All of us are trying to push the ship to her*
next port, but she insists on taking her own time about it. We are
all so anxious to get mail. I should have quite a respectable amount,
I only got two letters at the last delivery, and they were two months
old. If I'm disappointed again I don't know what I will do!

Here we begin to realize exactly how few letters Lester has been receiving, and therefore the reason for his recurring complaints and angry letters
to the Brooklyn Post Office.   He also describes the difficulty of having the
mail reach the correct port at the right time, in order to receive that mail in
as timely a fashion as possible, and how the navy can often make mistakes.
The couple, at this early point in their marriage, seem to celebrate their anniversary on the 24th of each month.

January 24, 1945
Churl Darling,
*   Besides being the 24th it is a Wednesday and hence doubly blessed.*
So a happy anniversary to you, my darling. And here's hoping that we
soon may celebrate them together. It is fortunate that today is our an-
niversary. I needed some ray of light to cheer me up. You see the navy,
in its incredibly block-headed way, did it again. They sent up all of
our first class mail to the port we had just left, despite the fact that
they had written instructions to hold it here for us. All that was waiting
for us here was a batch of Christmas cards and some packages. For my
part I received a couple of dental journals, and that package of mag-
azines you so thoughtfully sent to me. Don't think I don't appreciate
the magazines, I do; but I was looking forward to hearing from you
since it has been well over a month since the last letter. I'm sure you
can understand the disappointment, although, truthfully, deep down I
sort of anticipated this. The other set up seemed too good to be true.
You know, I figured it out today. Since I've been overseas I have received
to date 17 letters from you. Of those seventeen, five were written early
enough to have reached me in California before we left, but for some
fault in the postal service did not. That leaves 12 letters—12 letters
in four months' time. Now do you begin to see why mail means so
much to us out here?

February 6, 1945

. . . All of us have been anxiously awaiting news about the mail. There were lots of bets that it had crossed us and gone back to where we had just come from. Finally, word came through that that was what had happened. Most of our mail had been sent back, but there were three sacks still here.

February 16, 1945

. . . I have compared the postmarked dates on your letters with those you have inscribed, and I deduce you must have heard from me, suggesting that it works out, for in every case of a letter postmarked New York, the postmark is for the day after your date, and each envelope has a different postmarked date; whereas for those mailed from Brooklyn there are two for the fifteenth, three for the seventeenth, and then they are mailed from N.Y. It must have been on the 16th that you got my letters. To make it clearer I'll list your letters. Three are postmarked the 17th at Brooklyn. On those three you place dates of Jan 13, 14, 15. Of the two postmarked the 15th you placed dates of: the 10th and the 11th. Quite a delay (although not as bad some of the others—one of yours was held 32 days between the time of mailing and the time of postmarking).

Of the New York-postmarked letters: Your letter of the 21 is postmarked the 22. Your letter of January 17, is postmarked the 18, your letter of January 25 is postmarked the 26th. Your letter of January 29 is postmarked the 30. And your letter of January 28, Brooklyn, is postmarked the 30. I think that the evidence supports my point.

March 8, 1945
Churl Darling,

Another day gone by with no mail from you. Tonight's haul consisted of Christmas greetings from Chancellor Chase, and a bill for my annual dues from the ADA. How thrilling. Do you wonder that I am getting desperate? It is made all the worse because the mail situation for most of the ship has straightened out. Ralph, for instance, is receiving answers from Helen to letters he has written her from here. Many of the fellows are getting mail dated the 27th and 28th of February, and here I sit alone (except for the occasional copy of the N.Y. Times that gets through). I was looking over your mail today, and I note that I have received only three letters for December (1st, 2nd, 3rd) and that is all . . . another debt the post office owes me. Oh, well, Job bore up under his afflictions. I can too, since I must; but not with very good grace.

. . . I love you, and how I miss you! Please let the letters come through. I feel my manhood leaving me with each passing day that leaves no news. Goodnight dear.

By mid-March, almost eight months since their separation, the mail continues to frustrate Lester. However, as the following letter suggests, he thinks that he has found another possibility to explain his lack of mail.

March 11, 1945

Churl Darling,

The evening mail delivery has just been sorted. Tonight I received an assortment as follows: Dental Items of Interest, Journal of the American Dental Association, an answer from the Post Office Department to my complaint, and finally a letter from you dated the 30th of January. I already have letters from you dated the 1, 2, and 3 of February.

The post office department said they could find no reason for the discrepancy between the dates on the envelopes and the dates you had written inside, but they had cautioned all employees concerned to use care. As I was sitting listening to the radio, after having read your letter, my eye was caught by a peculiarity on the envelope. Written across the upper left hand corner of the envelope in heavy black pencil, in big block letters were the words AIR MAIL. This was peculiar because immediately over the address on the letter and a short distance under the stamp you had written "air mail" in script and under lined it a few times, also you had written air mail on the back of the letter in the same manner you had written it on the front. As you know, I have given a great deal of thought to the problem of the delay I experience in receiving your mail, and suddenly I had an explanation (I think). Consider: your envelope is an ordinary blue-gray envelope, not a distinctive airmail envelope with its red, white, *and blue border; the stamps you used were two ordinary three-cent stamps, not a distinctive air mail stamp: and finally the words "air mail" were written in longhand quite near the address, and actually were not very conspicuous at all. That this last fact is true is proven or at least partly borne out by the fact that some postal employee found it necessary to write "AIR MAIL" in heavy block letters in the space where ordinarily a return address is placed. Now it seems to me quite conceivable, and logical, that many of your letters in the hurried process of sorting are consigned to an ordinary mail sack instead of an air mail sack, and that is the reason my mail has been coming through late. The fact that this possibility may be the true explanation is further borne out by my recollection of other envelopes similarly marked. Obviously, the mistake is possible. Even though this is only a hypothesis, I want you to act on the suggestions that I give, and the mail situation is so urgent and so acute, and I feel its lack so keenly that I earnestly request no procrastination (in other words, darling, please do as I ask immediately because I am* plotzing *["collapsing" in Yiddish] because of the slow mail service I am getting). Stop using your monogrammed envelopes in writing to me. Instead of those, buy a stock of these special air mail envelopes (I suggest you use the stamped variety issued by the post office). Do not use ordinary 3-cent stamps; use air mail stamps only. Do not write "air mail on your envelopes in your ordinary script in plain black ink. For the meantime use a heavy red pencil and print. Do those things immediately!*

I never felt more sure about anything in my life than I do about this, darling, so please humor me in it. I feel the more sure about it because a couple of the officers to whom I mentioned my theory told me of similar cases where they received distinctively marked envelopes in a short time, whereas plain envelopes took ages. Ralph suggests that if that can be true your mail may be delayed until a ship sails through the canal for this part of the country. You can easily see how long that would delay the mail.

While we are discussing ways to improve the mail situation I have another couple of suggestions. Have stamps made up as follows: AIR MAIL; MRS. L. HALBREICH, AND 921 WASHINGTON AVENUE, BROOKLYN, NEW YORK (this last to be in two lines).

Keep the air mail stamp yourself and get a red ink pad. Now buy three or four dollars' worth of air mail envelopes, and you can stamp them all at once in bright red ink. Send the other stamps to me. I'll use them in stamping all my envelopes to you. It will save a lot of trouble. If you want to you can have a stamp made up with the Oxford on it (like my return address), and use it for mail.

And that is all, darling. I wanted to make sure that you get this as soon as possible so you can act on it. After all, as further evidence consider that the N.Y. Times your dad sends out is distinctively marked, and they seem to be coming through, whereas your letters supposedly mailed at the same place and the same time, are delayed (and I can't believe the post office has a special grudge against me). So good night, again darling, and remember that I love you to pieces, and I'm all wrought up for you.

Love,

Les

P.S. To show what I mean I enclose "exhibit A"—the envelope this letter came in. The date of the letter enclosed is Jan. 27.

All of a sudden, out of the sky fell several letters from Shirley, all at once. The Israelites could not have welcomed manna from heaven as much as Lester welcomed these letters from his much-missed wife. And he described his emotions when he has no letters in exquisitely painful terms:

March 19, 1945
Churl darling,

At long last a windfall of letters. I had just finished playing some bridge, and was walking to my office to write to you before turning in, when one of the corpsmen said, "You know, they've brought some mail aboard". I had just come from the wardroom and knew there was none there, so I ran to my office; but there was none there either. Back to the wardroom I dashed. They were distributing the officer's mail there. I pitched in to help. At the end of the job I had a letter from Herb Train, a letter from Roslyn, a letter from my folks, a letter from your dad, and the following letters from you: February 4, 6, 8, 10, 11, 12, 13, 17, 18, 21, 23, 24, 25, and March 7. Again, I believe, honestly, that a prayer of mine was answered. You see I knew that they had sent out after mail, although there was some scuttlebutt to the effect that the mail orderly hadn't been ready and therefore couldn't go. Naturally I was hoping all day and worrying about it. And at one time I actually offered a little prayer that this time my mail should arrive because I really needed it. And you can see what happened.

April 18, 1945

. . .We should be in port within a week at the outside, and already the prospect of mail waiting for us is sending the spirits of all on board way up high. I hope I do not get treated in the discourteous manner I have been in the past by the mailman. I am so hungry for news of and from you. Except for that letter of March seventh the latest consecutive letter I have from you is dated Feb. 26. If you'll compare that with the date of this letter you can easily see that that is quite a while.

April 22, 1945

It has been a long day, not hard, but exciting; and the result is that at the moment I feel somewhat pooed. I may not finish this letter tonight but the chances are that I will. Before going any further I want to reassure you. I did at last get mail from you. Oh heaven, oh bliss. And not only mail, but pictures. It is almost too much. And I mean that last statement. I hadn't realized how much of an anxiety complex I had developed over the mail situation. I thought that I had pretty good control over myself but actually, part of that pooed-out feeling is a result of the relaxation allowed myself when I finally did get the mail.

. . .I've had a grand, if very exciting, time reading and rereading your letters and looking again and again at your pictures.

April 24, 1945
Churl Darling,

Happy anniversary, darling. Even the mailman seems to have been affected by the spirit of the day for he brought me three letters from you: one from the 14ᵗʰ, the 15ᵗʰ, and the 16ᵗʰ. The first two were postmarked April 18, the last April 21. All from Brooklyn, *so as I say repetitiously, there is still some advantage in mailing from New York. What is phenomenal, however, is that a letter postmarked the 21st at Brooklyn is delivered to me here on the evening of the 24th.*

April 30, 1945
Churl Darling,

Today has been a fairly good day, made into an unusually perfect one by the receipt of five letters from you. As usual I'll deal with them individually; but I want to mention first a sentence from the first of the letters, that of the 20th: "You don't seem to believe me, but I rarely skip a day of writing to you". It isn't true that I don't believe you. I believe you implicitly, and I feel very badly that you have so interpreted what I've said. I knew that I was probably harping too much on the letters that didn't come, but never did I place the blame on you for not writing. I merely thought that you'd like to know which of your letters have gotten through, and the fate of the rest. Of course I couldn't help some genuine griping when I received no mail for long periods of time; but never was the griping directed at you, always at the post office. I still maintain that the New York Post Office probably gives better service than the Brooklyn one (your postman to the contrary). At the same time I never did blame you for the fault of the post office. It happens too consistently for it to be coincidental that I get your letters in groups of five and six, all of them postmarked the same time and date, and all of them written by you on different days. That is what I claim is wrong with the Brooklyn Post Office. Churl, darling, don't take what I've said as a criticism of you. Believe me, darling, I know that you write almost every night, just as I do, and I never intended for you to feel badly or apply to yourself criticism I meant for the post office. Please forgive me. What you say about undelivered letters and packages lying rotting in the warehouses, I know is true. I've seen some of these warehouses piled high with mail and packages. And besides that there is a war on, and much of that stuff is bound to be destroyed. I've developed what I think is the right attitude by now. I just relax as much as I can when there is no mail, I know that sooner or later I'll get a big batch of it all at once, so outside of a certain *amount of absolutely unavoidable blueness I really take it quite well, but still I like to let you know when I get mail and when I don't. You understand that don't you, dear? . . . Your letters are very good, and very well written. They are vivid, and manage to carry over to me surprisingly well a complete picture of Jeff's growing up, even with some of the flavor of being home; and always they carry something of you with them. I love your letters. They contrive some-how to make life aboard this ship something less than a boring hell. I feel good for days after receiving mail from you; and even when we have been at sea for weeks at a time, and I feel the pall of ennui and useless feeling closing in on me, I can always dispel it by taking out your letters and the picture album, and reading through the one and looking lovingly at the other.*

May 14, 1945

. . . I want to tell you now while I think of it that the next break of letters you will experience will be for quite a while, possibly for as long as three or four weeks, so don't worry if you don't hear from me for that length of time. We are going on a very long trip, but it is not perilous. Your letters on the contrary will probably be waiting for me at our first port of call, since they go air mail. Mine will have to wait until they can be discharged at this first port before they go airmail back to you.

May 26, 1945

. . . There is a possibility that the trip may be broken by another unexpected stop, so again the old question is argued, "Will they have mail for us here, or do you think it has all been forwarded to our ultimate destination." Time alone will tell; but in the meantime it is an intriguing subject of conversation.

June 13, 1945
Churl Darling,

This is being written early in the morning. I didn't write last night because I was tired, disappointed, angry, and a little unhappy; but I am reconciled to my lot now.

Journey's end, as you know, came yesterday. The first boat to leave the ship was the mail boat. Eagerly we awaited its return with the long awaited bags of mail, and word from home. In three hours it did come back with . . . no mail. Nope, there was no mail for us. Presumably it had been held at our last port. What a blow, what a disappointment. Each day we had been eagerly awaiting the end of the trip so we could hear from our loved ones, and now, because some no good so and so had blundered, there was no mail. It took some time to get over that shock, but now, I am finally used to the idea. It is just what one must expect I guess.

June 16, 1945
Churl Darling,

A trickle of mail arrived today, but none for me. By this time I have become inured to disappointment, so I didn't feel as badly as I might have. This was all recent mail. Our previous mail, I understand, has been sent to some place where we are not, and as is usual in these cases it will probably be a long, long time before we catch up to it or it catches up to us. However, should we be here for a few days I should get some of your recent letters, which in itself is something to look forward to.

June 19, 1945
. . . . The big event of the day was mail call. Yes, some of our mail is finally finding us. I received two letters from you, both written before we left the States, May 8, and May 15. I'll answer them in detail a bit later. I can't begin to tell you how good I felt. I read and reread the letters countless times. You write such marvelous letters, darling, and I love you for it. They brushed away the black mood I had been the victim of, and while they intensified my homesickness, at the same time they relieved it. Of course as is usual at mail call, Ralph got a tremendous number of letters, but I know what will happen. Mine will trickle in for a while until one day I'll get about twenty at once. That will happen for about three days. Then I'll be cut off again. But so long as I get mail I do not complain. And so you see, yesterday was rather a good one for me.

July 13, 1945

    . . . It looks as if that bonanza of mail I expected at this port will not materialize. But at least I got a few letters from you, and those pictures, so I can't complain too much. Tomorrow will probably be our last mail delivery for several weeks. Oh, well I can wait. The yield at our next port will be so much the greater. But think of it about six letters to last me for May, June, and now all of July, for it probably won't be until early August till we get mail. That's a long time for a man who loves his family to wait.

For a few weeks in August, Lester and Shirley had a reunion in San Francisco. However, even being together for a relatively extended time did nothing to stop Lester's ongoing cry for and about mail. It also includes new reasons to explain the absence of mail, this time not just for Lester but for the entire ship—including their commander, the weather, and the navy receiving their mail much more slowly than the army. Of these reasons, nothing could be verified except, of course, the weather, which did at times prevent planes from delivering that precious cargo.

September 5, 1945

    . . .When we got on board we heard the magic news that there was mail in the wardroom. We dashed below and there I found those wonderful letters you had written to me. Doesn't that make a fine day? I read them at the dinner table. Need I say that I didn't have much dinner? I can't get over it. As I commented to Ralph, "It is almost worthwhile being in the navy just for the pleasure of getting mail."

September 15, 1945
Churl Darling,

    There is still no mail for the ship, but we understand that that may be due to the bad flying weather which has held up the mail planes. No matter what the cause, the absence of mail is very real, and very much felt.

September 25, 1945
Churl Darling,

    Today at last it came true. The A.P.A. did bring two very full sacks of mail up from Manila. What excitement. What a thrill. I had no patients all morning because everyone was busy reading their mail. It took almost all morning before I got my full quota, but finally I had the full quota: August 28th, 29th, 30th and 31st. This delivery included mail up to the fifteenth of September, but as usual the Brooklyn post office fouled up. I didn't care, though, for I was so happy to get these few letters that I almost cried. I actually did kiss them. Your letters mean so much to me. They carry you across the country, and over the ocean straight into my waiting heart. How I love and miss you, my darling. I read the letters, and reread them, and then again. Then, after work today I read them again. Thanks for being you darling, and thanks for loving me as I love you.

October 10, 1945

. . . There are some vague rumors that our mail is on a ship that is at Okinawa. If that is the case we may get it soon, for it is probably that she put in there to escape the typhoon, and its center should pass tonight. Man could I do with a few letters from my wife.

October 21, 1945

. . . Ralph was there, and we talked about the mail situation. The most ridiculous thing about the whole affair is that the Army, who are our passengers, have been getting regular mail deliveries all along; but we have had none. I don't know how true it is, but I have been given to understand that the commodore in charge of this task force, and whose responsibility it is to direct the mail to be sent up to us, will not even permit a dispatch to go out enquiring about the mail so that we may know where it is. If that is true the only reasonable explanation for it is that the man is a lunatic. Oh, well, it does no good to rant and rave about it, one must be philosophical.

October 29, 1945

. . . And now for the news about our mail. There are tons of it lying on the beach at Linguyen. An APA came in today bearing the mail for the Montour, the commodore's ship. Through an error in

understanding they have brought only the mail of the one ship, and left that of the rest of the squadron at Linguyen. Oh, if I could only meet dear Commodore Graf as a civilian. What fun.

November 5, 1945
Churl Darling,

Miracles of miracles, the expected actually happened. We were hoping to get mail here today, and we did. It is the impossible come true. Of course the mail is not what we expected, it is a later batch; but after all, mail is mail. It is a blessing, it is water to we who perish of thirst, it is the staff of life, and the uplifter of our vanquished morale. In short, my darling, the four letters I got from you today made a new man of me. Your lovely letters were aided and abetted by a letter from Roslyn. Besides that I received my Battle Baby [Newsweek] for September 3. So you see I didn't make out at all badly.

Just a few days later the U.S.S. Oxford, with its dentist, Lester Halbreich aboard, embarked on its journey back to California and Lester's return home. For all of the eighteen months that Lester and Shirley were apart, they had relied on their letters to each other and suffered tremendously when they were deprived of this one lifeline to the other.

9

OTHER LETTERS

T HE MAIL BROUGHT LETTERS and packages from people other than Shirley, somewhat brightening Lester's days. Of these, the most important were from his parents, Charles and Esther, his in-laws, Sam and Rose, and his younger sister, Roslyn, who was a frequent correspondent. He also received letters from friends and other relatives, keeping him up to date on events in everyone's lives.

Charlie's and Essie's letters reflected their ongoing struggle to master written English, given that they had been born in Russia and lived among Yiddish speakers. Of the two, Essie, who had come to this country as an infant, was the better writer, but neither was fluent, and their letters tended to be short and simple. Sam and Rose did not have that problem, writing much chattier, longer letters.

Reading the letters from Lester's friends highlights the tremendous effects of the war. Each man was in some stage of service, going to or returning from a duty, their wives and children left behind, their careers put on hold. The sudden death of soldiers is evident in these letters as well, as the couple comment on who has been killed and how the widow is coping. The letters provide an intimate glimpse into the lives of young couples in the wartime 1940s.

"*Dear Lester and Shirley,*" Esther wrote to the couple when they were living together in Texas, between late 1943 and April, 1944,

> *We received your last letter and were very glad to hear from*
> *you but my darling son, you made me feel very badly [sic] when*

you said in your last letter that I am in the dog house. What should I say, my child? I only want to say this much. That I love you more than anything in the world and I pray to God that in this war you should be brought home safely, first to your darling wife and child and then to us. And darling, it goes without saying that I am ready to give up my life for you because you haven't yet lived. Darling, there is [sic] two reasons that I did not write. The first one is you can't realize, Lester dear, what a job it was to work and run a home. As you know Dad was not able to go to the store and get things ready-made. Everything had to be cooked and even I had to do my own baking. Dad was not able to eat the ready-baked cake and you know how Dad likes cake, so of course it was a big job, more than you realize. The second reason it was because my mind was content and very, very happy that you had your wife with you. I felt you are not alone. Not only did I feel that you are not alone but you have everything with you and that made us very happy. We often spoke of it. We said Thank God for that. Well, I think I said plenty for now because I hope to see you soon and explain things more fully.

My best love,
Mother

Lester's father, Charles, wrote on the occasion of Lester's birthday on April 7, 1944.

Dear Lester and Shirley,

It is quite some time since we saw each other or spoke to each other. I still can't get accustomed to this [sic] abnormal times when a parent can't see his child whenever he wishes or speak to each other according to their desire. But so long we are positive we have no part in bringing this abnormal times and plague to ourselves and to our shores so we have at least a salvation and that is that we are the surgeons and Samaritans and we have a duty to perform to operate on the cancer of the old body of the old world and bring piece [sic] and happiness to all of us that will enable us to see each other, speak to each other whenever we feel like. Amen.

Do you know, Lester dear, that April 7 is approaching. Do you

*remember what happened on that day just as it was yesterday? You
certainly looked swell. You felt so embarrassed that you would not
look at anyone so I had a consultation with the man who brought
you to this beautiful country and he advised to select a beautiful
looking blond nurse to take care on [sic] you and to our surprise as
soon as the nurse startit [sic] to make you comfortable and by the
way it was necessary to do it every five minutes you opened your
beautiful blue eyes and you started to smail [sic] and everything
was fine and dandy. And this lasted for a whole week and all of a
sudden on the eight [sic] day something awful happened. A man
with whiskers and yarmulke on his head came to the hospital and
did something terrible to you. You cried and you refused to open
your eyes again and you would not smail [sic] again. But the blond
nurse somehow managed to convince you that the man in the yarmulke has to support a wife and children and that is his livelihood
and you are very softhearted and sentimental and you forgave him
and all of us and you smiled again and you forgot entirely all the
wrong he did to you and there you are. All of this happened 27
years ago. Is not that wonderful? Good luck my boy for many and
many years to come. You and your wife be together in happiness
and joy with all of us together. Amen. As for myself I am still working on the first million. I am feeling better now. A happy Passover
to you and Shirley. Hoping to hear from you soon.*

*I remain yours,
Chas.*

August 16, 1944
   *. . . The rest of the time I've spent writing letters. I've dropped
a line to the Bodners, your dad, my folks, the Trains, the Schaeffers,
and you.*
   *Darling, will you send me the address of Jules and Jane? I'd
like to write to them.*
   *Oh yes, I had a nice letter from that sgt. And his wife, enclosing
a dollar bill and thanking me. I had a letter from Danny Lasmore,
and Herb Train's was waiting for me when I got back, as well as two
or three from Roslyn.*

September 18, 1944

...I wrote quite a few letters yesterday. Among others I dropped a line to Miltie[Milton Rosenberg, brother of Shirley's mother, Rose], Sid Cooper, and Aaron Richman. I ought to be getting some mail in my turn, but I rather doubt that I will. Most people just won't write. Those letters are my last attempt to elicit a response.

September 21, 1944

I wrote to the Schaeffers and the Vinsons this afternoon. That about brings me to date on my correspondence.

November 13, 1944

...Herb wrote me a typically Herb Train letter. I really couldn't help but smile at its tone. He writes about the dog and it seems that the kids are crazy about him, and he is crazy about them. I am very glad to hear that that is working out all right, even though I can't help but feel sorry that Roslyn didn't get the pup after all [Roslyn refers to Lester's sister, who was considering a puppy at this time].

December 30, 1944

... Esther [Esther Korchin, a relative of Lester's, on his father's side] wrote me a very lovely letter and enclosed a few pictures of Greg [her son]. He is really a good looking child. Don't you think so? Es writes a very nice letter. But talking of nice letters, my dad came through with one of his masterpieces. It really made me feel good to read it. It was so much like him that for a moment I was back home with you in the Bronx immediately after one of those Friday night kreplach [Jewish-style wonton] dinners. Pop was just lighting his pipe after tea and expounding his story. I don't know whether to send the letter on to you or copy it and send it on. In any event, save it.

The officers' packages haven't been distributed yet. One of the corpsmen says he saw a package addressed to me down below. Here it is now—Ralph just brought it up. It is a package from Miltie and Frances [Frances is the wife of Milton Rosenberg, Rose's brother]. I'm not as surprised as I was the first time; but I am just as pleased. I just appreciate these people so much. The package is of cupcakes, and are they delicious!!

January 3, 1945

. . . I told you, I believe, about receiving the first copy of the New York Times. It was a good feeling to read it even though the paper was a month and three weeks old. I wrote to Fran [Rosenberg], thanking her for her gift, and I wrote to Esther also. She sent me some pictures of the baby who seems very good-looking.

January 4, 1945

. . . Churl dear, I am going to type a copy of that letter of my dad's I told you about. I think it is quite good.

"Dear Lester,

"It is quite a long time we did not see each other or speak to each other. I must say that I am disgusted and tired of this whole set up.

"According to my thinking this mess should been over by this time and you dear boy would be home with us like before all together and this why I did not write to you thinking you would be home soon. I must admit I made some miscalculation somewhere regarding this matter. And now we must look at this tragedy more serious and work hard to bring this drama to a speedy successful ending so we will be altogether again the same like before. Amen Amen.

"Dear Lester, this week we Israelites celebrate the festival of Chanukah. You remember Hanukah, when you was a child, how you hoped to get some Hanukah presents from your relatives, especially from your pop? And now I am a grandpop. So I had to follow our custom. I explained to Jeffrey Neal all about Hanukah, about the Hasmonean Mattathias, son of Johannon, the high priest and his sons. How they with a small army and conquered our enemy because they believed in God and freedom for all. And now history repeats itself. But to you my dear I must say that with the help of God we will conquer all our enemies and we will have peace and freedom all over the world. And we will celebrate another Hanukah amen. Mother and myself gave to our dear grandson a Hanukah present a $25 liberty bond made to his name. So when he will get older he will also know what Hanukah means. As for myself and mother we are all well trying to make the best of everything. Hoping to see you soon I remain your

Charles."

Isn't that a nice letter?

And now, my sweetest wife, it is time to say Goodnight again. Sleep well my darling and dream of me. I know that I will of you. Kiss our son for me. And give my regards to all.

February 8, 1945

. . . Roslyn has written several letters to me, but you know how well she can say nothing in a page and a half. At any rate she hasn't mentioned anything about her affairs de coeur to me. Perhaps it is just as well. I certainly don't know what to tell her. I suspect that, if she is as unsettled as all that, neither one is the right one. On the other hand, who can say! Much as I love my sister, there is nothing I can do or say that could help her. Perhaps the example of our marriage means something to her. In any event, no matter what she does, I am behind her and hope (oh, I hope) that she makes a happy decision.

March 1, 1945

. . . Thank your father again for sending out the Times as he is doing. I find it very interesting to read about the things that have happened from the Times point of view. This one, for instance, had an article on the back of the page by Hanson Baldwin predicting the invasion of Iwo Jima, which, as a matter of fact, took place some time ago as you can tell by the papers.

March 11, 1945

. . . Did I tell you that I received a little note from Fran telling me that she had visited you and Jeff, and telling me what a wonderful baby he was, and admonishing me to keep my chin up. You know I think she must be one of the few really and genuinely nice people we know. She does so many little and small things that are so totally unexpected. And all the nicer because of that. You can tell her I like her a lot, but don't make her blush.

March 19, 1945

Your dad really wrote a lovely letter, in which he described, very vividly, a typical day at the Scheller mansion. I was very pleased with his letter, and with everything he told me.

My dad, too, wrote me a lovely letter in which he told me of your visit with Jeff to the Korchins and took occasion to remind me of the holiday of Purim. Undoubtedly these Bible stories of my dad's should be collected and published as Bible stories for children. He has the knack of telling them simply, movingly, and concisely. He's a good kid too, and I love him more than he knows. Every so often the thought of what my parents went through for my sake comes to mind, and I am overwhelmed with humility in the presence of such unthinking self-sacrifice. They truly have the stuff of greatness. They truly are wonderful people, but more of that some other time.

Herb Train's letter as usual is a rollicking, ribald sort of an affair. I wish we could see them often after this is all over. Between the four of us there seems to exist a Rabelasian sort of understanding that makes for good comradeship. Incidentally, there is a piece of news contained. Gladys is pregnant. It must be contagious. I was sure that they would stop with Marsha.

March 19, 1945

. . . Roslyn's letter of January 13 is nice, and much like most of her other letters. She tells me that she saw Aida, and liked it, and that she has added to "our" record collection. Aida must have been quite an experience. I have never seen an opera either. I don't know whether to feel sorry or glad.

March 25, 1945

. . . I wrote a congratulatory letter to my folks this morning on the occasion of their 34*th* wedding anniversary (April 1). I had thought of waiting till then, but I decided I'd best get it off now, even though I know it will not get there until later.

May 1, 1945

. . . I got back to the ship a while before dinner time. I had a lovely letter from Esther Korchin. She says that she likes you very much, and that each time she sees you, she likes you more, a fact that surprises me not all. She enclosed a picture of Greg in his Babee-Tenda, which was really adorable.

May 18, 1945

. . . I received no mail from you for the last two days. I suppose that it's been sent on ahead to our next port of call (in which case it will probably be a long time catching up). I did receive another package from Frances, though, a beautiful three-pound box of Lofts candy. What can I do or say. It's really too much. This time, in particular, it was almost funny. There I was lying in the sack with this upset tummy, I had whoops a few times in the morning, and all my roommates were coming in to console, and visit with me, and in the meantime eat all my candy, which of course I durst not touch. Of such things do the refinements of torture consist.

Shirley's father, Sam Scheller, wrote to Lester in the summer of 1945 from upstate New York, where he and Rose had gone on vacation. The doting grandfather's depiction of the baby must have made Lester wild with longing.

July 12, 1945
Dear Lester,

. . . Mrs. Scheller and I decided to spend ten days here so we could look around before we brought Shirley and Jeff and Elaine along. It is hard to find a place here, where they would accept a baby. Some places would accept, if the child was two years old, at least. However, we are not worrying because the old saying goes, for money, you get honey.

. . . Well, Lester, by the time you get this your son will be one year old. Whenever I think of him my eyes open up, my lips come closer, as if I would want to kiss him, and I am only 150 miles away and have see [sic] last week, so I am just thinking how you must feel. I can sit here all day and write to you about your son, but that is writing about the Grand Canyon or one of the other Seven Wonders of the World. You must be there to appreciate it. Shall I tell you when we got out for a [sic] auto ride, how he sits in his seat (he has his own seating contraption which is fixed onto the back of my seat), and every once in a while he leans over and blows the car signal, or trys [sic] to help me operate the car. And his hand is on the wheel. Well, Lester, can you believe what time does? . . . I could go on writing all

*day but one thing that stands out in my thought is how each morning
when I come into his room he may be lying in the crib, playing with
his blanket or some toy, and when he sees me he drops everything and
is up against his crib, waiting for me to take him, or when I get home
after business, he is usually get [sic] his dinner. Shirley is feeding
him and is telling him a good night story or why it is necessary to
eat. I come in and he forgets it. He tries getting out of his seat. He
can't because he is tied in, but he is eager to see me. Well, Lester,
these are some of the things you would see if you were home. I will
close with all the love in the world and all the luck that it won't be
long that you can be home and see Jeff and Shirley, your folks and
all those who are near and dear to you.*

Love,
Dad

In November of 1945, just before Lester is due to come home, his sister
Roslyn wrote to explain why she had not written sooner. He and his younger
sister had enjoyed an affectionate relationship despite their age difference.
Her letters kept him abreast of her romantic life, particularly as she began
to fall in love with Harold, to whom she became engaged, ending her earlier
turmoil. Previous letters between Lester and Shirley referred to Rozzie's
ambivalence over whom she should choose as a husband, and they were very
pleased that she had finally settled on Harold.

Nov. 3, 1945
Dearest Les,

*It's been some time since I've written you, I know. Please forgive
me and understand. Harold has come home for good now—his discharge becomes effective Nov. 15—and it just seemed so difficult
to sit down and write you. The days don't seem to be long enough—
to work, to go to school, and to be with Harold.*

*Harold, too, owes you a letter, and it's on his mind. We're all
hoping that there will be an end to this letter-writing very soon.
I'm hoping, Les dear, that you will be home for good by Christmas.
We're all waiting so very patiently and I suppose you understand
that Harold and I most of all. . .*

Danny Green came home Wednesday—with his discharge and

all. Herbert is expected next month.

Everybody at home is well. Mom and dad both look and feel fine—Jeff is as endearing and loving as ever and Churl is busy making him say "Daddy"...

Please take care of yourself and try to come home to us as soon as you can.

Love,
Roslyn

Shirley, writing from the home front, had a view of the people and the world that Lester had left behind. It is true that men always go off to war and suffer in their sacrifice, yet the women at home had their own unique perspective on the war, the lives disrupted, and the relationships altered by changing circumstances. Shirley's position reflected that of her entire cohort of mothers and daughters, wives and sisters. While they never served in battle, their world revolved around the shifting deployments of their men and the added responsibilities they themselves had to assume. They kept the home fires burning and the flow of personal and national news flowing in their letters.

Shirley very casually wrote about many of the men she knew, or knew of, who were in the service. It was so common for those men to be coming or going or actively serving that it drew little significant attention. Such items entered letters to Lester simply as news. Yet this very acceptance of military service only serves to emphasize its pervasiveness.

October 9, 1943
...I spoke to Rho and Aaron. He's reported [sic] for sea duty tomorrow morning at the Brooklyn Navy Yard.

October 16, 1943
...Milt doesn't think he'll be able to be in again for a long time. He's to go to Arkansas, escorting Nazi prisoners. He and Fran send you their fondest regards.

October 19, 1943
...I met Berry Hattenbach (the pretty girl on the 4th floor in our house), and I sat and talked with her until 2:00 in the morning. It

seems her husband is treated terribly in the Army as a private because he's Jewish, and she, too, has been humiliated. She's so thin and nervous with worry over him. She's afraid he's headed for a nervous breakdown.

October 21, 1943
     . . . Barney is stationed in Chicago now.
     Dorothy and Ken are home. Ken is now stationed near Providence, Rhode Island, and comes in weekends. He's working on experimental planes and it's a pretty permanent job. How do you like that for luck?

October 24, 1943
     . . . Tonight, we're having dinner with Mrs. Vogel in Lum Fong's. Dr. Vogel is somewhere in the South Pacific. Isn't that a shame?
     . . . Aaron left for sea duty yesterday, and you should have seen the crying.

October 25, 1943
     . . . Last night we went to Lum Fong's with Sydney and Mrs. Vogel. She looks wonderful, and I was fascinated the entire evening with her accent. I confessed the crush I had on her husband because of it, also. She's trying to get a job now that Dr. Vogel is in the Solomon Islands; but no one will take her because she didn't receive her citizenship papers as yet—although her husband is a citizen and in the Army. In fact, the Red Cross took her blood but will not allow her to do volunteer work for them. It's a shame, but I guess they can't be too careful in wartime.

November 18, 1944
     . . . Thelma's friend is, alas, the wife of a dentist—a former college roommate of Chester's. He has been overseas with the army about 10 months now. They also have a baby—whom the husband hasn't even seen. Thelma showed me a picture of her daughter, quite a cute little girl. She seems very optimistic about Chester's return in the next couple of months—for she said the usual span of duty for a medical or dental officer is about 10–14 months, and Chet has been away 10 months already.

November 26, 1944

. . . *Roz and I talked about various things, most important of which is her perplexing love life. She still isn't sure whether or not she loves Harold—even though she's getting involved with him to the extent that he is sending war bonds home in both their names which certainly means something. He is now stationed in Tampa, Fla., undergoing operation training, after which he most probably will ship out. And Leon still writes to her from France. Poor girl— it is true that she has scarcely had time to really know either of them.*

January 8, 1945

. . . *The wedding was held in the Essex House and Joel, the groom, is 4F—the army couldn't find one redeeming feature in him. (Now I'm not being catty, am I?) I was seated at a table of young couples, and some extra fellows (very nice), and all 4F. (Why, I haven't the slightest idea, as they were all healthy and good–looking).*

January 9, 1945

. . . *I spoke to Thelma Stoopack today. She says that Chet is now waiting for his orders, as his senior medical officer already has his. When does it count from, when you reported to your ship, or when the ship left for overseas duty? Oh, darling, if I could only hope that by next summer I'd see you. Do you write to Chet—also what about Lou Korchin? Did I ever tell you, I called Marvin Meister's wife. She seems very nice—expects her husband home soon. Imagine, he's already overseas 14 months. I made an appointment to go to the movies with Esther Korchin one evening next week. Her sister Pearl is also living at home with them now with her baby boy. But her husband is stationed in Washington, D.C., and so comes home every weekend. Esther expects Leo home by next summer, as that will make 2 years over the maximum policy for service in India. Do you know the various stations of the men in the family?*

Elliot—still here
Morty—Germany
Danny—still here

Herbert—Italy
Barney—Cleveland (was out at sea for a few weeks)
Bruce (Elsie's husband)—Belgium
Mary's husband—Washington, D.C.
My Uncle Milt—France
Uncle Sidney—Sidney, Australia (teaching English to the
    Armed forces—correspondence course)

January 10, 1945
. . . Berry's husband is touring the Panama Canal Zone, putting
on U.S.O. shows.

January 18, 1945
. . . I stayed in front of the house for a while and then, at 4,
Berry came down. They had received bad news this afternoon. Her
sister-in-law's fiancé called up to say he was being shipped, and
didn't know whether he'd get home to say good bye. Their big wedding was scheduled to take place in a week, and now, after 4 years
in the Army (stationed in Maryland —guarding the Coast), he's
being shipped so close to it.
. . .We met Dottie and Ken . . . Ken is in from the state of Washington on one of his innumerable leaves.

January 23, 1945
. . . Murray Kraus (her fiancé) is now ferrying supplies daily
from New Guinea to the Philippines in an unarmed plane; which
the army pilots blithely refer to as the "sitting duck" because of its
lack of speed and maneuverability. It's not the safest job in the
world—for they stand no chance against a Jap plane—and she's
plenty worried about him. He's been overseas already for 15
months, and, as she says, she is now about ready for Kings County
(I'm going to share a cell there with her soon).

February 11, 1945
. . . Berry and her sister-in-law Thelma came up. (Thelma is
the girl who got married last week. For want of better things to
tell, listen to this hot one. Her husband got a week furlough for his

honeymoon and then had to report back to his captain. But Thelma got unwell on her wedding night—it lasted the entire week—and so she is still a demure virgin; or so she claims!).

The following letter from Shirley describes to Lester her only personal encounter with the death of a soldier in the war, the fiancé of her close friend. Of those many thousands of soldiers killed in combat, this one death, striking a close friend, touched her deeply.

February 17, 1945
Darling,

For the first time since you've been away, I missed writing to you. I've tried to write for these past 3 days, but I've absolutely been unable to sit down to do it. For a pretty horrible thing occurred.

This Wednesday, Gloria Siegel received a telegram that her fiancé had been killed. Ever since then, I've been with her constantly. I'm just a mess of tears for all the tears I've shed since that night. It is the first time that anyone whom I personally know has been killed in this war—and I'm afraid it has hit me pretty hard. She's been with me all winter, and I have grown to be very fond of her. You must remember Murray Kraus—he was even at our wedding. According to the telegram received, he was killed in a crash on the island of Leyte, in the Philippines, on February 6. She was expecting him home at any time now, and they were to be married immediately. She's taking it terribly, poor thing. She can't stand to be alone, and begs me to be with her. I don't know how much help I am to her, for we both sit and cry constantly. Each night I've tried to sit down and write to you, but so far I've only dissolved in a spell of crying. Mother and Dad declare I'm growing morbid, so I'm trying to snap out of it.

After all, I knew Murray very well myself, having met him 5 years ago at camp. In fact, I was the one who introduced him to Glo.

After a winter of hearing her excited plans for her wedding, and their future together, and how much in love with him she was, it came as a cruel blow.

I was with her Wednesday night, when, after she came home from school, her parents told her.

I see I'm still not over it, for I can't seem to get away from the subject. He was a navigator in the Army Air Corps and had been flying supplies from one island to the other. The only ray of hope they have is the slim chance that it might have been a mistake, for about a month ago he wrote Glo saying that someone had erroneously reported that he had crashed, and he hoped a telegram hadn't gone through. But this telegram definitely says he was killed on Feb. 6— almost a month later. Her family has sent telegrams to the War Department, and also to the Jewish chaplain at Leyte, to investigate. Murray had an adorable wire-haired puppy he had bought in Australia, which always flew with him. They sent a request that, in case the dog by some chance didn't go with him that day, to please send it home.

Darling, she has been begging to please give you his address. If by any chance, you ever get to Leyte, would you please look up the address, find out the details, and if possible bring home the dog if he is alive. I know it's almost absurdly impossible, but she made me promise to ask you. Here it is:

> *Lt. Maurice D. Kraus 0-805172*
> *Headquarters*
> *V.A.S.A.C.*
> *A.P.O. #72*
> *c/o Post Master*
> *San Francisco, Cal.*

War is lousy—lousy—lousy!!!

Tonight, Gert Ginsberg, and Berry, and I have been up here, trying to cheer Glo up. So far, it's hopeless.

February 23, 1945

. . . Berry is so lucky. She has just gotten through speaking to her husband. They are allowed to call one another, even though he is in Panama.

Perhaps it is just as well I am unable to call you. I know if I ever heard your voice, I would get so choked up, it would be impossible to speak.

She had kept the baby up, and Eddy heard him making cooing sounds. They spoke for 15 minutes—and the bill was $40. And they do it often.

March 7, 1945
. . . Gloria Siegel came up just as I was going out, and she came with us. She also brought sad news. They received official confirmation of Murray's death from his commanding officer. He wrote that he had died in an accidental plane crash on the morning of February 6, and he was buried with Jewish services on the island of Leyte. Now that there is absolutely no hope left, she has broken down terribly. Up till now, they had slight hopes, but no more. It is lousy!

March 25, 1945
. . . She [Rozzie] has just come back from seeing Harold off at the train. His 5-day extension furlough was over tonight, and from here, he'll probably go overseas, unless he's lucky.

May 3, 1945
. . . I'm glad to hear that you have seen Al Sobel. Dad seems to think a lot of him; and from what I've heard, he must be pretty nice. I don't know if he knows, but his father isn't very well (don't mention it to him). One day this spring, I'd like to drive out and see his folks and meet his wife. How long has he been out at sea, and what does he think of his chances of any orders?

June 21, 1945
. . . Harold is still in Italy, doing nothing. Roz expects him to come home in August, for a 30-day furlough, and then on to the Pacific. So far, he's been pretty lucky. So far he's seen no warfare, and perhaps by the time he's due to go to the Pacific, the war may be over. Who knows? I certainly hope so.

10

AT SEA

AFTER THREE TEDIOUS MONTHS of training, Lester's ship, the *USS Oxford*, put out to sea, in October of 1944. There were no more practice drills or training runs; this was the real thing, at last. The Oxford was sailing from the West Coast for the Pacific theatre. Its primary purpose was to carry army troops to the war zone, and throughout the coming year this is exactly what the crew did; they picked up and dropped off varying numbers of men, getting them to where they were needed. The *Oxford* did not directly participate in battles—it was not a warship. Yet they came very close to danger and had several encounters with Japanese planes.

Nonetheless, life aboard ship was anything but tense. There was relatively little to do, and a recurring theme in Lester's letters about his life at sea is boredom. There seemed to be plenty of time for sleeping, for entertainment, for meals, for sunbathing, for reading, and for just plain gazing out at the sea, the stars and the moon.

The weather was usually unbearably hot, since they were sailing in the tropics. Lester kept talking about suffering the most when the ship was in port and the air was still. When the ship was moving a sea breeze at least constantly blew, which cooled those lucky enough to be on deck.

The tropical sun combined with the close quarters could wreak havoc on relationships aboard ship. So many men were crowded together in a metal vessel with only a few fans, and tempers occasionally and predictably frayed. It is perhaps most remarkable that arguments did not occur more often.

October 27, 1944

Churl Darling,

Well here we are at sea at last. The threshold of the great adventure; but it seems no different than usual. The sea is calm, and so are we.

We were waked this morning by the sound of the general alarm, and all hands man your battle stations. It was the routine general quarters that we have each day a half hour before sunrise, and a half hour before sunset.

It is violating no confidence to tell you that we have troops on board now; but I cannot tell you the type or their destination. For that matter, I do not know their destination, nor do they.

Now that we are at sea, I am forced to hold an election. Tomorrow is the appointed day. It shouldn't be too bad because most of the eligible voters have already used the state absentee ballot.

. . . The day has been very slow. For the first day or so at sea, that is to be expected, since it takes a time for routine to be established. I had my first two army patients this morning. They acted no differently than do the navy boys. One of the army doctors is a Major Glick, a Boro Park lad.

The day has been very cloudy, but with a calm sea. Despite the almost complete absence of roll, many of our passengers are experiencing all of the discomforts of sea sickness. They'll get over that in a short while.

The army brought along one thing to justify their passage . . . a supply of 16-mm motion picture features. We had no 35-mm projector, and no 16-mm features. Now with the army's supply, we can make up the slack and show movies on board ship. That is a definite aid to morale.

Now that we have the army on board, I cannot continue with a description of my fellow officers from a mess point of view, since our mess arrangements are now very different from what they were. But every once in a while, I'll pick someone out to tell you about.

By the next letter, Lester is already adapting, already becoming very quick at getting himself dressed when General Quarters is sounded.

October 28th, 1944
My Darling Wife,

This morning we were awakened by the clanging of the bell signaling routine general alarm and the passing of the words, General Quarters, All hands man your battle stations. Your husband is really learning to shrug into his clothes with amazing rapidity. Ralph usually beats me down, however, for he sleeps in his underwear whereas I sleep in the nude (don't blush, Mamma Rosie).

After General Quarters, of course there was breakfast. This business of eating your meals at regular hours has its drawbacks. If you miss a meal, you really start to get hungry after a while. For the first time in weeks, I changed from two soft-boiled eggs to hot cakes and bacon. As previously noted, I was hungry.

After breakfast I repaired to my office and started to make preparations for the day's work. As I shrugged into my gown, my eye fell on the duty schedule for the first time, and sure enough mine was the 0800–1200 watch. Without more ado, I put my shirt back on and climbed above to the coding room. It wasn't bad. I had a few messages to decode, and it was interesting enough.

I had to leave early, for today is the day I had to distribute federal ballots to the eligible ones. There weren't many, but it was a matter of an hour or two's work to get them off. Now I have to deliver them to the post office, and get a receipt for them.

. . .You remember how fond I am of platform rockers. Well I think after this trip I will be surfeited with them. Right now the whole ship is a platform rocker rocking back and forth and sideways. See, it's an ill wind that blows nobody any good. Now you won't have to be troubled with a platform rocker in our house.

Lester writes just one line in the next letter alluding to being joined by an escort carrier, yet it hints at the vast number of ships that are out in the Pacific with him.

October 29, 1944
Churl Darling,

Another morning ushered in by the rude demanding [call] to

General Quarters, another mad dash to dress and get below to our G.Q. stations, and another Sunday was initiated. It has been a beautiful day. The sea, while not rough, has been very roll-y, and since they come on from directly abeam (the side), the ship really rolls with them. It was too rough to do any work today, so I secured the office early. In the morning I took care of turning the executed Federal ballots over to the mail clerk and then spent some time leaning over the side, watching the waves race towards the ship, toss it lightly up, and pass under and on. Sometime during the morning we were joined by an escort carrier, one of the same type that Chester is on. He continued on a parallel course about a mile off our starboard beam. We watched him pitch and toss and roll for a while and then went below. When I came back he had changed course and gone.

Although the sea was calm, the swells caused considerable rocking. The crisis of seasickness had passed, but an epidemic of insomnia followed, and the heat and humidity increased.

October 30, 1944
My Darling Wife,

Tonight, my darling, there is just time for a few lines before turning in. The days are getting longer and longer, and the routine General Quarters in the morning are getting earlier and earlier, and since your husband has not yet become accustomed to the changing time schedule he has been getting tireder and tireder. Tonight I am really tired, so I'm going to turn in early.

. . . The sea is calmer, but the ground swells persist, so the net effect is the same as if it were quite rough: the ship rolls and pitches considerably. It is that roll and pitch that accounts for much of the inability to sleep. Say you are lying on your side. The ship rolls slowly to port. Up till a certain point you are comfortable; suddenly your whole body rolls to port also, and you are awake. As you become adjusted to the new position, the ship rolls to starboard, and the process repeats itself, and repeats itself again and again. The net result is a sort of half-awake sleep that is better than none at all, but not to be compared with the real thing.

Lester began to describe the effects of the tropical heat.

> *November 1, 1944*
> *Churl Darling,*
>
> *That General Quarters Alarm seems to grow more and more innocuous as we grow more and more accustomed to it. This morning I heard it as a distant far off bell trying to pierce a wall of sleep and failing to do so until Ralph yelled over, "Hey, Les. It's General Quarters". Then up I jumped and like the Blue Flash I was in my clothes and down below by the time you could say Jack Robinson.*
>
> *We can at last act as individual hygrometers now. As we make more and more southing the humidity becomes more and more marked. There isn't a stitch of clothes that can stay dry for any length of time at all. We wake up each morning drenched in perspiration, and I say wake up with an air of amazement because I never remember having been able to fall asleep at all. Our staterooms as I have told you before are quite small, and contain four of us. At night we have to darken the ship. That means that all doors and port holes have to be protected from giving away any light. That used to mean that they had to be closed, and the poor occupants would immediately smother to death. Now they have a device called the deadlight, which is put into the porthole and has openings in it arranged so as to admit air and prevent the passage of light. The result is that instead of smothering im-mediately, the process takes a little longer, but the result is the same.*

In this letter Lester mentioned a meal that he had. The navy certainly fed the men well, and as dining was the high point of most days, the men enjoyed describing every meal. This hit those at home hard, as they were being severely rationed. While Lester routinely dined on steak, his wife and in-laws could rarely indulge, causing some jealousy on the home front.

Inspections were another break in the boredom of shipboard life, pro-viding fodder for letters home.

November 2, 1944

... *It seems impossible, but this morning again the humidity is up. It seems as if your husband is destined to dissolve into a lake of perspiration. At almost all times during the day there are huge drops of perspiration all over my face, and my body is drenched. G.Q. was sounded a bit earlier, and breakfast was served immediately after that. There was time to get into the sack for about an hour before turning to the day's work, but it was really too hot. Ralph and I were standing at the starboard rail when word trickled back that a breeze was blowing; it was heaven to just stand there and be cool.*

We had quarters at about eight o'clock, and from quarters we had an abandon-ship drill. This time the troops were allowed to participate, and they practiced finding their stations. It was funny in a way to see them come up from below. Each had his rubber life belt inflated and bulging under his armpits, and from the belt of each dangled a water canteen and a first-aid packet. Many of them are still somewhat sea sick and the look in their eyes was pathetic as they stumbled to their places on the deck. One of the officers at the dinner table told me of a man in his company who is still sea sick. This man had been across seven times, he said, and each time has been sea sick all the way across. I said that in his place, I'd probably have gone over the hill before making another ocean voyage.

We had a good lunch today consisting of spaghetti and meatballs, with ice cream and frozen strawberries for dessert. After lunch I went to the room, where I sprawled out and read the startling adventures of Nero Wolfe, detective, for a while. Then at one, oops— 1300, came the pipe of the bosun's whistle, and "Turn to. Continue Ship's work. Sweepers man your brooms. Clean sweep down for and aft, and all ladders." So like a witch out of Macbeth, I manned my broom and flew madly below to my office where I proceeded to scare the daylights out of my patients.

Seriously speaking, though, I find that my office is one of the most comforting spots on board ship, and I am determined to spend a good deal of time here rather than soak in my room. You see, it is located on the outboard side right near the end of the port passageway, and the porthole opens up on the passageway. Well, the forward

*motion of the ship pushes the air back aft, where it piles up against
the bulkhead that ends the passage, and a good percentage of that
air comes through the porthole into my office. Of course I have my
ventilating fan in the porthole going at full speed in the attempt
to help pull the air in.*

*We are to have an inspection tomorrow, so I had the boys work-
ing to get ready for it. I knocked off work early so that they could
do their jobs without interference from me. You should see the place
now. It looks like an advertisement from an equipment catalogue.
Everything is polished, and shiny and bright.*

*After work today I sat in on the tail end of a class in Japanese
plane recognition, and then had a bull session or three with some
of the younger officers. That growing a bit boring I got into my
sack again and read some more about the adventures of Nero Wolfe.
Then I took a short nap until G.Q. time.*

Below, Lester describes a General Quarters that was not a drill but a result of an actual sighting of an enemy vessel. It caused quite a stir among all
the men, as this was the first such event. However, as the months, and these
events, went on, they failed to get a rise out the men anymore.

November 3, 1944
Churl Darling,

*After dinner I came back to the office to write to you, but first
I had to go below to the electrician's shop to see about changing
some bulbs. I was down there, passing a pleasant joke back and
forth, when suddenly there came the pipe of the bosun's whistle and,
"General Quarters. All hands man your battle stations!" Then the
bell, "Bong, bong, bong, bong." Up till now most of the men had
moved slowly and aimlessly to their stations, but not this time. I
was in the crew's berthing spaces at the time (the electrician's shop
was right in there), and those boys moved fast; and incidentally so
did I. I moved through the passage from port to starboard and forward along the starboard passage to the first water-tight door. I
stood there and whipped the men to move faster before I closed the
door. As soon as the last man was through I dogged the door down,
and it was going to stay that way. This was no drill. Our talker re-*

ported ready to the bridge and remained plugged in on the circuit, giving us a play-by-play account. It seems that some unidentified target (surface vessel) was someplace around us. We had a ticklish hour or so before we secured. Nobody knows what it was, and in this case no news is good news. While we were down there, the dogs that secure the water tight door started turning. Well, I turned them down as soon as they got they turned up; but this guy was persistent. I could see no future in standing there, so I decided to let this guy open the hatch, bawl him out, and send him back. I did that, and I had my mouth open to start eating him out when I noticed it was the army colonel. He was bringing us a few medical officers to help us man our stations. I swallowed my words, although I could have legitimately used them. No one is supposed to come through. I explained that to him as I let him and his men through; and then I battened down the door again. I had barely finished when I heard an apologetic voice in my ear saying, "I'm sorry, but I'll have to trouble you to loosen all of those dogs again—I've got to get to the main battle-dressing station." Colonel, I told him, there's a ladder here that goes up to the main deck, and then if you aft to the ward room you can get through to your destination; but this door must stay secured. He looked at me, I looked at him, and he went up the ladder. We were down there about an hour. In the meantime our radar kept tracking this vessel and giving us reports on it. Finally we secured from G.Q., and here am I writing to you.

As I say, it was hot down there, so I'm going to try to rustle up a Coke. I'll write more tomorrow.

November 10, 1944
Churl Darling,

Today was a red-letter day in our trip. We made a couple of landfalls. The fact that these landfalls were only a couple of islands is neither here nor there. They certainly did relieve the monotony of seeing the sea. The first was a small island sighted about ten o'-clock in the morning. I heard that land had been sighted, and ran up on the bridge to take a look. Dead ahead was what appeared to be a huge cloud on the horizon. Someone told me that the cloud was land, and I did him the credit of believing him. It turned out later that he was right. Everyone on board lined the rail of the ship to watch this infinitesimal speck in the bosom of the ocean slip slowly by. It was really an exciting event.

Today again was another of those typical days at sea. What I do to make the time go by I do not know, but surprisingly enough at the end of the day it was gone. Of course I have my work that keeps me occupied during the day. Then in the few spare hours left I try to get topside for a little air. Then I have chess, my bookkeeping, and always a book or two to read. It is amazing though how long the day seems (and, with a 5 o'clock G.Q., it is really long) at the beginning of the day, and how at the end it seems to have just flitted by.

We were surprised to have a field day today, so I knocked off work at 10 o'clock to let Lowman get started getting the place shined off. The kid really does a good job. It really shines after he gets done. Then at about two o'clock I started seeing patients again. I must have been in one of my extroverted, hilarious moods, because my three remaining patients that afternoon had the time of their lives laughing at and with me. At the conclusion of the day's work I went out to the rail to watch another island slide by, and a rather well-known one at that.

. . . The seas hereabouts are very calm. Every once in a while the desk quivers to the vibrations of the engine. That is the only way I know we are at sea.

Lester describes the excitement of first seeing land ahead. The entire journey, though, became one of hopping among islands, of being at port or at sea, and it no longer held the excitement that this first one created.

November 13, 1944
Churl Darling,
Well, we made our first landfall last night and came to anchor in the harbor of one of the South Sea islands, which one or even which group, of course I cannot say for reasons of security. The word

went around the ship in a minute: "Land dead ahead!" Everybody who possibly could lined the rail. There wasn't a bit of rail space available. We nudged our way into the harbor. Those who had glasses [field glasses] were continually being pestered, "Say, gimme a look for a minute, will ya?" I was among the pesterees. Sure enough, through the glasses we could see the coconut palms and thatched huts, and the high hills swathed in clouds that all my reading had anticipated for me. Through the glasses I could see a group of men, evidently some colored service troops, swimming around a raft. It was a pretty sight. We haven't been able to get ashore yet, and perhaps we may not be able to. That remains to be seen.

. . .Yesterday I did a little work in the office in the morning and afternoon, although the afternoon's activities were curtailed by our sighting land and the interest and necessary observation involved in same.

November 16, 1944

. . . Neither Ralph nor I got ashore at our last port. We came close, though. We were both of us in the boat and about ready to shove off when the exec ordered all officers in the boat to come back aboard. It seems that we had been placed on an urgent availability, and only those officers with official business ashore could hit the beach. Sightseeing isn't considered official business, so Ralph and I stayed aboard.

We took on some new passengers at this last port and it seems that all of the soldiers have nothing to do but make curios to sell to the sailors. They have coin bracelets, shell bracelets, rings, and so forth, nothing particularly beautiful or interesting. Much of it is like the typical Mexican tourist crap, and they ask and get exorbitant prices.

. . .Well, here we are at some other place in the South Pacific, but for all the difference between this and the last place we might as well never have moved. First off, of course, I must report that there was no mail awaiting us here. That means no letters for anybody. That being the case, I can't feel too bad.

The weather is really hot and stinkin'. What I mean is that we are doing the stinkin'. The day was rather uneventful.

. . . I have hopes of getting ashore tomorrow sometime. That will make the first time in several weeks I'll have touched terra firma. What a thrill. The funny thing is that you never mind not being ashore while at sea, but the moment you get in sight of harbor, and later after the hook is dropped, you get spilkas in tochas *[in Yiddish, "grow impatient"], if you follow me.*

November 23, 1944

. . . I got a sort of tough break today, although there is nobody to really blame for it. It seems that there is a shortage of mess attendants for the crew's mess, so each of the divisions has been asked to contribute a man or men, the contributees being chosen from the lowest-rated men of the division. My corpsman is one of the two lowest-rated men of the division, and he lost the toss, so he is elected. The reason it is a tough break for me is that I have to break in a new boy, and that is always a long process. And what usually happens is that, just when the kid is acquainted with what I want, he gets transferred again; but that's the navy.

We will be in port again in a few days, and I have been looking forward to getting some mail; but scuttlebutt has it that it is very improbable that there will be mail there. Oh, woe! This business of hopping all over the ocean is tough on the mailman. . . and me.

November 24, 1944
Churl Darling,

. . . This morning's activities consisted of decoding a group of messages using a certain-used system. Most of the messages weren't applicable to us, so after a long laborious labor of translation I'd show them to the communication officer, and he would glance at them briefly, then throw them aside, saying they didn't interest him. Life is really hell. This afternoon I spent the first hour after lunch in instruction for my new corpsman. The work necessarily went a good deal more slowly since I had to tell and demonstrate everything to this new boy.

In the next letter, Lester briefly describes the decoding machine that he has been using and he is amazed at its simplicity.

November 25, 1944

. . . Old man time zone keeps robbing us of our sleep. We lost another hour yesterday and again had an early morning G.Q. That is the one advantage of being in port. Usually we do not have to go to G.Q. then.

After chow I stood a four-hour watch in the coding room, and had some fun decoding a few strip messages and using that wonderful machine which practically thinks for you. All you do is set it up, then type the message in code, and it prints the decoded version. It is really marvelous. I was unable to be in my office for inspection of course, because of my coding board duties, but I am told it received very favorable comment.

. . . After I left the bridge I still had about an hour before evening G.Q. I used the time to censor my portion of the mail. They have a better system for mail censoring now than they did before. Each officer is given a small portion of the mail to read every day. That way the work is evenly divided. After finishing the ten or twelve letters that had been put in my box, I still had time for a few pages of that history of China I told you I was reading.

G.Q. interrupted the reading and sent me scurrying to my post with chessboard in hand. Lately they have been having casualty drills during G.Q. Tonight, just about as Ralph and I got into an interesting part of the game, the P.A. system announced a casualty for us to take care of. We dispatched stretcher bearers and broke out our supplies. When the casualty was brought to us, we gave him a mock treatment for his mock burns, and by then G.Q. was about over. Last night one of the battle problems announced was a submarine torpedo unexploded in the engine room. We were talking about it at the dinner table, and the exec asked me how I'd cope with the situation. "Sir, I'd run like the very devil to the nearest ladder and hop over the side as quick as I could. Unexploded torpedoes are not for me." There was some laughter but general agreement that was about the only sensible thing to do.

The wardroom has been enriched by the addition of a cigar

mess. The cigar mess merely is a convenience of having candy and cigarettes on sale at all times in the wardroom instead of having to go below to the ship's store to buy them. I am a charter member (to the tune of a ten-buck share of stock, which may appreciate or depreciate in value). Dr. Davey is in charge of the affair. He has arranged for a little candy stand to be set up in the wardroom and already it is heavily patronized.

Lester described a typical day for Shirley, summing it up by saying that there is usually little to do. Thousands of men were at war, but they all experienced it in their own way, depending on where they were stationed and what their duties were. Life on a ship, at least a troop ship, seemed to offer far less actual combat than being assigned to a forward attack unit.

November 28, 1944

    ...Today deserves little more than a paragraph. There was nothing to do and all day to do it in. In the morning I was supposed to have had the coding-board duty, but I was relieved after only a little while. In the afternoon most of my patients disappointed me. The most productive thing I did all day was first to take a nap this afternoon, and second to write home, which I am in the process of doing now.

November 29, 1944

Churl Darling,

    At this juncture life aboard the APA 189 is assuming an appalling, boresome aspect, more so with each passing moment. There is just so much repetition. Even reading becomes boring. And besides that it is so long since I've had a word from home. We have had no mail delivery since we arrived here, so I do not blame you or anyone else for the situation, but it is now well over a month since I've had any word, and as patient as man is, that is too long.

November 30, 1944

    ... I slept a little late this morning. One of the advantages of being in port is that there are no early morning G.Q's to disturb you. Breakfast consisted of juice, toast, and coffee, and then the morning's work, which was largely routine. At lunch Dr. Davey beat

me at acey-ducey, and in the afternoon I had a few more patients, and there you have the day till now. In about 30 minutes the liberty boat leaves, and Ralph and I will be on it. I expect that we'll have dinner ashore again. Today was pay-day but I've got enough money to see me through for a while, so I just let my couple of bucks ride.

December 17, 1944
Churl Darling,

At sea again, and it is almost a relief to be on the way again. Peculiar, isn't it, that a homebody, domesticated individual, like myself should be so impatient to stay on the move. It isn't that I am a wanderer either. It is just that, at sea, for some reason or other, there is a great diminution of tension.

I did a fair day's work for a change today, in spite of being interrupted by numerous drills. What spare time I had I spent in putting to use what I learned in my correspondence course in elementary bookkeeping, and figuring out the answer to a problem in the elementary course I didn't answer. Quite a job it was, too, but at last it's straightened out. You see, I have in addition to my other duties been appointed as the auditor for the cigar mess. Davey is running the cigar mess, and he gave me as incomprehensible a set of figures as can be imagined to approve of. I couldn't understand them at all. I suggested that we sit down together and try to work out a system of double entry bookkeeping from the start of the cigar mess until today, when we would take inventory and close the ledger. He thought it was a good idea, so we started it this afternoon. I opened up a General Journal for him. Then from the General Journal I opened up the necessary accounts. I balanced all of the accounts and proved cash, successfully. At this point, my headaches began. I suddenly realized that my course had posed problems involving only the sale of services, not of merchandise, e.g., the books of a dentist, or an accountant, etc. I didn't know how to keep the account of the stock. Was it to be a debit, a credit, an asset, a liability, or an expense? How to take inventory, and this, that, and the other thing. Things kept going from bad to worse, but we finally worked out the solution. I was quite proud of myself. I struck a trial balance of balances that balanced. Then, since I had no analysis paper, I prepared a separate

*profit-and-loss statement, and laid the groundwork for the balance
sheet, before knocking off. Tomorrow I will close all of the ledger accounts and reopen them. It was really quite a day's work. I believe
I'll keep on keeping the books. Perhaps that way I'll really remember
what I learned. I didn't intend to take the second course, but now
that I've had my interest involved, I believe I'll study it after all.*

Lester waxes philosophical:

January 4, 1945
Churl Darling,
    *Another day has passed under the ship's forefoot, flung into
the bottomless sea of time like the bow wave is flung to that passed
before, but enough similar so that casual observers might say, "Well,
what's the difference?" The difference is that a few different drills
were held today than were held yesterday. The difference again is
that, today at general quarters, I played chess again with Ralph
and won all of two games instead of losing one and winning one.
The difference is in the increased limpidity of the sea, and the increased uniformity of the swells. The difference is in the amount
and kind of dentistry I did today in my office. The difference is in
what I said and did with my shipmates. And that is only a partial
list of the differences between today and the one that went before.
So perhaps there is something new under the sun after all, at least
if we are perspicacious enough to see it.*

January 7, 1945
Churl Darling,
    *Our tempers are getting more and more frayed lately. A result
of too much living in cramped quarters. Luckily we all realize the
cause and excuse the occasional outbursts of temper. Aside from
these infrequent interruptions, the calm placidity of life aboard the
ship continues. The meals are regular, the hours of sleep are regular,
and so your husband thrives in a rather fleshy manner. At the present time, my hair is still too short to comb back but long enough to
present a mussed-up appearance. The result is very unfortunate,
cosmetically.*

Time often hung so heavily, despite the joys of sun bathing, talking to friends, playing cards, and eating, that Lester began to take a few correspondence courses, which he mentions in the next letter.

January 26, 1945

. . .Today was one of those ridiculous inspection days. I say ridiculous because it just kills the day. The boys turn to and spend all morning and part of the forenoon getting the ship cleaned up and prepared for inspection. Naturally you can't work until after inspection, because then you'll only dirty the area up. Toward the end of the day, the inspecting party comes around and looks in all the unlikely places for some dirt, finds it, makes a note of it, and passes on. Next week the process is repeated. The dental office always makes a good showing on inspection because of the enameled and chromium fixtures. Besides, it gives me a chance to relax, so I really shouldn't kick. This morning I read two of those Headline Books, Toward a Peace that Pays *and* The Roots of World Politics. *The last of the two was very interesting. After lunch I had time to read one of the essays of Charles Lamb. I have a collection of them in one of those handy armed forces editions and I read one every so often. After the inspection I had intended to take a sun-bath. But again weather interfered. It was dank and nasty rather than sunny, so I stayed in and played some more acey-ducey with Davey, again sharing the honors. I also started to read a book in one of these correspondence courses on* The Small Business. Course I. The Organization of the Small Business. *Oh, the life on the rolling main is academic indeed. What does it matter, as long as I keep myself busy enough to stay out of the cutthroat poker game that has developed onboard? I can lose 5 or ten bucks at a sitting with equanimity; but when the night's losses amount to 50 or more dollars per man, it is time for yours truly to find his way out. Why, I don't even enjoy winning that much money for feeling sorry for the people that have lost.*

At any rate I had time before dinner for a small nap which proved very refreshing, in view of our early G.Q. this morning.

And that, my darling, brings you abreast of the times on board

*the APA 189. Good-night for tonight, my lovechild. Take care of
you and hold Jeff for me.*

Love,

Les

January 31, 1945

Churl Darling,

*It would seem that we have been here too long. As evidence of
that I offer last night's horrible excuse for a letter. At least we are
under way and there is the sensation of motion and the accompanying
illusion that something is being accomplished, that we are going
somewhere (which of course is a delusion); but here at harbor with
the same routine, the heat intensified, the ship still in the water, the
sensation of monotony is heightened. All of the creative depths of
an individual seem dragged out, used up, vanished. So it has been
these last two days or so. Everything seems stale and gray-tasting.*

February 2, 1945

Churl Darling,

*I didn't write to you last night because it was one of those hot
stinking days in port during the course of which we did nothing
but sweat and feel miserable. Today at last we are underway and on
our way (we hope to that long-awaited mail). There is a different
feeling about the ship now as she rolls to the swells of the sea; and
the cool sea breeze has swept away most of the ugliness of temper
induced by the sultry stay in port.*

Here, Lester unexpectedly encounters the ship's commander, and they
actually hold a conversation. Also, they watch the ship's navigators do some
star shooting, which is a time-honored method of determining the location
of the ship, still used then, despite more modern technology.

February 5, 1945

*. . . After chow today I excused myself as soon as I decently
could. The sun started setting a little early tonight, and I didn't
want to miss it. As I turned aft on the navigation deck I faced the
skipper coming onto the bridge. As I didn't have a hat on, I couldn't*

salute, so I contented myself with a big hello. He responded, and to my surprise, since usually he seems very preoccupied, he stopped to chat with me for a while. We passed a pleasant 15 minutes in chit-chat. Of course most of our talk was about the war. I was the first to tell him that Manila had become ours, so we talked about the Japs for a while. While we were talking, the navigators came by to do some star shooting. We joined them for a while, and then, under the theory that working men should not be forced to be socialites, I excused myself to let them do their work in piece [sic]. The rest of the time until now I have spent in watching the sunset. It was very brief tonight, but full of lovely soft shades of colors. It was a cozy, intimate sort of a thing, rather than the flamboyancy of earlier days.

Incidentally, the captain mentioned that we may get mail tomorrow. God grant that it is true. I am so hungry for news of you and home. And now my sweetheart, Goodnight, and God watch over you and Jeff.

February 9, 1945
Churl Darling,

After writing to you last night I intended to go get some sleep since I have a 12–4 watch in the morning. Somehow or other I got inveigled into a bridge game, and the first thing I knew it was time to go on watch; and me with no sleep. I finished out a sleepy watch, and managed to get a little catnap before G.Q., but I was still rather tired. Today was inspection day so I wasn't allowed in the office. On these days it belongs to the corpsman to get ready for the afternoon inspection.

After inspection (about three o'clock) I went above and got into my shorts for a little bout of sunbathing. While engaged in this pleasant pastime, I noticed the captain's inspection party, which was assigned to the weather decks, working its way from the main deck upward toward me. I decided that it would be undiplomatic to be caught in briefs by the captain, so at an opportune moment I skedaddled below to my bunk to wait for the announcement that inspection was completed. Guess what happened. Of course. The last thing I heard was the boatswain's whistle and some word about inspection; the next thing I knew I

*was being awakened for dinner. What a pleasant nap that was.
It is so good to awake cool and refreshed for a change instead of
hot and sweaty. The only trouble with all of that is that we have
an early G.Q. tomorrow, and I'm not at all sleepy now. The punishment of mankind comes home to roost; but it was worth it.*

How does an anchor actually get raised or lowered? It seems that this
was something that he was quite interested in. He devoted a good deal of
the letter to this procedure, which did seem to fascinate him.

March 4, 1945
  *. . . Not since the ship has been in commission have I ever once
seen the anchor raised or lowered. Today the ship had to change
berths, and I resolved that I would be up in the fo'castle to watch
the hook come up. I was fortunate, for within the space of a couple
of hours I saw both operations consummated. Usually the anchor
is lifted at the start of a voyage and let down at the end, quite a
time interval as you can see; in some cases, as in mooring to a dock,
the anchor is neither lowered nor raised. So you can see how fortunate I was in seeing both operations in the course of a few hours. I
made my way to the fo'castle shortly after the word had been passed
to set the special sea and anchor detail. I was almost too late. Already the anchor chain was being drawn up. I won't go into detail
about the operation. Suffice it to say that there is a very powerful
winch that controls the raising and lowering of the anchors (one
on the port, one on the starboard—one anchor). The anchor chain
is made up of a series of giant links, each of which is braced in the
middle by a cross-piece. At the command from the bridge, the bosun
gives the winch operator the order to start hoisting the anchor. As
the winch puts tension on the chain, the ship is drawn up to the
anchor, which at the beginning is buried deep in the mud of the
bottom. Finally the ship is directly over the anchor. In this position
the resistance to the upward motion of the anchor is at a minimum;
and it is a comparatively simple matter for the powerful winch to
break it loose and start it upward through the water. The bosun
has his head hung over the side all this time, watching the cable
and giving the appropriate orders to the winchman. And of course*

your husband had his head hung over the side also, asking foolish questions. As the chain is drawn up, two men armed with hoses flush off the caked mud with a powerful stream of water. As you look down there is a lighter green that seems to flash through the dark green water, for all the world like a gigantic fish at the end of a line. Slowly this sparkling green gets closer to the surface, getting brighter and taking on form as it does so. Finally, just before it breaks surface, the outline of the flukes may be discerned. The next moment there is a flash of white water, and there she hangs, black and massive, immediately over the water. The winchman is given the order to stop, and word is passed to the bridge that the anchor is clear of the water. A short time later, the upward motion is started again. And now about halfway up on the hull the anchor strikes a projection built into the hull and sloping slightly from fore to aft. As the anchor comes up she rides along this projection and suddenly, flip, the massive anchor is turned over into exactly the right position to be received in its nest. That was really ingenious, and for the first time I realized the purpose of that projection. Now the anchor was drawn securely into position. The winch was stopped, and a safety lock clamped across the links of the chain. The anchor was in. I suppose it doesn't sound like much, but really it was very interesting. Letting down the anchor was exactly the same process in reverse, and I will say nothing about that.

"Man Overboard!"

March 12, 1945

The day was uneventful, by which I mean that it was just like a million other days (a little exaggerated) with a little work, a little reading, and a little bridge. I spent some time rereading some of your old letters. I read again about Jeff's ½-year birthday party, of your preparations for it, and of its tremendous success. And when I read of your little prayer for me to be with you for his 1st-year birthday party, tears came to my eyes as they did the first time I read your letter. Please God that this be so.

We had a moment of excitement this afternoon. I was getting ready for an extraction on my last patient when the word over the *loudspeaker came: "Man overboard on the starboard side." We dropped everything and went out in a rush to the starboard rail. Nobody could see nuttin. We assembled at quarters. All personnel of this ship were accounted for. Could the man have been from the ship ahead of us? No, it finally turned out that the wrong signal had been hoisted by accident by the ship ahead of us, and we had acted on it. For a while the situation was confoosin, but not amoozin; but no great harm was done.*

. . . It is starting to look like the beginning of the rainy season. We have had several hours of a downpour that gives no sign of abating. If that is the case, it is one time to be thankful we are aboard ship. It must be hell in these land bases with all the mud, and muck, and dampness.

March 13, 1945

. . . Today was rather easy for me. The ship was moving from place to place in the harbor, and the constant setting and unsetting of "special sea and anchor details" interfered with my scheduled appointments to such an extent that, in the morning, I was almost altogether idle; and in the afternoon I had only two patients.

Chow is served at 11:30 and 5:30 now that we have troops aboard. That gives us a long lunch hour and takes away my excuse for not playing chess during the time.

. . . Due to the new seating arrangements I have been moved from the foot of my old table to the head of the new one. I am now a person of some importance, the one the mess boy serves first of all. From this you can easily see that my figure will not suffer from lack of food. Across the table from me sits a captain from a surgical team (but I do not believe he is a physician); next to him sits our chaplain. To my right is another chaplain. Can you hear your profane husband carefully choosing his words in the dinner conversation, and can you see my occasional embarrassment when, despite all precautions, some cuss word inadvertently slips out.

The great cultural mixing bowl that is the military provided many opportunities for collisions, especially at mess. Lester first hears about lasagna at one meal, and provides a lesson on the Irish in New York to a priest at another.

March 16, 1945

*   . . . As each meal takes its rightful place (within the belly) I am developing a closer comradeship with those who share it with me. Dr. Coniello, who sits opposite me, is a Fordham man. He is a small dark type, with a thin moustache. Yesterday at lunch we had spaghetti and meat balls. Naturally this precipitated a discussion of Italian foods and cooking. Together we reveled in fond recollection of spaghetti with different kinds of sauces, prepared and served in a true Italian style. We talked of chicken cacciatore, of veal scaloppini, of soups and salads, of fried green peppers. He described something I'd never heard of. It is a very involved dish built up of several different layers of macaroni, this, that, and the other thing, and finally placed in the oven and baked. The discussion made my, and his, mouth water. Curiously enough it evidently had a different effect on our seat mates. Chaplain Noland however, a staunch product of the middle west—Oklahoma, and Kansas City—couldn't help but turn up his nose in evident re-vulsion at the very thought of such outlandish dishes (I have heard him speak gloatingly of hog chitlins and the "cheese they make of hog brains"). Which all goes to prove something or other.*

Chaplain Noland (he is the ship's chaplain) and I got a little smile out of another bit of table conversation. This took place at dinner last night (which incidentally featured some good steak). Chaplain Regan, the army Catholic chaplain who sits at my right, turned to me and enquired if I knew whether or not it was St. Patrick's Day. I professed ignorance, as did the others all around us. Then Regan asked if we knew the date (by way of background: Regan is a fellow of about 24 or 26 years of age. He is about 5'9," fairly huskily built, with a fleshy character to his body and face, that betokens an appreciation of good food (indeed at every meal he comments on how wonderful it is to be eating good chow again. He is blond and wears glasses that give him a rather studious expression. In all of his conversation he affects a deep rolling timbre to his voice that, while appropriate to the pulpit, is out of place in table conversation). We were able to supply the date for him. Then he said, "Oh, yes, tomorrow (or today—I don't remember) there will be a tremendous parade in New York. Practically the entire police force will be there (as the Order of Hibernians). Everyone will be marching. Indeed many of the Jews will close their pawnshops, put on a green ribbon, and parade themselves." At that chaplain Noland caught my eye, and we smiled. It really was a little funny—the idea of the Jewish pawnbrokers, and the idea of New York's entire police force being Irish (which is something the world likes to see). Neither of us made any direct comment, but I pointed out that Boston undoubtedly had a noteworthy celebration on that day, and that they had a much greater Irish population than New York. I also commented that the percentage of Irish, while undoubtedly great on the N.Y. police force, was nowhere near the percentage it once was, and so many people now took the police force for a career. And from this we went on to a discussion of the comparative cost of living in the New York area as compared with other sections of the country, and the relative advantages of each. And with that supper was over.

March 29, 1945

. . .With so little to do professionally, you can see that I had a lot of time on my hands. I spent some time this morning watching the deck divisions engage in the practice of "streaming paravanes". Paravanes, as you probably know, are devices intended to cut the cables of moored mines, causing them to float free when they can be destroyed by rifle fire. The paravane itself looks like a small "robomb". It is lifted over the side of the ship by a special boom and it is so constructed that it trails out at about 20 yards from the ship. In this position the lines of the mines are engaged by the paravane lines, and thus guided to a wire cutter on the paravane which cuts the mine wire. All very complicated in description, and actually not too simple an affair.

April 7, 1945

. . . Please note the date above, and please note by the same sign that I am evidently becoming an "alte kaker" (and that isn't a relation of Skipper's either). For my 28th birthday, the day has been actually very uneventful. I did a little more work than usual, as I got my schedule rolling again, but that has been the only departure from the ordinary course of affairs, if departure it can be called.

. . .And that, my darling, is about the summary of the day. Not very much, is it? But at least there isn't usually very much (thank

god for the inaction). So goodnight for now, my darling. I love you and miss you.

April 17, 1945

. . . The weather remained fresh today. The swells, while not so high as formerly, were more choppy, and as a result, as the ship crashed on through them, she left a wide wake of churning white water.

I almost forgot. There was a little excitement today, but I saw nothing of it. It seems that a man fell overboard from the ship directly ahead of us in formation. We could do nothing but clear out of the way. A couple of the men on the fantail threw him a life ring or two, but he was actually picked up by another ship. And even that momentous occurrence hardly made a dent in the serenity of our daily routine.

May 20, 1945

. . . Today has been a mild, peaceful one. I had an impaction scheduled for this morning, but my patient showed up, a very sick lad, so we postponed it for a while. I saw a few of my other patients for a while and spent the rest of the morning in a bull session with Drs. G., G., and V. Lunch was good, fried chicken, of which I managed to secure a couple of breasts (trust me for that). After chow we went back to the room to continue the bull session but came below after a while to grab a Coke and play our new quiz machine. This last named device is rather an ingenious affair. It looks like a pinball machine. There are a number of cards, each bearing a question and several possible answers, which are numbered. Pressing a button discloses one of these cards. The player reads the question, selects his answer, and pushes the button that corresponds (from a row on top of the machine). If it is correct, a yellow rectangle with the word correct is lighted up, and the number of points scored is ticked off in the appropriate box. If it is incorrect, a red light shows behind a square with the word incorrect on it, and you go on to the next question. It really is quite interesting.

After our little game we all went into Dr. Golden's office to talk for a while, and then I excused myself to come in here to read and write.

May 22, 1945

. . . The routine of sea life is so deadening and so easy to fall into. Do nothing. Just look forward to meals and sleep. I wonder how I'll adjust to shore duty again. I'm afraid it will be quite a strain, but I'm sure that given the chance I'll make it.

June 2, 1945

. . . As I've mentioned before, Dr. Golden is quite a conversationalist. So that usually after chow, both in the morning and evening, I find we are out on deck talking. In the evening the conversation is usually interrupted by eight o'clock reports, and by that time the evening bridge game is ready to start. When the bridge game breaks up, I usually feel too rocky (from the hot, close atmosphere of the blacked-out wardroom) to want to write a letter. Last night we played no bridge, but we did have an old fashioned gab-fest (the four of us medical department officers), which lasted until about twelve last night, and then it was bedtime because of the early G.Q.'s we have been having. I used to like to write to you after dinner each night, but now, when I finish dinner, Dr. Golden usually gives me the high sign and we go out to get some air. That isn't a bad idea, because that way I get on deck a lot more than I used to. I really like this guy Golden. He's a slow- talking, very agreeable fellow. He doesn't sound at first as if he knows very much, but his fund of knowledge on certain subjects is very amazing.

. . . The weather gets cooler (thank God) and rougher, which I rather enjoy. I much prefer the ship to have some definite motion. This business of sailing on an absolutely placid sea merely adds to the boredom of the voyage. When we have some weather the monotony can at least be broken by such obvious comments as, "Say, she's rolling, isn't she?" Of course it is perfectly obvious that she really is rolling, but it makes a good conversational gambit.

In the next letter, Lester attempts to describe the vast size of just his own convoy of ships. His ship, like all troop ships, traveled in a convoy for protection. The ships were able to communicate with one another and to share their supplies and expertise.

June 3, 1945

. . . This business of being at sea is really amazing. This convoy is actually a floating city. Today, for example, a pharmacist's mate on one of the ships fell down a ladder and suffered severe head injuries. In a very routine manner, the short-range radio was used, and a consultation of medical experts was held from ship to ship by means of it. Then it was decided to shift the lad to the ship on which the S.M.O. was a specialist in these things. It was only a matter of minutes until the lad was aboard. All this in the middle of the war, with scarcely a disturbance to the routine of the convoy.

As usual I spent some time on deck with Dr. Golden today talking of this, that, and the other thing. Today a new Alnav came out that seems to restrict all future promotions. Naturally we discussed the implications of this. I got quite a respectable burn on my face, for I forgot we were out of doors. But it is not uncomfortable.

June 8, 1945
Churl Darling,

Remember how the old dime novels used to talk about going onward into the face of the setting sun? Actually that is what we are doing now, but it is far from being romantic. Each day seems to be an impossibly few degrees warmer than the one which went before, and somehow we manage to adjust, and not only stay alive, but reasonably happy too.

It is amazing to note the difference in attitude that now exists from that which was evident on our first trip through similar waters. Officially we are now in "dangerous waters"; but whereas, on our first trip, there was an element of tenseness everywhere, now there is really a bored acceptance of the fact that we have to do a ferry job, and a somewhat general scoffing at the term "dangerous." That is not to say that all precautions are not observed, and that our escorts do not continue to be very diligent and investigate every contact, for they do. It is merely that the first sharp edge has gone, and a realization of the hopeless position of the Jap navy as compared to our own permeates all ranks, and rates.

By this point in the year at sea, the sounding of General Quarters, even for a true sighting, no longer elicited the initial thrills of fear or excitement that it originally had.

June 17, 1945
Churl Darling,

Another Sunday. This one started peaceably enough. I slept some later than usual, for I had no patients awaiting me, came down to my usual juice and coffee breakfast; enlivened this time with some left over coffee cake, and schmoozed for a while. Then I got ambitious and wrote a couple of letters: one to my folks, and one to Grandpop Scheller. About that time it was time for lunch (early lunch for early liberty, you know). We sat down at the table, and the main course was served immediately: roast chicken, stuffing, green peas. Sounds good, doesn't it? It tasted good too, the first bite. Just as I had the first mouthful on its way down, the clanging of the general alarm bell sounded. There was a moment's silence while we looked at each other with a questioning surprise. Then came the purposeful sound of chairs being pushed back as all hands went to their general quarters station. Our movements were expedited by the sound of the coxswain's voice: "All hands, man your general quarters stations. Flash yellow, condition red." (May I add parenthetically that I took my plate below with me.) The G.Q. didn't last long. It was probably caused by a Jap snooper plane. We came back to a dessert of vanilla ice cream, which isn't a bad dessert to come back to. The alert did serve to delay our liberty. Ralph, the chaplain, and Mr. Parsons, invited me to a game of bridge, which I happily accepted. We had time for about three-quarters of an hour of playing before liberty was announced. Ralph and I made the boat with minutes to spare.

July 7, 1945
Churl Darling,

Another day at sea. It would seem that in that sentence I have summarized the entire letter, and that all I'd have to do would be to sign, "Love, Les," and that would be that. But, strangely enough, that isn't exactly the case, for as much as I complain of the monot-

ony of life at sea, each day differs from every other day in certain small, but very significant ways. Ordinarily that might not be so; and the fact that it is so, and consequently interesting, I owe to you. For it is my daily letter to you, and my attempt to bring you close to me over the thousands of miles that separate us, that cause me to observe the minutiae of the day's happenings, and to note their significance so that I can retell them to you later on. It is true that today, as usual, I overslept by a few minutes, came down to the office, treated my usual routine of patients, ate the same meals, passed my time in much the same way I have almost every day on board; but different things did happen. For example: This morning we had quarters for muster, instead of muster on stations. There we found out that some of our convoy was to leave us. Later in the morning I managed to make a couple of soft eggs for my corpsman and myself. That doesn't happen every day, no sir.

For another thing, just before chow this noon I made the acquaintance of an eight-week-old bull terrier puppy that one of the army doctors has with him. That was quite an interesting experience. The little fellow is already quite husky and muscular and with needle sharp teeth. I got nipped quite sharply by teasing him. It made me feel good just to play with the pup.

July 13, 1945

. . . I expect that this will be the last letter you'll be getting for a couple of weeks because we will probably be at sea tomorrow, for how long or where nobody knows. It will be a relief to get out to sea once again. I've had about enough of port. The weather is very hot, and the liberty is uninteresting, so I've been staying aboard and sweating it out. At least at sea it should become cooler above decks, I hope.

July 21, 1945

. . . And coming to anchor in a new port is a good way to break the monotony of being at sea. It's funny how when we are in port for a long period of time, the prospect of getting to sea is so inviting. Then after a day or so at sea, it seems that there is nothing quite so desirable as getting into port again. How the days seem to stretch

out. The one consolation is that someday, not too far off, I hope, this whole thing will be just a memory. Will you drink to that, my love? And now goodnight.

Lester's excess of free time inspired him to acquire new knowledge and skills in other areas, in addition to his correspondence courses.

July 26, 1945

. . . Today has been a day of finishing and preparation in the office: finishing the work on several special patients, and preparing the office to get painted. Our deck is pretty shoddy about now, and in honor of our new skipper, who should be coming along soon, we should brighten it up. After I got below, I showered, then got into the sack with the trombone mouthpiece that Sherman Davies (the trombone instructor to be) loaned me. You see, we have no trombone on board, so I am improving the time by blowing through the mouthpiece in an attempt to develop my "embouchure," or the relation between the trombone mouthpiece and the lips. The exercises are also supposed to develop the lip muscles, and aid in breath control. Quite imposing, isn't it? I seem to be making fair progress with the mouthpiece. I've had it a few days, and I've developed to the point where instead of sounding like a flatulent horse I sound like an asthmatic old man (but it's fun and it is a constructive way to pass the time away).

We had some choice filet mignon for dinner tonight, thick and juicy. My, oh my. After dinner, Dr. Golden and I went on deck. It was just after another rain squall, and the water was comparatively rough. We wandered back on the fantail to watch the other ships with us lift high out of the water and then, with that irresistible slowness, plunge their bows deep down, lift them ponderously aloft, and go through the cycle again.

The ship sailed back across the Pacific to San Francisco for refitting, which allowed Lester and Shirley a two-week reunion in early August. The *Oxford* then set sail for the Pacific once again, this time going to the Philippines prior to sailing into Japan, and then sailing home again, this time permanently, at least for Lester.

September 12, 1945
Churl Darling,

Once again we approach journey's end, and as ever in such a circumstance hearts are lighter and gayer, for the end of the trip means a discharge of cargo and troops, more room on board, a more comfortable ship, movies at night, liberty; but more important than all of these together is the prospect of getting mail from home. How much that means to us!

The days have been very ordinary with the usual routine of office work, sun, and evening bridge alternated with snatches of reading.

October 1, 1945
Churl Darling,

Well, we are still here in Linguyen Gulf, but the best scuttlebutt has it that the typhoon is moving off toward Foochow; and that we will get underway before sunset tonight. This very moment the boatswain passed the word, "Now go to your stations, all the special sea and anchor detail." That means we are due to get underway within the hour. I think that this time we will really start for Japan, not merely change our anchorage as we have been doing the last few days.

October 3, 1945
Churl Darling,

The sea, the sea, the beautiful sea. There is so damned much of it! The typhoon has blown on its way, and we are following in its wake, northward to the tip of Luzon, then west through the Luzon Straits, and finally northwest toward Japan via Formosa and Okinawa. Just a short haul of some thousands of miles. The 21 ships of the convoy are spread over several miles of ocean in three rather ragged lines. Some of the ships have never traveled in formation before, and station keeping was rendered even more difficult by the almost mountainous seas which are a legacy of the typhoon that passed.

October 10, 1945

...The fleet is still anchored here in the harbor with an extra length of anchor cable waiting for the full force of the typhoon. It *started to blow up about five o'clock tonight. At last report the wind was blowing fifty knots and still going on. We are anchored in a comparatively sheltered location, but still there are very high swells, and the surface of the sea is a froth of white from the spume picked up by the wind, and a couple of the ships have started to drag their anchors.*

October 16, 1945
Churl Darling,

Today I broke the monotony of life aboard ship by going ashore. Dr. Golden was supposed to go with me but was unavoidably detained. It seems that, just before chow, a soldier, who also was bored with life aboard ship, broke the monotony by falling through an open hatch. The interesting journey through space between two decks resulted in some minor head injuries, which required Golden's attention. So you see that there are many different solutions to this problem of boredom.

October 26, 1945
Churl Darling,

Can you believe it? At 1300 today this squadron of ships got underway for Nagoya. Everyone had expected a last-minute change of orders, so many things have occurred to delay us already, but nothing happened except that the twenty ships formed a tremendous single line as they left the harbor, and they were underway. We still don't know where we will go from Nagoya, but it will probably be back to the States with another load of troops. Oh, joy. The trip is a short one. If you have a map handy you can see that all we have to do is round a finger of land to reach our destination. We should be in the harbor tomorrow morning.

October 27, 1945
Churl Darling,

Well, things must be moving on for at last we are here. Nope, I take that back. We are not yet at Nagoya, but are very close to it. At 8:30 this morning we made a turn, passed through a narrow channel and started to make our way into the port. It is evidently a tremendous bay, because we didn't drop the hook until about

1400, and then we were some fifteen miles out of Nagoya, anchored off the industrial center of Yokachi.

October 29, 1945

. . .We will probably finish unloading tonight and move out into the stream tomorrow. Where we will go and what we will do after that, we do not know. We all think that we will load troops to return to the States, but where will we go to get them? If we pick them up here it will be a short run back to the States. Here's hoping.

11

SHIPMATES

ESTER RELIED UPON HIS well-developed writing skills to paint a verbal picture for Shirley of his many friends and shipmates during his tour of duty. He tried to recreate his daily life, so that she could share in the experience and understand the men as if she, too, were there.

Ralph Goldman, his bunkmate, friend and foil, was Lester's favorite subject. They spent much time together, censored each other's mail, discussed every aspect of their lives, and came to know every quirk of each other's personality. Shirley certainly got to know Ralph – his pomposity, his views on marriage, and the reasons for and resolutions of their disagreements. More than having lived on opposite coasts seemed to divide these two men, yet they maintained a close connection, and Lester spoke fondly of Ralph for years after the war's end.

Lester also described the other men in his sphere, initially discussing one in each letter, chosen by their position at the dinner table. He named the "person of the day," described where he sat, then moved from a physical description to an ever-broadening set of other characteristics about each one, in the hope that Shirley would come to know each man as a unique person.

September 13, 1944

I haven't told you about Mr. Adams yet. I met him first while waiting for a bus to Tongue Point. His wife had just left, and he was moving into B.O.Q. out there. It just so happened that he was assigned the room next to mine. In the ensuing week we often

*bought drinks for each other and really became quite clubby. I use
the term advisedly because it is just about what you would expect
from him, if that conveys any meaning to you. He is about my
height, baldish around the temples, and with the wisps of hair in
the center line gray. He is a southerner, a Virginian as a matter of
fact, and has impeccable manners. He is quiet, courteous, and pleasant at all times. Most noticeable is his diction. I can't describe it
to you. It isn't nasal, but it seems to be. It is quite pleasant to
listen to. At any rate, I am quite fond of Mr. Adams, and note, too,
that he is still Mr. Adams, and I am Dr.*

September 14, 1944

*. . . This bunkmate of mine, Ralph Goldman, plays about the
same type of chess game that I do, so that makes it a lot of fun, of
course. He is one of the two junior medical officers on board. He
is a bit shorter than I am but is built much broader and heavier
than I am. He has a full face, a full behind —what I mean is that
he is a bit broader in the beam —and is quite a cheerful soul. Altogether a compatible individual. He has been married about three
years, and his wife is now two months pregnant. How does that listen to you?*

October 14, 1944

*. . . I promised in my last letter that I would try to give you a
thumbnail sketch of each of the officers on board, the completeness
of the same depending on how well I've gotten to know each of the
individuals. I think that the best way to do this is to take them as
they are seated at the tables in the wardroom and work down from
the exec. through the warrant officers. Before starting in on this
enterprise I think it is well to describe the wardroom. There really
isn't much to the description, for essentially it consists of a room
about 40 feet long by 15 or 18 feet wide with about eight rows of
tables running the width of the room. At one end is a little alcove
with a table in that. On one of the walls (bulkheads) is a radio
speaker which plays one of two programs that the radio central picks
up and relays to us. On the overhead (ceiling) run the rather low
beams that force all of us who are near the six-foot mark to walk*

*with a perpetual stoop. Along the front of the room as you pass
from fore to aft are, first, a hat and coat rack, then a small desk or
serving table, then a group of silver and linen cabinets, then a scuttlebutt (drinking fountain), then an exit. The room is located on
the starboard (right) side, and approximately amidships. As you
know the wardroom is the clubroom of the ship. Meals are served
there; all large conferences are held there; when you are tired of your
stateroom, you go down to pass the time with the other officers there;
and it is utilized for similar purposes whatever they may be. At
meals we are seated according to rank. The center table seats the
ranking men on board, and the tables forward and aft of the center
table hold the junior officers. The exec. sits at the head of the center
table then down the after side are seated: Lt. Cmdr. Thomson, Lt.
Borden, Lt. McNeil, Lt. (JG) Carter, Lt. (JG) Schaeffer.*

*I have already told you something about the executive officer
in one of my letters from Bremerton. He is a man about 35 years
of age, and as is usual in such cases has a receding hairline. He
stands about the same height I do and has that characteristic stoop
associated with those trying to avoid braining themselves on the low
overhead. He is slightly built with a bit of a belly emphasized by
the lifebelt he wears. His nose is a bit prominent, and his face tapers
from back to front rather sharply, not sufficiently so to be hatchet-
faced, however. I guess he is what would be called aquiline featured.
He is not very popular with the officers and men; but I suspect that
that unpopularity is part of his job. After all, he has to serve as a
foil for the captain; and all unpopular decisions, such as those involving liberty, work, etc., are pictured as coming from him, whereas
they are in reality, in all probability, coming from the captain
through him. I come into very little contact with him, and what I
have had to do with him has in all cases been conducted in at least
a courteous manner, so I cannot join with those who condemn him.
He is working hard, and in all probability he is making some mistakes; but it is his first position of this type, and I think he is just
trying too hard. You remember I told you that he is an alumnus of
the Cornell Graduate School of about a year previous to me, and
he had the same professors I did. That of course gave us a common
ground and something to talk about, but that is as far as our fa-*

miliarity goes. I've played about three games of chess with him and
been badly beaten each time. One good thing to be said about him
before leaving is that he dislikes Dickey. Of course Dickey ranks
him and so goes over his head to the skipper; but at least the dislike
is there.

More tomorrow in this fascinating series. Tune in early for the
breathtaking description of the great I AM .

October 15, 1944

...It's about time for the nightly character sketch. Tonight we
will discuss the chief engineer, or as he is called by those he loves,
"Chief." The chief, Mr. Thomson by name, sits to the left of the executive officer across the table from Dr. Dickey. He is a short, broad
man with a rather full belly, full enough to almost justify the ad-
jective "squat." His hair is black and is baldish topside; around the
edges it still grows rather vigorously. I understand that he is quite
popular with the officers and men who work under him. He has an
exceptionally calm disposition. I have never seen him get ruffled or
upset; and there have been times when he was unmercifully teased,
or things just seemed to go wrong despite himself. I am told that
he is very competent and has just performed wonders with our en-
gineering plant. In summary a good, equitable fellow, handy at his
job, and good to have around. Prognosis: will have to get to know
him better.

October 16, 1944

...And now for the guest star of the evening, Lieutenant Warmington. There isn't much I can tell about him because I don't know
him very well. He is about 34 years old, with sandy red hair; but
he looks about fifty. He is a regular navy man of many years' standing, having worked his way up from the ranks to where he now
stands, ranking lieutenant on board. He has many duties, and many
important duties. He is a pleasant enough chap, and we are very
cordial and affable; but between you and me, I don't think too much
of him as an individual. The mark of liquor and dissipation is too
deep on him to suit me. But aside from that, he is a decent enough
chap and a good shipmate.

October 18, 1944

 . . . *Tonight I believe we will take Lieutenant McNeil for our subject. I met Mac, as he is popularly called by the other officers, the day I came on board. He was to share the stateroom with Ralph and myself; as a matter of fact for the first week or two we did bunk together. He is a fellow of about my height and build, with darkish, albeit thinning, hair (you see I am not alone in my trouble). He is very husky and has a ruggedness and almost a bluffness about him that carry over to his voice. His civilian occupation was insurance. How that fits him to assist Mr. Warmington in the management of his beach party I do not know, but that is his job. He is a pleasant companion and proved to be very easy to get along with. He lives in Philly, although his wife and child are now in San Diego. He is definitely a nice guy.*

October 19, 1944

 . . . *And now, darling, before closing for the night I want you to meet our communications officer. Darling, this is Lieutenant (JG) Lester Schaeffer. Mr. Schaeffer, my wife. Mr. Schaeffer is a Philadelphia lawyer, and one of the hardest-working men on board ship. His position is one of great responsibility. He is the message center of the ship both within and without, and a wrong move on his part could prove disastrous. He is about my age, smallish, with a thin face, thinning hairline (what, again!) and a bouncing verve to his walk. He is usually cheerful and ready with a bright word or bon mot; but occasionally he gets very upset, either because of adverse criticism or because of poor work on the part of his subordinates. Then his tongue becomes caustic indeed. Les is my superior on the coding board, so of course I have to be nice to him, not that it is difficult for we get along very well.*

October 20, 1944

 . . . *Before saying* adieu *for tonight, or should I say,* buenas noches, *I want you to meet Chaplain Noland. The chaplain is what is known as a big man. He is about as tall as I am, but he gives a much bigger impression, and with reason, since he is a good deal heavier. He is a reddish-haired man with a florid complexion. He is an Oklahoman, and listening to him talk you would guess it. He has a homely, folksy way of expressing himself. Cheerful, very much so. I have never heard an angry word from his mouth, although, as I've mentioned to you, I have seen him when he was hard put to it to rest in his Irish temper. He is a very sincere and God-fearing man, and withal I believe a very tolerant one. I won't say that I am very friendly with him; but I can say that there is a definite feeling of warmth and understanding between the two of us, and that is good. He is well-liked by the men, as I've noted both in talking to them, and censoring the mail. Frankly, I think we are fortunate to have a man like him for the position. It would have been so easy to have an obstreperous individual instead.*

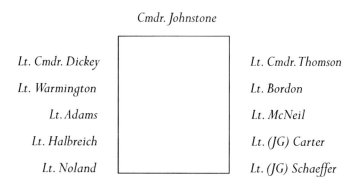

Cmdr. Johnstone

Lt. Cmdr. Dickey		*Lt. Cmdr. Thomson*
Lt. Warmington		*Lt. Bordon*
Lt. Adams		*Lt. McNeil*
Lt. Halbreich		*Lt. (JG) Carter*
Lt. Noland		*Lt. (JG) Schaeffer*

October 27, 1944

. . . Tonight for example I'll tell you something more about Bob Bastian, or "the marine," as he is commonly called. Bob is our transport quartermaster, that is, he has been especially trained to embark troops on board and meet their problems, act as a liaison officer between the army or marines, as the case may be, and the navy. He is about my height but of slimmer build. With glasses, he appears to be quite the student. He is of a very retiring nature, is shy, sensitive, and withal efficient. He is by way of being an artist. Frequently he is to be found sitting at the desk indulging in his version of doodling, which is to draw New Yorkerish figures on a sheet of paper. At other times he is busy with water colors. His work of course has just started, but judging from the smooth way he has gotten it rolling, it ought to keep on fine.

October 28, 1944

. . . Our disbursing officer is a nice fellow. His name is Something-or-other Christopher, commonly called Chris. He is a small, slightly built lad, about 25 years of age, and looking younger. He is usually cheerful, and always with an appreciative joke. He is one of the hardest working men on board. It is his job to pay the officers and crew, and take care of such things as travel, etc.; and he works quite hard doing it. It's nice listening to him talk in his deep Southern drawl. He's a nice guy, too, so you can see we have a pretty good set of officers on board.

November 1, 1944

And now, before turning in, I may as well take this moment to introduce you to Dr. Davey. I'm sorry, but I do not know his first name, but if it helps his initials are V. V. He is the fourth member of our rooming association in 0103. Frankly, he is not well liked by any of the others. As I say, Davey is not a particularly nice boy. He takes credit for work Ralph has done, keeps quiet when he should speak, and vice versa. Luckily, our paths have crossed but little. He sleeps below in the sick bay most of the time. On one or two occasions when our paths have crossed he has tried to be obstreperously overbearing with a few poorly chosen remarks. On each of these occasions, I have not hesitated to use my rank to put him in his place at once. The result is that, while he doesn't exactly like me, he doesn't bother me much either, which is exactly what I am hoping for. I imagine I can best sum this poor example of a big Texan up by the phrase, "A small mind in a small body."

And on that rather minor note I'll call it quits for tonight. Good night my darling. Keep well and write soon.

November 9, 1944

. . . I think that this is probably a good time to tell you something about Butch Allan. Robert "Butch" Allan is our pharmacist warrant officer. It is his job to see that our organization as a hospital runs smoothly from an administrative point of view, and he does just that very efficiently. The moment you look at him the appropriateness of the name, Butch, is evident. He is some shorter than I am, about 5'10", and weighs about 190 pounds. He is broad in the shoulder and wide in the chest. His belly, while not unusually large, cannot be denied. His arms are heavy, and his hands are large. He gives an impression of great strength, and he is a powerful man. His head is large and firmly stout, full and rounded. He has a baldish (there are still a few hairs straggling around) dome with a fringe of black hair, something like my father's. What is very noticeable about his face are the prominent, deeply engraved laugh wrinkles at the corners of his mouth and eyes. Butch is really a jovial fellow in a Rabelaisian sense. It does not pay, however, to be misled by his joviality into thinking him a fool. He is one of the most intelligent fellows I know. He is just lousy with native intelligence and common sense. His formal schooling is limited to a high school education and what courses he has taken in the navy, but he knows an awful lot. He particularly knows a lot of medicine. I have much confidence in the man and respect for his abilities. He talks in four-letter swear words, a habit, incidentally, that I find myself relapsing into more than I should; but on him it sounds good. He tells an awfully good story, and all of them are true although somewhat incredible. He is married, apparently very happily, and has a son whom he proudly refers to as "Butchie," or "You know that little son-of-a-bitch." He is a regular navy man who worked his way up from the ranks to his commissioned warrant officer's rank the hard way. He has lots of interesting stories to tell about his life pre- and early navy, but there is no place for them here; sufficient to say that, at 18 years of age (his age at enlistment), he must have been a good tough boy. He has had some interesting experiences recently, too. His last tour of duty was on board the Hornet, the aircraft carrier with Doolittle's Fliers, when they bombed Japan, and which was sunk off Vera Cruz during a naval engagement with Japan. He wears a purple heart for his part in that last. It seems that he was in a compartment which was hit by a shell. Of thirty men there, he and two others were the only survivors. Then, although bleeding from many wounds and in a state of shock himself, he instinctively (only through the promptings of a naturally brave and fighting heart) set about attending to the other wounded, among other things amputating a leg on the flight deck with a pair of *bandage shears as his only instrument. There you have Robert Butch Allan, Warrant Pharmacist, USN, all man.*

November 13, 1944

. . . Since our messing arrangements have been changed I have some new table buddies. Ralph sits directly opposite me, and on my right hand (note that I now sit at the head of the table) sits Mr. Orlich. Mr. Orlich is our gunnery officer. He is a fellow just a little taller than Leo Korchin with a fine, solid build, and an ever-present, pleasant smile. His hair is thinning in the middle (about how many people have I said that!). He is the man responsible for our guns, and he seems to have a good background of experience for the job, having just come off an aircraft carrier of the Essex class, which latter are rather heavily gunned. He is a quiet sort of fellow, very unobtrusive, and withal very good-natured. He is a pleasant guy to sit next to at meal times.

December 19, 1944

. . . Have I ever mentioned Chips, our carpenter, in any of my letters? I am sure I must have. His name is Youngblood, but you very seldom hear that mentioned. It's always Chips. Chips is undoubtedly one of the characters on this ship. He would be a character on any ship. He is a college man who joined the regular navy after he got out, and that was quite a while ago. He is ready for retirement now (he's only making this last trip for some personal reason, which I don't know). He is fond of reminiscing about how much better he has done in the navy than his classmates who stayed civilians. He is about fifty-five years of age, I guess, baldish, with deeply wrinkled face and a smile that looks as if it were chopped with a meat cleaver. He is probably about five six in height, but is very broad in the shoulder. His face is deeply lined, and he smiles frequently, exhibiting his dentures, of which he is very proud (he helped construct the press they were molded in in Alaska). In his conversation he is very pontifical, using sonorous phrases to describe vulgar things. He loves to sit back and reminisce over the past years of the navy. And it is really something to sit there and listen to the tales of past orgies, narrated in a real thick whiskey voice, issuing from a

red-nosed, weather-beaten face. He has drunk a lot of whiskey and is evidently prouder of that than almost anything else. He has the Purple Heart medal, wounded at Pearl Harbor and carrying on despite his wounds. He never talks of that. A more opinionated man you never met, no one more convinced of his own worth. And that is Chips; what he is actually worth, it is hard to say. At this stage of the game, I think he is just an old man who has done too much drinking in too little time; but one thing he definitely is—a real product of the sea, a real old sea-dog.

In this letter Lester mentions the first of several arguments that he had with some of his shipmates, some more serious than others. Living and working in such close proximity with so many men, with no break, was bound to cause some friction.

January 8, 1945
 . . . Had some words with Chief Gerraghty the other day. It seems that he is a red-headed Irishman with a temper, and is oh, so sensitive. He has a degree and a year of medical school, after which he quit. He is about 33 years old and evidently resents his position very much, particularly in relation to a lot of punk kids, the junior medical officers of the department. We have all along realized his disposition and tried to make allowances, bending over backward to do so. He, on the other hand, has never hesitated to use the rough side of his tongue. All in all, a peculiar situation. Well, the other day a question came up concerning my dressing station, and he became very loud and abusive, questioned my authority to do certain things, claimed that by doing them I was endangering the ship, and raved for a while. I told him that, to the best of my knowledge, the authority for my action was in navy regs. He said that he knew the regs a lot better than me, and that I was wrong. I said that might be so but that, as senior officer present in the compartment, I intended to do what I had been doing until directed otherwise by competent authority. That night I spoke to the executive officer, the first lieutenant, and his assistant. It was their unanimous opinion that I was right in every instance. That's all there is to it, but the poor man feels mortally insulted. To which I say the hell with him.

*I'm tired of being the considerate guy that gets his behind kicked
for his pains. If he intends to act like a damned fool, he can reap
the benefits of such a course. Of such small things is the life aboard
ship made of.*

A description follows of Lester's friend and bunk mate, Ralph Goldman,
with whom he frequently engaged in intellectual arguments, with a few actual
disagreements, as well:

January 15, 1945
*. . .Yesterday Ralph and I had a little talk about ourselves and
our wives. As usual he introduced the subject, and as usual he used
the conversation as a sort of psychological mirror to posture and
primp in front of. Now, don't misunderstand me, Ralph is a fine
fellow, but like all of us he has his faults. One of his is his view of
himself as a psychological peculiarity, a little different from anyone
else because of his background and upbringing (an only child and
social conflict); another is his assuming the mantle of authority on
no better basis than his own say-so and his own pretensions to in-
tellectuality (which last is much overdone). Naturally, when I spoke
of you and me, I did so with a great glow, and a great deal of fervor.
As I told you much earlier, Ralph is much concerned over the success
of his marriage. As is usual when he starts off on a subject like that,
he found it difficult to stick to one subject, and we kept coming back
to what evidently interests him "more than slightly" (Damon Run-
yon): Ralph Goldman. He reminds me of me as I was about five
years ago, only much more so, but he cannot admit that his attitudes
are something he may well leave behind him. He said among other
things that he had had a nightmare that Helen had taken up with
someone else while he was gone. He insisted on discussing it from
an intellectual point of view, insisting that, under certain circumstances, he wouldn't mind, particularly if, after it was all over, she
wanted to come back to him. (You remember some of things I told
you at the beginning about jealousy, and how it didn't take me long
to change—well, his discussion was along similar lines, only more
so). I kept picking holes in his arguments. After all, who can do so
better than someone who not so long ago fervently advocated the*

same theories? As we talked I spoke of you and me, not intending to draw a comparison either. But he couldn't permit it to go at that. His had to be better than that. Les, he said quite seriously, your marriage is very physical. I had to laugh. The comparison he meant was plain. He and Helen lived a life of the intellect, communing in spirit and in art while you and I, alas, poor souls, could never appreciate the delicacies that these two (for all their self-confessed unhappiness, and incompatibilities on various spheres) could enjoy. The answer was too obvious, and I didn't want to punish Ralph by making him feel bad. So I merely said that it was difficult for me to see how he could make such a statement when I myself still wasn't sure of exactly what it was that made our marriage without a doubt the happiest I have seen. It is doubtless true that a goodly percentage of our relationship is based on sex, although I have never been able to separate one part from another; but if by your statement you imply, which you obviously do, that that is the sum total of our relationship, then just as obviously you are wrong, for I can tell you what it isn't, even if I can't quite describe what it is. I had to leave soon after that for a 12 to four watch in the morning, so we let it go at that. I was glad he brought the subject up because it brought back a rush of happy memories I occupied my mind with while I engaged in the mechanical things I had to do and made a pleasure of what otherwise would have been a boresome four hours.

And on that note of you, which is always a glad and joyous note, I'll say so long for today my darling. (Every time I think of the definite, and defiant, way Ralph phrased his statement . . . and how uncalled for it was . . . I have to smile). I love you, my darling.

January 16, 1945

. . . Another of my corpsman trainees has been transferred out. I don't remember if I told you about Anderson. He is a big fellow, raw-boned, I guess you'd call him, of about 19 yrs. He is very quiet, nice, and easy to get along with, and very eager to please. I am very sorry to lose him, and he is very sorry to go. That incidentally is one of the things I am rather pleased about. All of the boys I have had in here are anxious to stay, to come back after they go; and *those that haven't been in are anxious for a try at it. Andy is a North Dakota boy. No, he is from Lincoln, Nebraska, which incidentally is a very nice little city. I called you from Lincoln when I was driving to Seattle. Remember? He wants to go back to college after the War (he already had a year of it) and make something of himself, an ambition I heartily endorse.*

March 1, 1945
 . . . I don't believe I told you that we have a new doctor aboard. Dewitt True, by name, and a product of Harvard. He is about my age and is married, with one child. He started off on the wrong foot, it seems; but for my money seems to be pretty much all right so far.

The following letter concerns an argument that Lester and Ralph Goldman had, disrupting their shipboard friendship and good working relationship. Had they not been forced into such close and constant proximity by shipboard life, it is doubtful that the argument would ever have arisen.

March 9, 1945
 . . . . As Ralph was getting ready for inspection, he handed me a sheet of paper (which he had done a few moments earlier) with a request to put it away. I told him (as I had a few moments earlier) that I would bring it down to my office later. Whether it was because the loss of the chess game rankled or what, I don't know, but he has made some remark about the neatness of the desk. Now, Ralph, like the pedant he is, has been throwing his weight around about the neatness of the room since we got aboard, and he has done as much as any of us to keep it unneat. So far as the desk in particular is concerned, I keep very little there, using the desk in my office almost exclusively. As I had so often before, I gave him a soft answer; but he persisted. I regret to say that I lost my temper and really told him off, not only for this one time but for his entire attitude from the beginning, which had rankled the three others in the room more than once. He tried to say something in his defense, but he was absolutely wrong. There was nothing he could say, and the more I said the more upset I became, so I really handed it to him hot and heavy for a while. There is no question but that he has been asking for it

for a long time with his unconscious assumption of a righteous air, and a guardian spirit; but I suddenly realized the triviality of the trigger incident that had set off this tremendous emotional outflow, and shut up. So did he. We read our mail for a little, and then both offered, sheepishly, our regrets. Everything is so magnified on board ship, and being without mail as I have been undoubtedly contributes to the situation. Immediately afterwards, the inspection started, and by now the whole thing is over. Doubtless I got too excited, but all of what I said is stuff that badly needed telling, and if he takes a lesson from it the incident will not have been entirely bad.

April 12, 1945

The night before last I stood at the rail as the sun set and had an interesting talk with our new intelligence officer (he it was, incidentally, whose tooth I extracted today). He is man of about my height, possibly half an inch taller, well built, with eyes set deep in his head, and handsome in a hard, craggy sort of manner. He is very pleasant and really a nice guy. It seems he spent some time in New York while training, and met a rather good-looking gal there whose pictures he has posted all over his room. We started speaking about her, and then with one thing or another we went into a discussion of the trials and tribulations of young unmarried men. I was a very sympathetic listener. A little later Boats came along, and the conversation became more general, touching on other things— on the efficacy of horse shit as a therapeutic agent. Both men contended stoutly that it was wonderful. "All right," I admitted finally, "you've convinced me, Mr. Taylor. I'll pack your socket with horse shit after we extract the tooth tomorrow." That ended that discussion.

While Ralph and Lester were good friends, there was sometimes a competitive edge to their relationship.

October 20, 1945

. . . Ralph noticed the Spanish book on the desk, so of course we talked of the advantages and disadvantages of going to South America, and in his usual categorical manner (which I dislike so intensely), Ralph declared that I'd never get you to go. Now I admit

that the whole idea may be very silly, and merely a justification for me to study Spanish as a way to pass the time; but he certainly does- n't know that, nor is it good form for him to assume that he is the only individual who may do some postwar traveling. And, well, lots more; but that's enough. I got angry, of course, but had sense enough to hold my tongue, and merely changed the subject. About that point of view we can only say with Christ, "Forgive them, my Lord, for they know not what they do."

Shirley also tried to paint the same kinds of pictures for Lester, although in her case Lester already was at least acquainted with most of the people who Shirley would write about. Therefore, her point was not so much to introduce them to Lester, so he could understand her daily world, as to fur- ther his comprehension of the personalities who inhabited her sphere.

Shirley described her changing emotions toward two of her long-time friends, Florence and Rhoda, an issue that will permeate her letters.

November 19, 1944
. . . Sometimes I feel so strange with them [Rhoda, Florence, and other single friends], as though I have passed beyond their in- terests, and that we haven't much in common any more. Indeed, we have almost nothing in common, except our friendship through the years. I feel, though, that I don't want to break off with them as yet, as that would leave me with hardly any close friends. In my silly stubborn way, I am trying to hold on to friendships, for I don't want them to end. We are fond of each other; I really like them; yet sometimes their constant talk of clothes and money drives me mad, whereas they can't understand my willingness to tie myself down with a baby. I would like to dress well, too, someday, but in the meantime the lack of it doesn't bother me, for I am satisfied and content. They know how happy I am, and envy my contentedness, and so they are constantly searching for it but can't find it. They envy me, and yet because I am satisfied with what is insignificant to them, they scorn it. Oh, well, perhaps someday they'll know.

Shirley wrote often about her friend and neighbor Berry. She seemed to have a confused relationship with her, not really enjoying several of her characteristics, such as her constant chatter, her disorganized style and her overwhelming interest in sex, yet she sometimes defended her and saw her frequently.

> *January 10, 1945*
> *...I met Berry downstairs and we took a walk together—she jabbering away, and I patiently listening. Her husband is touring the Panama Canal Zone putting on U.S.O. Shows—while she raves and rants that no one has been harder hit by the war than she. And she loves Eddy more—she's more sensitive, and all that bash.*

> *January 12, 1945*
> *...Berry is such a nit wit, you can't help liking her and feeling sorry for whomever she has to live with. She is a spoiled brat. Her parents cater to her every whim. For instance, she actually forgot to prepare the baby's formula for tomorrow, so her mother said she'd do it.*

> *January 16, 1945*
> *Darling,*
> *I have finally met my match in Berry. She was up here all night—I finally got rid of her 5 minutes ago (it's now 1:00 in the morning). She talks so fast and so much that it is impossible to get a word in edgewise to tell her it's time for her to go. SEX is all she lives for, it's the air she breaths. Why, she and her husband have a huge collection of the best pornographic pictures and literature that can be had—did you ever hear of anything like that?*

In the following letter, Shirley reacts to Lester's description of some of Ralph's ideas and views on life.

> *January 30, 1945*
> *...Poor foolish Ralph—how full of inconsequential nonsense he is. If our marriage is based on sex—why, who can divorce the mind from the body? I'm sure we can both be attracted physically to others, and be mentally stimulated by still others, but to find, as you and I have, perfect coordination and mating of both—why,*

that is our marriage.

I'm sure he is not really in love with his wife, for he wouldn't be so indifferent to her supposed infidelities if he were. For we both found out that love wants complete possession, and jealousy is one of its manifestations. Also, he would graciously condone and take her back under certain conditions, but she supposedly doesn't even mind if he has affairs while she is carrying his child. You can tell Ralph to stop worrying, which he admits he does do, despite his mask of indifference—Helen is in no condition or mood to have any affairs right now. If he admits to doubts of the success of his marriage, than there is something basically wrong. So perhaps we, with our bourgeois acceptance of sex and complete happiness in it, aren't so wrong. And also tell Ralph that I am not all body but do possess a small fraction of a mind and am eager to learn (for a penny). We don't only talk about the "lower things of life." We too, can commune with the arts. But why, in God's name, don't they try talking to the devil once in a while. They might enjoy him.

Also inform Ralph that I could interest him both mind and body. I don't know whatever gave him the idea of the purely barbarous aspect of our marriage. He's full of "phooey." It's the speech of a college senior who hasn't experienced yet that which is to change his whole stereotyped philosophy of life.

Whatever it is that makes our marriage so happy—it is the one stable, permanent fixture in both our lives. It has made me whole—and I know we were both greatly enriched from the mere fact of having known it. A true "pair from God."

February 11, 1945

. . . For some reason or other Florence and Rhoda have taken a dislike to Berry (and vice versa), and so the evening was full of fireworks. Rhoda started it off by saying, "Berry, didn't you get that dress in Loehman's for $4.98 four years ago?" At Berry's affirmative reply, Rhoda then brightly remarked, "Why, I gave that to my maid, years ago." Well, that started off an evening characterized chiefly by sweet and catty brilliant sayings. I, wisely enough, kept quiet, but I was rocking back and forth in hysterics. But dumb little Berry gave them back as good as they handed out. And frankly, my sym-

pathies lay with Berry. As crazy as she is, she doesn't have the money-warped viewpoint on life that those two have. She nearly hit the ceiling when Florence said she'd be damned if she'd pick up Sydney's socks, or even wash them, or that he should ever get a cent of her money without a strict I.O.U. attached to it. They're nice kids, but I don't know who to feel sorrier for, they or their husbands.

Glo Siegel is another friend, one whose fiancé was killed in the war.

April 8, 1945
    . . .When we got home I went down to Berry's for supper. Her father brought home chow mein and so we had some delicious egg rolls, fried rice, chow mein, and barbecued pork. Hungry? I wish I could send you some.
    Glo Siegel came up too, and the 3 of us sat and schmoozed. The talk centered mainly about sex, as it does all the time when Berry is around. Her husband must be a marvelous lover—all she raves about is how perfect he is (knows all the tricks of the trade. He ought to; he knows practically all the "houses"). And how perfect a pair they are. And how only frigid people do it only at night. They do it morning, noon, and night, and never skip! Whew! Glo and I kept discreetly silent, and did we learn things. Berry talks too much.

The next two letters continue the theme of Shirley's increasing disillusionment with her friends Florence and Rhoda.

April 21, 1945
    . . .Then Gert came over at 8, and we settled down for a quiet evening of gin rummy and talk. For some reason, we were very giddy and laughed hysterically at each other's inane cracks. I like her a lot; it's nice of her to stay in with me occasionally on Saturday nights. I can see who my real friends are now. For instance, Rhoda and Aaron have never asked me out with them yet (and Aaron has been in now almost 2 months).

Florence displayed a cavalier attitude about the war until it began to affect her, when she suddenly turned her attention to it again, but just to a degree.

May 7, 1945

...*Flo Cooper called up tonight and got mother and me angry by declaring, in her usual selfish way, that as far as she is concerned the war is all over. She doesn't give a damn for those thousands who are still fighting in the Pacific. She'd sing a different tune if Sidney now had to go to the Pacific.*

May 9, 1945

...*Florence just called up. For once, she is slightly worried about her husband. She hasn't heard from him in over 3 weeks—since the start of the last offensive in Italy. She thinks that they may have sent him to Japan, and so now realizes that the war isn't totally over, as she so blithely assumed on Monday. And yet she has still found time to rave to me about the 2 new hats she bought today! Some mighty funny critters inhabit this world.*

Shirley's good friend Gloria has recently lost her fiancé in the war.

August 26, 1945

Gloria Siegel came home from camp today, and she rushed up to see the baby and me. Jeff didn't remember her, but he soon was his old friendly self. His teeth tend to make him sort of cranky during the day. Last night, too, he got me up at 3:00 A.M. for a little while. However, he is so darn cute right now that I can't help but grab him and hug him impulsively in his most adorable moments—and he has many.

I spent the evening with Glo, rehashing the summer. She had a fairly nice time; but with every boy she went with, she couldn't help compare them with Murray. Poor kid, I feel so sorry for her. Victory hasn't much meaning for those who've lost the ones they love. It's a wonder it hasn't embittered her more than it has.

October 8, 1945

...*I was expecting Gloria up tonight, as I was supposed to meet her boyfriend. It's amazing that this has developed so soon. I'm afraid she's rushing into things too quickly, for how can she fall in love so soon after Murray's death? I really don't think she is in love with this boy—she's practically admitted as much—but she is very fond of him, and love is growing. He must be very nice, for all I've heard. However, I don't think that if she had been married to Murray for any length of time, she would be able to think of marriage to someone else, in so short a time. Marriage binds two people together for all time, no matter what happens in the future to separate them. But all this is Gloria's affair and not mine. She'll most likely be very happy with Jasper (ugh, what a name), for already I can see that her frequent moods of melancholy and blue have all but passed away. It will probably be the best thing for her. And what did poor Murray die for? It's best not to dwell on such thoughts. She just wants to get married, and so she has accepted practically the first one. Fear of being an old maid, I guess. Well, enough of that. Here's to their good luck.*

October 19, 1945

. . . A platterful of glorious days, and today was another one. Vivian came over, and we had lunch out while Jeff slept in his carriage. Later, we met Gloria on Eastern Parkway, and we spent the rest of the afternoon there. Gloria came with the good news that she had passed her teacher's exam and had received her license today. She is now a qualified substitute art teacher, eligible for high school teaching. She'll start in Girl's Commercial next week. I'd love to be in the classroom when she teaches, for she looks younger and smaller than most of the amazons who will be her pupils.

Tonight she brought up her fiancé so that I could finally meet him. Mother and dad went to my aunt's new store, and Elaine was out. He is incredibly ugly, as Vivian had said, but he is so charming and nice in other respects that I soon forgot all about his looks. He's negroid in features, bald, and wears thick glasses. He really looks moronic, until he begins to speak. Then you can tell that he really is an intelligent boy. I like him very much, and so would you. He speaks, somehow, in almost the same way as you. In fact, when he was telling a story I could have sworn it was you who was narrating.

They stayed until 10:00, at the end of which time I settled down for some reading—and here I am (at your beck and call, my Lord, as always).

November 5, 1945

... Les, please tell Ralph for me that, whether I go to South America or not, it's none of his damn business. I don't see that his ideas and future plans are grinding out so smoothly that he can afford to butt into those of other people. That little boy doesn't know what he wants, or what life is yet about. By the way, his wife never answered my letter or my card.

12

DENTIST AFLOAT

E VERYONE UNDERSTANDS WHAT IT means to be in the army or navy, or so they think. Military life during wartime generally conjures thoughts of land and sea battles, interspersed with quiet times. Yet, a great deal of effort is involved in clothing, feeding, housing, transporting and arming the servicemen, so that in reality, there must be huge numbers of people in the military who are not directly involved in combat. The actual ratio of combat to support personnel is surprisingly imbalanced, and it raises the distinct probability, that for any one person, service very well might not involve direct contact with the enemy.

Such was the case with Lester, a dentist in the navy. Nobody automatically thinks of a navy dentist, yet the crew and their passengers all required both regular and emergency dental care. When he enrolled in the naval ROTC program as a Cornell undergraduate he would probably not have realized that, in a relatively few years, that is exactly what he would be doing. Dental officers are not the stuff of drama. Physicians might qualify, but nobody romanticizes the navy dentist.

What did Les and his dental colleagues do all day? Arriving at the base in Washington, there was, in fact, little to do, and Lester seemed to have plenty of free time. He did set up his office, which included ordering instruments and unpacking and arranging them according to his preferences as they arrived. He also slowly began to see patients.

The men of the ship arrived piecemeal, it seemed, and had other tasks assigned to them. Lester's services at that early stage were only needed if an emergency arose. When this did occur, he often excitedly wrote about it to Shirley. He was, after all, just two years out of dental school, a novice in his profession with sufficient enthusiasm to still become excited by emergencies, or by how other dentists treated them. He might quote the textbooks or his own professors. One can only hope that Shirley was equally as fascinated as he was by these dental procedures.

Once the ship was underway and on its assigned voyage, Lester and the other dentists regularly performed check-ups on the men, held daily clinic hours, and continued to respond to emergencies. The men made appointments to see him, just as in civilian life, so that he could continue to work on and complete whatever had been initially identified as requiring attention.

Emergencies seemed to occur frequently, considering the size of the crew and the limited availability of good dental care for many of the young men in pre-war civilian life. There were repeated infections, abscesses, broken teeth and impactions, some of which were of sufficient severity to require medical surgery, with Lester in attendance and assisting. On occasion heroic actions were required, and Lester saved at least one young man's life. These episodes provided great intellectual stimulation and challenges to this newly-fledged dentist. And his loving wife, Shirley, probably heard much more about dentistry than she ever bargained for.

In this early letter written from Texas, Lester was just a year out of dental school and was reacting well to praise from a superior:

> October 14, 1943
> . . . Did a root end amputation yesterday with Dr. Levin observing. He said he was quite pleased.

Lester set up his new office upon arriving on the newly built *Oxford*, which was still in dry dock in Washington State.

> July 25, 1944
> . . . Today in the clinic the first group of patients from my ship came in. They sent in too many for me to do more than just examine them and put in a filling or two, but at least it is getting the ball rolling.

> September 14, 1944
> . . . The dental office is about as complete right now as I can make it. Now I have to wait for the services of an x-ray technician

to test my x-ray machine, and some ship fitters to fit my compressor to the unit and to install a few things on the bulkheads. Today therefore was mostly a matter of filling in time. I did this mostly by reading the table of ship's organization. Besides that, I did a little reading in one of my texts.

. . . Right now we are just about squared away in the dental office. I am waiting for the x-ray expert to test and approve my machine and for the roper individual to connect my unit up to the air compressor. After that I will need a few drugs for the shelves and I will be ready to start operating.

They've really fixed me up quite nicely here. I have a Ritter senior unit, and a Ritter chair. The unit is pretty generally considered to be the best available, it is the type I will probably have in my office afterwards. The chair is fine, but of course it is one of the Victory type, hard-seated, you know, but contoured so that it is really quite comfortable. Then I have a good sized sterilizer, and a large white enameled cabinet to keep my supplies in. The big deficiency is in the lack of an instrument cabinet. Somehow or other this very vital item was left out, and replaced with an eye, ear, nose and throat cabinet, which is very unsatisfactory. What I have done therefore is stowed most of my gear down in the hold, used the E.E.N.T. cabinet to stow a small amount of supplies in, and am fixing the supply cabinet up as an instrument cabinet. Not good, but it is better than nothing (I think).

September 23, 1944

. . . I told you, I think, my dental stool was repaired. Already I've been using it and find it to be quite a help. It was really a new experience to be operating at sea. But it wasn't bad; and I soon got used to it, stool and all.

One of the things that I was not provided with by some oversight was a bur block. It is a small item, but really almost essential to keep a neat operating room. All that it needs is a block of wood with some holes in it. Well, you should have seen the trouble I had in getting it. As a matter of fact I still haven't gotten it, but the carpenter is working on it.

September 25, 1944

. . . I had a few patients this afternoon. The men are starting to discover that my office is open, and as the ship's business allows them, they came in to take care of their teeth.

September 26, 1944

. . . I had a lot of patients today. Mostly it was a case of treating trench mouth, but there were a couple of fillings thrown in and an extraction besides. All very uneventful, but going to make up a full day.

October 13, 1944

. . . Today has been a rather usual day as far as routine is concerned. It differed from the preceding days in the absence of drills. So for a change I was able to get a day's work done. Nor was the operation made easier by the poor quality of the instruments. One of my elevators broke the first time I applied it, and with very light force. I had to finally split the crown of the tooth, and then remove the roots. I wanted to turn him into sick bay so that by the use of cold packs and proper medication I could reduce the after swelling and pain I expected the patient to experience. To admit him, I had to get Dr. Dickey's OK. The first thing he asked me was, "Is it elective or pathological surgery?" Meaning was there actual infection or could I elect the time to intervene. I answered that it was elective and started to say something else. "Very well, Doctor," he said. "You may admit him this time, but in the future there is to be no elective surgery to be performed on board without my permission" (you can see who runs the dental department). Later, while I was admitting the patient, he came over to explain why. Leaving out the verbiage and pompousness of it all, the explanation had a degree of logic so far as medical surgery was concerned, none at all so far as dental surgery was concerned. He claimed that elective surgery should be postponed until the patient was on the beach so that no one else would be forced to do the work of the patient. Well, that's fine in the kind of case he treats, but in the case of these impacted third molars, in almost nine cases out of ten, you can't interfere where there is pathology, so it is always elective surgery. Nevertheless, unless you elect to interfere at the right time, the area becomes pathological so that you can't operate again; and thus the cycle continues, eventually causing more loss of time than if the offending tooth had been removed at the first opportunity. That is what I had tried to tell HIM at the beginning but he was too busy to listen.

October 16, 1944

...While all this was going on, one of the men reported to sick bay with a temperature, and feeling bad, and with a previous history of malaria. I ordered a smear taken, and while that was being done my visitor departed. The smear was positively diagnosed for malaria so I ordered him to bed. I got out the old textbooks and looked up the treatment, but seeing it was close to five o'clock decided to wait to let Dickey see him and prescribe for his condition (after all, he is a physician). Well, Dickey came on board with two guests, and he was just too busy to look at the patient. "You take care of him, Doctor," he said to me quite graciously. Well, I was boiling. The son-of-a-bitch wasn't even physician enough to take a look at a sick boy. In the meantime, Al Sobol, whom I had invited over for dinner, showed up. I'm afraid I made a very poor host. First I was too busy taking care of this boy, and second I was so mad at Dickey (not because he mistreated me, because he really hadn't) for his lack of professional conscience that I could talk about very little else. During supper one of the other junior medics came on board, and I checked my treatment method with him. It was all right, so I felt better.

October 31, 1944

...And so the day goes by. Work is increasing slowly as the ship enters upon its routine, and the men can plan their schedules to come visit me. Besides the crew, of course, I have the dental care of our army passengers, and there are always one or two emergencies a day to disrupt any planned routine. I make good use of the operating stool. Yesterday and the day before, for instance, I was able to work sitting down when I know that it was much too rough to operate standing up. Dr. Dickey and I appear to have

*reached a stage of mutual obliviousness. I pretend he is non-ex-
istent, and so far he has done the same to me. I don't believe I
say ten words a day to him, nor does he to me. That being the
case everyone is happy.*

November 5, 1944
  *. . . Incidentally, I was my own dentist yesterday. One of the
ensigns gave me a piece of chewy candy after the morning's festivities, which I just finished describing to you. I was happily
chewing away when I felt my teeth strike something harder than
usual. Investigation disclosed that the filling had fallen out of
one of my teeth. I ran down below, got a corpsman to assist me in
the mixing of cement, and, looking at the mirror, I sterilized and
dried the cavity and inserted the filling. After it was all over and
I was giving myself a mental pat on the back, I suddenly remembered that there were four army dentists on board who undoubtedly could have done a better job than I did. The pat turned
immediately into a kick.*

November 11, 1944
  *. . .We had captain's inspection today, and the dental office
again passed admirably. There was very little work today, the most
arduous being two extractions, one of which was complicated by
the most awful hook on a root I've ever seen, but it finally came
out with no trouble.*

November 13, 1944
Churl Darling,
  *. . . One of my patients today was the chaplain. I've told
you about him and how big he is. Well, all six feet and two-
twenty pounds of him were curdled with fear. I thought I'd make
things easier by giving him an inferior alveolar injection. Well,
I gave him three of them, finally, and each time he got the classical symptoms of anesthesia, but no sooner would I start then
he would moan and groan and writhe in the chair. I got disgusted toward the end and just finished out. I know damned
well that he wasn't being hurt.*

November 20, 1944
Churl Darling,

It is so hot and muggy nights down here that we never even bother to strip down the bedspread, just get undressed, stretch out on top of the spread and go to sleep. Absolutely bare-assed, if you know what I mean. Well, this morning Dr. Dickey came by to wake me up. "Got to get up and get dressed, Doctor, we just got the word on the blinker. There is a boat load of dental emergencies on the way over from some other ship right now." So I lazily opened one eye, then got up and got dressed, and hurried below to get a cup of coffee. At about nine o'clock these emergencies came in. They weren't really emergencies, but I spent the morning doing the work anyhow. On the last patient I had to extract two teeth. I gave him the correct injections and he gave the symptoms of anesthesia, but when it came to leaning on the tooth the kid felt pain. It dawned on me then that the kid had a pericementitis and would require a general anesthetic. I was about to send him ashore when Butch, who happened to walk in, suggested that we use Pentothal sodium. I was agreeable, so he went off to get Dr. Davey. To cut the story short, Davey gave too much in too little time, in too concentrated a dose. I got the one molar out all right but I refused to go after the other tooth because the kid was showing signs of difficulty. We had quite a time with him, and coming out of the anesthetic, which he finally did all right, he went through a prolonged excitement stage. It took seven or eight corpsmen to prevent him from hurting himself. Of course, Dr. Dickey took a fit, he says he doesn't blame me, but, I don't know, although as I say, I wasn't responsible for the anesthetic, and the dental end of the deal was all right.

December 12, 1944

. . . The reason I was so listless last night was my concern over one of the officers, who reported to me with an elevated temperature, a swelling of the right ramus of the mandible, and an inability to open his mouth very wide. I'm pretty sure that he has an infection of the same type you had around the third molar. I put him to bed and started treatment, but his temperature continued to rise slowly, as did the swelling. There was nothing I could do, and I was in no

way responsible for this condition, but I felt badly about it never-
theless. This morning his temperature is down, the swelling is greatly
reduced, and he can open his mouth somewhat wider.

December 13, 1944
Churl Darling,

It seems that later in the day, after I wrote you in the morning,
this Ensign Miller's temperature went up. Now I don't know why I
should be worried or concerned about this boy. After all, he is the
medical department's responsibility, although the mouth is involved;
but I can't help it, I do worry that he is a medical department case.
I know more about these things than they do. At any rate, I talked
it over with Dr. Davey, who is handling the case, and suggested that
it would be better for all concerned, for a variety of reasons, if Mr.
Miller were to be sent ashore to a base hospital here. The ship would
probably benefit. Mr. Miller would be in a better position to get
what treatment he needed, and our medical department would be
left free for more urgent duties. We talked about it all for quite a
while, and then decided to wait until morning and get Dr. Dickey's
OK on it. Incidentally, I made sure by direct inquiry that Dr. Davey
had informed Dr. Dickey about the case earlier, and I knew for a
fact that he had seen an x-ray I had ordered for the boy.

. . . Mr. Miller, it seems, felt some better last night, and this
morning his temperature was normal, but it has climbed slowly dur-
ing the day till now it is about 100.2. I expect that that will repeat
the next few days until it stays normal. I still think he should go
ashore, but I'm done being concerned about it. The medical depart-
ment has my recommendation. Dr. Dickey has been informed of the
case, and hasn't bothered looking at it as yet. If he isn't concerned,
I surely have no cause to be. If Miller stays on board, and this case
resolves sufficiently, I'll extract that wisdom tooth. It is going to be
a tough job, and he'll probably be good and sick postoperatively,
and not be much good to the ship (which is the main reason I want
him ashore now, so that we can get a replacement easily). But "the
hell with it." That is an attitude I have been forced to adopt. You
remember what I used to say about ". . .it all." I must adopt that at-
titude on board.

December 18, 1944

   . . . *Late in the afternoon I had a patient come in with a deep lateral abscess near a lower molar, and immediately in front of that a bicuspid which had to extracted. I took x-rays of the teeth, anaesthetized the area, and extracted the teeth. I noticed that he bled a little more freely than is usual. I asked him if, when he bit himself, he usually clotted right up or if he bled freely. "I bleed a lot, Doc," he said. "The last time I had a tooth extracted I bled for 26 hours before they stopped it." I immediately put a pack in place (something I do routinely anyhow), took him next door to the sick bay, had him lie down, and left directions for the packs to be changed every half hour, and for him to keep an ice pack on the part 20 minutes in the hour. I told him not to leave until I returned. Finally I had to pack the socket with gauze and have him bite on a gauze sponge placed on top of that. At this stage the bleeding seems to have stopped.*

December 22, 1944

   . . . *I spent most of the morning, however, treating this fellow with the long bleeding time that I wrote to you about. I removed the pack from the socket, and he started to bleed again. I tried some topical pressure in an attempt to stop it and was about to give up and repack the socket when I noted the blood showed a tendency to flow more slowly. So I continued with the pressure packs. They seemed to work all right for when I sent him below at 11:30 the bleeding seemed to have stopped.*

   This morning too, I had to treat an officer from another ship. He had a toothache and came over to have me extract the offending member. Examination disclosed a deep cavity, but it seemed as if the tooth might be saved. It was. I took out the decay, sterilized, and filled over a cement base. The fellow was much relieved, and very pleased at retaining a tooth he had given up for lost. It seems that some other dentist had previously informed him that it would have to come out.

   Lester's detailed descriptions of his surgical procedures reflected the enthusiasm and pride of a very young man, very new to his field. He is eloquent about impactions and three-rooted molars, often rhapsodizing over "a lovely surgical extraction."

> *January 4, 1945*
>   *. . . and then came below to my office. Here I performed a very lovely surgical extraction of an upper second molar. So far I am proud of myself, and if it doesn't kick up in the next day or so I'll continue to be so. Without going into too much detail I can say that the tooth was non-vital (therefore very brittle) with a hollow crown. The three roots were thin and tortuously curved, and ran at right angles to each other (as shown in the x-ray). Therefore I made a flap, removed buccal (side toward the cheek) bone to the bifurcation of the roots, cut them both from the crown. Then I applied forceps to the crown and by the careful application of force succeeded in removing the crown and the lingual root intact. After that it was a simple matter to elevate the two buccal roots individually from their sockets, and remove them with a forceps; and follow that by suturing the flap back to position. Is that too detailed? Anyhow it worked out very nicely.*

Not all ships had their own dentists, which meant that Lester had many unexpected patients whenever they were in port. Yet, despite the extra work, he was proud of what he accomplished.

> *February 6, 1945*
> *Churl Darling,*
>   *I am afraid that this will have to be a short letter. I just completed a very full day, of which the last four hours have been the most difficult, and I find that I am very tired. In brief explanation, it happened that I had to treat 3 patients from another ship. Each of the three had a lot of emergency work to do, and I was working under a time limit. I could have said "the hell with it," done a little and let the rest go; but that would have meant much pain and agony for these lads, who didn't have a dentist aboard. I pitched in and did manage to complete all of the urgent work, including some rather difficult extractions. My only reward (and the only one I wanted) was the satisfaction of knowing that I had really helped those lads*

out. *They came over quite late, and I had to work right through supper. I had a bite to eat. I was too tired to be very hungry, and now
after a quick line to you, I'll shower and get into my sack.*

Lester described, in all modesty, his good standing among the crew, offering a few possible reasons for it.

February 15, 1945
*. . . Incidentally, for not writing last night, there was simply
no time. And for a change that is actually true. I put in a full day
at the office yesterday, made all the longer by the unscheduled appearance of three patients from another ship, the same ship I had
some patients from previously. It seems as if I have made a hit there
because I understand via Anderson that the boys expressed a definite
desire to come back here for their dental work rather than go to another ship. Of course it means more work, but such a tribute is worth
it. While I am tooting my own horn, I may as well mention the fact
that it seems to be the consensus of opinion on board that I am a
good dentist and the officers and men are glad to come in to have
me do their work for them. I can scarcely offer this as proof of professional competency, after all, these people are not dentists; but I
do like to think that it is an indication of professional respect and
impression made on a patient that will stand in good stead as a
carry-over in civilian life. After all, the most valuable asset in a
practice is simply the conviction of the patient that you are doing
what is best for them in a fairly adequate manner, and with a fairly
pleasing personality. That seems to be the case on board. I am at
least fairly well liked, despite the fact that there exists no great in-
timacy between anyone else on board and myself, with the possible
exception of Ralph Goldman; and the men, especially the officers,
have, almost without exception, offered unsolicited praise of my
work, not so much to me, as praise which I have heard through a
rather circuitous route. Frankly, I am rather proud of that. I think
this good opinion is primarily because of my attempt to retain a
conscience. The boys know that actually I am doing my best for
them. So much for that which I mention only because I know you
will feel just as good about it as I do.*

February 19, 1945

. . . Today was a fairly nice Sunday. I had four patients over from another ship in the morning. They didn't have much work to do. As a matter of fact I finished them just before afternoon chow.

. . . I had a pretty full day today. The first thing in the morning a boat from a ship without a dentist pulled alongside and asked me to care for the five fellows they had with them. I was set for the day. While working on those lads, a message came across from another ship asking me to take care of a dental emergency. That being accomplished I was requested by the same ship to take 14 more patients during the week, and by the first ship a similar amount. What a life.

February 25, 1945

. . . . In the morning I took out an impacted wisdom tooth for one of the boys, who has been having some trouble with it. I'm developing a pretty fair technique on those things. This one came out very nicely.

. . . I have been doing quite a bit of dentistry for a number of the smaller ships in the vicinity. I try to complete the boys as well as I can at one sitting. It's a little hard on the boys, and me; and they really appreciate it. Just yesterday the exec of one of these LST's sent me the nicest letter of appreciation. That was all the pay I needed. I'll send the letter along by separate mail. I know you'll like it, and you'll want to hold onto it.

Here, Lester recounted the fact that other people were praising his skill as a dentist.

March 1, 1945

. . . I don't mean to brag, and what I say I tell you only because I know how pleased you will be to hear about it. But honestly I have been collecting unsolicited praise lately from officers and enlisted personnel alike. I am told that my work for the men of the other ships is highly praised and much appreciated, and yesterday Ed Davies told me that he had heard a number of enlisted men discussing the medical department, and they all agreed that I was the *only one who deserved the title "Dr. " Things like that have been coming to my ears more and more frequently of late, and frankly I like it and am proud of it. Indeed I am now consciously trying to act in a manner becoming to my reputation. How do you like me?*

A huge abscess, and a lawyer without the knowledge of floss.

March 15, 1945
. . . One of my patients, an army boy, came in with a complaint of toothache. Examination showed two abscessed teeth, which I x-rayed, injected, and extracted. With the teeth, and with the curette after the extractions, I removed one of the most extensive abscesses I have yet encountered. It was really phenomenal. That's one boy that should feel a lot better with his teeth gone and that source of infection with them.

Our communications officer has been complaining of a peculiar pain brought on only by chewing gum. The teeth concerned looked perfectly sound, they weren't being traumatized. Yet he insisted he had a legitimate, honest, pain and made much of it. The last time I examined him we decided that it might be merely that he forced some of the gum between his teeth while chewing, and thereby caused pain (although it hardly should have caused the degree of pain he complained of). Today he came in after lunch saying he had just chewed gum, and he had a splitting toothache. I took him to the office, passed a piece of dental floss between his teeth, removed a small shred of food, and miraculously he was cured! I offered him a pack of dental floss for his own use. "No," he said, "I can't use the stuff." I actually had to give him a personal demonstration in the use of the floss. And he a successful lawyer. Tsk, tsk.

A little lesson in humility after all the praise.

May 8, 1945
. . . Today, I found to my surprise, was Sunday. I say surprise because I had already anaesthetized a patient for the removal of an impacted lower third molar. Every once in a while, about as soon as I start to think that I'm getting pretty good at those things, some-

thing comes up to show me that there's still room for improvement. This was a complete boney impaction, but the x-ray didn't make it appear unusually difficult. Indeed it started out fine. The incision was clean, the bone was removed nicely, I applied the elevator, the tooth was loosened in its socket, and then when I thought I had it out, the tooth structure in which I had inserted the elevator point just crumbled. That happened several times. The tooth was of a chalky consistency and wouldn't resist pressure. It was really a problem. The tooth was loose enough so that it could have been lifted out if I could have grasped it with an instrument, but it was slightly wedged in under the second molar. Anyhow, I worked for about 1 hour after it was loosened, trying to devise some way to get it out. I finally succeeded. What a relief it was to lift that tooth out its socket intact. The aggravating thing about it was that all along the tooth was so loose, and yet resisted dislodgement.

...I am pleased to report that patient whose third molar I labored so hard over is feeling fine today, and seems but little the worse for wear.

However, Lester's confidence bounces back. It is interesting to note that he was still close enough to his dental school days to refer to what he learned in his text books.

May 19, 1945

...I had an average day in the office today. In the afternoon I had an impaction to do which served to restore my confidence in me. I thought it would be real tough, but after splitting the tooth the roots responded to the leverage of the elevator just like the textbook says they should.

Only after this complete description of the dental procedure did Lester ask Shirley if she was interested.

June 10, 1945

...I looked over a couple of patients on whom I had performed recent extractions, this morning. After that I removed a completely impacted upper left cuspid from one of the lads. He came in a couple of weeks ago complaining of a third tooth; and palpation did show a bump over the first bicuspid. The cuspid had never erupted

*and was not making itself felt. I took x-rays, and after a little hes-
itation decided to remove it. I hesitated because I had never removed
an impacted cuspid, and this one was atypical in being located ex-
ternally, rather than internally; and the x-ray showed it to be in
close relation to the maxillary sinus. But the tooth had to come
out, and if I went into the sinus, so would anybody else, and there
is always a first time. So this morning I gave him a single injection
that blocked off the entire area (an infraorbital, if you are curious),
made a long incision medially, and a short one distally, turned back
a generous flap, removed the bone overlying the crown, and a portion
of the root, loosened it with an elevator, applied forceps and with a
complex series of movements (the root had several twists) removed it
intact. I then replaced the flap and inserted two sutures, one medial
and one distal. It really wasn't bad at all. For a while, when she
wouldn't come even after it was loose, I was afraid I would have to
really dig deep to overcome the curvature; but she finally did yield
to pressure and came out intact. Now if there is no infection it
should be fine. Are you interested in my technical experiences?*

The ship was often docked at an island, and liberty was then frequently
called for all the men. Imagine choosing liberty over a dental appointment.

June 14, 1945

    *. . . Since we've been here the liberty policy has been rather lib-
eral. The result is that I get very little work in the office since the
boys are either getting over or getting ready for a liberty. By this
time I am enough of a veteran to realize that* nothing *is as important as liberty, so I do not mind the broken appointments.*

September 9, 1945

    *. . . Today was supposed to be a quiet Sunday, but as usual with
planned quietness, events decreed otherwise. I spent a busy morning
seeing a succession of unscheduled patients. This afternoon Davey
and the exec played a little bridge with Major Mitchell and me. We
were having a nice quiet game when I was called out to care for a
dental emergency. The kid had a badly infected central incisor and
his face was blown up. I extracted the tooth and put him in the sick*

*bay with directions to administer penicillin. Immediately after that
another fellow came up complaining of a toothache. He had symptoms of a sinusitis, besides. I extracted the aching tooth, which was
pyorrhetic and had to come out anyhow, and put him in the ward
on a sulfa regime. I hope they come along all right.*

The following is an interesting encounter with a patient who required
more psychology than dentistry. For any dentist, an understanding of the
psychology of fear and pain is basic to practice.

October 24, 1945

   *I had a peculiar one this morning. I noticed a temporary filling
in the mouth of the last patient I had for the morning. The kid told
me it had been put in by a dentist on another APA about a month
ago and was to last until he got to the States. I had to x-ray another
tooth anyhow so I x-rayed that one while I was at it. It turned out
to be exposed and I thought I'd better extract it. It has club shaped
roots, and I knew it would be a toughy, so I tried to prepare the patient for it. I gave him the injection, and got the anesthesia fine.
Then I put the forceps on it, but as I expected it didn't yield to pressure of the forceps, hardly at all. I put down my forceps to insert a
burr in my contrangle (I was going to divide the tooth at the bifur-
cation of the roots and deliver each root separately). I suddenly noticed that the patient's hands were shaking like leaves, and that it
seemed to be spreading to the rest of him. I put my instruments
aside and started to see what was the matter. The kid sat up in the
chair, put his head in his hands, and wept great salt tears. "It isn't
you," he insisted, "it's me. I'm terribly afraid." And he said I wasn't
hurting him. Obviously he wasn't going to faint on me, so I tried
to encourage him. However, instead of getting better, the nervous
palsy increased in intensity, and the lad seemed to have difficulty
in understanding what was being said to him. To play it safe (I was
afraid that he would work himself into a self-induced hysterical
form of shock), I sent for Ralph and told him that that was the end
of the morning's work, that I'd do nothing further about extracting
the tooth. Then I gave him a Nembutal. In a little while he calmed
down, and I let him return to the ship with the tooth still in his*

head. That was an interesting reaction. It seems that, when he was in boot camp, some dentist extracted a tooth for him and failed to keep his promise of "freezing" it, and it turned out to be a very painful procedure. The result is that he is terribly apprehensive of any dental procedures.

13

THE SUN, THE MOON,
AND THE STARS

FIGHTING BOREDOM AND LONELINESS was a daily struggle. Lester's days began quite early, usually around 5 AM for those morning drills. Yet he was awake long into the night talking with friends and writing to Shirley. The long days seemed even longer when the ship was at sea, and while the routines of the day helped to structure the time, the monotony was unavoidable.

Everyone must have coped with it in their own way. Lester found relief in writing, reading and passing the time with his shipmates. Being both the observant scientist and a romantic at heart, he often spent long hours on deck watching the sea and sky and commenting upon the weather. Many letters described the sunset that day, the oppressive humidity, the appearance of fish, or the way a wave broke along the ship as the bow cut through the ocean. All of this he wanted to share with Shirley.

In these sections of the letters, Lester gave free rein to his poetic side. Far from being factual, dry recitations, the language often flowed and sang.

Time on deck entailed a degree of personal risk. Lester was blonde and blue-eyed, with the fair skin that never tans but always burned. His paeans to nature were often accompanied by tales of his attempts to avoid sunburn, and his success or failure in preventing it.

Lester spent time topside to escape the build-up of heat below deck, but the Equatorial sun was relentless, and there was no real escape. Being above deck also provided a temporary respite from the crush of people inside, a short break of solitude, a rare commodity. Others often had the same idea, though, spoiling his attempt to find some momentary peace. He would try again later.

Lester tried to express for Shirley something of what he was seeing in the world around him. The natural world was a very real and rich aspect of his everyday life.

Lester had just arrived at his base in Bremerton, Washington, not yet having gone out to sea, but the vistas all around him must have been vastly different from those in Brooklyn or Texas.

July 25, 1944

. . . The sun has been setting as I write this, and it is indeed a beautiful sight to see. This bay which we see from the verandah on which I now sit is as calm and peaceful as a lake. It is immediately ringed with a line of spruce trees. In the middle distance is the top of a small hill, also covered with trees. Then, making up the background, black and majestic in the rays of the setting sun, which silhouettes them from behind, are the jagged peaks of the Olympian Mountain range.

October 1, 1944

. . . It was a lovely night. A great big full moon shone brilliantly on the water. And the ship rocked slowly and majestically to the movement of the waves. Standing where we were the moon appeared right over the mast, and instead of the ship moving it seemed as if the moon was describing circles about the ship.

. . . Before turning in last night I took a few turns about the weather deck, about all the exercise we get on board. It was another one of those moonlit nights such as I told you about in the last letter. It brings to mind a line from "The Highwayman":"And the moon was a sliver of light / on the highway," or words to that effect. It is beautiful. The air clear and cold, the stars swinging back and forth, back and forth as the ship rolls to first one side, then another.

October 14, 1944

. . . I stood at the extreme end of the fan tail and leaned on the rail watching the wake of water churned up by the propeller. The Pacific is a funny ocean so far as colors are concerned. I've seen in it more shades of blue, green, and gray than I imagined existed. Today the wake was a beautiful light turquoise blue. While I was standing there Ralph came out and we talked for a while. "I'll have to have a boat after this," he said. I agreed with him.

After reading this, one can almost feel the ship move through the churning sea.

October 28, 1944

. . . The sea in this area seems to be unusually rough. And some of the army men are reacting in the usual way. Seasickness is a pretty sad thing. Our G.Q. station was rather close and for a while down below I felt rather queasy myself. I love to stay outside on the weather decks, however, and watch the ship plow through the rollers throwing tons of water in a graceful arcing loop to fill in a welter of white spray on the green solidity beneath. The wind was from just a little off the starboard bow and standing on the starboard side you can watch the sea as it coils and recoils making and unmaking the waves. The waves approach the ship at what seems tremendous speed, actually taking a long time to reach the side. As they get closer they increase in size; but the increase seems to be more a relative than an actual one, for the waves, far from seeming to add to their mass, the sea seems to drop away from in front of them. And as the wave draws nearer the depth of this trough seems to increase. Then it seems as if the ship dips sidewise into this deep hollow, the rail rolls sideward towards the wave until the crest seems to be over your head and it appears as if the ship will be swamped. Then suddenly the wave passes under the ship and there is a quick lift of the deck under your feet as it passes backward. I can stand for hours just watching these waves roll along.

October 29, 1944

. . . I stayed topside and got some sun for a while. While I was standing there Mr. Powell came up to join me; then Mr. Slemmons

came by, and finally Mr. Warmington joined our gossip circle. We stayed there and shot the bull for a while in the sunlight. It was a good feeling. I kept my head back and watched the masts describe crazy circles in the sky in response to the urging of the insistent waves, or dropping my eye suddenly I would follow the course of a wave as it raced along the side of the ship from fore to aft. How relaxing it was. I could close my eyes for a moment and imagine I was on a palatial pleasure liner on a cruise around the world. In another moment I would ring for the steward, to bring me a refreshing drink.

. . . I finally made it to the forecastle, the forepeak, the eyes of the ship, this last so called because of the eye like slits on each side of the bow for the passage of hawsers. It is the extreme forward part of the ship. Standing there the ship did not seem to roll near as much as it did along either of the rails amidships. The reason became apparent after a moment. Amidships, near the rails, the rolling motion of the ship is multiplied by your distance from the center line, which acts as the horizontal axis along which the ship rolls. When you are far forward as I was, you are standing right on the center line and hence, although the ship rolls, you do not feel it. I put my feet up on a support and leaned far enough over the bow to watch the ships forefoot cleaving sharply through the water, and sending a beautiful gossamer-thin wave arcing clear and white over the more turgid water below, and finally regretting even a short absence from the mother sea dropping hastily back, there to mingle itself indistinguishably with the body of its progenitor. Ahead of us another ship, as if to belie my impression of calm, was rolling heavily from starboard to port, and then back again. While I stood there a group of enlisted men wandered forward to join me and we talked for a while of this and that as we watched the sun make its preparations to set. The first thing it did was to take a face cloth of a cloud and scrub its face thoroughly with it, changing the bright sunshine of a moment before to an effulgent light, caressing in its softness, and broken here and there by the straight harsh bars shooting halo like from the periphery uncovered by the cloud. The rest of the sun's routine for setting I cannot tell you for at that moment general quarters sounded and we had to man our battle stations. Ralph brought his chess set below with him, and although G.Q. was short

*it was long enough for me to revenge myself for this morning's defeat
by decisively winning this encounter.*

Lester spied schools of fish and also found yet new ways to describe the
sea and waves to Shirley.

October 31, 1944

*. . .Yesterday, while standing on the fo'castle, I saw a couple of
schools of flying fish. At first glance I was really amazed. I knew
how far we were from land, and here were these swallow-like creatures
skimming the waves. A moment after, the sun shone on them from
the right angle and lighted up their brilliant blue iridescence, and
the filmy, gossamer-like fins. Then I could see them for the fish they
were. They would take off, fly darting-like over the surface, and then
suddenly plunge into the water. It was really very interesting. There
is something very soporific and peaceful about the sea. I like to walk
to the extreme forward portion of the ship, where the port and starboard rails come together at about the level of my shoulders. There
I lean my arms on the rail, put my head on my arms, and just stand
watching the water. As the ship rolls I roll with it, as it pitches my
knees bend and straighten as the occasion demands. With my head
down I can see the wall of white spray thrown up by the bow of the
ship. Further out the body of the sea undulates as it gathers itself in
to form the swells. Watching the swells take shape and move on and
disappear and reappear is something I can watch for hours on end.
It is so mysterious. Out of the calm smoothness of the water a rounded
mass takes shape, small and insignificant-appearing. As you watch
it, it rolls toward you at a deceptively slow pace. Suddenly it approaches the ship, and by some magic it has been transformed into a
speeding, irresistible mass of ton upon ton of water. Its side towers
as high as the rail. It seems as if it must come aboard. Then suddenly
the side of the ship rises high in the air, the stern digs in, the bow
lifts up, and the masts cant crazily to the side as the swell lifts the
ship as if it were a toy. As it passes underneath and from fore to aft
the direction of tilt changes, and suddenly this rail that a moment
before was so high above the water is lowered, lowered with a thun-
derous "OOOOMMM" as it crashes on the breast of the sea beneath*

and throws a tremendous wave of foam and water to the side. And as this bow wave rolls aside, it meets the next swell head on. There is another formation of spray and foam as the two tremendous bodies of water meet. It seems that the bow wave has neutralized the swell; but the next moment shows that the neutralization is merely an optical illusion, for again the ship heels to the stimulus of the swell, and again the process is repeated. And there I stand for hour upon hour, watching this play of force against force, to a soothing hiss of the passage of the ship through the water. Perhaps that is why doctors so frequently recommend long sea voyages for people with distraught emotions.

November 5, 1944

. . . The sky tonight was the first one that approaches the dime novel description of tropical skies studded with stars. There were just thousands of stars in the sky, their brightness emphasized by the blackness of a few low-hanging clouds. The wake of our ship was a milky white and amidst this whiteness were occasional shining flecks that grew more and more numerous as I looked at them. These were the first manifestations of phosphorescence we had seen. I understand that as we make more southing they will become more and more pronounced. We talked a while there and then came below to turn in.

Lester spotted, and described, a volcanic island.

November 16, 1944

. . . Last night, just before G.Q., I was up on the flying bridge while we were passing close aboard one of the numerous volcanic islands that dot the ocean. This one with all its peaks, and the clouds around its summit, others pouring over its shoulder like a slow motion waterfall might have seemed to step right off the silk of a beautifully done Japanese print. Without doubt it was one of the most beautiful things I've seen on this voyage.

Lester's view of the various islands in the Pacific.

December 23, 1944

...We have been getting around quite a bit of this section of the Pacific, and of course, have seen many places that by now are familiar names to everybody. It is surprising how similar they all look from aboard ship. An island formed by a mountain dipping to the valleys in filmy mists; along the sea shore a mass of vegetation or in some instances a palm grove. Here and there a beach marked by a stretch of white sand, and the froth of the breakers spoiling the uniform blue of the sea. Tropicalia. However worked and overdone it has all been. And yet certain parts of it are beautiful. Occasional sunsets are memorable.

January 3, 1945

...The night was lovely. There was a lovely sunset distinguished chiefly by some beautiful pastel shades of pink and blue, and a darkening gold against which the blackness of the night came rolling in from over the horizon.

January 8, 1945

...We have been having many different types of sunsets of late, some flamboyant some quietly pastel-like in character, others a bastard mixture of the two; but all well worth seeing. One thing most of them seem to have in common, that is long banks of clouds rising from the horizon like dark bars with the colors of the sky showing between, these bars seeming to blend at a common point on the horizon (like rail road tracks run together in the distance).

Lester pondered the life of the seaman.

January 14, 1945

...Last night as I watched the water slide by from my vantage point, aft on the cabin deck, I couldn't help but wonder what manner of man would chose to follow the sea for a life work. What compensations does it have to offer for that which it steals from a man: his wife, his children, his home. Certainly the romance of the sea is a myth. It is beautiful at times, but no more so than many places. And although there are many seaports I am not familiar with I be-

*lieve that most of them are about the same, offering chiefly rough-
ness, much liquor, and cheap (or in some cases expensive) women.
No, I am afraid that it is not the life for me.*

January 16, 1945
*   . . . I have developed a new habit. After chow each night I try
to get above on the upper deck to watch the sunsets. Unquestionably,
they are beautiful and colorful. The character of the sunset at sea
seems to change as one goes from north to south and vice versa. That
is, as one goes north they tend to be less flamboyant (although equally
colorful in pastels) than they are in the south. About now they seem
to be compounded equally of both types. They start with pastel blues
and light greens. Then unobtrusively a cloud bank seems to develop,
first the fingers, then the arm, then the shoulder, then the body of
night. But this cloud bank of course acts like a prism and breaks up
the rays of the sun into deep passionate reds, purples and blues, with
black splotches of cloud interspersed amongst them. The louder colors
seem to seek the horizon. The pastels linger higher in the vault of
heaven. Indeed, although the evening is but brief (15 minutes after
the sunset begins it is too dark to read), the light seems to linger in
the heavens. Thus, while in the East it is fully black and stars twinkle
gaily in the skies, in the West it is dark only at the horizon. High in
the heavens, the light blue lingers on for an astonishing length of
time. Really, I have had some pleasant, if solitary, evenings up there
watching the night draw on. Frequently, the chaplain plays some
records over the p.a., and every so often he plays one of ours. And
there am I stretched out on an ammunition box looking at the sky
and being very homesick. Isn't that a sad picture?*

Lester had great powers of both observation and description, as shown
in this letter about their first storm.

January 20, 1945
Sweetheart,
*   There was no letter written last night for a variety of reasons.
Mostly it was the storm. You see, there was nothing to do during
the rough weather but lie in the sack and try to sleep. Oh, yes! We*

had what passed for our first storm at sea, and I will admit that it was rather rough for a while, too rough for a while, too rough to even try to work. Aside from the fact that the ship rolled violently and frequently, it was nothing unusual. The sky was gray and overcast the entire day. The wind whipped the waves to respectable proportions and the old Blue Ox rolled like a cow with the bellyache. I spent some time on the bridge watching the ship react to the storm. The swells were coming at us from directly abeam. This of course intensified the roll. First the ship would roll a little to port as it slid into the follow of the oncoming wave, then it would quiver for a moment as the force of impact of the mass of rushing water hit it, then slowly the wave passed under the ship (slowly to judge the almost dignified gyrations of the mast). First, the ship would lie way over to starboard, taking its own sweet time about getting there. At the limit of its swing, it would hesitate for a moment like a pendulum at the apex of its arc. Then slowly back to port we would careen, and away over on the port beam we would go. And so it went back and forth and back and forth. For variety, occasional seas would hit us on the bow instead of on the beam. In this case the forward part of the ship would lift and roll while the after part would fall, and the after part would lift and roll. This would impart a peculiar, plunging, corkscrew-like motion to the ship.

Lester never seemed to tire of either watching or writing about the waves and the sunsets. That seemed to be his primary means of relaxation. The following letter concerned the effects of a storm on the other ships in the convoy.

March 29, 1945
Churl Darling,
     The weather continued quite rough today. There really is quite a sea running. Fortunately for most of us we are running head on to it most of the time. Thus we merely pitch from fore to aft (like a seesaw). If the ship were from the beam or on the bow or quarter, the ship would roll, or, most probably, roll and pitch, both producing a corkscrew, plunging sort of motion, which is supposedly very efficacious in causing sea sickness. Even as it is we get an occasional

sea on the beam with sad results for many of the men. It is really quite a sight to be on deck and watch the other ships of the convoy making heavy weather of it. One moment their bows are lifted high in the air or the sea passes under it, the next the stern is lifted high and the bow plunges low. If, as is frequently the case, the next swell arrives at the right moment, the bow is driven right into it and the wave breaks with a roar over the fo'castle. It is fun, too, to hold your head over the side and watch the tons of water flung aside by the forefoot of the ship as it slaps down on the bosom of Mamma Sea after a high toss. The gray water mass is broken into a million particles, which so distort the light as to appear white. Each particle is cast far to the side in a beautiful arc to fall into the bluish wake of the ship in front of us. It is consoling, too, to realize that as heavy as the weather may be for us, it is treble that for the lean destroyers and other escort craft that so doggedly maintain their stations on the flanks of the convoy.

Shocked by common occurrences.

April 1, 1945
      . . .The other day, while standing at the rail, I saw a fish jump. It was a fairly large fellow with a forked tail. "Look at that fish jump," I exclaimed, tugging at the sleeve of the fellow next to me. "I saw it," said he, in the same tone of amazement. The really amazing thing about this "amazing" incident is that both of us should consider it amazing to see a fish in the ocean. How uncommon a thing that is!

May 26, 1945
      . . .We are getting back into the flying fish territory. Those I saw this evening were numerous and big. Familiarity hasn't bred contempt for these graceful fellows. I still get a big thrill out of watching them break water, skim the waves, and finally plunk in again.
      Yesterday, while I was talking with Dr. Golden and the skipper on the bridge, word came that one of our escorts had a "contact." The skipper said he had just seen a school of whales go by, and therefore wasn't particularly alarmed. Sure enough, a few moments later the report came that the contact wasn't a sub.

Lester's literary skills reported to Shirley on "the questing eye finding momentary magic," which is far from the typical declarative statement.

June 3, 1945

. . . It is still hot, but we seem to have moved to an area of more pronounced winds, and cooler nights, which is something to be thankful for. The sunsets are still assuming their usual gorgeous hues and shades. Blue skies forming a background for smoldering cloud masses of fiery red and orange, that gradually turn into purple and black as night falls. The evening skies are not as glorious as before. The stars seem to be smaller and further away. But the hiss of the water in the quiet of the night, as the ship cuts its way forward, is still as mystically pleasing to the ear as before. And still the questing eye finds momentary magic in the sudden phosphorescent gleam appearing in the white water of our wake. I have again taken to spending a few minutes on deck before turning in, and usually I can build up a mood of home and you, before coming below, and hitting the sack. That is good.

Lester was taken by atolls.

June 7, 1945

. . . Churl Darling,

Yesterday was another of the infrequent days I missed writing to you. That was because I had a bit of a sunburn, which tired me out. You see, we went ashore yesterday, on one of the famous Pacific atolls. It was the first time I had actually set foot on one of these unique formations, and it was quite interesting. Any dictionary will tell you what an atoll is and how it is formed; but no book can tell how small these things actually are, especially when viewed from the sea, and how miraculous it is to the uninitiated (that's me) that men not only exist there but set up relatively tremendous and permanent installations. These atolls, as you know, are made up of a group of small islands arranged in a circular fashion about a central body of water, the lagoon. The islands act as a breakwater, and the water in the lagoon is fairly deep, so that it serves as a good anchorage. Viewed from the sea, the atoll at first appears like a reef that at another tide will surely be submerged. Even from the center of the lagoon, this appearance of tininess persists, except that usually from closer in the vegetation may be distinguished, and the sight of palm trees assures you that the land does not entirely submerge. As the shore is approached in a small boat, and when you look up from marveling at the clearness of the water it becomes even more apparent that these are actually fair-sized islands, and are several feet above sea level. Some of these islets are sandy and barren; others seem to support a rather luxuriant growth of palms, ferns, and other tropical vegetation. This particular one that I visited was really very pleasant. It had a nice beach which ended a few feet inland in the bases of a grove of palm trees. We walked around it (with a couple of beers for nourishment) and saw a few interesting native cemeteries. They evidently bury their dead in a shallow grave, and then cover the graves with stones for protection. The natives had moved off this island so that they would not be interfered with by our forces (and vice-versa).

June 29, 1945

. . .We came in alongside a dock yesterday and thus got close enough to see the countryside at first hand. I had my glasses to supplement my naked eyes. The country side is very impressive. Right here there is a shallow coastal plain that rises abruptly to very steep foothills, beyond which the tall peaks of the mountains thrust up into concealing masses of clouds. Near the base of these mountains wisps of fog and cloud hang low, and fill in the definitive outline of valleys and defiles. It is strictly Hollywood-ian in appearance, the kind of thing you think never exists; but here it is. You remember in Lost Horizons how the clouds swirled around the mountain tops? That is something like it is down here. It is refreshing merely to stand on deck and smell the good greenness of the land. For a few yards inland there are a few houses in a clearing; then suddenly the jungle closes in. And it is just like that. One moment you are in civilization, abruptly, as if a curtain fell, you are cut off from all this by thick jungle. What a place.

He and a friend sat and watched flying fish.

July 7, 1945

...At one o 'clock I returned to my office for another session as patient. This lasted until about four o'clock, the work and the bull session. Then Dr. Mace and I went to the fo'castle to watch the flying fish. They seem to have increased both in size and number. They would take off in schools of fifty and a hundred and fly along to either side of the ship. It was fun to watch them from the bow. The water was clear today, so we could see them swim swiftly along just below the surface, gathering speed. Then with a flurry of white water they break the surface and they are off with a final flick of their tails. They glide swiftly along for incredible distances; and the blueness of their bodies contrasts brilliantly with a gold segment they have at the base of their fins. As they fly along they bank sharply so that their colorful dorsals disappear, to be replaced by their gleaming white bellies. Then, all of a sudden, they "plop" into a wave (you can almost hear the sound), make one or two fast circles downward in the water, and then disappear from view. This process they repeat continually, and it is one of never-ending interest to me.

August 25, 1945

...At the close of the day's work I went out on the fan tail to look at the ocean and the sky. As usual, when we are about this far out we have two gulls that follow the ship. I guess they live on what we throw overboard, but in the meantime they tirelessly fly along behind us, taking brilliant advantage of the air currents to soar and swoop along the waves. They seem to delight in making wheeling movements just above the surface of the water, following the contour of each wave, and seemingly seeing how close they can drag the tip of the lowermost wing without getting it wet. It is a wonderful pastime to watch them at their work. This afternoon for the first time I saw one of them light on the water.

September 14, 1945

...We arrived here in Manila this morning. The trip through the straits was lively, but I've already described that to you. There were lots of flying fish showing the way to the ship, and off to each side numerous schools of porpoises lazily rolled and arched in and

*out of the water. I spent a lot of time at the rail watching the shift-
ing landscape, made the more interesting yesterday, because of the
heavy rain clouds that blotted over some sections of the shore line.*

Just about a month away from sailing home, Lester still found beauty in
the routine, and still found arresting language to describe it.

October 3, 1945

*. . . Dr. Golden and I spent about an hour on the fan tail before
dinner last night just at the time we had entered the straits. On
each side of us were the peaks of the mountains that formed the islands lining the straits. The seas, about fifteen or twenty feet from
trough to the top of the swell, were coming from directly astern. We
stayed there and watched them gather height and speed as they approached the ship, then, passing underneath, caused the fantail to
lift as if our lumbering old gal was a saucy wench flicking her hips.
About two miles away, and headed on an opposite course, came another APA. She was riding light, and, heading into the sea as she
was, she seemed to be making much better time than she actually
was. The seas would lift her bow clear of the water and then let it
drop heavily back again. We were practically on to her, and from
that vantage point she looked long and lean, like a destroyer. She
passed in front of two stalagmite-like pinnacles of rock that jutted
up out of the ocean, and the scene was really one of true marine
beauty.*

Sam Scheller, 1915, age 19

Shirley Scheller, 1924, age 1

Rose, Shirley, and Sam Scheller, 1926

Shirley and her sister Elaine, 1932,
ages 9 and 4

Shirley, 1929, age 6

Sam Scheller, 1932, age 36

Rose and Sam Scheller

Rose and Sam Scheller, 1930s

Lester, 1934, age 17

Shirley, 1940, age 17

Shirley's graduation from Erasmus Hall High School, June 1941

Shirley, age 18, at Stevensville Hotel, 1941

Shirley and Lester while courting at the Stevensville Hotel, August, 1941

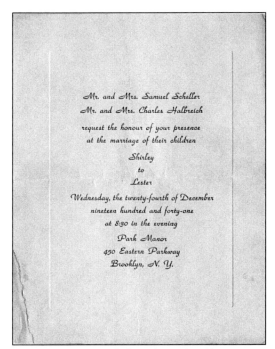

Invitation to Shirley and Lester's wedding

Shirley and Lester at their wedding, with their mothers, Rose Scheller and Esther Halbreich

Shirley as a bride, December 24, 1941

Lester as a groom, December 24, 1941

Shirley as a glamour girl, Spring 1942

At Lester's NYU Dental School graduation, June 1942

Riding mules in Mexico while stationed in Texas, early 1944

The USS Oxford, the ship on which Lester served August, 1944–November, 1945

Lester aboard the Oxford

Wartime V-Mail holiday card sent home to Shirley. Notice the censor's seal in the upper left corner, with the initials "R.G." (Ralph Goldman, Lester's bunk mate).

Shirley with newborn son Jeffrey, and Skipper

A proud Shirley with Jeff

*Shirley with Jeffrey, age 7 months,
outside on a cold day*

Jeffrey as a toddler, soon after the end of the war

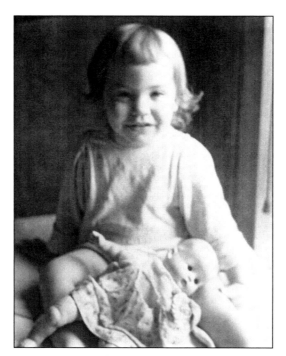

Daughter Terri Beth in 1950

Terri with Mike, the beloved family dog, 1957

Jeffrey and Terri at home

Lester at his dental office desk. The office was attached to the house.

Jeffrey at his bar mitzvah, with his parents, Shirley and Lester, September 1957

Jeffrey and Terri at Jeff's bar mitzvah, September 1957

Jeff shaking hands with Grandpa Charlie Halbreich at Jeff's bar mitzvah, September 1957

Essie and Charlie Halbreich, Lester's parents, 1958

The author at camp, age 8

David Martin, 1959

Shirley and Lester at their 20th anniversary party, December 1961.
Her MS is evident in her choice of flats for shoes.

Shirley, 1964

The Halbreich family—Terri, Shirley, David, Lester, and Jeffrey—at Jeffrey's wedding, June 26, 1965

Terri dancing with her older brother, Jeffrey, at his wedding

Both grandmothers at their grandson Jeffrey's wedding—Rose Scheller (left) and Esther Halbreich

Shirley and her sister, Elaine, at Jeff's wedding

Shirley and Lester dancing at their niece's wedding, July 1969

Shirley and Lester during the 1970s

Lester and Terri at her doctoral graduation, NYU, June 1986

Lester and Shirley on their way to their 50th Wedding Anniversary party, December 1991

Lester and Terri at the 50th anniversary party, December, 1991

14

THAT'S ENTERTAINMENT

WHAT TO DO TO fill the long hours of each day when you are apart from your wife, your family, your work, and everything familiar? And the same was true for the wives left behind, in the same familiar surroundings, but with an absent spouse. For the thousands of people touched by the war, the questions of how to carry on became the most important questions.

People living today, especially younger people, assume that filling those empty hours would be much easier now, taking into account the vast array of electronic devices and other forms of entertainment now at their disposal. This may be true; people in the 1940s had no computers, smart phones, video games, Netflix, IPads, or IPods. They did not even have television or stereo music, and the only way to see a movie was to go to a theatre. With such limited options, how did couples separated by war manage to pass their free time – those hours not consumed by work or military duty?

Apparently, they managed with great ease. As the letters show, the most common amusement involved socializing with other people. People typically interacted with each other to an extent that might seem extraordinary today. Possibly due to the very absence of electronic options people turned to one another for company. In fact, this had been true for most people in most places before the very recent introduction of electronic entertainment. Humans are said to be social beings, and this is reflected in their entertainment choices.

A good percentage of time was spent in conversation. Day after day, Les wrote about conversations after hours, as the men usually congregated in a general location to relax. With little else to do and nowhere else to go, their conversations were often prolonged, touching on personal, political, religious, or other topics, all explored in depth, over and again. They described the lives that they left behind, their wives and children. They talked about the progress of the war and what they expected, especially as it might affect them personally, such as their discharges from the navy. They discussed politics at home and in enemy countries. They delved into each other's faiths and religious practices. They endlessly dissected superior officers, especially those whom they disliked. And of course they discussed the movies, shore leave experiences, daily events and rumors.

While the men were talking, they also enjoyed other activities. Les and his friends played endless rounds of bridge, almost every day. When it was not bridge, the choice was often chess, also endlessly, game after game, day after day — but talking among themselves all the while. Sometimes, they took breaks and snacked. They snacked constantly in their free time, and food went with drinking. Beer was the usual beverage, but Coke was also popular. Often, someone would produce a record player, and the games, eating and conversation would then take place against a musical background.

This was mostly true aboard ship, but the ship often docked at island ports, where it remained for either a few days or an extended stay. Once in port the men were given regular shore leave, and they usually went ashore in large groups. So the socializing continued, but the venues changed. Les and his friends would usually wander the streets of the town, exploring and shopping for souvenirs. Shore leaves were in fact typically social, not isolated, activities, and they usually ended at the officers club for drinks and a meal. Occasionally, they ate at a local establishment. In later years, Les often reminisced about his time on New Caledonia, which he particularly enjoyed, and about his time in Japan, which aroused more complicated emotions.

The ship showed current movies on a regular basis, as the navy's answer to boost morale. It seemed to work, as Les and his companions frequently attended, watching movies which may now be considered classics, such as Arsenic and Old Lace, and others which were much more forgettable.

Even these social and gregarious naval officers did spend some time alone, Les being no exception. He rather enjoyed time by himself, which he liked to spend reading. He had always been a voracious reader. He used to tell a story of having read the dictionary for fun, when he was young, and another about his mother cutting his meat for him at the dinner table so that he would not have to stop reading. So reading was as natural to Les as breathing. What was remarkable in the letters was how rapidly he went through books, especially considering how much time he spent on all of his other activities and duties. He frequently mentioned that he was starting or finishing a book. He also plowed through dental journals and several correspondence courses. He took many of these while he was away, on topics such as accounting and auto mechanics. He hoped to use the accounting knowledge some day in his private practice to enhance his business skills.

When he was not reading or writing, he enjoyed working on crossword puzzles, which became a lifelong habit. Decades later, he and I solved The New York Times puzzle together over the phone, during our daily conversations. He also loved listening to music, mostly classical and opera, which he played when he was alone in his bunk or in his office. He began early what he later often indulged in — singing opera to his patients while working on them.

Thus, while he missed Shirley, he managed to fill his hours with a wide variety of activities.

This was a letter written while still in Texas.

> *October 12, 1943*
> *...They opened up the bowling alleys yesterday, so I bowled a few frames at lunch time, and a few before dinner.*
> *After dinner, I hung around, thinking I'd go to the movies, but it was that stinking* We've Never Been Licked *picture, which we'd seen. So I invited Paul and Neil to the room. On the way, we picked up Fred Holmberg, that red-headed marine flyer, who, incidentally, along with Howard and a few other marines, received their first lieutenant's yesterday. Arrived at home and we made up some rum and Coke. I broke out some crackers and cheese and peanut butter, and we had an orgy. It broke up about 11 o'clock. Had a lot of unexpected fun. That bonding left me a little stiff-limbed; but I'm going back for more today.*

Here, Lester was already on the *Oxford*, on the West Coast.

October 18, 1944
Churl, Darling,

The picnic yesterday was grand fun. I left at about 12, driving alone, but met the truck that the corpsmen were using, and parked my car and piled in with them. And a good thing, too, because it was about 30 miles out. One of the men had brought a football, and another a baseball and bat. So we threw them around for a while, drank some beer, sang, told stories, etc., etc. We got back about 10 PM. I piled right into bed and dropped off.

Neil came to the house Saturday night and listened to the Vic.

July 22, 1944

I met another Brooklyn boy and his wife, Eddie Zuckerman. We talked for a while and got acquainted. . .I'm invited to Sunday dinner at their house this week.

After the reception, we went to the movies on the base to see Going My Way. I really enjoyed it.

July 26, 1944

. . .After writing to you last night, I dropped in at the Zuckermans'. She was finishing a pie, and he was helping her. It was a nice night, so we all piled into the car and took a drive for half-an-hour.

I let them off at 10 o'clock, and drove up the hill to the house.

Socializing, eating, talking, driving, drinking and reading—all on the day that his son was born, but he did not as yet know that.

July 28, 1944

This evening I have the party for the ship's officers to get acquainted. I have an idea that they will be a nice bunch. I also have an idea that the wine will flow free.

The night before last I decided to just stay home and read instead of going out as usual. I had a Life, and Mrs. Iverson had a Reader's Digest. So I came home, showered, and turned on the radio, and settled down in the living room to read. No sooner had I started than I heard childish voices outside. It was three little children, neighbors of mine. . .putting on a vaudeville show for me. They sang, danced and told jokes for about thirty minutes.

August 19, 1944

We had no lectures after lunch. . . Then we went to town. I had some beers with the boys at a place called the Rathskeller (there will always be a Rathskeller). The first thing I knew, it was 5 o'clock and we were hungry, so we had a small spaghetti dinner. We hung around there. . .and then went to the movies. You will never guess what I saw. Snow White and the Seven Dwarfs. *It was really a lovely thing. I had seen it before, but you know me with my childish enthusiasm. I had to see it over again.*

After the show, there was nothing to do but walk around town and watch the drunks. This pretty little pastime soon lost its interest, and we got on the bus to come back. As usual, there was standing room only, and unfortunately I was standing in front of a tanked-up soldier. Before I knew it, he spewed. I got out of the way just in time.

This place is a little more lonely than was Bremerton. As yet I have made no comparable friends, although I have lots of people to talk to.

Movies in color were a relatively new phenomenon and certainly something to be noticed and discussed.

August 21, 1944

I don't believe that I took the time to tell you that I went to the movies on the base last night to see Greenwich Village. *It's a Technicolor job and for a musical was really quite good. I think you will enjoy it. They have a girl singer whom I believe they are trying to build up to compete with Betty Grable.*

August 27, 1944

I'm glad you're going out with the girls. I certainly do not want you to become a stay-in. Go out frequently.

. . . Later in the afternoon a group of us fellows chipped in, rented a car, and went for a drive. We had dinner out and then

drove to a spot near the lake. One of the fellows had a bottle (I can't stand the taste of hard liquor, but the others didn't share my prejudice), and we sang and joked until quite late. As the only fellow (sober) in the party I had to drive going back. After we returned the car, we were unable to get a taxi, and the buses had stopped running, so we walked back to the pier. It wasn't so bad, because halfway there we got picked up.

September 18, 1944

I started to town to see Pin-Up Girl but was sidetracked by the local O-club, a not too difficult job since I remembered that you said that the picture was lousy. There I had a couple of drinks, and one of the boys bought me a couple of drinks, and we had a good time. While we were there the exec and the captain walked in, so we joined them and shot the bull back and forth for a while. I can't begin to tell you what a swell fellow the skipper is. It is really unusual to find a man in his position so warm and human.

...After supper I went into town ...I stopped into the hospital to say hello to Ralph and his wife. I found them both there. I stayed for a while and we talked of this and that, of politics, God and personality. As usual, nothing was settled, but it was fun. I left early. She's going to leave for home tomorrow, and I wanted them to have their last few moments together as one. I walked down a few blocks to the bus and came on back to the base.

September 28, 1944

...Last night after I got into bed, Ralph and I talked for quite a while about quite a number of things. It was almost like being back at Cornell a while, such philosophic talk. My, oh, my.

September 29, 1944

As I left the table for dinner, the exec asked me to play a quick game of chess with him. I agreed and dug up my little pocket game. I didn't think I had much of a chance, because he had said he was "quite" interested in the game, and usually the man who so describes himself is quite good. Unquestionably, he is a better player than I am. He plays with somewhat more of a fixed idea than I do, but *with all due modesty I must admit that I gave him a bit of a tussle. The game took a bit longer than 10 minutes, and when he did checkmate me, it was with only a rook and a king left for him, and only a king left for me.*

Toward the end of that game, or rather while we were still playing, one of the ensigns brought down some records and started to play them on the Victrola we have here in the wardroom. So I walked over and started to listen with them for a while.

Shades of homesickness—guess what they played? First they played excerpts from Porgy and Bess, including "Bess you is my woman now." After that they played Tchaikovsky's Violin Concerto. *You can guess how I felt. Toward the last movement of the concerto, Ralph challenged me to a game of chess. Here I salved my injured pride by trouncing him unmistakably.*

As a matter of fact, he just left a few moments ago. Most of this letter was written between moves of that game. You don't mind, do you?

October 3, 1944

. . . My spare time, of which I usually have plenty, is spent, reading, playing chess or bridge, occasionally acting as a mail censor; and now and then making a tour of the ship so that I will know what makes it tick.

Men from home might find themselves assigned to the same bases and visited each other.

October 7, 1944

I suddenly remembered that today was laundry day, so I started to count my laundry. While I was engaged in this soulful task, a messenger came up telling me I had a visitor. I couldn't imagine who it could be, but while putting on my shoes I said, I bet it is Dr. Malinak, and sure enough that's exactly who it was. We talked for about an hour, and then he had to get a boat to return to his ship, which was moored nearby. It was really a very pleasant visit.

October 11, 1944

. . . At G.Q. in the afternoon, Ralph and I played our usual

chess game, and after that it was time to secure for the day and go to chow. After chow Ralph and Butch Allan (our warrant pharmacist), Dr. Davey, and myself played some bridge. Some of the bridge was good, some atrocious, some hilarious; but the time did pass.

October 31, 1944

. . . I just finished playing a game of chess with the exec, and he beat me again. This time though he had to fight me for it. The games get more and more difficult as we got along. I think that before the voyage is over I'll be able to win about 50% of the games.

November 1, 1944

. . . After dinner tonight Ralph and I played some bridge with Butch Allan and Dr. Davey. We took them into camp very handily, although I must admit that we did get the cards. After the game Dr. Davey suggested a few minutes of poker. I wasn't keen on it, but I didn't want to be a spoil sport, so I joined in. We played about an hour and I ended up about 2 bucks losers, which renewed my resolve to stay away from such games, not that the two bucks itself was significant, but I didn't enjoy playing for it and that was that.

November 3, 1944

. . . I spent the morning in the room doing a bookkeeping lesson. By this time I am quite a bookkeeper. I think that I am up to lesson five and already I know about journalizing, posting, and keeping a ledger. I've gotten perfect grades on all of the self-testing problems given so far. I am so proud. Tonight I have to learn about proving the ledger by trial balances.

November 10, 1944

. . . I was joined by Ralph, who challenged me to a game of chess. At first I was loathe to accept, but I came above in a little while and we set to. The game kept us busy until dinner time. After dinner we had time to get a little of the evening breeze at the port rail before evening G.Q. Tonight I brought a book with me to read, continued reading it after G.Q. and finished it a few moments ago. It's one of those sexy detective things. I took it from the ship's library *because it was by Thorne Smith entitled* Did She Fall. *I'm still not sure, but it was nice light reading.*

November 16, 1944

. . . I finished The Grapes of Wrath *last night. Parts of it were very good, and parts of it, of course, were very lousy. I enjoyed reading it, however. Dr. Davey is an Oklahoma lad, so I asked him to give us an eyewitness account of the terrible dust storms. He did too, and a very graphic one. From there he went on to discuss the background of what he called the typical Oklahoma family. This led into a discussion of the Okies in California. And here the bitterness, which before now he had only hinted at, came frankly out in the open; and the next thing he was ranting a little of sectional patriotism, and talking of such nonsense as the Oklahoma kids being smarter than the California kids anyhow, and then he wished all the foreigners were kicked out of the country because they were the real cause of all our trouble anyhow. I listened for a while in amazement, at first amused a little, then sad, for here was a product of the educational system, and a talking testimonial to its failure. Then I started to lead the talk away from the subject, and a few moments later the lights were out and we were asleep.*

November 20, 1944

. . . I have almost finished with this elementary bookkeeping course. I proudly report that I have caught the book in several mistakes, and proved them, too. Not that the presence of mistakes in a teaching text made my work any easier, but I feel good at having proved my own work to be right.

November 24, 1944

. . . After working hours I went to the room determined to get in a short nap before evening G.Q. Ralph and Bob were there and it developed that we had quite a conversation about contraceptives, children, life, sterilization, and the advisability of having money. As you can see I didn't get a hell of a lot of sleep during that period of time.

I spent most of time during G.Q. this evening trying to find something to read. I had to settle on The Soldiers Manual, *which one of our recent passengers left behind. It wasn't very satisfactory.*

After supper I went out on the flying bridge to get some air and watch the sea, a thing I have been too remiss in lately. There was quite a breeze out there, and it was quite refreshing so I stayed out there for a good while talking of this and that to a group of the watch officers. After a while of this I went below. My old corpsman was explaining some things to my new one, and helping him clean the office up. I decided the best place for me was out of his way, so I grabbed my typewriter and went into the wardroom. I sat down next to Bob and in between letters we discussed the perennial contest between regular navy and reserves, the science of meteorology, the difficulty of earning a living, what people do to earn a living, and the probable mission of the ship. Quite a bit of discussion for one evening. Despite all the talk I did manage to get those letters written.

December 1, 1944

…This evening I saw Holy Matrimony *with MontyWooley and Gracie Fields. It was good even a second time. We had seen it before.*

December 3, 1944

. . . I'm going to knock off now darling to see the movie, Gov't Girl *I think it is, and after that I'm going to turn in. I miss you and love you terrific like, darling. Good night my sweetheart.*

December 4, 1944

…There wasn't much to do this morning, either before or after GQ, and the same held true for the afternoon. I used part of the time to read Ellery Queen's novel CalamityTown, *which is really a good detective story.*

January 7, 1945

. . . In the past few days I've read The Thin Man *and* The Maltese Falcon. *Both were excellent mysteries. This evening I started to read* Strange Fruit. *I think you told me that you had read it. At any rate, there are a couple of copies aboard and it is well thought of.*

January 14, 1945

...*I am poking tentatively at this second bookkeeping course. I don't really think it is worthwhile, but in the meantime I have learned about the purchase journal, and how to record sales in cash and on account. This is certainly one aspect of my education that has, until now, been neglected.*

...*Have I mentioned that I finished* Home Sweet Homicide, *a mystery that is no better or worse than a good many others. I have started Phillip Guedella's* Wellington, *and I find it well and interestingly written so far. Incidentally, I think this is a good time to put in a plug for these paper-covered volumes that are issued "For the Armed Forces Only." They are for free, but would be a bargain even if paid for in cash. They represent an extensive library of diversified literature, in a very handy pocket form. When I go to G.Q., I always carry in one hip pocket a pair of leather gloves, in the other one of these convenient books. I have passed many otherwise dull hours in profitable (or, if not profitable) at least interesting reading.*

January 18, 1945

...*Today I finished reading* Wellington, *and not a bad book either. Indeed I enjoyed it thoroughly. It served to give me quite a new picture of European history of that period, and combined and settled into place a group of what had been unrelated impressions.*

Also I managed to read through the rest of the textbook on bookkeeping (course two). I didn't bother with the exercises past the third lesson. It is not that they are difficult, but they are tedious, and my purpose was served by gaining an understanding bookkeeping meaning and method. I feel now that I can look at a set of books and figure out what they mean. And that, after all, is what I wanted. In the final analysis I do not intend to become a bookkeeper. Each man to his own last, and I already have mine. So I think I am done with Bookkeeping *for the present. What my next course will be, I don't know. But rest assured I will keep you informed.*

January 22, 1945

...*In the last couple of days I have read* The Fleet in the Forest, *a novel of the building and use of Perry's fleet on the shores of, and in the waters of, respectively, Lake Erie. Beside that I've read most of the stories in a* Pocket Book of Dog Stories, *and some excerpts from a collection of Ogden Nash's verse. Today I am in the process of finishing* Hotel Berlin, '43, *a Vicki Baum novel. None of the stuff is particularly good, and the truth of the matter is I am getting tired of reading. As a matter of fact, there is little aboard the ship that retains my interest. Chess is not particularly attractive, acey-ducey is about to make me scream, and all in all I am on the edge of a good attack of boredom. I haven't succumbed yet, and am fighting in every way I know. I think that by tomorrow it will wear off. These spells come periodically, last a while, poisoning my outlook on everything and then go away.*

January 24, 1945

. . . Tonight we had quite a movie program. First they showed a March of Time *about the part the navy has played in winning the war. This was followed by an army comedy about the gentle art of potato peeling (as humor, it made a fine tragedy). Then we saw Jon Nesbitt's* Passing Parade, *featuring the World of Tomorrow, which was interesting, even if somewhat inaccurate. And now the Grrrrand feature,* Once Upon a Time. *The picture didn't mean anything in particular, but it was good to sit and watch, so it served its purpose.*

Yesterday I read a good mystery, The Judas Window. *It was really very baffling, and very thrilling, and very ingenious. Today I filled in the idle hours by getting most of the way through* Report From Tokyo.

February 13, 1945

. . . I managed to read in the last couple of Days Hervey Allan's The Fort and the Forest, *a novel of early American history, and to finish one of those thin, emotional, semi-stream-of-consciousness novels about a girl who married a flyer someplace in California. How tense and impressive it was. I didn't like it. Of course, no day is complete without a page or two of economic geography, and today's stint carried me through England to the Continent, and a little discussion of the German chemical industry. Très interés-*

sant. Vraiment.

I had no time for sunning today since I had a four to eight watch this afternoon. The monotony of that watch was relieved by a break at dinner time. As I left the dinner table I was informed that Ralph and I had been invited to play against Bob Powell and Earl Slemmons at eight (bridge). I accepted the invitation. We played some interesting bridge. Unfortunately, we didn't get the cards hardly at all, so the final score was against us. It was fun nevertheless.

April 28, 1945

. . . I have finished reading the first part of King Henry VI. *I'm really enjoying it. The drama is so tense, and the swearing so delightful. In one place where a certain duke protests that his ass is good as another, the second answers, "Ass good and I am: My grandfather's bastard." Priceless (I think).*

May 3, 1945

. . .We made rather good connections coming back, and arrived on board in time to see the movie Winged Victory. It was a little too sloppy for me.

. . . As I was coming out of the wardroom after the show I ran into Davey. "Come on up," he said. "Bastian's had a baby." It was true. Bob had a message flashed from shore. His wife had a baby girl. I broke out my remaining bottle of wine, and we killed it in celebration of the event.

May 4, 1945

. . . As I mentioned once before, the ship's library has been renewed. I've gotten my Shakespeare, the wardroom magazine subscriptions, and my dental publications have started to come through so you can easily see that I'll have plenty to read for a long while.

May 8, 1945

. . . I have been reading in my Shakespeare, slowly, but withal making progress. How now, varlet! Doubtest thou my word? Know then that the three parts of the History of King Henry VI, *have*

I thus far thoroughly pursued, and the Tragedy of Richard III, *to boot. And after mature reflection on the bloody genealogical struggles therein described, I cry with another of the bard's characters "A plague on both of your houses." Seriously though, I have gotten a good deal of pleasure out of these plays.*

May 9, 1945

. . . For the rest it has been a matter of eating, sleeping and reading. I finished King Richard the III *last night, and this afternoon laughed heartily at the farce of the* Comedy of Errors. *In between times I read a few short stories by Arrel. I would have read more, but Ralph had to return the book from the man he borrowed it from.*

May 10, 1945

. . . Today I read Titus Andronicus *in my Shakespeare. What a bloody tragedy. It's almost as bloodthirsty as the present war. Tomorrow I'll start the* Two Gentlemen of Verona. *Now I'm starting to get his more mature stuff.*

May 18, 1945

. . . I have started to reread Hemingway's The Sun Also Rises, *primarily, I think, because it is in a convenient-sized book. I had read it before, but so long ago that only certain names and situations arouse a sense of familiarity. So I am quite occupied with readings now, what with this and a few other books that are in the room, my Shakespeare, the new ship's library, my periodical literature, and a new textbook on oral surgery I bought.*

June 19, 1945
Churl darling,

Last night after the show I came into the wardroom with my typewriter to write to you, and bumped smack into a bull session involving as the participants: Mr. Mitchell, Chaplain Noland (Battling Bob from Oklahoma and Kansas) Dr. Golden, and me (the Pitkin Avenue Commandos). I add myself because I was irresistibly and immediately drawn into the vortex of this whirlpool of conversation. And to add to the already tremendous flow of words the chaplain contributed six bottles of Coke, which, appropriately iced, and served in a silver pitcher by myself, served to smooth the path of egress of the punctuated sound, we laughingly referred to as conversation. We talked of many things, some serious and some ridiculous; but to each we gave our earnest attention. This babble of words lasted until about one o'clock in the morning, at which time it was deemed feasible to retire. So I didn't write last night. There was but little to say. The big event of the day had been the movie, National Velvet. We all enjoyed it. The story was more than a little overdone, but the color was magnificent, and the horse was really beautiful. It made me a little nostalgic too, for the days of long ago when I was a fairly accomplished horseman. Once again the pictures of rides along the beautiful bridal paths at Cornell in the crisp autumn days came flocking to my mind: the glorious colors, the scuffle of the dead leaves under the horse's hooves, the exhilaration of the jumps, the thrill of riding at full gallop along the narrow curving, path amidst the trees when the turns were possible only by throwing your own weight into the effort at the right time; and the comic instances, especially the falls, brought forth their chuckles. So you can see I did enjoy the movie of the day.

June 22, 1945

    . . . After a while we came up to the room, where I started the Vic going and played a couple of recordings of classical music programs. They weren't very good, except for certain passages of intermezzo, which of course made me cry for you. (Miss you? Well, a leetle, yust a leetle bit.)

    This evening at our usual bridge game our winning streak continued, and we won four of five rubbers. That's very unusual. Next week our luck will change as we will be on the losing end.

June 24, 1945

    . . . I've started to read Beard's Republic, and so far (about 130 pages) find it rather interesting. My reading was interrupted this afternoon by a meeting of the bridge club which I was urgently

invited to attend. I did, but found that as usual the cards were running rather poorly. Just a few short minutes ago the game broke up.
July 1, 1945

...Then we went below to the galley to see what we could scare up in the line of food. One of my patients was working down there, and he made up a couple of filet mignon sandwiches for me which were absolutely delicious. Indeed they were so good that I had seconds. Ralph had one, too, and Butch made himself a plate of ham and eggs. So you see we are not starving to death. After the snack we went up, showered, and turned in.

We had holiday routine today, but I saw a few patients this morning, and spent some time schmoozing. After chow this afternoon I went on deck for a little while, then turned in my sack to read a book of short stories by Sholem Asch. How I enjoy reading some of his stuff. Certain portions of his writings actually bring tears stinging to my eyes. Why I should be so moved by his tales of life in these Polish villages I do not know. Actually, I have no background to make me appreciate it, but the moistening of my eyes is a fact which cannot be denied.

While reading, I felt the tiredness resulting from last night's late hours, so I reached up, turned off the light, and took me a delicious nap, which lasted until just a little while before supper time.

This evening we played some more bridge, with some rather favorable results for our side.

July 3, 1945

.... After dinner I went on deck, where my ears were gladdened by the sound of merry music. I followed it to its source. There, on number-two hatch was a 16-piece orchestra busily engaged in beating it out. And man, they were really good. And what an audience they had crowded on the forward boat deck, and on the higher decks looking down. There wasn't a bit of room left. Men were perched on the boats, the davits, and winches, the rails, everywhere there was a place to stand. The boys gave a good performance, and the men were a good audience. They really gave with that old applause.

A little while after the concert was over the movie went on, DuBarry Was a Lady. It was old but good. Everybody enjoyed it.

Later, the evening ended in a bridge game. Bob and I played Ralph and Slemmons. It was a lot of fun. All of us made terrible errors, but the game's the thing. We schmoozed for a while after the game, and finally at about one o'clock turned in.

. . . I finished that book of Sholem Asch's I told you about, Children of Abraham. *I think you would probably like it. In the meantime I am still reading in my American Democracy, and my Blair and Ivy. In the former I am up to the period of Roosevelt, and in the latter I am reading the section on tumors.*

July 21, 1945

. . . If you promise not to laugh, or to snitch to anyone else, I'll tell you about the latest project I embarked upon. I had my first lesson tonight. I am taking music lessons from one of the corpsmen. I might even get to play an instrument in time. I wonder how long the urge will last. Tonight I learned of scales and intervals. And I've even got a homework assignment.

We played a little bridge tonight and last night. Last night we broke about even, but tonight we got swamped. Ooh, did they lick us.

July 24, 1945

. . . The most interesting thing for the time being is that secret I told you about, my preoccupation with music. I am studying the harmony book carefully, and am getting introductory lessons on the trombone. Are you surprised? I know I am. The idea is that we have a kid on board who is by way of being a trombonist. He can teach me the elements of it. Right now we have no instrument on board, but he has loaned me a mouthpiece and I am practicing tone control and lip vibration. In my spare time I am reading the harmony book, and doing the exercises. I find it slow but interesting. For some reason, I have always been convinced that I have no musical talent. Various persons (especially the members of the upstairs Korchin family) have not hesitated to assure me that I have no sense of rhythm, tone, or music at all. Probably they are right. Possibly they are wrong. If I learn enough to be able to read some music, perhaps even play a simple tune on an instrument, it will be a tremendous source

of gratification to me. I'm sure you understand that. There is no particular reason for picking the trombone other than the easy availability of a teacher with various books about it. On the other hand, there is no reason why I shouldn't pick on the trombone. It is a nice instrument, and should be nice-sounding. The book on harmony is by Preston Ware Orem, Student's Harmony Book. *It is very simply written. In the last day or so I've learned all the scales of the treble clef. Last night I learned a little about the base [sic] clef. Tonight I study something about intervals and chords. It's a lot of fun. In the meantime I have this trombone mouthpiece which I carry around with me and practice blowing into. I have achieved a relatively great amount of success in the sounding of tones, relatively great because yesterday all I could make was a suspicious sounding buzz, like a horse letting wind.*

August 24, 1945
   . . . As usual we played some bridge this evening. As you can easily imagine, it is coming out of my ears by this time, but what else is there to do?

September 19, 1945
   . . . This evening we had a double feature, Arsenic and Old Lace *and* Footlight Glamour. *I enjoyed seeing the former over once more, and the latter was an amusing, typical Blondie and Dagwood affair.*
   During the day I read a little in the Blue Book *magazine,* The Flesh, the World, and Father Smith, *and* Foreign Policy Begins At Home. *Of them all I think I enjoyed* Bluebook *the best of all.*

After a year on board ship, it was becoming harder to be truly entertained by the old stand-bys.

October 5, 1945
   . . . Finding sleep to be impossible I spent some time finishing Life With Father, *which I rather enjoyed, and reading a couple of clever profiles from the book,* Take Them Up Tenderly.

The evening's bridge of late has been rather on the successful side; but like everything else we do on board grows monotonous through constant repetition. At this stage of the game all of us are going stale and so rapidly, that it is apparent even to ourselves.

October 9, 1945

. . . I finished reading Fer-de-lance *by Rex Stout. Like all of his novels I enjoyed this one very much. Nero Wolfe is a fine detective with a healthy appreciation of money. After that I started to read* The Education of Henry Adams. *It is fine reading, but rather slow. I find that since we've taken these troops on board I've read less than usual. For one thing Dr. Curly is in my office very frequently and times when I would ordinarily be reading I spend talking to him. When he isn't around Dr. Golden is usually around and we rehash some subject or other that we talked out a long time ago.*

October 10, 1945

. . . I am still reading The Education of Henry Adams *and find it to be very entertaining and instructive. At present he is acting as private secretary to his father Charles Francis Adams, who is our Ambassador to England during the trying times of our civil war.*

October 20, 1945

. . . After dinner I got in a little bull session in the medical office until the movies were announced. The show tonight was a musical stinkaroo the name of which, I am glad to see, I have forgotten already. I came down to the office to study some more Spanish after the show, but found Dr. Curly seated in the chair reading. We had some coffee in the wardroom, then returned to the office, where we started in talking a bit of shop. At this time Ralph came in, so we broadened the base of the conversation to include his profession, and kept on talking.

At about 10:30 they left. I didn't feel sleepy so I continued to study lesson 10 of Hugo. I finished studying the conditional and imperfect tense. Then I took a half an hour to review the regular endings of all the tenses I had learned so far. I must admit that I am very confused at the multiplicity of endings right now, but at the same time I realize that individually they are very simple, and I merely need the practice to recognize and use them with facility.

When I finished the verb review I went back to Henry VIII. *I had left him when he was in the process of accusing Ann Boleyn of adultery and before going to bed I read of how he had her beheaded. What a great life these personages lead. And after all, things are scarcely any different today. In their fight for money and power too many lose sight of the idea of true happiness, and when they achieve their object they are bereft of any value. My sweet wife, I ask nothing more of God and the world than that I continue in as great a degree of happiness with you and Jeff as we have enjoyed thus far. They can take the rest of it and do what they will with it. Only let me have you and your love next to me for as long as I live, and I will be content.*

October 27, 1945

...Tonight's movie was Tonight and Every Night, *a serious attempt on the part of Hollywood to prove that Rita Hayworth has a body. I think that everybody, including myself, was convinced. After the show I came down to the wardroom for a cup of coffee. I got to talking with Golden, Chaplain Noland, and myself. We got started on an interesting bull session (the Protestant, the Catholic, and the Jew). I started it unwittingly. In the movie the hero's pop, a preacher, proposes to Rita for his son, by bringing to her a bible his son has left behind with a picture of Rita pasted on a page of the* New Testament. *From the picture an arrow is drawn to a particular passage. I lay no claim to clairvoyance, but in this case I predicted the passage, and I was part right; part right because they only quoted it in part. The quotation was (in the Hollywood style), "It is better to marry." And Rita accepts that as a proposal of marriage, and everything is fine. What tickled me, however, was the neat way that Hollywood misquoted by omission. Actually, the passage is from one of Paul's epistles, and in this particular part he had been running down women of being no particular use anyway, and pretty much sinful creatures, and a drag on man's spiritual progress in general. But he was smart enough*

to realize that for the ordinary man they were necessary, so he said, "It is better to marry than to burn." Well, I asked Bob Noland if he had noticed the passage, and he said he had. Then Golden spoke up, and we were off on a bull session that carried us through ancient history, idolatry, the early beginnings of Christianity, whether or not Christ had a brother (that is still unsettled, it seems), various items of the Old Testament. From there we branched off into Hebrew and Yiddish as languages, and then into a discussion of languages in general. I argued with Golden on the value of studying Latin as opposed to the study of one of the modern languages. Then we touched on the relative moralities of small town against large city, and from there into a discussion of homosexuals, and about that time everyone got hungry so we all made ourselves melted cheese sandwiches, ate them and everybody went their separate ways. Garrulous people, aren't we?

I filled in the hour before dinner tonight by studying another Spanish lesson. It still goes fairly rapidly, and with use the proper interpretation of the various tenses seems to be a little easier. Tonight I learned to count to the millions, learned also the days of the week, and the months of the year. I also in the same hour read another act in King Henry VIII. *In this play I am reading, for the first time, about Falstaff, the boon companion of the Prince of Wales, and a jolly rogue indeed. Tonight's discussion served to emphasize a desire I've had for quite a while, to reread the Bible, so tonight I borrowed a copy from Bob Bastian and left it in the room. I intend to read a few pages every night, and thus get through some of it at least.*

October 31, 1945
. . . Life on board is much the same as usual. I am reading the bible nightly, and am at present with Moses in his efforts to persuade Pharoah to "let my people go." In between times at the office I have managed to finish King Henry IV *and start the* Vth. *My Spanish has suffered from a little neglect the last few days, but still makes progress.*

Shirley, too, filled her time with friends and family, despite being very busy caring for their newborn son. Her parents had insisted that she and the baby move in with them, so she was living with ready-made babysitters, allowing for more free time and flexibility in her routine. She was also living in the same area in which she had grown up, which was also near her long-time friends, so spontaneous get-togethers, even with Jeff present, were possible.

She kept late hours, with visits often starting at 9:00 PM and going late into the night. Even then, Shirley would still usually finish the evening with a letter to Les, then drop into bed for a few hours of sleep before Jeffrey awoke, around 6:00 AM.

One particular friend in the apartment building was frequently mentioned, but there were also visits to nearby homes for conversation and coffee. Also, Shirley would often be accompanied by friends on her walks with the baby, and there were frequent visits with relatives. She would sometimes go up to the Bronx to see Lester's family, sometimes sleeping over and spending time with Rozzie, her sister-in-law. Being two years older, married and a mother, Shirley felt protective of Rozzie, often taking her shopping or offering advice. There were also visits to a nearby nursing home to see her maternal grandmother, Tibey, who was quite frail and in deteriorating health.

One advantage of living in Brooklyn was its proximity to Manhattan, which allowed Shirley to often attend the theatre, Radio City and the Ice Capades. These were special nights out, but she often went into the city just to have dinner with her parents or friends.

When she was alone, Shirley felt the time drag, but she spent time reading and listening to music, just as Lester was doing aboard his ship. Then there was the baby, who provided a great deal of entertainment but who also took up much of the day of this twenty-one year old single parent.

Noticeably absent from Shirley's social life was her younger sister, Elaine. There was a five-year age difference between them, and they seemed to spend very little recreational time together, despite living in the same house. The developmental differences between the married war bride and the sixteen-year-old high school girl caused them to move in separate social circles.

This first letter was written from Camp Brookwood, after Lester was taken ill.

August 1943
. . . Last night, I and the other members of the Hen Club went to Barryville to the movies. We saw The Magnificent Dope—*if*

ever a picture was aptly titled, that was the picture. But anyway it was a relief to get away from Camp. Ruthie, Doris, Shirley Manheimer, Shirley (from the office), Sylvia (the nurse), and I made up the gay little party. It was the only time this summer that I traveled in comfort and peace in a Dunlop's cab.

October 15, 1944

. . . I may go away with mother and Dad to the Grossinger Hotel next weekend.

Tonight I'm invited to Marilyn's house for dinner. I took Rozzie shopping yesterday. We covered practically all N.Y; and I was dead last night. She didn't get anything, as the prices are so high. I took her to lunch at Schrafft's. She told me that you wrote that you won't be in until the first of November. Will it really be so long? I hope not.

October 16, 1944
Darling,

I've never seen such rain in my entire life. Last night I went to Marilyn's house for dinner in a terrible storm. I arrived looking like the step-sister of the original drowned rat. Mrs. Chester made a delicious dinner, and I had a grand time. Gaby made his famous ice cream cocktails, and I got slightly woozy. Mike showed me her trousseau—I was flabbergasted. Her mother spent $400 for her linens alone (which was the cost of furnishing our entire apartment)!

I got so jealous watching Mike and Gabe make love. Why weren't you with me! (I'm writing this leaning on Skipper's back— that why it's so shaky.)

. . . Right from Grandma, we went to New York, to meet daddy at 6:00 in Longchamp's. It was really good. I ate the meal for you, honey—now don't you feel full.

We went to Radio City to see Lassie Come Home, a dog picture. I cried my eyes out. But I resolved to teach that son of mine that beauty alone isn't enough. He must be as intelligent as the Collie was.

The stage show was really a treat, staged as only Radio City can do it. The orchestra played a most beautiful selection—from La Bohême *by Puccini. I wish we could get it. I'm enclosing the program, to make you feel as if you were there.*

Sitting next to me was a badly crippled man with a huge brace around his neck and a terrible limp. As he got up to go, I saw he was a naval Officer with a purple heart pinned to his chest. Darling, how I cried for him. It's a good thing the picture was sad too, so I wasn't so obvious.

October 21, 1944

. . . Tomorrow, Florence is coming over the house. Flora Leopold may also. I saw her at school yesterday, and she's still the same Flora. Her father has 4 dentists working for him now. What do you say honey, let's be unethical. It's more fun anyway.

Saturday, Flo and I are going to Rhoda's brother's bar mitzvah. Remember the fat little Henry? I can just see him saying his prayers.

October 22, 1944

. . . It's raining today, for a change; and I'm staying home. I finally got hold of A Tree Grows in Brooklyn. *Williamsburg is really like that. You should read it. Are the books in the base library any good?*

November 18, 1944

. . . I got there a few minutes before Thelma (aren't I good). Broadway will ever and ever continue to amaze me. But never have I seen it so mad, and feverish and full of servicemen and war money just flung any way.

There is a long wait in all restaurants, and lines that wind around the block for any old movie. But it's still Broadway—the same temporary fascination it effects on all of us. By some lucky chance, we were able to get seats in Radio City after only a half-hour wait. That is because we were fortunate enough to come just at show break. We saw Mrs. Parkington. *Not bad, but the book was much better. The trouble with Greer Garson is, she is still Greer Garson, no matter in what picture she plays. But the stage show was absolutely the loveliest I have ever seen there. The whole show was in tribute to the works of George Gershwin, and the final triumph was a ballet interpretation of "Rhapsody in Blue." It ran the gamut of moods and glorious colors and sensuous dancing that is so wonderful to behold.*

After the show, we stopped in for coffee and a bit of schmoozing. Thelma's friend is also the wife of a dentist, a former college roommate of Chester's. He has been overseas with the army about 10 months now. They also have a baby—whom the husband hasn't even seen. Thelma showed me a picture of her daughter; quite a cute little girl.

November 21, 1944

. . . Gloria Siegel came up tonight, and after I got through washing the baby's clothes, and gossiped and knitted, I agreed that a few more months of our Puritan existence and we'll be ready for any institution.

November 23, 1944
Darling,

First, I'd like to apologize for not writing yesterday.

I went out unexpectedly with Dad last night and didn't get home until 2 A.M., much too pooped to do much of anything except sleep.

Yesterday was another of those typically New York winterish nasty days, and I stayed up with Jeff all day. I washed his clothes and played with him for the remainder of the day.

At night, Dad came home with 2 tickets to the Ice Follies of 1945 at Madison Square Garden. Mother said she didn't care to go, but that I should go instead. Nothing loath, I said I'd love to.

We went to Longchamp's for dinner. I was all dressed up, and Dad said the other men looked very envious "thinking you're my mistress, and I'm just an old geezer." Imagine dad being so wicked as to say a thing like that!

I had dinner in real style: a cocktail, steak, parfait, and coffee. How relaxed and glamorous I felt for a change.

Then we went to Madison Square Garden. Our seats were wonderful, 2 rows back and right in the center. And Les, the show had me fascinated from start to finish. I, frankly, never expected to care too much for an ice show, but it was wonderful. It's supposed to be much better and more lavish than the one at Radio City. The girls and costumes could put any of Billy Rose's productions to shame, and the set-

*tings and skating were grand. I'm so sorry that we never went to one,
but perhaps you'll take me to the Ice Show of 1946. We met a lot of
people we know there, as Dad bought the tickets through his lodge.
Afterwards we went for a drink, so, tired and happy, I came home. The
first thing I rushed to see of course was my little snooks. It's amazing
how much I miss that little one when I'm away from him.*

November 26, 1944

*. . . Roz left about 5—she had an appointment. Then Dad
came home. We had made reservations for* Café Society Up-
town—*the folks were taking me out. Nora, our colored girl, very
kindly offered to stay in with Jeff, as Elaine had a date. The folks
were feeling sorry for me after all these weeks of moping alone on
Sat. nights. So they finally decided their million- dollar grandson
was getting old enough to be trusted, but only with Nora.*

*Dad drove me to N.Y., where we picked up Mother. The night-
club was a small place but very lovely. It was surprisingly inexpensive—no cover or minimum, and a complete dinner for $3.50. I
had a turkey dinner, and very delicious. It is a club rather on the
style of theVersailles Restaurant. There was no floor show in the sense
of girls but we did see Hazel Scott, Jimmy Savo, and Mildred Baily
entertain. I laughed myself sick at Jimmy Savo. Hazel Scott is the
colored singer you and I and Roz once saw at the Roxy Theater. There
she sang a Jewish song, but here it was evidently too swank, for she
just played various swing selections on the piano. She lost a great
deal of weight and looks stunning. She's getting married to a colored
congressman from N.Y. Mildred Baily is quite famous also—she's a
very tall woman, with quite a good voice. All in all it was very enjoyable, but how I missed you. Even more than usual, for everyone
was in couples, and mostly all men were in uniform. I would have
given 2 molars if I could have danced just one dance. But it was a
grand evening, and a swell change for me. We came home rather late
and I was too tired to write—so forgive me, won't you?*

January 12, 1945

*. . . Berry asked me to go to the movies with her tonight, and
as none of my other friends could go; I reluctantly agreed to go with*

her. But—and I knew it would happen—when I called for her at
8:30, she was just finishing bathing the baby and hadn't dressed
or eaten yet. So I impatiently waited for her, while she wasted more
time by talking a mile a minute and arguing with her poor mother
(her usual occupation). Berry is such a nitwit, you can't help liking
her. We finally left at 9:30, went to see Marriage Is a Private Affair. It was pretty amusing and appealing to me, for it had a baby
in it. And I am more than ever convinced that Lana Turner is gorgeous. Oh, well.

We stopped in to Schaeffer's for a soda and talk (it was jammed
as usual there), and then came home, finally.

January 13, 1945
. . .Well, love child, I have rambled on, haven't I? Let's see what
happened today? Gert Rudnik (neé Ginsburg) came over in the afternoon. We were going to walk to Loehman's but it started to snow
for a change. Later on, Gloria Siegel dropped up. Then my Uncle
Arthur dropped in for a minute to see the baby. (He's crazy about
him, thinks no other baby can compare with him. A fact which
makes my cousin Lillian rather angry. But her baby is nice, too.)
We put records on and danced, and Arthur did the Samba with Jeff.
He loved it and giggled with delight. In the evening, Elaine decided
to stay home; so Gert and Gloria and I went to the movies. We went
to the Kings and saw Charles Boyer and Irene Dunne in Together
Again. It wasn't much as a picture, but that guy still appeals to
me. What the hell has he got, I still don't know. We broke up a pair
of lovers in front of us by giggling out of sheer cussedness and frustration. And that is all for tonight.

January 17, 1945
. . . Gloria Siegel and Berry came up tonight and kept me company. The usual dirty jokes were told by Berry, and we had a good
time laughing, as she is funny.

January 20, 1945
. . . Elaine and her friend have 2 boys over the house and so I
could have gone out if I wanted to, but no one is free tonight.

So I went down to Gloria's house and am writing to you while she is studying for her finals for N.Y.U.

January 21, 1945

. . . The girls came up and sat with me while I washed Jeff's clothes (it seems as if I'm forever doing them, doesn't it? Berry's maid does hers, but ours won't. It's all right, though. Jeff promised that, next week, when he's 6 months old, he'll wash them for me). We gossiped and told the usual jokes. Then Mother and Dad came home, and we had a discussion with them. They claim that we take our woes too hard; that there are girls who haven't seen their husbands for much longer than we; and I agree. But it doesn't alleviate our rights to complain.

They stayed till 12 and so that ended today and another weekend, thank God.

January 23, 1945

. . . Tonight after dinner the family got together, for a change, in the living room, even including Elaine, for some gossip and jokes and friendly arguments.

After a while, Gloria Siegel came up and chimed in just like one of the family. She really is a nice kid, very good-natured, and a lot of company for me.

. . . I've about finished reading A Bell for Adano, *by John Hersey. It's very good.*

January 25, 1945

. . . Toward evening the weather dropped to zero, and a terrible wind sprung up. I had an appointment to meet Thelma Stoopack in N.Y., and as it was too late to break it, I bravely fared forth. You can well believe me that, before the wind had shoved me two blocks, I was wishing that I wasn't such a fool as to leave the house on a night like that.

I was to meet Thelma and friends of hers in the lobby of the Hotel Taft at 7:15, and believe it or not, I was early. While waiting for them, I had the craziest assortment of attempted pick-ups. They finally arrived 15 minutes later. There were 6 of us altogether; we

ate in the Taft, accompanied "to the strains" of Vincent Lopez's or-
chestra. Believe me, it was torture to hear the music and watch oth-
ers dance, and not be able to. It's hell to be a woman!

We schmoozed over our dinner until 9:30, and then, with a
rush, headed next door to the Roxy, as we were determined not to
walk outside any further than we could help.

The stage show was the entire floor show of the Zanzibar Night
Club, and it was excellent, an all-colored cast.

Louis Armstrong's orchestra and many swell acts and Bill Robin-
son, at his best. The picture, too, was delightful—Sunday Dinner
for a Soldier. *It's a very human and sweet and totally different story.*
Also—John Hodiak was in it! Oh, I have finally decided he is my
new screen heartthrob. Ugly, but as sweet as can be.

. . . I stayed up with the baby today, too, and tonight Glo Siegel
came up to keep me company. We're really a good pair—we cry on
each other's shoulders and swear that, in one more year, we will
start knocking our heads against the wall.

I'm going out tomorrow night, too. This time with the folks
and the Sobels, so I had better turn in now.

January 27, 1945
. . . I had an appointment to meet Mother and Dad and the
Sobels (Al Sobel's parents) at the 34th St. Longchamp's at 7:00 o'-
clock. Luckily for me, Jeff finished his supper in time, and I left the
house at 6:15, leaving Elaine to mind him.

Well, as luck would have it, there was a 35 min. hold up on
the B.M.T., and there I was, leaving the house in time for practically
the first time in my life. And so I had to wait in the freezing outdoor
station until 7:00, when the train was finally fixed. I arrived half
an hour late, but they luckily had already ordered my dinner and
we were able to get to the theater. The Sobels had also brought
along their 2 daughters, altogether a lovely family. You'd like them.

Dad had miraculously gotten us tickets for Anna Lucasta, *one*
of the best plays of the season. It has an all-Negro cast and is the
story of a colored prostitute. Very well done and very enjoyable. The
girl who plays Anna Lucasta is really something for the boys. It was
a wonderful evening but marred only by the fact that, whenever I

see a play, I keep thinking how you would enjoy it, and how much more I would enjoy it with you beside me.

Another successful play on Broadway this year is Trio, *the story of two lesbians. Broadway is really growing up and becoming broadminded!*

February 1, 1945

. . . This evening Gloria and Berry came up, and we schmoozed over some gin rummy.

February 6, 1945

. . . Tonight I went down to Glo Siegel's apartment for a change, instead of her usually coming up here. We played some gin, and gossiped, and looked at old pictures, and talked of you and her Murray and all our future plans.

'Twas a nice evening, and now I think I shall toddle off to bed for a little shut-eye.

Goodnight for tonight, sweets—remember I love you.

February 10, 1945

. . . Berry and Gloria Siegel were up tonight to keep me company. As per usual when Berry is around, the talk turned to sex. It is the only subject she can speak upon with authority. Hereupon, I quote a famous sentence she came out with tonight:"Eddy and I have done it every way including hanging from the chandelier!" Also to further illustrate the point and one of the ways,"Have you ever heard the story of the private who got $25 every time he bent down to tie his shoelace?"

February 12, 1945

Darling,

Today Gloria Siegel and I took turns pushing Jeffrey the cherub to Nostrand Avenue. What a walk! Mayor La Guardia had the bright idea to have all the streets cleaned of the recent snow storms by opening all the fire hydrants and flooding the streets. We practically swam through! I had to go to a trimming store on Nostrand to get some buttons for a dress. And then while the "Angel?" slept his allotted twenty winks, Gloria and I repaired to Schaeffer's for a soda. For after all, we logically figured, don't we need strength for the walk home? And so we prepared to fill out our figures with a total lack of conscience.

February 21, 1945
Darling,

I couldn't write to you last night as Mother and Dad took me to Madison Square Garden for the Israel Orphan Asylum Benefit. It is like the "Night of Stars," consisting of famous stars and people and lasting till all hours.

When we left at 2 A.M. it was still going strong, and most of the people were still there. It's a wonderful affair, darling. I know you'd like it. Perhaps next year, we'll be able to go together.

We had dinner at Longchamps, with another couple, and then we joined a big party at the Garden. They started with a fashion show, which still has me drooling. And then they had the following stars, of which I'll name just a few: Milton Berle, Henny Youngman, Jimmy Savo, Mary Small, and so many others I can't even remember them. Most of the leading orchestras played, and they showed bits from most of the Broadway shows and vaudeville acts.

All in all, I enjoyed myself so much, and laughed heartily.

. . . Today has been very raw, so I only took Jeff out for an hour. After that I brought him into Gloria Siegel's house, for a "Special Visit." She's crazy about him, and he cheers her up as nothing else seems to do.

Tonight I read, the whole night. Usually, the only chance I get is after I write to you—in bed, each night, until all hours in the morning. But this evening, I was in a very rebellious mood. I shoved aside all the things I had to do and declared a holiday. I read and read, finished Presidential Agent, *and now I'm starting* Der Führer, *by Konrad Heiden. You'd enjoy both of them.*

April 14, 1945

. . . I tried to write last night, but I had to skip yesterday's letter. Roz took me out for my birthday, and when I got home at 2:30, I was so exhausted my eyes were shut, even before I stumbled into bed. Please forgive me.

We had a swell time. I met her in front of Radio City. She had already bought the tickets, and so only after a 20-min. wait in the lobby, we were able to get seats. We sat way down in front, as the stage show was about to go on, and as we knew that Dorothy Shoen was going to sing a solo we wanted to be able to see her. We saw the Easter Show. It was gorgeous. Dorothy has quite a good voice. She sang the opening hymn for the show. The picture, With- out Love, *was amusing.*

Roz and I went in for a bite at Child's after the show. She gave me a very nice pair of earrings—which was lovely of her. We sat and talked until almost 2, and then I traveled home but not by my lonesome. I was surrounded by 2 persistent sailors, quite drunk, who pestered me to show them around the town, as they were very lonesome. When they were getting too much for me to handle, a Lt. Com'dr stepped over, and spoke to them. In a very chastened mood, they left the train at the next station. So many naval men, but none of them are the one I want most to see.

April 20, 1945

. . .Yesterday afternoon, Flo Cooper told me she could get hold of 2 tickets for On the Town *for that evening, and would I care to go. I was delighted, as it came to break up the monotony of the evenings, and as I haven't seen many shows at all this sea-son.* On the Town *is one of the hit musicals on Broadway. It was very clever, and very entertaining. We sat in the orchestra, 8th row (that is really the only way to enjoy a show), and had a swell time. The play was written by Betty Comden and the music composed by Leonard Bernstein (he's now conducting the Phil-harmonic). Esther Korchin knows Betty Comden from Tamiment, and she says that you went to school with her brother. After the show, Flo and I strutted into Lindy's and had a marvelous time staring, and being stared at. Ah, my cosmopolitan soul, how it relishes a fling like that. But the normalcy of everyday living is more to my taste these days. I develop my bitchy streak when I see other couples together and I come home alone. Honey, I'm afraid I really don't deserve that halo of mine. Its luster is get-ting dimmer.*

April 21, 1945

...Then Gert came over at 8, and we settled down for a quiet evening of gin rummy and talk. For some reason, we were very giddy, and laughed hysterically at each other's inane cracks. I like her a lot; it's nice of her to stay in with me occasionally on Saturday nights.

May 4, 1945

...Roz left at 8:30 and I walked her to the station. Then I had an appointment to meet Gert Ginsberg at the Patio, to see A Song to Remember. I enjoyed it so much. The glorious strains of Chopin's music were played throughout the picture. It's a crime that he died at such an early age. They portrayed Georges Sand as quite a vicious bitch; but in reality, she wasn't quite as they pictured her. I still have his "Polonaise" running in my head, as I write this.

May 7, 1945

...Yesterday was Elaine's 17th birthday, so the folks took her out to dinner, along with the Ginsbergs. Jeff and I were supposed to go, but none of the better places had highchairs, so the two orphans (oh, 3, I forgot Skipper), stayed at home. I stayed out with him until 4 o'clock, when it started to rain. I took him up to Gloria's house for his "social hour," and he promptly charmed her folks and their company by his antics.

I had an appointment to meet Esther Korchin at the Savoy to see A Tree Grows in Brooklyn. It can't compare with the book, but it was very enjoyable, nevertheless; and I know you'll enjoy it, if only for its locale.

May 10, 1945

...I spent the evening playing gin rummy with Dad. This time I underestimated myself, and beat him to the tune of $23, which I magnanimously refused to accept. In the middle of our playing, the lights went out for a while, but the two dauntless card sharks continued playing by candle light.

Vivian called up today and invited Mother, Dad and me to her *housewarming Saturday night. She's having 70 people—ah, a little social life, a chance to get all swanked up. Norah promised to stay in with Jeff as Elaine is already going to the party.*

June 24, 1945

. . . After walking them to the subway, I met Bernice Lapper, and she persuaded me to go to Schaeffer's for a drink. Always willing, I consented. We passed the Park Manor [where Shirley and Les got married] on the way, where a wedding was taking place. What wonderful memories that place evokes. We stayed out talking until almost midnight (it's wonderful how much we two can talk about—we get along, or click, so well. I'm really very fond of her). Her husband was minding the baby. So here it is past midnight, and your very lonesome wife must say a reluctant goodnight. Thank goodness one day nearer to your homecoming. It had better be soon, for I miss you and love you so much.

July 1, 1945

. . . On the way home, Jeff only insisted on leaning out from his car seat, and helping daddy steer the wheel. He's fascinated by that and by the horn. I got through with him early, for we had to leave by seven o'clock. Nora came to mind him. Dr. and Mrs. Vogel came, and Francis, and my uncle Sammy, and Gloria Siegel and Elaine and I. We went to the Persian Room of the Savoy-Plaza. It was wonderfully cool there, and the dinner was delicious. Hildegard was the sole entertainment, and she held us spellbound for an hour and half. I'd like you to see her someday —she was simply marvelous. I danced with Dr. Vogel, and Daddy and Sammy—oh, rapture. (There is no dance that is truly en-joyable unless I dance with you.) As I said before, we got home late, and then Fran and I sat with our noses glued to the fan, sipped Pepsi-Colas, and talked.

July 2, 1945

Gloria left for camp this morning and already I feel quite lost without her. As Gert goes away to her bungalow each weekend, I will be sadly lacking some friends this summer.

August 29, 1945

. . . *Esther Korchin came over for dinner. She was suffering from a severe attack of hay fever and hardly stopped sneezing all night long. I served a consommé, chicken salad, potato salad, and peas, and iced stewed pears and iced tea. Nice! We ate dinner in our slips, and had the fan on, in full blast, blowing directly on us. Draft or not, it was heavenly. She now expects Leo home sometime before Christmas. That will be two and a half years that he will be overseas.*

September 4, 1945

. . . *I went down to visit Berry tonight. Darling, that girl is absolutely nuts. She's under such high tension that she drives everyone around her batty. When I left her at 11:00 she still had to sterilize the baby's bottles and finish eating dinner. However, her incessant chatter is good for my nerves. I just have to sit back and relax.*

October 14, 1945
Darling,

Please excuse me for not writing last night, honey, but I came home so late and so tired that I absolutely couldn't. It seemed that I no sooner undressed and put my head on the pillow but what it was morning already with Jeff yelling, "Ma, ma." You really can't have a night-life habit and be a good mama, full of energy and pep, at the same time.

Mother and dad took me to see La Traviata *last night at the City Center. We all enjoyed it immensely. This Opera Company may not be as famous or as awe inspiring as the Metropolitan, but believe me, it was darned good. I loved every minute of it. It was impossible to get a sitter for the baby, and, as Elaine had a date, Gloria's brother consented to watch him. It was very nice of him, for I'd been looking forward to seeing it for many weeks.*

After the Opera, we went to Rumpelmaier's, my favorite place. I had my favorite waffles and chicken—it was delicious. You must try it with me some day, I know just what you'll like, and that's it.

November 3, 1945

...*I had a nice evening with the folks and Mildred. We saw* Weekend *at the* Waldorf *at Radio City. It was pretty entertaining and brought back such memories of the night we danced on the Starlight Roof Terrace with my big belly as a silent partner. I love you so, sweetheart. We've shared such marvelous times together, intimate or with a crowd—and we have so much more to look forward now.*

We all went to Rumpelmaier's after the show, and now my evening is over. My glass slipper is taken away, and Cinderella returns to the kitchen.

It's awfully late now, my dear, and I must get some rest.

Goodnight, for now, keep well, return to me soon. My arms are open and waiting for you.

15

THE GREAT I AM

ONE MAN DESERVES A chapter all to himself, for all the wrong reasons. The aptly named Dr. Dickey dominated Lester's days, nights, and dreams for a very long time. According to Lester, Dickey was the very personification of evil: a malicious, prejudiced, manipulative, and angry man, the worst type to have as a commanding officer. Yet there he was, in all his glory, greeting Les when he first arrived at the ship in Washington, and he soon began tormenting him and the other men, constantly and for months. The ship had few places to effectively hide, and Dr. Dickey would eventually discover most of them. His name would darken many letters during their months together at sea as he came to represent all that was wrong with a rigid bureaucracy. Even many years later, Lester could not joke about the infamous Dr. Dickey, and he would explain the man was probably the single most important reason that he chose to work in private practice. Never, ever again did Lester want to be in a subordinate position or to answer to anyone who could wield such arbitrary power.

Dr. Dickey was a physician, not a dentist, and he was in charge of the medical department. However, to Lester's continual torment, the dental department was subsumed under it. Dickey could initially charm a new man with his false smile, as he did Lester in the beginning, but his true character would soon emerge, enraging all who were under his command. His superiors were often unaware of these problems, as part of Dr. Dickey's *modus operandi* was to be overly deferential and polite, creating as positive an image of himself as possible. And, for a very long time, he was successful in this—

until he finally failed.

Most people have had a Dr. Dickey in their lives, but to encounter one in the armed forces, with its demand for unquestioning obedience to superiors, makes for a particular hell. Les, in later years, spoke of his ruminations about an eventual confrontation, either verbally or in an actual fight, aware of but no longer caring about the very real and dangerous consequences. Luckily for his future, he never acted upon these thoughts, but he said that he had come exquisitely close.

The most harmful effect of working for a man like Dr. Dickey is the sense of powerlessness that it engenders. Employees serving under such people can never hope to find any sense of fairness, compensation, evenhandedness, or understanding. One is always subject to sudden, inexplicable whims, which can suddenly crush a person.

Les would usually attempt to handle their confrontations by becoming icy in his tone and emotionally removed rather than losing his temper. The angrier that Dr. Dickey became, the colder Lester turned. However, Dickey was not affected by this, or any other approach, so that Lester constantly harbored fantasies of confrontation and revenge.

Lester's first meeting with Dr. Dickey, without any idea of what was in store for him, was described in this letter.

> *July 21, 1944*
> *...About an hour ago I met the senior and junior medical officers of my ship. The senior is Lt. Cmdr. Dickey; the junior, Lt. (JG) Davey. They seem to be nice. So far, they know as little about the ship as I do.*

However, it did not take too long to figure Dr. Dickey out. He seemed to be even worse than Lester could describe, yet the tried to cope with it, partly by telling himself that he did not care.

> *September 20, 1944*
> *I need to say it because my original idea of Dr. Dickey is correct, not the modification, but the original. He has turned out to be a pure unadulterated bastard. He has given me not the least bit of cooperation since coming on board. In fact, he has obstructed me at every opportunity, as for instance in my request for several items (each of my requests*

*must pass through his hands as department head). He has merely ig-
nored them, and has never presented them to the proper authority. He
has given me directions and then bawled me out for following them.
My dental office was open for business about four days ago, but he refused to let me see patients until today for reasons of his own. I don't
mind. I saw some time ago the kind of fellow he was and made up my
mind to stay out of his way as much as possible and to pay absolutely
no attention to his guff. What I mean is that he is not only as bad as
I say, but more, but I have my own office to which I retire and I can
mostly keep out of his way. When I can, his rantings affect me not at
all, anyway. Besides this, he has to be careful not to overstep the bounds,
so I don't object but do what he says. After all, I figure it is no skin off
my neck if I requisition certain material and he says no. It simply
means that the quality of the service that I can offer the crew is im-
paired. Well, that's too bad. I've done my part. I've ordered the material. The rest is out of my hands, and I don't worry about it a bit.*

*So as I say it doesn't concern me much at all, but poor Ralph
is right under his thumb, and he grinds him harder every day. You
remember the helpless rage I used to get in once in a while when
Levin would pull one of his famous tricks? Well, it's the same way
now for Ralph. Believe me, I feel for him. But enough of that for
this letter. There'll be more of this character later.*

Lester stood up to Dr. Dickey, initially believing that he had made some
headway.

September 26, 1944
*. . . It's a very long story and the details are scarcely interesting.
Suffice it to say that he [Dr. Dickey] bawled me out one morning
for something he thought I had done wrong, namely going ashore
that day, and not coming aboard until late. It so happened that
everything he thought was wrong was right. I was a little tired of
being pushed around so I requested a private conference with him
in his office. It was soon apparent that I had gone ashore on official
business in my capacity as voting officer for the ship, and had
arranged well in advance for my watch to be stood; but he was not
beaten. Give the man credit. He is very clever. He changed the*

subject at once and accused me of non-cooperation in the setting up of the medical department. You know, for a while he had me, for afterward as I was thinking about it, the validness of the things he said were painfully apparent. After all, I set up the dental department by myself, with my corpsman to assist, in record time, and was ready to go (but he refused to give me permission to start operating). He said I was not there offering suggestions and being helpful in the work of getting things going. Well, that was true. When I had seen his reactions to my suggestions about the organization of the dental end of things, I straightway decided that it would be much wiser to say nothing about the medical end of things. And after all, for what he wanted done, he knew I was in my office at all times, ready to do what I was told or asked to do. But this morning Ralph told me that Dr. Dickey told him, "Well, Dr. Halbreich and I had a man to man talk yesterday. I told him I hated his guts and he told me he hated mine. But I think that we'll get along better now." So perhaps I did manage to gain a little of his respect by standing up to him. I would have had to do it sooner or later, for as I say he was really beating Goldman and me, and I wanted to do it while I had definite right on my side. After putting up a show of resistance for your own self-respect, I had very little to lose. The worst he could do was to put me on the beach, and is that bad? And today I have been working, and he has been almost pleasant to me. I believe I will be all right from now on. Particularly now that the patients are starting to roll into my office. He will stop picking on me and start on Ralph again. After that he will let Ralph alone and start picking at me again, and so it will go. But as I say, I don't mind it. I just stay as calm as I can and let it slide off my back. I do my job and forget the rest. As I've told you before, I have too much to live for to let aggravation of that sort bring on heart disease and an early demise. So that's all there is to it. Don't you worry about it, darling. I assure you I won't, and I assure you that everything will be all right.

Lester began referring to Dr. Dickey using various monikers, sometimes just calling him HE, sometimes using the title, The Great One, and sometimes THE GREAT I AM, as in this letter.

October 4, 1944

...About an hour before lunch Ralph asked me to X-ray an extremity (foot) for him. One of the men had dropped a packing case on his foot. We were proceeding with the job when Dr. Dickey, The Great I Am, came bustling in, in his impatient way, and took over from Ralph completely. It is too bad that such a vance [Yiddish for "pest"] should exist. He insulted poor Ralph right and left all the while he handled the case. He kept asking Ralph questions and receiving correct answers. This got him angry, of course, because only he is supposed to know the answers. Finally he looks up at Ralph and says, "Pretty smart, Goldie, but after all, with two years of internship, why not?" Me he gave the silent treatment to, ignoring me completely. That kind of treatment from that man is like manna from heaven. Later on he gave Ralph a terrible bawling out for the way the report was written out. Immediately thereafter he found that the report was correct after all but there were no apologies. Ralph was again trembling with rage this afternoon.

Lester and Ralph decide to request a transfer because of Dr. Dickey.

October 6, 1944

...Today was a little uninteresting. There was some work, and some drills. Dr. Dickey pulled a few of his typical boorish stunts, but none involved me so that was all right. Ralph and I have about made up our minds to request a transfer. About all that remains to be decided is shall we apply at the same time or separately.

Part of Dr. Dickey's animosity is underlying anti-Semitism.

October 16, 1944

... On my way up to bed I met the chaplain. The chaplain is another man who has run afoul of Dickey's foul tongue. We had quite a long talk. I won't go into detail, but I will say that the talk confirmed the very first thing I suspected about Dickey, namely that he dislikes Ralph (and I presume me) because he is a Jew. He said as much to the chaplain. So there you have it. About that there is nothing to do but ignore it. And that is all to that.

October 20, 1944

. . .This last week or so has been very peaceful, the more so, for because HE has spent almost all of his time ashore. Unfortunately when we put out to sea again HE will be on board and the idyllic period will be over.

The anger toward Dr. Dickey is evidently widespread. A conference is held, which results in a decision to discuss this issue with the executive officer, who would then bring it to the captain's attention.

November 6 & 7, 1944

. . .You remember I told you about the soldier that got socked or kicked in the groin during the initiation ceremonies. Well, he was examined by Dr. Dickey. After he had looked at him, Dr. Dickey left, and in the meantime Dr. Davey took a look at the kid. He suggested that the kid be given some morphine to ease the pain. Dr. Dickey blew up in one of his psychotic rages. He stormed into sick bay, threw the kid's wet overalls on the floor and his shoes after him. "Get up and get out of here. You're just a coward. It's guys like you that fuck up the army and the navy." Word of that incident passed around the ship in about a half hour. But aside from that, Dr. Davey was really upset. He had been getting a sample of the Dickey treatment for a while now, and he didn't like it. Among other things, Dr. Dickey had told the warrant pharmacist that he would do surgery in preference to the two younger doctors, and many other things too numerous to mention. He came into the room (Davey) all wrought up and claiming he couldn't take it much longer. What to do and so forth. Well, I was trying to sleep, and Ralph was there. The upshot of it was that we had quite a conference. We finally decided that, if Butch would go with us, we would go to the captain (despite his liking for Dickey) and put the situation into his hands, explaining that an intolerable situation existed in the medical department and why. We had much information to back us up as, for example, all of the corpsmen are ready to apply in a body for a transfer. Butch, however, is a regular navy boy, and he was a little leery of getting into this thing too precipitately. Well, we talked and talked and finally decided that we would ask

the advice of the executive officer. We sent Davey to invite him to
the room, but he talked with Davey separately and with Allan after
that, and promised to bring it to the attention of the captain if we
would let it alone for a day or two. So that is the situation at pres-
ent. In a couple of days there should be an explosion to be heard
round the world.

Ralph does put in for a transfer, despite the politics and knowing the fu-
tility of it. Sometimes, just taking action, any action, can improve one's sense
of control.

> *November 22, 1944*
> *. . . Yesterday was notable because Ralph, fed up to the gills*
> *with the treatment he had been getting, and the treatment he an-*
> *ticipated getting from Dr. Dickey, handed in for forwarding his ap-*
> *plication for transfer. Of course Dr. Dickey heard of it immediately,*
> *and Ralph is very upset about it right now. What will probably*
> *occur is that the request for transfer will be refused, and Ralph will*
> *feel that at least he made his protest and did what he could.*

> *November 23, 1944*
> *. . . Ralph was pretty low in the slough of despondency because*
> *he heard that the skipper had turned over his request for transfer to*
> *Dickey for endorsement and forwarding. He feels a great deal better*
> *today, however, because he realizes that, after all, his letter cannot*
> *alter his situation for the worse. It was as bad as it could get before*
> *now. He doesn't expect much results from it, but it does represent*
> *at least a protest against the sordid type of treatment he has been*
> *undergoing.*

Yet another run-in. It illustrates that the ongoing stress of this dysfunc-
tional relationship led to deteriorating behavior on Lester's part.

> *March 30, 1945*
> *. . . There hasn't been much to keep me busy in the office; but*
> *there have been a few people coming in with various complaints. I*
> *had a little run in with Dickey this morning on the behalf of one of*

them. To my own satisfaction I came out on top; but the man, merely by being, annoys the hell out of me. This officer came in complaining of a sore mouth and throat. Examination revealed the presence of a developing pericoronitis (inflammation of the tissues around the third molar, and frequently extending into the throat). I treated it locally, gave him hot saline rinses at half-hourly intervals. Then I thought I'd like to put him on sulfa or penicillin. To do this I had to go through Dickey. He was talking to Mr. Allan (his sycophant) when I came over, and immediately set the tone by saying, "Well, what d'ya want?" Than in an aside to Allen, "This ought to be good." I told him that his officer has pericoronitis. "What, what's that? Explain it to me," he said. He obviously wanted to upset me. Instead of getting excited or flustered, I took the opportunity to painstakingly explain to him exactly what pericoronitis is, using one syllable words, and a patient tone of voice, much the same as if I were addressing a not too bright child. At the same time I tipped Butch a wink which, while not obvious enough to be called insulting, left a definite implication of same. Butch couldn't help smiling in return. That aspect of the engagement having obviously turned against him, Dickey again tried to be rude and abusive by interrupting me and suggesting treatment. I met rudeness with rudeness. Just as he interrupted me, so I interrupted him. I finished my explanation (which he had asked for), dismissed his suggestions for treatment as being non-essential and behind the time since I had already undertaken local therapy, and gave him to understand definitely, that I wanted no advice from him but merely his approval (which since he's head of the medical department he had to give) for the start of sulfa or penicillin therapy. That about finished him. He stomped off to his office, and that was the end of that. Actually, nothing was gained from the engagement, but a little salve to my self-respect (and the unexpectedly rapid response of the patient to my treatment—which last makes both of us very happy).

April 4, 1945

. . . Life aboard is much the same as usual. A common hatred for Dickey unites the medical department and many of the other officer personnel and also provides much material for conversation. Aside from that, time passes in a fairly aimless, and fairly pleasant manner.

April 11, 1945
Churl Darling,

Had trouble falling asleep last night. My mind was occupied with thought of how best to tell Dickey that I would decide what dental treatment the skipper needed without his interference. I found this morning that the skipper had decided to wait until we reach our destination before attempting anything, which is what I had in mind. In the meantime, I have fixed him up with a comfortable temporary filling.

That fellow with the Leukoplaquia that I told you about was in this morning. I looked at him, and his mouth had evidently been burned by the application of the silver nitrate. I went to see Dickey and told him about it. He said to reapply the silver nitrate. I told him that I wanted to make it plain to him that I considered this to be a case of Leukoplaquia, and that silver nitrate was probably contraindicated. We had a long talk, he trying to show me up and being very supercilious, among other things, trying to make me give my diagnosis of the lesion as cancerous. I knew my ground, however, and did not yield on a point. I insisted that the lesion was precancerous in nature, and that the application of such strong nitrate solutions was contraindicated by the authorities I had read as tending to produce a fulmination or infiltration of a benign lesion into a malignant one. He finally came into the office and took a look at Richard's mouth. He said nothing to me, but instead of applying silver nitrate he applied Gentian violet. There is absolutely no rational basis for the use of the last-named drug at all, but at least it will cause no harm.

Dr. Dickey's resentment of Lester took a personal turn, and Lester chose his own interpretation.

April 18, 1945
. . .We had an inspection today but by arrangement I worked right through. I prefer it that way. It was a head of department inspection, and Dickey tried hard to find something wrong, but my boys had really made the place beautiful (in spite of the fact that I was working all the time) and he could find nothing to say. As he turned to leave he looked again at your pictures, and at the

enlargement of Jeff that I have mounted on my desk, and, as each time previously, I caught that fleeting, hard-to-describe look with its clearly defined element of envy and meanness. Then he suddenly turned to me and rapidly (and loudly) said, "I won't have any personal pictures around during inspection. I have told you that nine times." I didn't say a thing because I knew how consumed with rage and jealousy he must have been. Besides, I didn't have time because he was out of the office before I could say a word. That was all. I'm rather proud of the fact that I didn't get at all upset over this incident. In respect to that man I can honestly say that I consider his hatred in the nature of an accolade. He resents me, the things I stand for, and the things I have: namely, you and Jeff and the happiness you bring me, so much that he can hardly stand it. And I wear that happiness that the two of you mean to me as a protective armament through which his arrows of meanness, scorn, envy, and sadism cannot penetrate.

The beginning of the end.

April 30, 1945

. . .And now to start at the beginning. I did a little work this morning, and received permission to go ashore to visit the fleet dental officer (the senior dental officer of this area). I got off the ship at 11 o'clock and reached his office about 15 minutes before 12. The captain was out but I had a very interesting talk with his aide. We were discussing some forms, and I mentioned that I had help in making them out from a chief warrant officer who was experienced in that sort of thing. He said, "You get along well with the medical department, don't you?" I couldn't help it. I gave him a very emphatic "No." When we got done with what we were discussing, he asked me some questions, and I mentioned some of the grievances I had against Dickey. He was very interested, and asked me to return tomorrow, bringing Dickey if I could. I don't know what will come of it. Probably nothing but trouble, but it is started now, and I can't stop it. I'll keep you posted as events unfold.

As is his habit, Dickey got up from the table and dashed off. I followed and tendered the captain's invitation to him. He evidently thought nothing of it, for he said very friendly-like, "He wants me to give him the two bottles of whiskey I can get on my liquor ration."

May 1, 1945

. . . As I was finishing off there came a knock on the door. It was Gherkin, one of my assistants, with a message that Dr. Dickey wanted to see me. I put my shirt on and went below to his office. Butch Allan was there. Evidently Dickey had stayed awake last night, thinking, for he wasn't quite as affable as usual. As a matter of fact, as he questioned me about this invitation from the fleet dental officer to visit him, there was a definite background of menace in his voice. I remained entirely at ease, however, and disclaimed any knowledge outside of what I had already told him, that the captain's aide had forwarded through me an invitation for Dr. Dickey to visit him. He went into a dissertation to the effect that his loyalties were with the ship (in the last six days he has spent a total of about six hours aboard), and that if the captain really wanted to see him he would have sent him an official message to that effect. I said nothing, and I was dismissed. Dr. Dickey wasn't going with me to visit the captain. Frankly, I felt better for it. At the same time I have to give the old son of a bitch credit for smelling a mouse. I spent the rest of the morning doing some work. Then after lunch we went ashore.

Both the captain and his aide were out when I got there, but I spent a pleasant 15 minutes chatting with Gale Curran (Chet's old S.D.O). Then after a while the aide came in, and in a short time I was shown in for an interview with the captain. He asked for my story, and I gave him some of the details. He was very sympathetic and evidently believed me implicitly. He asked me to do certain things, on his promise as an officer and a gentleman that my name would not become involved in this deal, and very casually he mentioned that the surgeon general of the navy would probably be interested to hear about this because he had said before Congress that such things do not happen in the navy. When I left he shook hands with me, and thanked me. You can understand how good I feel. It may be premature, but it looks as though my "friend" may get his comeuppance. Hallelujah!

Will wonders never cease?

May 4, 1945

Churl Darling,

Rejoice with me, darling, for a very good thing has happened. Good for the ship as well as for me, which makes the cause for rejoicing so much the greater. I won't hold you on tenterhooks any longer, I'll tell you. Dr. Dickey received orders today. He is to be replaced by a Lt. Comdr. Golden and is to be sent to an island base. I do not think it is wise to go into details about the thing now, but I think that you can put two and two together. It will make an interesting story for me to tell you when finally I get back. Isn't that great news? Now, sea duty should start to be as enjoyable as any duty away from you could be. I suppose I should have led up to the news a little more dramatically but I had to tell you about it quick-like, all at once.

. . . Ralph and I were talking of sex in general, and inevitably his problem in particular, when the news came to us of Dr. Dickey's orders. First, in came Ed Davies. He said he had just seen the message, that no one was supposed to know about it but that Dr. Dickey had received his orders. We thanked him and spoke gleefully for a while. Scarcely had he left when Mr. Schaeffer came in. He too told us the news, adding again that we were to tell nobody. We registered the proper surprise and glee, and he left. A moment later Butch Allen came into the room. He tried being mysterious, trying, I think, to find out what we knew. Ralph and I pretended ignorance, and finally he told us he had just left Dr. Dickey, and that the old man had his orders. We registered the proper emotions. Before he left he asked us to keep it quiet. We said we would, and then went down to dinner. In the wardroom everybody was talking about it. Dr. Dickey himself had spread the news. And that is how the great news was passed. It will be interesting now to see how Allan and Davey react to the new man. Davey has been very friendly with Ralph and me in a sort of self-defense, and in some ways I have grown to be fond of him. What will happen now? Tune in tomorrow night at this same time for another thrilling episode of this great story.

May 5, 1945

Well, here we are at sea again. I can't tell you what it is like out on deck, because I haven't been out on deck. I can tell you that Dr. Dickey's relief got on board just before we cast off. It was too late for Dickey to get ashore, so he came along with us. The new S.M.O. is a Brooklyn boy named Golden. He hails from Bay Ridge. He is rather young for a lieutenant commander, having come into the service directly after his internship in 1941. He seems to be a very swell guy. I understand the captain is moving heaven and earth in an attempt to keep the dear Dr. Dickey on board, but I don't believe he will have much success. From the point of view of congeniality this sea duty ought to be much more pleasant now. Incidentally, Dr. Golden is a graduate of Long Island Medical College, and an interne of Kings County.

May 12, 1945

. . . and I returned to the ship to find that Dickey's appeal had been answered with a dispatch to "carry out basic orders", in other words the detachment holds good, and he should be leaving in a few days at most.

Paradise descends to Earth.

May 14, 1945

. . . Today you know is "D" day. That is, it is the day the great Dickey checks out. I can hardly believe it.

The effect, for good or ill, that one man can have on a group.

May 19, 1945

. . . Now that Dickey is definitely gone, and Dr. Golden has taken over you should see the change in atmosphere in the medical department, from the lowest corpsman on up. Everyone is anxious to work, and at the same time relaxed and happy. It is amazing the degree of tension that that tyrant created. Mr. Allan and the Chief are still not sure about how or where they stand, but they are being

slowly educated. Drs. Davey and Goldman, especially, are elated. For the first time since we have been aboard they are acting like doctors, and assuming responsibility. The changes are coming about gradually. Today the duties of the corpsmen were changed around so that I get back my original dental corpsman. He will bear a little stern treatment at first, and then he'll be all right. Also Dr. Golden returned my x-ray viewer, which Dr. Dickey had appropriated.

16

LIBERTY!

WE HAVE ALL SEEN movies that include raucous scenes in which men long cooped up on base or on board ship are finally granted leave or liberty. Think *Mr. Roberts*—drinking, beautiful women, dancing into the wee hours, maybe a brawl or two. . . . This seems to be the typical Hollywood portrayal of leave, a light-hearted, comedic break from the tension-filled days of war.

It certainly seems true, from Les's description of his various liberties, that they served as a distraction and as an emotional outlet. These were care-free times removed from the drudgery of daily life and the ship's routine. However, the activities during Lester's liberties, along with those of his friends and companions, bear little resemblance to those cinematic images so familiar to us. They were fairly tame, probably because most of Lester's companions were married and already officers, considered even at age twenty-seven or so to be the older, more mature crew members, not the most likely candidates for drunken revelries.

Yet there was a fair amount of alcohol consumption, which was a standard part of each liberty regardless of its location. Whether the men were Stateside, on a large island with well-established facilities, or on a small island with few resources, there was always an officers club available for a round (usually several) of drinks. A liberty might begin with a visit to the local o-club or end there; there was no established pattern for how one spent liberty. In addition to the joys of the o-club, the men also frequented restaurants and bars at each island. They had good meals with friends, often with alcohol, although sometimes just with sodas.

These forays into wining and dining establishments were interspersed with a few other activities. Most often the men would shop, either for souvenirs to send home or for items they themselves needed. Lester often described these shopping sprees and the gifts he had decided to buy for Shirley or other family members. On occasion, he compared his purchases to similar ones his friends made, explaining why his were superior or, rarely, the opposite. The couple compared notes about these gifts, their prices, and how to get them shipped home.

Les and his friends would often tour an island, and he would describe what he saw in letters home. These tours were not limited to native, pastoral scenes; he included descriptions of post-battle devastation as well, delayed in time to pass the censor's requirements.

When the ship was docked for long periods at one island, liberty became a regular feature of naval life, often occurring as frequently as every other day. Although Lester's letters give the impression of men doing almost nothing else, it should be remembered that censorship proscribed the discussion of many topics. At other times, there were long periods at sea during which liberty was impossible. The men continued to have off-duty hours but could not escape the trials and anxieties of shipboard life as completely as when they literally left the ship.

At the beginning of Lester's tour, while his ship was docked in California, he used one liberty to visit Ralph's parents at their home, which he described in particular detail.

> October 9, 1944
>
> . . . Then, surprise of surprises, scuttlebutt for once proved to be fairly accurate. It had been rumored that there would be early liberty, and sure enough the word was passed at lunch that there would be one o'clock liberty. I rated liberty, and there wasn't much time, so I dashed upstairs (oops, topside) to get into my blues.
>
> Ralph had his dad's car parked near the landing, and we drove immediately to his house, which is in a city somewhat inland from the sea, a distance of about 25 miles. Ralph has spoken to me often of his parents' home, the view, the location, the grounds, the contents, etc., but really he hadn't done it justice. The city is situated among the foothills of a coastal range of mountains, and parts of

it therefore are quite precipitous. Well, his folks found two lots near the summit of one of these hills, from which a beautiful view is had. Directly in front is the valley, with another of the hills rising on the opposite side, and prettily and geometrically decorated with the precise patterns of city lots and varicolored slate roofs, with perhaps its most prominent feature being a flight of steps that goes steeply up the slope of the hill. Then on your right hand as you face across the valley there is, first, the calm blue water of the lake in the foreground, and beyond that the craggy, majestic sweep of this coastal range of mountains with its slopes deeply etched with canyons and deep crevices, seeming to be near yet having the haziness about them that distance lends to the view. As your eyes traverse this view in the manner of a movie camera making a panorama, you pass again over the valley, then come the geometrical shapes and tall buildings of the city within a city that make this particular metropolis partially what it is, followed by the restful suggestion of a lovely residential district, and finally a corner of the mighty Pacific, looking on this lovely clear day so peaceful and tranquil.

They have built their home on top of the two plots—what I mean, of course, is at the highest point of their property. There are about two flights of steps laid out through his garden so as to ease the climb (the price has to be paid for the view, and well worth it). The garden has no grass but consists of some kind of vine that grows with long covering strands, like long but thinning hair, and is interspersed with lots of colorful plants and different types of shrubbery. Ralph assures me, and it is easy to believe, that many of the smaller types of wildlife just naturally abound there, and it is a fertile place for nature study. I was too interested in the view and the garden, and too impressed by the news that Mr. Goldman cared for this tremendous project by himself, to take note of the front elevation of the house. I won't go into too much detail about the house, except to say that it was designed with their particular needs in mind and fulfills them admirably. There are five rooms consisting of a living room, dining room, kitchen, library and den, bathroom, and bedroom. Then there are two dressing rooms of large-closet dimensions. In the rear of the house is a large patio. And not least of all is the open fireplace in the living room.

We were of course cordially welcomed by his parents and wife, *of whom I have told you about previously. His folks are really very lovely. His father is a man who Ralph tells me is interested in what we have come to call the finer things of life and has surrounded himself with them. For example, he has a library of hundreds of books of all kinds. He has a large collection of coins, of prints, of woodcuts, of pictures, of porcelains (including some lovely Wedgwood)—and all of this not at all ostentatiously but with a simple enjoyment that is quite refreshing.*

After talking for a while, Ralph and Helen and I got into their car and they showed me all over the city. It was very beautiful. The residential sections were uniformly nice, particularly so a bit further out where were to be found not homes but mansions, and where, according to popular supposition, a place is a shack unless it has its own private swimming pool. They drove to their old alma mater and were properly nostalgic reliving lost years. I suggested they allow me to take them to dinner, and, the idea being good, we ate out. Helen, who is rather well acquainted with these places, made the suggestions. We tried two or three before finding one that was open. This one proved to be a happy choice.

A typical liberty for Lester on his own, while still in California:

October 19, 1944

. . .There is so much noise and confusion on board that I took liberty today at 4:40. I caught a cab into town and spent the afternoon looking around. It is quite a good-sized place, and had several large stores. I walked around several of them thinking to get you something nice, but I saw nothing you would be sure to like, so I didn't get you a thing.

I wended my way across the Strasse to the Friars, the place I called you from the other night. There was a wait for seats, but it wasn't long before I was seated, and it wasn't long after that until I was eating the usual inch-thick steak (quite good, too).

Feeling comfortably replete I left this eating joint and strolled back to the center of town, debating whether or not to venture up to the Sky Room, the rendezvous of most of the officers on board ship, to see who was there, or to see a movie. I didn't feel like drink-

ing or staring at women (honest, I didn't), so I decided in favor of the latter course. The only thing in town I hadn't seen was a double feature: Kismet, and a Charlie Chan detective feature. Both were mediocre but enjoyable in their way. This business of color photography becomes more amazing every day. After the show I grabbed a cab back to the station and reported on board, the proud possessor of a mild headache, mild heartburn, and bearing gifts for Jeff. So here is your fat husband, wondering how you can love him; and thanking God at the same time that you do.

Liberty with a good deal of shopping.

December 1, 1944

. . . As I expected the liberty yesterday was rather nice. It was rather choppy on the bay and the boats were shipping quite a bit of water so a tarpaulin had been rigged up over the gunnels. Into the boat and under the tarp poured the first liberty party officers and men to leave the ship at 16:30. It was a decidedly uncomfortable position we had to assume, neither kneeling nor standing but someplace in between, and the choicest bit of scenery available was your neighbor's butt. Nevertheless, an air of happiness and good fellowship prevailed, for "Were we not going on liberty?" Ralph and I were eager to walk around the town, so we left early and walked rapidly towards the center of town. We walked in and out of a couple of shops, looking at the souvenirs. We were particularly interested in a certain wooden mask made hereabouts. Ralph had bought one yesterday made of light wood, which he was very taken with. I had seen it previously, and some made of dark wood besides, but I didn't think too much of those I saw. I showed Ralph those that were offered by the shops I had been to without him. Then we wandered into the shop where I had showed him the light-colored mask the last time we were on liberty. There were two dark-colored masks on display. I asked to see them. They were fine examples of this type of work, and were unblemished. I bought both of them and am sending them on to you. They'll look nice in our home, dear. Really, they are very attractive things, and will look nice flat against a wall. You'll like them when you see them, I am sure. After this purchase we wandered over to the Post Exchange,

where Ralph bought a pair of wooden clogs and a pair of the same for Bob. While there, we had a snack of a malted milk and a few donuts, neither of which were particularly good. They were selling cartons of chewing gum. I know that stuff is comparatively rare in the States, so I bought four cartons, two cartons for you and your folks, and two cartons for my folks. I got spearmint and Juicy Fruit. My idea is that you'll keep a carton of each and give a carton of each to my folks when they come over. I send all of this to you direct because it is difficult to get the materials to make a proper package on board, and two packages are just that much more difficult to provide for.

After we left the PX, we walked around the public square of the town and at the same time did some more window shopping. This square is about three blocks long by about one wide and has lots of curving walks running through it. The main tree has a beautiful red flower. It is really very colorful to see a group of these trees. Under the trees and at strategic intervals along the paths are benches. Here the local populace, native and white, comes to sit and schmooze, like Union Square. It is really a peaceful sight, though, and to make it more homelike are the numerous mongrel dogs that run all over the place. We left the square after a while to walk around some of the back streets of the town, and while walking speculated about the recency of the architecture and the probable fate of this place after the war.

It was getting late, so we decided to look the local cathedral over and then head for dinner. We walked up the hill, at the summit of which the cathedral was situated. It was growing dark and the fading light coming in through the windows was softened and made beautiful by the tinted glass of the windows, which in turn, robbing the light of part of its spectrum, was made beautiful, too. We stood in contemplation for a while and then left. Ralph had arranged for reservations at this officers club, thinking that we would get local cookery there. It turned out to be exactly the same type of meal we would have on board, or at the corner of 14th and Fifth Avenues, for that matter.

December 13, 1944

After dinner we made our way through to the landing. We were passing by one of the military office establishments when we saw a man working on something in one of the windows. He was stuffing animals. We decided to go inside and talk to him. He was very nice, and told us a lot about himself and his work. It seems he is a zoologist and spends all his spare time getting specimens of the local fauna, which he prepares and makes collections of, and sends back to the States. He was particularly interested in bats. Sure enough, on the table were a half a dozen small bats which he was in the process of skinning and stuffing, and off to the right of these were four or five huge bats, about the size of a large rat, with about four- or five-foot wingspreads. Some people have the most peculiar hobbies. I can understand most hobbies, but bats are one animal that repulse me most satisfactorily. He can have all of them. At this stage I observed a claw-like talon moving from a black mass hanging on the back of a chair close by. I asked about that. "Oh," he said, "that's Oscar. He's my pet." And so saying he reached down and picked up this black mass, which turned out to be a bat with about an 18-inch wingspread, and let him hang from his shirt. The bat started crawling all over him. Frankly it was a nauseous-looking sight at first. Then, after a while, the bat just hung head down with his rear claws supporting him from this fellow's shirt, and I discovered a peculiar rat-like likableness to his countenance. I can't understand it. This fellow insists that this pet of his recognizes him, and other people, and understands and responds to affection and love. We spent an interesting half-hour there. When we left, I was more than ever convinced that Skipper is an ideal pup.

We had hopes of catching an early boat back to the ship, but the boat schedule was all fouled up, making a wait of an hour necessary.

In later years, Lester often spoke of New Caledonia as having been his favorite Pacific island.

January 18, 1945
. . . It seems to me that I have told you most of interest about New Caledonia. It might be interesting to you to check up on me in the encyclopedia. I don't think I mentioned that the island is

French, Free French now, and in many ways is a reminder of the old world. The architecture, for instance, is a transplantation from France, with solid fronts to blocks of houses in some instances, broken occasionally by a fence that walls in a patio. The more well-to-do have what corresponds to our middle- class one-family house. These of the upper brackets live fringing the bay, many of them preferring the heights for the view it affords, and the cool breeze that blows up there. There is a sizable French population, and of course a sizable native population, besides which there is a liberal admixture of Javanese and Tonkinese. One habit is very noticeable here. The men quite unconcernedly walk along the street holding hands. This is a bit shocking to us of the Anglo-Saxon tradition, but I am assured by those who are used to the continental manner that it is quite common in Europe. One of the more interesting sights of town was to ride by the government office and see some colossal bearded Negro, with a bayonet-mounted rifle, clad in a white uniform with short trousers, standing guard at the entrance.

Most of the souvenirs I got are just small little things, but something had to be gotten. I think those letter openers are a particular happy thought (they are sandalwood, you know). I think the real find is the pair of heads in ebony. They will really look good on a wall of our home. We placed them against the bulkhead in our room and found that the more we looked at them, the more we enjoyed them. They (as well as the rest of the stuff, the beads, the mats, the charms, belt, etc.) are all authentic native workmanship. Most of them come from the isle of Tahiti, which is not far from here. I left five bucks with a friend of Ralph's. He promised to send me a set of bookends when they got a shipment. They may be waiting for me now.

Here, Lester and his friends found evidence of earlier Japanese invasions.

January 29, 1945
Churl Darling,
Today was a little unusual. I had a liberty this morning, but that wasn't what made it unusual. The unusual thing was that the coxswain knew the right beach and how to get there, and we got

there all right. The liberty party had been given a recreation beach on this island which only a few months ago (about 9 I guess) had been Japanese. The signs of our preliminary bombardment were still painfully obvious— coconut palms with their tops shot off require more than nine months to heal. On the beach there were belts of small caliber ammunition strewn around, and fronting the sea, both on the beach and some way inland, were the famous coconut log bunkers of the Japs. They consist of a hole dug in the earth, usually with the entrance from the rear being flush with the earth (sometimes the entrance is through the top). The sides of this excavation are lined to just below the level of the top (a matter of about 3-4 feet) with heavy, tough, coconut logs, locked in position. The sides of the bunker (especially the front) slope away shallowly, so that it blends very nicely with the surrounding terrain. The shallow slope also serves to pick up a good thickness of earth in front of the logs, which serves the admirable protection against shellfire. As is usual with islands of the type (coral), the approaches have a small reef usually marked by a thin line of breakers, a smooth "bay," and a sandy beach, which is lapped by the gentle waves, more like the shores of a lake than waves on the beach such as we are more accustomed to in the Atlantic.

The first thing we did was cache our beer in what we thought was a safe place and start exploring. We had heard about a wrecked Jap plane inland, so we struck out to look for it. We had quite a walk. We passed through an army encampment, saw their crude but effective motion picture theater, and shower, all out of doors, of course, and finally ended up at the air strip. There we saw several planes both in whole and in part. We walked along, seeing several different types of lizards on the way. At long last, we headed back. We were hot and tired and sweaty, and anticipated the cold beer waiting for us back on the beach. Like Mother Hubbard. When we got, there the cupboard was bare. Some of the enlisted had stolen it. There was nothing to do but swear for a while and bear it. We were due to return in about an hour. I spent the time taking a swim, the first I've had in the Pacific. It was really almost tepid, but at that cooler than the air. Then I walked up and down the beach for a while, looking at the thousands of seals, watching the sand crabs

*and snails take cover as I approached, and marveling at all the de-
bris around. Finally it was back to the ship, where I showered, had
a bite to eat, and . . . but that's a little later. Most of the time on
the beach I kept my shirt on, but despite that I got quite a burn.
My face (especially my ears) is as red as a beet.*

April 23, 1945
Churl Darling,

    *Today has been a big day indeed. My first liberty in this new
port! I wish I could describe it to you and tell you about it all, but
that will have to wait. After that we took a bus into town, the very
center. Ralph stopped in to have his shoes shined. While waiting
for him, I strolled up the street. I was attracted by a set of small
prints hanging in the window of a curio shop. I went to inquire
about them. The girl who waited on me was a very slim (skinny)
Oriental lass with a lovely cultured English voice. She explained
to me that these scrolls came in sets of four but were for sale individually. I was rather taken by them, so I ordered four. I'll mail
them out tomorrow. If you like them we can keep the entire set. If
not, you might want to make a gift of a pair of them to someone,
but only to someone who deserves them, for I really think they are
lovely. I'll also send out a pair of earrings I bought in the same
place. I'm afraid I was a bit extravagant because I paid more than
a dollar or two for them, but I thought that you'd like them. They
are made of the very hardest ivory from the tusks of African ele-
phants, and carved to an original design of the house where I bought
them. This particular model is modeled after the leaves of the
frangipane, a tropical plant. Translated, frangipane means "bloom
of love." I assure you that I had picked the earrings out before being
told the meaning of the word, but I was very pleased by the appropriateness of the definition. Ralph wandered in while the gifts were
being wrapped. I asked him if he liked the scrolls. "No," he said, to
which I replied that I was glad I had purchased them before asking
his opinion.*

    *After we left that place we hunted for a public phone for Ralph
since he had a few calls to make. While he was busy on the phone,
I located a couple of Momma's Day cards. I sent one to you and*

one to my mother. I'm sorry, but the choice was very limited. That didn't take long, so I spent some time wandering through the aisles of a rather nice department store. I stopped to buy some handkerchiefs there, rather lovely ones, I thought. There is one in particular I want for you to keep, the one with the rose motif, and the green border. For the rest of them, distribute them as you will. Keep one or two for yourself, I suggest, and give a couple each to Roz and Elaine. This business of souvenirs is mostly a pain in the neck. Most of the stuff is junk. But this time I think that I got some rather nice stuff. Oh, yes, I bought a couple of sport shirts: one for Pop S. and one for Pop H. I didn't know what size they wore, so I bought one medium and one large. I hope the fitting problem gets straightened out satisfactorily.

May 1, 1945

. . .After I left the dental clinic I walked over to the club and grabbed off a couple of beers, after which I made a ship's service. There I bought a pair of khaki trousers (I may as well wear out what brown shoes I have with me) and a set of Lt.'s. bars. Also, I bought a very lovely sterling silver charm bracelet for you. I'll be able to mail it out so you should have it soon. At the uniform counter I saw exactly the same shirts I had paid four bucks for downtown for sale at $2.65. I bought four of them. They only had the medium size. I hope they fit. I suggest you give two to each of the pops, and save two for me because they are pretty nice shirts (I'll send six altogether). I am looking for a little photo album to use when I have no more room in this. They have only some tremendous ones which aren't suitable, and which are very expensive, so I'll wait.

Censorship rules affected the descriptions of liberty.

May 3, 1945

. . .Today was an early liberty day. Ralph and I left the ship early and managed to do quite a bit of sightseeing, and there were some beautiful sights to see. We took bus trips to different parts of the island. I wish I could describe them to you, but you know. At *any rate it is safe to say that this is really by way of being one of the loveliest countrysides we have ever seen. The downtown portion of the town isn't very much, but the residential district is very nice. One of our trips ended at a naval station. We walked into the ship's service there, and I saw a rather attractive slack set I bought for you (size 14). I hope they fit, and I hope you like it.*

On this island Lester sees more evidence of previous Japanese war activity.

June 13, 1945

. . . Liberty was declared at 1530, to expire at 1800 on the dock. That left only a couple of hours to see this town, but it was an opportunity to stretch my legs, so I took the proffered chance. This was a large city once, not so long ago, and fairly modern. Today it is gutted by bomb and shell fire. It is perhaps the most sobering and realistic glimpse of the effect of war on a metropolis that we have yet seen. And the bombed cities of Europe must be a hundred times worse. The populace is very happy and friendly, however. They are industriously engaged with hammer and saw, putting up shops, most of them souvenir shops, and trying to regain once more the atmosphere of a bustling city. Surprisingly enough, they succeed. The trip through the harbor made the liberty worthwhile. On each side, no matter where you looked, you saw the masts of sunken ships breaking the surface of the water. There must have been hundreds of them, Japanese, all of them. How they can continue to carry on a war that involves sea communications is beyond me, in the face of this mute testimony to their inability to resist our blows. So we walked through the streets of this busy city, and it really is busy, looking at the people, and at the souvenir shops. The natives were selling everything. The children offered packets of Japanese occupation money for sale, and packets of stamps. The money was so common that it was blowing around the streets. Others had packages of the local fruit to offer. None of them were insistent; if you said no, they wouldn't bother you any further. Politeness seems to be almost a national characteristic here. As we came into the harbor, we passed many of the little outrigger fishing boats which are so characteristic of the area. Each one that was at all near would paddle

madly to approach the ship, although they knew we would not stop to trade with them, then rest their paddles, take off their big brimmed hats and wave them madly at us in greeting. I liked that. Others of the natives had some of the local birds in pairs in little cages, and mighty attractive they were, but there is no place for such things on board ship, and besides no animals may be brought back to the States. The shops were filled with a miscellany of objects, but we weren't buying that day. Most of us only had a couple of bucks and lots of energy to dissipate. As we walked along I saw in a window of one of the nicer-looking shops a set of large red and white chessmen, carved in Chinese style. You know how I've always wanted a little Chinese chess set (exactly why, I don't know). The boys were walking fast, so I had no opportunity to ask about it. On the way back, however, I stopped in. The store was closing for the evening, and the owners had left, but they had evidently seen me, for they returned. I asked the price of the set. "Oh," she said in a French accent, "zat iss 700 'underd dollars." I rapidly made my excuses, cut off any further efforts at salesmanship, and caught up with my party. I had a borrowed 5-dollar bill in my pocket. The set was hand carved out of ivory, and included an inlaid chess board. I didn't get a chance to study them closely, but it may have been worth anywhere between one and three hundred dollars as object of art. That's still a little too much for them. Shortly after that we were due at the dock to catch the boat back to the ship. On the way we stopped in at the American Red Cross for doughnuts and lemonade. Then we made the boat for a wet trip back to the ship.

There is ever more evidence of destruction from the war, and Ralph and Lester disagreed about the quality of their respective purchases.

June 14, 1945
  ...Today Ralph and I caught an early liberty. We each carried a canteen, for the drinking water ashore is still not safe. The ship too, in a burst of unusual thoughtfulness, had provided beer for both officers and men. It was ready and waiting when we got ashore. The boat trip had been a bit hot so we wasted no time in quaffing a beer. Then we slipped a can apiece into our pocket and shoved.

We first went to see that part of the town where the Japs had holed up and had to be dug out. What incredible devastation! Words cannot describe it. Nothing left but a few shattered walls, the space between filled with pulverized rubble. Rebuild? About all that can be done is to save the foundations. Well, that's one way of modernizing a city, although it is a bit drastic for my taste. We poked about these ruins for quite a while. There were the usual empty shell cases, and battered guns, both Jap and ours. Incendiaries had evidently been profusely used, for many empty cases were found, and frequently glass was found to have been fused, melted by the heat. There is no need to go into all of the gruesome details. The newspapers can do a better job of that than I can.

We left this place of demolished buildings after a while, and repaired to the active part of the city, busily engaged in rebuilding itself. We strolled along looking at the souvenir shops. Most of the stuff is junk, as usual, but there are some fine figures carved from ivory. After all, the Asiatic influence is strong here. The prices for everything are exorbitant, and actually the same items may be obtained in New York for comparable prices or less. But it was fun to stroll along and examine the merchandise displayed, and observe the people at work. Here in one shop a cigar-smoking grandmamma dangled her grandchild on her knee. Next door an eager soldier was talking with obvious intent to a bashfully smiling young girl (in appearance about 14 years of age). "Pompom" is one of the most reasonably priced and abundant commodities to be found hereabouts, and judging by the prophylaxis lines each night the boys take advantage of it. The street is alive with soldiers and sailors out to do the town. There is a higher than usual proportion of bad drunks, but on the whole, the atmosphere is bustling and good natured, made the more so by the blatant sound of the corny bands playing in the second story night clubs. I took Ralph to see the 700-dollar chess set, and we both decided it was greatly over-valued, although it is rather nice. The popular mode of conveyance here is by a two-wheeled carriage drawn by a very small, scrawny horse. How he ever pulls the carriage and the people in it I will never understand. It is like the Mexican burros. Indeed it was all I could do to keep from shouting, "Burro, burro." Remember? I love you so, darling. And I have such happy memories to make your hours bright. If only I could take you in my arms for a moment (but that's another story).

June 17, 1945

. . . *I have told you how expensive things are hereabouts, but the barter system makes things more reasonable, and I was able to put it into effect in a small way. The result was that I managed to obtain two rather nice souvenirs at not too great an expense (I think). I bought a snakeskin (python) purse for you with a wallet of the same material. There were several styles available, but none as neat or as nice as the one I bought for you. I think it will go well with a sport outfit. Indeed, it should look good with that gray gabardine suit of yours. Then, later in the afternoon, I bought a piece of ivory. I bought a long cigarette holder for you, with a beautifully carved flower design on it. It was rather expensive, but I was quite taken with it, and I think that it is probably not exorbitant. I smoked a few cigarettes with it this evening, and already I am so attached to it that I debated a moment about keeping it for myself, but I want you to have it (the more so because I like it). The pleasure of sending it to you is intensified just that much by the small amount of personal sacrifice involved. So use and enjoy it, darling. And when you smoke your first cigarette with it, and get that odor of burnt tobacco lingering within, remember that it was a cigarette of mine that caused it, and in remembering, come that much closer to me. Indeed, I'll light up another one right now. How exotic you will be with those ivory earrings, and this long, long holder (I'll measure it. Wait a moment. It is 6 and a quarter inches). I like the picture.*

Well, the story of the souvenirs got me a little ahead of my story. We got ashore and as usual prepared for our excursion by having a can of beer apiece, and taking along a couple for reserve. Actually, there is little I can tell of the afternoon's activity without violating regulations, but we did do quite a bit of walking and seeing several interesting things, places and people. The kids would run after us yelling, "Hi, Joe," and even the littlest ones would usually add, "Got a cigarette?" We saw a group of kids playing some kind of a game involving choosing, the winner drawing four lines to form the outline of a flag, then within the field of the flag drawing two semi-circles to complete the diagram of the Japanese flag. It was a game they had learned during the Jap occupation.

As usual we ended our trip with a visit to the Red Cross for some very welcome lemonade. Then we went down to the dock to wait for the boat. Poor us. A sudden rainstorm blew up and lasted until we were once more on board ship. There was absolutely no protection. Soaked. I have never been so wet.

September 5, 1945

. . . At 10 minutes before three we heard that there would be liberty starting at three. Of the department, Drs. Golden, Goldman, and Halbreich, and Butch Allan made the boat. We were put ashore at a pier about a mile down the beach from the club. The walk there got us all thirsty, and we really piled into the first couple of cans of beer. After that we found seats and sat down to enjoy ourselves. This club isn't a bad one. It isn't as sumptuous as some of the others, but it was cool, had a nice long bar, and plenty of room to accommodate large numbers of people.

About an hour before we were due to go back to the ship, Ralph, Dr. Golden, and I walked on down to the local ship's service to see if there were any late magazines we could bring back. We did manage to get a couple of copies of Yank and a Time. Then I saw another line. I got on that and ended up with four boxes of Cheese-its. Just before we left I saw some model outrigger canoes with a lateen sail rig. They were broken, but the clerk sold me one for a buck. I took it back to the ship with me, and I'm going to arrange for one of the ship's carpenters to fix it up. It is really very nice. Jeff will like it when he gets ready for that kind of thing, and he'll be able to tell his friends, "That's what my pop brought back from the Pacific for me." Won't that be grand?

The trip back to the ship was a riot. Most of the officers were slightly on the squiffed side, and as usual the trip was a wet one, complicated furthermore by the necessity of towing back one of the other boats which had bent its rudder. We finally made it with no mishaps, and a thoroughly wet-down group of passengers.

Some observations on local life.

September 22, 1945

. . .Yesterday I went ashore with the liberty party. The liberty party consisted of Dr. Golden, Mr. Allan, Thomas, and Miller, and me. We had five cases of beer with us (not a bad percentage). On the way in the boat crew slung out a board with a line attached to it (an aquaplane) and jokingly asked if anyone of us wanted to try it. What was their surprise when I said I would. I stripped, dove in the water, and mounted my trusty steed. At the signal, the coxswain opened the throttle, and as soon as we had weigh enough I knelt, then rose on the board. It was great fun. A short way out from the beach he slowed down, when I came into the boat. I dried off and got dressed. When we got ashore we hitched several rides to the beach party tent. There we found a thirsty group of sailors who made short work of all but one case of the beer. While we were there the exec drove up in the jeep, and went back to the ship. No sooner had he gone then we appropriated the jeep and drove inland to the town of San Fabien, which is nearby. It was quite interesting. It was a much more typical approach to island life than that found in Manila. We passed several caribou, of course, and saw the thatched huts of the natives, and the ramshackle structures that they had thrown together from available materials. We took a case of beer with us, and found an inn, the Cozy Corner, where, for payment of a couple of pesos, we were provided with glasses and permitted to drink our own beer. There we spent the afternoon drinking and talking. The two girls who waited table there were very chummy with the chief, who had taken us to the place (he was there yesterday).

They were rather pretty Filipinos. They had a great time poking fun at Butch Allan's bald head. While we were sitting there, a native funeral passed in the road in front. First, there was the music of a brass band, very loud and gay. Then a small coffin, carried by two youngsters (it was evidently an infant that had died), followed by a rather cheerful crowd. In a moment it was passed, and only the sound of the drum remained to remind us of it. If the girls hadn't told us it was a funeral we would never have known.

We managed to polish off the case of beer. This involved several visits to the head, of course, then started back for the beach, where we caught a boat to the ship.

Lester described local life vividly. The Japanese scrolls and samurai dolls that he bought here remained in the family for the rest of his life, and were toys for his children to play with.

October 14, 1945

...We moved back into the harbor yesterday to our old anchorages. The center of the typhoon had passed and there was nothing more to fear. In the afternoon liberty was called. Dr. Golden and I went ashore in our turn. I changed about five dollars' worth of American money into yen in the morning and, before going ashore, loaded myself down with cigarettes and soap to trade. As I got into the boat I heard that the fleet commander had issued an order against barter. It was too late to go back, so I stayed in the boat. Dr. Golden and a few of the other boys were similarly provided. As the boat came close to the landing, I noticed that the shore patrol was searching the liberty parties from the boats preceding ours. There was nothing to do but leave our cargo in the boat. We went ashore and walked around the town. It was the same as I had written to you before. This time we walked up the hill and out towards a small fishing village that was located about a mile beyond Waka-nura (the city of Wakayama is inland further and is out of bounds). We reached the village by walking along a footpath cut into the side of a steep hillside. It reminded me very much of the Cornell gorges, the same type of sedimentary shale was exposed; but whereas at Cornell at the foot of the gorge we had had a rambling stream, here at the foot of the cliff was the Pacific Ocean. On our way to the village we passed a few of the local cemeteries, which are quite compact and neatly laid out. We noticed also that into the side of the cliff had been cut numerous caves. We don't know, but we suspect that they were pill boxes to be used in defense of the coast. We reached a point overlooking the village which consisted of a group of houses constructed with the typical Japanese architectural plan, reaching inland from a beach on which reposed a score or more of

small fishing boats, and which boasted a small pier extending into the bay. Overhead wheeled a flock of gulls searching for something to eat. We would have gone on further but at that moment the first few drops of an imminent rainstorm fell, and we deemed it advisable to retrace our course to the club.

What I haven't told you, though, is that I got two of the nicest souvenirs of the voyage during our wanderings. Remember I told you that some of the shops had these typical Japanese scroll drawings? Well, most of them are rather trashy, more or less like the American calendar art. I saw one yesterday that I thought was rather nice and managed to get the guy to take a yen for it (most of them will only trade for cigarettes and soap, you know). It is hand painted on silk and bears a verse of a Japanese poem. I won't try to describe it to you except to say it is a rather typical example of this particular art form, and is really very simple. I had our Japanese language expert, Mr. Scallopino, translate the verse for me, and it fits in very well indeed with the subject matter of the scroll. I find that looking at it is very much like listening to the Tchaikovsky Violin Concerto. The more you look at it the more pleasure you derive from it, just as the more you listen to the concerto the more you enjoy it. I think you will be well pleased with it.

I also bought two native dolls, a samurai warrior and a warrior woman, both in full costume. I rationalized by saying that I'd bought them for Jeff. Actually I'm crazy about them myself, and he will be permitted to handle them. The dolls are mounted on sticks in a little box with a glass front to it and are dressed in richly brocaded and embroidered costumes in the typical style of the period. Every detail is complete, to the fierce look in the warrior's eyes. They are too hard to describe, but I don't think they need a description on paper. If I remember correctly the Brooklyn Museum has a rather large collection of such dolls in its Japanese section. You might find it interesting to walk in there one afternoon to see what I mean. At any event, I know that you'll like these dolls as much as I do and that is a lot.

October 29, 1945
    . . . The portion of Nagoya where we now are is highly industrialized, and from on board ship the scene looked like any typical

waterfront view with the buildings and chimneys of the industrial plant being the prominent parts of the skyline. We might have been anchored in the river off downtown Brooklyn, for all we could tell. The place looked so untouched that Ralph at lunch time commented that he couldn't understand the much-vaunted accuracy of our force, for apparently very little damage had been done. Well, this afternoon after work, Dr. Golden and I went out on the dock (to inspect the rat guards) and from there managed to walk off the pier into the city (we weren't supposed to, but what the hell). The reason the place looked so neat from the ship was that it had been completely flattened for block on block, and the rubble had been neatly sorted and arranged in piles. Here there was a leaning chimney, or the charred trunk of a tree, or some sagging trolley lines, all bearing mute testimony to the fury of the bombs and fire which had gutted the place. The people here are different than they were at Wakanura. The latter place, being a small fishing village of comparatively little importance, had been left untouched, so the people were comparatively cheerful and friendly, but here the people walked along with no cheer at all showing on their faces, rather showing the strain of the constant gnawing of hunger. And in support of the fact that food was short there were everywhere that a plot of ground could be found little plots of vegetables growing. We walked into town for quite a ways, and then returned to the ship. On the way back we stopped by a warehouse. This particular place had been stuffed full of Chinese coins by the Japs. They were going to use them to get copper for arms. Now the doggies were loading up with all they could carry. I took a handful along to give to the corpsmen on board ship.

This was Lester's last liberty prior to the final voyage to California and home to Shirley.

November 7, 1945
. . . I didn't even intend to go ashore, but Golden said he was going over at about 3:30 and I was feeling bored and disgusted, so I went along. We came ashore at the town of Guiuinar, on the island of Samar. On the way to the club, we stopped off to inspect the

town's cathedral and fort, a rather imposing though simple structure built of coral blocks, which were painted with limestone. Inside we saw the usual devout few on their knees, praying, and flying around the eaves were a few twittering songsters. The effect was impressive and lovely. From the church we went on up to the club, which was a ramshackle structure. We spent an hour or so drinking beer, then headed back to the landing to catch a boat. As we might have foreseen, a drenching rain started to fall the moment we left the pier. The result was that all of us were soaked through when we got on board.

17

LIFE GOES ON

AR MAY BE RAGING, soldiers may be dying, battle plans may be drawn up, and couples may be torn apart for the duration, yet the obligations and concerns of daily life never disappear. Movies only portray the glory moments of war—the battles, the brilliant strategy sessions, the romances—but never show the ongoing issues that make up everyday existence. How do bills get paid? How does the income get divided? How does the soldier get whatever he needs—money, clothing, books? In general, how do decisions get made even about mundane concerns, if thousands of miles and a relatively inefficient postal system separate the couple?

These questions may not be the stuff of cinema, but they do occupy a good part of the daily lives and daily dilemmas of the many thousands of couples who went through World War II—and all other wars. Lester and Shirley were no different in this, as is evident from their very first letters.

One issue involved a rug that they no longer wanted. Should they sell it, and if so, for what price? This question went back and forth for a surprisingly long time, complicated by the fact that neither wanted to decide anything that would go against the other's wishes. They were still newlyweds, after all, trying to be tactful and considerate of each other.

Money in general took up a routine residence in their letters. Lester was the one earning the salary, though it was not a very large one. He was trying to save some of it, to buy U. S. savings bonds on a regular basis, and to send a good amount home to Shirley. He kept as little as possible for himself and for whatever needs he may have had, which varied depending on whether he was in Texas, on the West Coast, or at sea. When Lester was alone in Texas, he had to pay rent, buy gas for the car, pay the utility bills, buy some food items (even though he really did not cook for himself—he made coffee, had some sort of breakfast, and some snacks), and pay whatever costs were associated with his entertainment. He occasionally needed items of clothing, too. Lester's letters frequently and very specifically accounted for all such expenditures. He also tried to send money to Shirley for her own indulgences, possibly to buy herself a new dress, a hat, or a coat.

Shirley was running the household, so to speak, though she was living with her parents. She had checking and savings accounts, and she would often write to Lester about how she was managing them. Her letters also included descriptions of unexpected financial windfalls that came her way— usually when her father gave her some extra money.

Apart from finances, Shirley always described Jeffrey's daily antics as well. When he was ill or teething, or when Skipper, the dog, was misbehaving, she had to face it alone and was reduced to writing about her worries or the events as they unfolded. For his part, Les could only write back to show his support and offer advice, which often arrived too late to matter.

Early on, Shirley had written concerning her worries about her struggle to conceive, and Lester had attempted to assuage her anxiety. Another issue that kept recurring was interpersonal in nature, as one, then the other, had problems getting along with a particular friend or relative. Each one in turn would write to describe the events and their feelings about them, and, weeks later, the other spouse would try to console and employ reason to effect a broader perspective. This was never satisfactory, since it could not be discussed in the moment, and remained another issue of daily life not captured by the movies.

This letter covers some of Lester's daily routine while he was in Texas, some bills that he had questioned, a request for Shirley to buy new clothes, and an acknowledgment of funds he had received from her.

October 10, 1943
. . . This morning I had juice, toast, and jam, and a cup of
Bellar coffee for breakfast. Oh, yes, I've cleaned and polished my
gold braid and buttons. They look like new now. I brought the car

down to Garza's, and we got rid of the squeak.

On the financial end, I received a bill from the "O" Club, which I shall not pay because I wrote a letter of resignation last month. And Rarmeg had the nerve to send me a $21.00 bill for work on the car. He deducted $7.00 for engine overhaul. But I'm only going to pay him $8.50 for the cost of cleaning the tank. Boy, that guy gets me sore.

Darling, there are two things that you must do while you are in the city.

Replenish your wardrobe.

Get Elliot's address and send it to me so I can write him about you, and also see Esther and have her father look you over, and ask him to write me a summary of his findings.

P.S. I received your telegram and money order.

P.P.S. I finally got that rear license plate holder. We don't have to hide from the sheriff anymore.

The rug problems begin.

October 13, 1943

...About the rug, I don't know what to do. We certainly don't need it now; and when we furnish when this war is over, it may not be what we want. But then again, it may be. See if my folks are using it. Then ask your dad. If you sell it with the pad, you should get at least as much as we paid for it, probably $5.00 or $10.00. I have the bill on it at home. I think that altogether it cost us $80 or $90. I'll let you know more after we've looked it up.

October 14, 1943

P.S. The rug stood us $80. Sell it for no less than that!! If you decide to sell, and I think that you may as well.

More on the rug, and on their checking account.

October 21, 1943

...About the rug, if you don't want to sell it for $80, don't sell it at all. I'm not interested in making money, but I'm not in-

terested in losing it either. Its real value is far more than that. And the extent of its wear and spotting I'm sure is negligible. But I don't think you ought to sell it. If we keep it, everyone will be happier.

Lester had driven across the country to report to duty and was providing Shirley with the costs of that trip.

July 16, 1944
> *. . . The expenses on the car came to about $32.*
> *Storage, $1.50*
> *Grease, $1.00*
> *Oil, 2.10*
> *Gas, $1.71*
> *Wash, $1.50*
> *Fix Horn, $11.67 (about $6.00 more than if I'd done it in Corpus)*
> *Balance, about $27.68*
> *I had to buy a new tube for the spare since the old one was split wide open (that flat we had in St. Louis). The new tube, together with the five gallons of gas, came to another five bucks.*
> *I decided that I better have more money to take with me, so I cashed a check for $50.*

July 22, 1944
Churl Darling,
> *After lunch yesterday I walked over to the administration building and picked up my check for travel and my original orders. I am enclosing a check for $135 endorsed for deposit only.*

Lester tried to live on less than his salary, and he also asked Shirley to reimburse his parents for a call that he had to make collect.

July 28, 1944
> *I sent the $135 check in another letter. My salary will be more than sufficient to live on—don't be concerned about that.*
> *I'm glad to know that you received the pearls at last and it*

made me happy to know that you like them so much.

... Oh yes, on those pictures of mine. I'd like my folks to have a print or two. Will you arrange it for me, please? One more thing, when I called last time, and switched the call to the Bronx, it was a collect call. Please try to pay for it.

P.S. I haven't heard from my folks yet. Find out why.

August 2, 1944

I spent the day before yesterday and yesterday trying to sell the car. Like a fool I went to the dealers first. You've probably heard them advertise on the radio, "Bring your car to us." "Highest ceiling price paid." Well, to cut down on a long story, I got offers ranging from $950 to $1,050 with a favor. The ceiling price is $1,090. So I advertised, and despite the fact that the ad was placed in the wrong classification, I got several calls, and sold the car to the first party that came along, for $1,090 cash. I closed the deal today. As soon as I had the money, I had a cashier's check for $1,100 made out to Dad.

Well, we lost some money on this car, but in our total automobile operations we realized a respectable profit and besides had the use of the car for a year and a half. That's not a bad record, of course. If I had sold before the ceiling we might have made more, but then our transportation costs would have been more. As it is, when I add my per diem money to this $1,100, and then collect your transportation money, we will not only be out of debt entirely, we will be ahead of the game. When you stop to think that, besides that, we've got a tidy sum in the bank stashed away I think that the both of us deserve considerable credit. My very best congratulations to you, Mrs. Halbreich, and a hearty hug and kiss.

Lester is concerned that Shirley should remember to take care of her teeth, which she later writes to him about.

August 27, 1944

I had to cash two five-dollar checks. This business is going too far. My money just seems to disappear, although I did do some shopping.

... Let me remind you again to get to the dentist. And don't *put it off. That is very important, darling. I am working at the clinic tomorrow night and am going to take care of my own teeth. What I mean is that I am going to have the other man fill some teeth for me.*

September 3, 1944

It is a little hard staying on $45 every 15 days. As I told you, that is primarily because I have so much damn time on my hands now. I don't like to hang around this dive all day merely to be able to eat, so I go to town. Well, even if I eat only two meals a day, they come to close to three dollars. In 15 days that is almost the entire amount of my pay check. Then of course there are other expenses. And so I've written some checks. On board ship of course it will be different.

Churl, you don't have to pay the uniforms yet. Although if you want to you can. The check for your travel will be about $86. And I owe them, as I recollect, about $81. So let that wait until I get your travel money, then we will pay them. It doesn't make much difference, although if you want to pay them now write a check out to the order of the "Naval Uniform Shop."

While on the subject I want to remind you to change the form of our hospitalization policy so that the pregnancy clause is eliminated. We do not need that for the time being, and it will save a dollar a month. Also, while on that, make sure that Jeff is included in the provisions of the new policy. I am sure that he is covered until 18 years of age without additional charge.

I would do that for you, but I made you the family representative while I am in service and you have all the papers at home.

Lester, concerned about Shirley's level of fatigue as a new mother, asks her to hire a maid.

September 26, 1944

I think that I've answered most of the questions already . . . except the one about the watch. I think that you had better have the pocket watch fixed and send that along. The Gruen is too good to spoil, or be stolen, on this voyage.

. . . Darling, you sound to me as if you are working too hard in

the house. Why don't you try to get a girl to help you with some of the work, at least? I was thinking of taking the extra $21 a month of sea pay, and getting another $18.50 bond, but if you can use it for a maid, I'll just enlarge your allotment by that amount. Let me know what you prefer.

. . .Yes, I received the laundry that was lost. It finally caught up with me, and a good thing, too. I can use it all. As things stand now, there is just about enough room for my clothes with three of us in a stateroom for four.

I hope that I didn't do too wrong about the sea chest. I thought that it could surely be stored in the basement.

I thought for a while that I had lost my lighter, but I had it in my pocket in my blues. The little elektro-lighter is really good, though. You know the type. It's one of those flameless affairs.

The money situation is fine. As I explained to you, I am thinking of either putting it into a bond or increasing your allotment, but as I write this I think more and more of the idea I was telling you about before I left. I think I will take out a separate $18.50 bond in our name. That series of bonds is to be kept separately from the others and is to be used after the war to buy, for the most lovely of all wives, a beautiful stone martin three-quarter coat. I can see you in it now. Yep. Now that I've written it on paper I am going in to see our disbursing office about it tomorrow. Wear it in good health, sweetheart.

Lester signs up for a war bond plan, wanting Shirley to splurge on something for herself with that money.

September 28, 1944

This morning, in line with my recent decision, I went to the disbursing officer, and registered an $18.75 allotment for war bonds in both our names. I have your father as the mailing address. They should start coming through in November (about the first). Now, darling, those bonds are yours to do with as you please. I consider them as resulting from your own efforts at economy. Of course, I still like my idea of putting them toward a nice Stone Martin three-quarter jacket; but if you have a better suggestion, why you go ahead and use them as you please.

December 12, 1944

... By this time the socket of that third molar of yours should be all healed up, or very close to it. How I understand and sympathize with what you went through immediately before and for a while after the extraction. It must have been hell for you. Phil is right of course in trying to avoid having anything fall into the socket, and from the description of your dental appointments with him it would seem that there was always something interfering with work getting done. By this time he should be able to make rapid progress with your work. Ask him to use Novocain, and explain to him how difficult it is for you to get out there frequently. Perhaps he can arrange to give you longer appointments, and accomplish more work at a single sitting. Dentistry is a pretty slow and tedious job anyway.

Lester always wants Shirley to buy luxuries for herself.

December 15, 1944

... Besides that, honey, I had part of my salary paid to me as a 30-dollar check. I am going to endorse it payable to you. Fifteen of that thirty is for the hat I told you to buy yourself; the other fifteen is for you to pick out an anniversary gift for yourself with. I haven't many ideas, but possibly a fur-trimmed hat to go with your beaver would be suitable, no?

February 8, 1945

... I'm glad you managed to get yourself a nice- looking coat (Nov. 16). I always think of you in beautiful clothes. In looking through the Times, *for instance, I say, "How well this would look on Churl. I'd like to see Churl in this." Is that silly? I don't think so. At any rate, I hope you are not stinting on your wardrobe. I want you to look lovely and beautiful at all times. Your picture of Jeff in his bath is priceless. Talking of pictures, Ralph showed some pictures of Helen in color and some in black and white. The contrast was amazing. So I suggest that, if in the future you can get any color film, use it. And don't stint on pictures. Take as many as you can. Next to a letter they are all what we all want most out here.*

Lester found that he did not need much money. He therefore decreased-his allotment while increasing Shirley's, reminding her that this was intended for her to buy herself a coat.

> *February 15, 1945*
> *. . .While I am rambling like this I might as well mention two things that I've skipped: (a) the new executive officer's memorandum which is the laugh of the ship, "Sleeping in the nude is prohibited because it is unsanitary, indecent and something else." I will not confess the fact we in our room (all of us sleep in that awful nudity) look indecent, but he is going to have a hard time convincing us that the indecency is worth giving up comfort for. The other matter is financial. One of my patients this afternoon was the paymaster. After I worked on him I returned to his office with him to check over my pay account. I decided that I am drawing more money than I need out here. I have therefore made out the following allotments: (a) I increased the $37.50 allotment to $75.00; (b) I increased the $18.50 allotment to $37.50. These changes will take effect about May (it takes that long for them to be put through). You understand that the $18.50 bonds earlier (and the $37.50 bonds of the future) are earmarked for the stone martin jacket for you. They are to be considered as saved from my personal allowance. I had considered saving for one of the ruby-and-diamond wedding bands for you, but one thing at a time, and I want you to have the coat first, because I promised it to you and I mean to see that you have it. Saving this money and earmarking it now for future use is the ideal way to make that promise good. You don't need a coat now anyhow with your fur jacket and coat, and by the time you are ready for it the amount of money we have put aside for it should buy a beautiful garment, and perhaps the proper accessories, too. I think it is absurd to buy little. What we save now will undoubtedly buy much more for us at a later date. That will be true even if there is a period of prosperity rather than a slump after the war.*

It seems that the Dental Society still expected its annual dues, even from men in uniform. Also, Lester was bemused by a bill issue about a book.

September 18, 1945

I am enclosing the bill for my dues at the Second District Dental Society. Would you please write them a check for $6.00 and mail it to them? The third enclosure is really funny. It is the bill, and the letter, from the yearbook publishers. Last year at Beeville, I ordered a Yearbook of Dentistry, which I received and paid for. This year, while we were at Leyte, I received a copy that I hadn't ordered. I thought it was a courtesy they extended to men in service, and read the book. Later on, I kept receiving bills, all kinds of bills. No matter what mail I didn't get, I continued to receive their dunning letters. Of course I got mad, and after a while I didn't open up any of them. I got the last one at Eniwetok. I just opened it tonight to find the enclosed letter, which is explanatory. It's too damned much trouble to wrap the book and send it back. As a matter of fact, I don't think I am obligated to do so, and I am tempted to just forget the whole thing, because they did get me mad with their "please remit" letters. You read their letter and, if you want to, send them a check for three dollars with a note to send no more books unless ordered. I believe they've spent over three dollars in time and trouble, and postage. They've probably learned their lesson. Dad will like the story I think.

The following letters are from Shirley, from her perspective. The first two are early, pre-separation letters, from when they were both working in camp but Lester became ill and was sent to a hospital in New York City, leaving Shirley behind to write to him.

August 1943

. . . I packed your trunk, and it's going off this morning. I think one of your bathing suits is missing. How many did you have? Tell me also how many instruments you left at the clinic so that I can check them. I'm enclosing a $25 check which I can't get cashed here as it needs your endorsement. Sign it, dear, and cash it in the city. Daddy is sending me up $7, which I need until I can get the check money.

. . . I gave the nurses $5. The canteen bill was close to $9, so I'm pretty short on cash. I haven't enough to pay the waiters as yet, until I get the check from Daddy.

August 1943

. . . I have followed all your instructions. The trunk was sent off yesterday, I got the instruments from Dr. Stitch, and I have collected your belongings from the four corners of your bunk. Joe Palonni helped me—he sleeps there now. I have withdrawn all your salary, with no objections. In fact I have been a very good girl and done all you told me to do, even before you told me. Your precious electric razor is quite safe in your trunk and so are your navy papers. By the way, I put the proper heading on your assignment which was due in August and sent it off.

The only thing that presents difficulty is trying to get your tips. It is virtually impossible for me to stay near your children as they reach the station, and I have to stay with my kids. But I promise you, I'll try.

. . . Daddy sent me up an $8 money order, which I shall cash in the guest house and use to pay the waiters. That will leave me a dollar and change with which to come home, which will be more than enough. Daddy said in the accompanying letter that he was sending me a $10 money order, but instead I received an $8 money order. I can't understand it.

This is the origin of the rug issue and who wanted to buy it.

October 9, 1943

. . . Marilyn and Gabe were here all night, so I had a very nice time. Marilyn and Gabe both kissed me and called me "darling." They're spending over $1,200 to furnish their room and a half. They'd like to know if we'd consider selling them our rug, as they can't get any all-wool ones, and as the size and the color are what they need. I told them I'd ask you, and if it is O.K., then for how much should we sell it? Answer me on this, soon.

October 12, 1943

. . . Honey, is that money dad sent you enough, or do you need more? And how are your chances for a 15-day furlough or for a plane ride?

. . . Dad is giving me money to buy clothes with. Even he said I needed some. So I guess I'll buy a few.

That rug just kept popping up.

October 13, 1943
...You know, honey, I asked you about selling the rug to Mar-
ilyn, and then said not to because your mother is using it in the
dining room. Well, last night, they told me to sell it if I possibly
can, as it's only a nuisance to them. What do you think? Marilyn
would love to have it. But do you think we ought to sell it, or not?
And how much do you think I ought to ask for it?

And the rug does not go away.

October 15, 1943
...As to the rug, I wouldn't sell it for what we paid for it, but
less. After all, it's spotted and worn, and I'm not out to make a
profit on them. With the mat, we paid $81.

October 18, 1943
...As to the rug, I don't know whether I want to sell it or not.
But I definitely won't charge them $80; after all, it's worn and
spotted. Also, we may need it after the war ourselves. What do you
suggest?
As to Raimey, they told you they'd fix the car free of charge, so
why are you paying at all?
... Mother would like to get a washing machine through the
navy. How can we go about it? I'd like to get the same kind that
Mrs. Levin has. Also, Marilyn needs an iron, and I guess I can get
her one through the navy also. After all, if they don't have one,
who does?

October 24, 1943
...We stopped off and sent you a $100 by Western Union.
This hundred, the fifty we sent you, and a hundred that Daddy is
giving me for clothes, is to be a gift to us. But no more after that.
This hundred we sent you is for bills, for coming home, and for our
allowance in the city, and for return tickets and expenses home. I
hope it'll be enough. How about our rent for this month, though?

I only hope you get my allotment check before you leave, so that we'll have enough. How in the world did our rent check bounce? I feel terrible about it. How did you pay last month's rent, then— out of the fifty I sent you? If so, you'd probably have had no money to come home with and pay your bills. That's why I borrowed another $100. I'm really worried about it. But that's enough of that.

. . . I guess I'll go to the doctor this week. I have to pay him out of the $100 I have for clothes, and also use it for my allowance, and for sending the salamis and lipsticks back home, so I guess there won't be many clothes. But I really don't care, darling. I know we're in a tight spot for money right now, and I don't want to ask Daddy for more. After all, he's already given me $250 as a gift.

October 13, 1944

. . . Do you remember the hurricane your folks had in the Bronx, in which our couch got water stained? Well, we're collecting very nicely from it. Dad got $385 for the damages. I'm going to give your folks $100 (for they weren't covered with their policy by storm insurance, and a few of their things got water stained. I haven't told them as yet—let it be a nice surprise to them. With the $285 I'll get, I'll pay dad the remaining $200 we owe him, and pay the uniform debt of $80, and then we shall be free and clear of all debts. Isn't that a wonderful feeling? (I'd like a nice little hurricane like that, once a week.) Trust Dad to have us covered in any emergency. No one thinks of taking out storm insurance until they actually get struck by one.

Darling, did you collect your travel money yet? How are you set for money—do you need any? Have you cashed any more checks?

November 16, 1944
Sweetheart,

Now I, too, can strut my stuff. I bought me an officer's-style coat, but, ahem, it has a little more to it than the usual men's coats.

Mother and Dad took me tonight to get a coat on Belmont Ave. (the Pitkin Ave. district). And there I saw the same coat I admired so much in Russek's (for $200) for $44 without the fur. It *is gold, and I am having the caracul fur that mother has made into a collar and buttons. Quite chi-chi, but I had better not get stout, for you can only get away with that style when you're thin! They'll give me material, and I'll have a hat made up to match. It's no use my shopping in department stores in wartime, for I simply can't spend the prices they ask, and you know how I instinctively like the expensive ones. The only thing to do is to duplicate their models, which I have done the same way I copied my winter furred suit.*

Well, baby, that's enough of clothes for the moment.

January 12, 1945

. . . However, I did manage to send off the check for your life insurance policy. I now pay it once a year ($20.61), as Daddy informed me it's a couple of dollars cheaper that way. Also, I sent a revised ownership blank to the Sugar's in Corpus Christi as to who owns Skipper. It seems we made a mistake, and said we both own him, whereas only you do. So the American Kennel Association wants the correct ownership listed before they will recognize Skipper's puppies as being legitimate! So I signed for you (by my power of attorney) and sent the corrected slip on to them. Did you know that Skipper's wife gave birth to 6 beautiful blonds—3 males, and 3 females. Our little dog does all right for himself. Also I wrote dad a check for $112.50, the amount I am now saving each month. That buys $150 worth of bonds adding to your $75 bonds, makes our monthly bond allotment quite impressive. We now have saved so far $1,625 worth of bonds since you're in the navy. At this rate, we'll have about $4,000 by next year in this time. Filthy rich, ain't we? It doesn't leave me with too much money each month, but I get by, and at least I know we are saving a nice amount.

April 10, 1945

. . . And speaking of vacations, I decided to bank that $79 travel check you sent me, as a basis for the vacation we'll take when you come home. And we'll need plenty. Isn't that a good idea to build up a fund for it? It will be a separate savings account, in the Washington Avenue Bank. All I keep in the Franklin Ave. Bank is enough

money for my living expenses. The rest of my allotment goes into bonds each month— for Dad tells me you can cash a bond very easily. But you're not tempted to as much as if it were plain cash. I give him a $93.75 check each month, which buys me $125 worth of bonds. That leaves me just enough to live on for Jeff and me. Added to your bonds, we have about $2,200 worth (face value) saved since you've started your allotment in the navy. Now I'm first beginning to realize how long it takes to save thousands.

Shirley loved Lester's attempt to buy shoes for her, and she told him what she spent her birthday money on—sexy black lingerie.

May 1, 1945

. . . Now, onto the other events of the day: I received a letter from you dated the 26th of April. I was hysterical when I heard that you bought me a pair of shoes. It was so unexpected but such welcome news to me. I was wondering where I could ever manage to find a pair of brown-and-white spectator shoes. And so I am very grateful to you for thinking of it. However darling, I'm sorry to tell you that my shoe width is B, and my correct size is 6½ B (my foot grew half a size since I had the baby). However, if you aren't allowed to exchange it, send it on anyway, as Vivian said she'd gladly buy it from me, as that is her size. If they do allow you to bring it back, then do get me a 6½ B. I hate to be such a bother to you. Also darling, Elaine and I use a size 16 blouse, although the 14 is perfect for Roz. If this is too much of a nuisance to you, or you can't do it, don't worry about it. We'll make it do. Poor Les, our personal shopper, and so far away. I do love you for your thought-fulness in selecting those just-right gifts. We have a complete edition of Shakespeare at home. Are the stores there nice? What do you think of the place altogether? Is it all it's supposed to be? Don't miss the big hotel there which is world-famous for its beauty. Darling, can I compete with the Hula girls?

I told you what it was I bought for my birthday with the money you sent me, but I guess you didn't get it as yet. I bought what I've always yearned to have, a luxury but so "warming to the cockles of my heart," a complete set of black lingerie—brassiere, girdle, slip, and panties. They really are necessary though, for my summer black sheers, and for a low-décolleté dress I recently bought. I love them, and I know you will, too! It's something we'll both get pleasure out of, so it was money well spent.

Shirley, even as late as November 1945, had no idea that Lester would soon be home, and discussed making banking arrangements for the future as though their separation would continue.

November 7, 1945

. . . I finally received my allotment check this morning, with a note to the effect that it will be mailed on the fifth of each month from now on. It came just in the nick of time, for I was practically down to my last dollar. I've been living on very little money for these months, as I've been paying Dad back at the rate of $150 a month, which leaves me barely enough. Tonight I gave him a check for another payment, which now leaves us but $300 to pay. It's far better that way.

18

SO MUCH IN LOVE

T IS FAR FROM surprising that couples, especially the young and newly married, would miss each other constantly when separated by war. Yet in reading someone else's intimate letters, there is still something surprisingly personal about the expression of raw emotion, as if one is eavesdropping on a very private conversation. The feelings of loss and loneliness, sadness and yearning, come through very clearly.

Lester made his love for Shirley palpable and often painful, so that the reader, seventy years later, is there with him, in his mind, his heart and his dreams. His feelings rise off the page eloquently and convincingly, still meaningful so many decades later.

Les and Shirley loved and missed each other. The mere fact of the almost-daily letter itself testifies to that, but the descriptions of Lester's soaring and crashing emotions, his depictions of physical loneliness and emptiness, add depth and breadth to that basic awareness. A few of the letters could even be described as love letters pure and simple, since he spoke directly to her of his love, adding nothing else. More often, there was a sudden, startling paragraph, a switch in topic from something ordinary to a long, heart-rending prayer for her presence. At times, he wrote about her absence from his bed, his desire to hold her, or a dream he had of her, only to awake to reality. Once he had vented, he would return to more routine topics, or would take leave of her at that point in an emotional farewell.

Shirley's writing style was not as poetic or literary. It is more straightforward, yet clear and forceful. She, too, misses her other half and often needed to give voice to her loneliness. She may summon memories from their shared past or tell him about her eagerness for his return, but her dominant theme was her sense of loss. She was only twenty-one years old but had already experienced great love, marriage, pregnancy, birth, and the enforced separation from her beloved. These were deep, roiling emotions that she had to express, despite her pledge not to unduly upset Lester by writing to him of her sadness. Small wonder that she often could no longer relate well to her single friends.

In hindsight, the separation was sixteen months long, with one short reunion, although they had no idea how long it would be last at the time. How they would have coped with an even longer separation is hard to imagine.

Even in Texas, and only apart for a few weeks, Lester cannot help but miss Shirley.

> *October 10, 1943*
> *...And that, my darling love, brings the narration of events to date. But my sweetheart, no words can tell you . . . each day that passes is significant only because it brings nearer the time we two will be together again. So long for today, my sweet.*

> *October 25, 1943*
> *...As always, I'm too nervous and jumpy to sleep. But I've got to get to bed early tonight so I came home. . . I certainly need to catch up on sleep. I miss you so much, darling. I'll stalk up and down in impotent rage trying to get close to you. Hold me in your thoughts till I can hold you in my arms.*

> *August 17, 1944*
> *. . . I miss you terribly at all times. I needn't tell you how much. You know from your own experience that it can't be done; and from your own experience you know how much I miss you. All that I do is try to keep busy all day and at night I try to prevent my thoughts of you from giving me the miseries.*

This is a letter completely devoted to loving and missing Shirley.

August, 1944

(1100 Sunday night)

My Darling Wife,

And I mean my darling wife. My roommate is reading right now, so I am ready to sit up for a few minutes and write to you to tell you how much I love you, and how much you mean to me.

I know that I've told you this a thousand or more times, but it bears repetition. I love you, my darling, with all my heart and with all my soul and with all my might. As I sit here typing this, I have both your pictures in front of me, and my heart goes out to you in the deepest of passion, and I could die of unrequited love because you are not here with me.

All day I've missed you. I've tried to fill in the void. I've played checkers, bowled, gone to the movies, drunk beer with the fellows, laughed and kidded (as best as I could), but all the time there was that great emptiness which nothing but the feel of you in my arms, and pressed close to me can fill. I miss the warmth of your lips against mine, the nearness of you to me in every way. I am frightfully and desperately lonely for you . . . and I am glad; glad because I know you miss me as greatly as I do you; and glad in the anticipation of our reunion.

Oh, darling, how lucky we are to love one another. Every day (or almost every day) I meet people who are married and not in love, and what does life hold for them. Nothing. But for you and I my sweetest darling, life holds everything. Why, only the prospect of being together with you makes it worthwhile.

I don't apologize for being passionate. I feel passionate. If I had you with me now I would love you passionately (as I could love only you amongst all the women in the world, and as you could love only me). All day long I've sat thinking of you. I tried to call you this evening, but there was too long a delay so I sit down to you and send myself to you as best I can via a typewriter.

I won't write this way again soon, my life, my excuse for living, but this once I had to let all the love I feel for you pour out unstinted.

I love you. You are my "raison d'être." Without you, life is mean-

ingless; with you it is a perfect sonnet, a fine-cut gem, a beautifully conceived symphony. Or to descend to the other end of the ladder of words, I was no damned good before I met you. And life is only worthwhile while I am with you. Away from you I am as nothing. How well this has been shown in the last month.

I could rave more. Indeed, darling, that is what I want to do. To sit here and look at your picture, and drink in your beauty of soul and body, and revel in the thought that as I love you so do you love me; but rapt as I am in thoughts of you, the wishes of three roommates must be respected, and they want to sleep. So, goodnight, my dearest love, sleep well, and think of me, please, each night, before falling to sleep, as I do of thee.

This letter mentions the derivation of Shirley's nickname.

September 3, 1944
My Sweetest Churl,

I have to smile when I address you like that, smile tenderly and reminiscently, for each time I call you "Churl" there is immediately projected onto my mind the picture of an early July evening, you and me walking, and me calling you Churl because . . . it is exactly what you are not (if you can follow the reasoning involved), and then you laugh and say, "Well, then I'll call you 'sucker.'" And then we both laugh. Tell me, my sweetheart, when did we not laugh during those happy months? That little vignette is only one of scores which keep recurring in memory. Every phrase, gesture, or word brings back another. I swear we have no kick coming. We have had in our few short years together more pure unalloyed happiness than most other people have in ten lifetimes. . .and we will have more, much more. We will have happiness for ourselves and now happiness for Jeff, too.

You know, my darling, how, every once in a while when one gets blue, one starts bitching at the deal he has gotten out of life. I used to be that way, and of late again I find that occasionally I complain, but honestly, darling, I can't really complain. I have had so much happiness with you that nothing else really matters. God moved in his subtle way, indiscernible to us poor mortals, to bring you close to me and to make the most perfect wife in this or any other world.

Even this while I was complaining most vociferously about this or that I was being moved slowly and imperceptibly to union with you. That's a happy thought. I've dwelt on it often, especially of late when we are forced apart as we are, I've tended to feel bitter and blue; but when I do think again of the magic way we two were brought together, and realize that there will in the end be compensations, then, while I must admit I cannot feel happy about being away from you, at least I feel better than before.

September 19, 1944
    . . .Well, that is all for tonight. Goodnight, my darling, and happy dreams. Kiss my son for me, and tell him his pop misses him. Then go look into the mirror and project my thoughts into your mind so that you can know how much I miss you. Then think of me, and reminisce about the delicious moments in darkness in bed, and feel as I do, lonesome but happy. Goodnight, my sweetest love, sleep well, aurora, dream pleasantly, curly bumps. I love you so.

October 4, 1944
    . . . I helped him unpack, and now here I am. And there you are right above me, so radiantly beautiful in your wedding finery. How nice it is to love and be loved, beloved. Can you ever forget the thrill of that night of nights? The deliriously delicious conscious unconsciousness of all else but you? How my heart and arms yearned for you. How I sensed a kindred emotion in you (you didn't even try a little to hide it). Our hearts dwelt in our eyes. And no part of that has changed. It is only that, looking again at your slim, girlish beauty, I recapture just a shade more vividly the spirit of that time. I can do no more but tell you again I love you, and to repeat it with the same monotonous but strengthening regularity. And you likewise. And so, my beloved, good night for now. Sleep well, kiss and love Jeff for me—after all, is he not the tangible living proof of our love? Before he came, we could only tell each other of our love for each other and seek its elusiveness in each other's arms; now we have it personified, and we can actually take our love in our hands and kiss it, and

caress it and fondle it. Oh, lucky we are, and how much more so we will be when soon we will be together again. So good night, my love.

A little late-night free association.

November 22, 1944
Churl Darling,
    It is late, and I am slightly pooped, having just finished a long twelve-hour day. The clocks are going to undergo an adjustment, robbing us of an extra hour of sleep, of which already we have about two hours too little. So tonight I shan't go into detail about the day's activities. I should go right up to my little trundle bed and pillow my head on the shoulder of Morpheus, but I cannot do so without my nightly communication to you. I want to tell you again how much I love you and adore you and miss you. I love you more than that. I love you more than Coke after a hot airless G.Q. (how much that is you will never, Thank God, know). I love you more than liberty after a week in port. I love you more than beer in a beerless tropical paradise. I love you more than you, and I love you more than me. I just love you with all my heart, and with all my soul, and with all my might, and more besides that. My love for you transcends reason. And why not? How can any thing infinite be based securely upon the finite? In short, my darling wife, I love you . . . and that is all. And what makes it so perfect is that you love me as I love you. And on this note, my sweetest darling, I'll give you a fond kiss goodnight, and with a last look at your picture go to sleep. Good-night, my love, my own, my sweetheart. God bless you and keep you.
                                                              Love,
                                                              Les

On their third anniversary.

December 25, 1944
CHURL DARLING,
    I capitalized purposely this time as just another way to indicate

the increased significance of this day and the day that has gone before. Indeed it was so close to the 25th when the ceremony was performed that we are quite justified in celebrating both days as our anniversary, and surely such an important event deserves two days of celebration. Very proudly, and very joyously, then, with all the love I possess, a happy anniversary to you, my darling, and thank you again for being you. And thank God for making you you, and then making you mine.

It is no news to you to learn of how much I think of you all the time, nor is it a surprise that as our anniversary drew near I should think of you and me and Jeff even more. Even more than before are such thoughts ever with me, more than before because now they are not so far in my subconscious mind. Most particularly, of course, do I indulge in these thoughts in the time I lie abed immediately before going to sleep or getting out in the morning. Then indeed do the nebulous thoughts and phantasmagoric pictures take possession of me. I think of us as we were at the beginning, at the various times we were with each other and dream of the future for the three of us. I project impossible courses for the ship so that, in the words of Dr. Dickey, "I shall have plenty of liberty in Brooklyn." I have pictured my homecoming a million different times, in a million different ways. Of one thing I am sure; this separation is enough to last us the rest of our lives. Never again shall I leave you, for so much as a day.

Lester and Gertrude Stein.

February 10, 1945
. . . Darling, they've made me darken ship (that means close all outside ports and vents), and it grows stifling hot in here. Will you excuse me for tonight? There is really nothing left to say anyway, that wouldn't require more detail or elaboration than there is paper in the world. I love you. That is the beginning, the ending, and middle of everything. Nothing else matters besides that. Thank God you understand that because I could never explain it myself, since myself, I do not understand it in a comprehensible way, al-

though I do understand it. I start to sound like Gertrude Stein. Goodnight sweetheart.

> *Love,*
> *Les*

May 8, 1945

. . . Do you know that you go to bed with me every night? Well, your pictures do, anyhow. I have your album at the side of my bed, and always thumb through it before turning out the lights. Good night, sweetheart.

Lester waxes poetic.

May 25, 1945
Churl Darling,

How much affection I lavish into that salutation. As I write it, there races through my mind a multitude of endearments, in the Joycean style: Churl sweetheart, Shirley love, my darling. How the name of a moment has held on through the years, you are first my sweet Churl, and then my darling Shirley, and always my own loved wife. I love you so, darling. You are so much of my life. How can I tell you in awkward phrases? Would I even try if I knew not in advance that you know before I speak, that our love brings a knowledge above and beyond words. So I murmur, Churl darling, Churl sweetheart, I love you, I love you, I love you, ad infinitum. And to you these words, even these formless, unaspirated, written characters, must serve as a gesture, as a bridge between the two of us. And it does. Is there not something truly immortal in this, something above and beyond the two of us; perhaps something of which the fused duo of us is a small part of? I think it must be so.

Lester interweaves being torn from Shirley and his daily life in the war.

June 3, 1945
Churl Darling,

It is harder for me to write "June" at the top of the letter than any other month for it brings home hard the fact that next month is July and it will be a year that we have been apart. It has been such a long, empty, year for me. I know that it has been a hard lonesome year for you too, but it has been mitigated somewhat by Jeff, I'm sure. I resent the loss of this year so much. It has robbed me of the pleasure of watching our son grow, and taken you away from me. In the place of those two things (to me the only worthwhile things life has to offer), I have had the "excitement" of being at war. What a dull prosaic business this business of war really is. Hot, sweaty, monotonous. Occasional moments of danger, and even during those being tucked away somewhere, or so busy at your job, that you are not conscious of the peril until it has passed. Well, there is one consolation, even if it is a negative one, at being apart so long; we are definitely on the homeward stretch now. The first half, at least, is definitely behind and each day now is one that brings us closer together. God speed the day.

Lester is even grateful to Shirley's parents.

July 6, 1945
. . . . I love you so, darling. And I'm so happy in loving you. I wish I could manage somehow to let you know how much just thinking about you makes me a happy and better person. Thanks again, darling, for being you (and thank your mom and pop for me for their part in making you you). That's the most important thing I have to tell you today (or any other day for that matter). And with that I'll say goodnight for tonight my sweetheart.

Lester thinks back over Shirley's months of pregnancy, as Jeffrey's first birthday approaches.

July 26, 1945
Churl Darling,
Hello, Mom. I can't help thinking of how last year about now, the only thing you knew about motherhood was that you had a big belly (and on you it looked good . . . believe me). We did have fun while you were pregnant, didn't we (except of course for these two uncomfortable times you were ill); but on the whole it was a damn

*nice nine months. It had an element of surprise in it from the be-
ginning when you told me you were pregnant. Poor Jeff, what a
rough time he had of it the first three months of his life. Why, it
proves that he must be a rough, tough, tenacious kid (like his old
lady). And you were so wonderful and so beautiful. I can't understand it, sweetheart. Each moment it has seemed as if I loved you
as much as a human possibly could without busting, and yet as each
interval passed by I realized that I loved you even more. I'm still
not used to it. I suppose I never will be. That is what I meant from
the beginning, and mean now when I say, "Even more than that! So
again, and again, I love you darling, even more than that.*

Lester had been on duty for over a year and was impatient for it to end.

*September 19, 1945
       ...Damn but I'm anxious to get out. There are so many things
I want to do with you, and talk with you about. A letter is a horrible second best for being with a person, isn't it, darling? Of
course your letters are heaven to me. I mean it. I get so much
pleasure from them, and they stand rereading so well. I wish that
I could write a letter half as good, so that I could carry myself to
you, as well as you carry yourself to me in your letters. I try, but
I know I fail miserably.*

Shirley was much more direct in her language, yet already misses Lester
after just a few days apart due to his illness while at camp.

*August, 1943
       ...Do I really mean that to you? You'll turn my head if you
continue to tell me of what's in your heart. I really do love to know
all of it.
       Seriously, I miss you as I never thought it possible to miss
anyone. The letters are but a substitute, but I'm so grateful to
them—for a few minutes, anyway, I almost forget that you aren't
with me.*

A view into what war wives must have experienced.

October 20, 1943

. . .You know, when the operator called the first time from Texas, and said she'd call back later, as you had stepped out for a minute, I developed a beautiful case of first-class jitters until I actually spoke to you. I thought you were calling to tell me that you had received orders, and was I frantic.

Shirley, as well as Lester, kept remembering their shared past.

October 26, 1943

. . . Darling, last night I laid awake for a long time. Scenes of my meeting you, and our subsequent courtship and marriage flashed before me so completely and wondrously. Sweetheart, I am indeed blessed to have known and loved you. Accept this as a declaration of my love for you, and for my complete happiness in my two years of my married life.

I'll have to close now, darling, as we must leave. Come home quickly and safely, and never be away from me anymore. I need you too much.

November 18, 1944

. . . I came back alone to Brooklyn and got in the house about 2:00 a.m. Sweetheart darling, how I missed you. Broadway, the theater, all the glitter and excitement of New York paled into obscurity besides the overwhelming feeling of desolation I experienced on the subway back to Brooklyn as I watched the other couples. I love you so, and need you at all times. All that fills my mind is thoughts of you and hopes of your coming home soon. I pray God this war is soon over and we are together again—I miss you terribly. I promise you, I'll never let you out of my arms, once you come home to them again.

Shirley was writing to observe the five-month mark of their separation. In this letter she freely discusses with Lester that which she never discussed in later years—her pain upon his leaving for the war.

January 13, 1945

Darling,

It's incredible, but I just realized that today makes 5 months ex-

actly since I said good-bye to you at La Guardia Airport. In one way, it seems as if every day has 48 hours and the months seem like centuries, and yet (Thank the Lord), the time in retrospect seems to have flown. Five months, and I always thought I couldn't do without you near me for 5 days. It's amazing how much we can take when we have to. But what a shameful waste of months. There have been actual moments of real pain when I long for you and want you near me, and so many times when I wish you could be here to see one of the many adorable things our son has done. Our first baby—he is more than we ever dreamed of, in reality a love child born out of our great love for each other. Mother always says, "Tell me, what do you have to do to make a baby like this?" But he is our secret formula, isn't he? Do you remember that night when he was most probably conceived—something marvelous had to be the result of our love that night!

Well, darling, I don't mean to sound too reminiscent or stray from the subject, but this day marking 5 months only makes me more poignantly aware of how incomplete I am without you. I pray God you come home to me soon—safe and well. You are my love; nothing else will ever come near to taking the place you have in my heart. You know that, don't you? I love Jeff, really adore him, so much that I am amazed sometimes how quickly the intensity of that love grew. But he is so cherished, not only for himself, but because he is part of you. He looks and acts exactly like you, but so exactly, it's almost ludicrous at times. And not only is he a good-looking baby, but he is very mentally alert and full of life. I'm very happy with my family; and very lucky to be so blessed.

Darling, now that 5 months have passed I can write of that night, August 13, without too much pain. I felt so hopelessly and tragically alone; the misery of that night, I hope is never to be repeated. I tried not to break down in front of you, but when I saw you kiss Jeff goodbye, I couldn't control myself any longer. I'm sorry I behaved like such a coward— it only made it harder for you. The sight of your plane taking you off and carrying you away from me will remain with me forever. I don't usually allow myself to dwell like this on our separation, in time I've achieved some measure of stoicism, but on special dates like this, the dam bursts.

Forgive me, Les, I don't mean to make you unhappy —it's just a letter of memories and regrets for this damn war. I am calm and content most of the time. Thank God for the baby. He doesn't leave me much time to think, which is a good idea. But what an uninviting thing is an empty bed at night. I swear I'll even follow you into the bathroom when you get home. I'll never let you away for a moment, until finally you yell for mercy and privacy and peace.

Shirley is unhappy whether she stays in or goes out. She cannot escape her loneliness.

February 4, 1945
   ... Nora, our colored maid, stays in with Jeff once a month on a Saturday nite, thus letting me go out big-timing. (I don't know why, but Saturday is a particularly miserable day to get through, and I do feel better if I can go out and forget for a little while. But then I usually come home feeling worse than ever, for it really strikes hard to see other couples. It is better to stay at home. (I think, when you come home, I won't let you get out of the house. We won't see anyone, just talk, and love, and laugh, and dance all by ourselves. We always did have the best times all by ourselves.)

Shirley finally shows her long-hidden emotions to a friend. Later, she wears her birthday gift to bed, on Lester's birthday.

April 7, 1945
Les Dearest,
   Happy Birthday, my darling. Many, many happy returns. My only wish and prayer—next year we shall be together again. This last year is a wasted page in our lives, but all the others should be so much more the beautiful. We have so much on which to build our happiness; you are the total answer to mine. We're a swell family, darling, God willing, we'll be together for many more birthdays.
   Gert Ginsberg was over today, and for this evening. I guess the day got me a little. I talked and talked of how wonderful you are, and shed a few tears on her sympathetic shoulder. She, game soul, joined me in the deluge. All in all, we had a very satisfying system.

Shirley celebrates having met Lester on this date four years ago.

July 13, 1945
Darling,

Happy anniversary, sweetheart. Do you remember? Four years ago today, I met you. Hallelujah. Therefore let me dedicate this as a love letter to you. For I do love you, so very much. Thank you for making these past four years so very beautiful. We have a wonderful marriage, and now we're a wonderfully complete family, you, Jeff, and I.

You've been so sweet and thoughtful, and so patient with me for all the mistakes I may have made. I'm a lucky girl, Les—all because of you. So thank you, dear, for everything. Praise be to Stevensville, and let's drink a toast to that glass of milk (by the way, I can't remember whether or not I actually ever did drink that down). To me, our meeting is one great big, lucky miracle. If I've made you as happy as I've been, that's all the reward I'll ever want. And because of us, something as adorable as Jeff has been created. It's a little awe-inspiring to think that we're responsible for this precious life. So God bless you, darling, and keep you safe. I'll love you forever, and even more than that.

Churl

In the summer of 1945, the *Oxford* came to the West Coast for repair and refitting, allowing Lester and Shirley a brief reunion in San Francisco.

August 29, 1945

Darling, it's getting pretty late and your lonesome wife is both hot and tired. My single cot looks repulsive somehow, when the memory of you lying next to me always projects itself, especially when I'm lying awake late at night. Our two weeks were so perfect. How in the world did I ever observe the social amenities enough so that I was able to walk with you with decorum suitable to a lady. I love you at all times as your wife, and even more than that. Goodnight, darling.

Churl

Shirley recognized Lester's language skills and wished that she had similar abilities so that she could more artfully express her love to him.

October 5, 1945

. . . I've read and reread your letters today at least a hundred times. The baby and the innumerable duties have been grossly neglected. There is one letter that I especially cherish, the one in which you tell me of your love for me. Sweetheart, I wish that I were gifted enough to answer you and tell you how completely you are my life. But as you concluded, "I love you" seems to convey all that I could say. When you get home, I'll attempt to show you just how much I mean those three little words. Thank you for everything you said, darling. I really feel humble to know that I have given you this happiness, as you have given me mine. I love you, Les—I love you all that is humanly possible, and even more than that. Yes, I thank God for allowing us to meet and love and create our family the way we have. We have so very much to be grateful for.

> *Love,*
> *Churl*

October 19, 1945

. . . I'm lonely for you, darling. I admit it unhesitatingly. I'm in love with you, so very much. These few months that remain until you return are barriers that must be passed somehow. The time goes by so very slowly.

Goodnight, my love. God bless you, and keep you well. Letters are so inadequate to convey all that I want to say to you; all that you mean to me. I'm sick and tired of being wedded to a fountain pen, and being married to a sheet of stationary. However, as a substitution, they serve to bring us together over the miles that separate us tonight. I feel so very close to you, as I write; a mood of tranquility settles over me.

This is what it comes down to—a man and a woman, trying to lock out the world.

October 28, 1945

. . . Darling, there is nothing more to say about today. What could there be? The same truth: I love you, so very much. Since I received your letter yesterday, I'm a far better, and an entirely different person. Darling, please, please be home by two months from now. I think I can exist for the 61 more days without you, but no longer. What a hell of a war to fight for—trouble in South America, and now Chinese Civil War. Can we say that it will ever end? I don't give a damn about the world anymore. I want you home — for you are my world.

Love
Churl

19

THE PIN-UP GIRL

BETTY GRABLE WAS THE famous one, the one whose likeness so many soldiers had pinned to their lockers. There were other glamorous stars as well that soldiers and sailors pined for. Pictures of those lovely ladies got many a lonely soldier through the long and dangerous months away from home.

There was none of this in Lester's cabin. He did not need it, not when he had his cherished photos of his wife. Hollywood sirens paled in comparison to her. And he was far from alone in this opinion. Since Lester hung her pictures in his cabin and in his office, in full view of the men, many got to see them and generally commented on them. Lester often reported to Shirley what those love-starved men had to say about her, not to make her feel egotistical but to tell her of his own pride in her. The photographs not only helped to assuage his loneliness but also gave him a chance to talk about her with his friends. It was a clever strategy.

> *October 18, 1943*
> *. . . I showed him our pictures and he was impressed by my wife, "Glamour Pants." He told me to be careful or he'd fall in love with you. And I wouldn't blame him in the slightest.*

> *September 13, 1944*
> *. . . I have your pictures on top of the instrument cabinet. Without exception, everyone coming in has gazed, and either whistled or*

thought of whistling at you. One said I must have talked mighty fast to get you, and I agreed without a moment's hesitation.

September 14, 1944

I wish you could stand here in the office, invisible, for a moment to see the reaction that your pictures produce on the men coming in and out. It varies from person to person, but the emotion is one of admiration, disguised to a greater or lesser extent. I, of course, swell with pride, but try to be very matter-of-fact about it.

October 20, 1944

. . . Incidentally, your pictures, both the large ones and those with Jeff, are still arousing tremendous exclamations on the part of visitors to my office. Indeed, things have reached such a stage that the different corpsmen are proudly bringing men in from the other departments to introduce them to the doctor's wife. I must admit that I thrive on such adulation.

November 10, 1944

. . . I want to tell you how much the pictures of you and the baby mean to me. I look at them every day, and they help to bring you nearer to me. You in your wedding gown with your gorgeous smile are by this time well known to all the corpsmen. Most of them by now call you by your first name. One of them comes around every morning and leans against the door, looking at your picture, which is on top of my instrument cabinet. When I look at him questioningly, he says, "Oh, I just came by to say good-morning to Shirley, Doctor." This afternoon, after inspection, Abe Lowman asked me, "Should I put Shirley back on top on the instrument cabinet, Doctor?" How do you like being a pin-up girl? I was washing up today when I looked in the mirror and was struck with an idea. I took out the album and checked on it. It is true. With more hair, closed cropped as it is now, I look more like Jeff than ever.

May 8, 1945

. . . As is my habit, I enjoyed my album of photos last night before turning in. Only now do I realize how wonderful this series of

pictures really is. How much Jeff has changed with each group of snapshots. It's marvelous, the exclamations of wonder and praise I get from everyone who sees your pictures and Jeff's. I have a lot of explaining to do about how I persuaded you to throw yourself away on me (something I'm not quite sure of yet).

September 3, 1945

. . . I forgot to tell you, baby. In the last three days, three different officers have stopped me in the passageway to tell me (entirely without prompting) how lovely they thought my wife was, and what a charming person she was. Of course I told them that they were greatly mistaken, but they didn't believe me. What's your opinion?

20

THE WAR AND ITS EFFECTS

HINDSIGHT IS A WONDERFUL thing. We view past events and wonder why the people who lived through them were not as wise as we are. In every biography, Abraham Lincoln continues to make the same mistake of attending Ford's Theatre that fateful night of his assassination.

The war was winding down. Shirley and Les wondered how it would end, and they hoped it would end soon given the nature of events overseas, but they couldn't be certain. Reading their letters, you want to call out and tell them to hold on, the end is near—but that is as impossible as warning Lincoln.

The great news of the day was not history to them, it was current events, and they had front row seats. Les and Shirley viewed most of what happened in the context of how it would affect their reunion. So they dwelled upon every bit of news that might hasten the war's end. Lester, especially, enjoyed the sweep of history as it unfolded before him, and frequently commented on it.

There were also logistical problems—he was both too close and too far away from events to truly understand them. He was living in real time, seeing events as they unfolded, lacking the perspective that time provides, and not always able to integrate them meaningfully. And he was at the same time too far removed geographically, aboard one ship in one spot in the vast Pacific, far from the battles in Europe and from most of those in the Pacific, and without the benefit of regular news while at sea. Added to this was the great uncertainty about what the enemy would actually do and about how events would play out and affect other aspects of the war.

Yet some of Les and Shirley's observations are well worth noting. For instance, anyone who has seen the movie *Patton* will recall the scene in which the general slapped a soldier for perceived cowardice. In their letters, that event is discussed in real time, just after it happened, and they debate its impact on other soldiers, and the judiciousness of Patton's behavior. Recurrent discussions also pepper the letters of when the war might end and how that might happen. Even after V-E Day and the surrender of Nazi Germany, the Pacific war dragged on, with Japan showing few signs of willingness to surrender, and since Lester was serving in the Pacific, this was more essential to their peace of mind. In fact, V-E Day received little mention in their correspondence. The death of Franklin Roosevelt, whom both had strongly supported, was written about in greater depth and with deeper feelings.

The next letter contains the first reference to the possible end of the war and the shift of attention to the Pacific front.

> *July 25, 1944*
> *...And the parting is made to seem shorter than I ever had dared hope by the rapidity with which events in Europe are moving. It begins to appear as though Germany may crack, after all, sooner than I had anticipated. That being the case, it will be to turn our undivided attention upon the Japs, this God-damned affair will soon be over.*

Here is the news of General Patton having slapped that soldier. One detects that Lester is not too pleased with the general's behavior.

> *August 22, 1944*
> *...Incidentally, isn't that European news wonderful? And tell me, are the NY papers playing General Patton as a great guy? They are out here, and I think that they are trying to cover over that face-slapping incident.*

Sometimes enthusiasm can lead to overly optimistic predictions. The European war dragged on for a lot longer than the four to six weeks that Lester had thought.

August 24, 1944

> *...I came back here to read the papers. The news is wonderful: Romania out altogether, and Bulgaria and Hungary on the way. I never believed it would go so fast. How long Germany can exist now is extremely problematical. I believe now that it is pessimistic to believe that the European war will not be over before Christmas. Indeed, it may well be over in four to six weeks. I shouldn't be at all surprised if that should prove to be the case. That being so, I cannot figure out the effect on the Japanese. The war in Europe would turn a terrific war potential into an actuality, so that it begins to look as if Japan will follow Germany soon. God grant that it be so.*

Not only did the naval troops actually listen to Tokyo Rose; at times she was their only source of news, and they had to factor in the evident bias in her reports.

January 14, 1945

> *...We have picked up Tokyo Rose and several other Japanese English broadcasts recently. She has a very pleasing voice and an effective delivery. Of course her version of the news is slightly colored (about 2 or 300% wrong), but of late it has been our only source. All I can say is that I hope she is as wrong about the European Situation as she has been about ours.*

More guessing follows about when the war in Europe will end, clearly months after Lester's initially over-enthusiastic estimate.

January 24, 1945

> *...We on this side of the ocean are listening to the European news with a great deal of interest, and there is much speculation as to the probable end of that conflict. I am starting to set it at a very early date. I don't believe it can last more than two months, but so as not to be disappointed I say surely it must be over in four.*

Lester and the crew of the Oxford heard about the Russian advance on Berlin, though they were unaware of the eventual outcome.

January 30, 1945

. . . The news from Europe daily hits a new peak. Today the Russians are only 90 miles from Berlin. It is like a crescendo with the audience breathlessly awaiting the finale, the collapse of Germany, and its aftermath, the surrender of Japan. May it be soon.

With the Russians continuing to close in on Berlin, the excitement about the war's possible end grew greater. Yet could the Nazis fight on even after that?

February 3, 1945

. . . Each day we are thrilling to the inexorable Russian advance on Berlin. At last the end seems to be in sight. It is conceivable that they can keep on fighting after the fall of Berlin, but it is a remote possibility that they could accomplish anything. This may yet be the last of the war. Please God.

The Battle of Iwo Jima, with its unimaginable gunfire, impressed Lester and brought the fear that the entire Pacific theatre could see action similar in nature. And everyone was daily waiting for the news from Germany.

March 11, 1945

Among my patients yesterday were a couple from a ship that had been up at Iwo Jima. They tell me that that was really a rough deal on the Marines, that the island was one gigantic fortified position. It must have been hell. How an area as small as that cannot only withstand the withering rain of bombs and shells that were poured into it over a period of time, but besides, come up and, in turn, heap upon the attackers a devastating return fire, is more than I can comprehend. I imagine that that will be the pattern of things to come. Small islands or areas will be extremely well prepared and soldierly. Larger areas, as Luzon for example, which it is impossible to fortify so extensively, will probably yield with less effort.

All of us look with bated breath to Europe. How much longer can those bastardly Germans hold out? Now that the Rhine has been breached at the Cologne bridge head it seems that they can, at best, have a short time left. The rolling plains that stretch to Berlin should offer ideal terrain for our tanks. I imagine that the Russians, at least, may make an effort to extend their flank in the south before going on to Berlin, to try to prevent any sizable retreat of the Nazi army to the mountains of Austria. There remains much fighting in store, and many lives to be lost before the finish can be written, but now I believe the end is definitely in sight. Please God let it be over soon so that we may be together again.

Lester mentions General Eisenhower's military surprise and then waxes patriotic about how victorious the Pacific forces will be with even a fraction of the arms that flowed to Europe.

April 1, 1945
. . . The news from Europe is truly amazing. I believe Eisenhower pulled the surprise of the war by forcing a crossing of the Rhine so soon after reaching it. It cannot be long now before that thing is wound up, and even before the definite termination of that affair they may start shifting men and materiel to this theatre. When that happens, Tojo may as well throw in the sponge. We have accomplished so much with comparatively so little here that, with a flow of arms and men even remotely approximating that which gets to Europe, it is hard to conceive how even the most fanatical of minds can conceive of a chance to stave off sure and horrible defeat.

The censorship that restricted all correspondence concerning battles deprived people on the home front of the information they most desired, but Lester was able to assure Shirley that he had come through a skirmish.

April 7, 1945
Churl Darling,
The censor has given us permission to write saying that we have been in a recent invasion, and that we are all right. I therefore take great pleasure in informing you that I took part in a recent invasion and that I am all right. See, I told you not to worry. Seriously though, honey, I wrote you a long letter about this last operation from my point of view. Unfortunately there are too many

details that are censorable, so I can't send it on, but at least with the first two sentences of this letter you can compose yourself for a while.

News of Roosevelt's death affected the men around the globe, who had all been fighting for their commander-in-chief.

> *April 14, 1945*
> *...P.S. I fail to mention Roosevelt's demise not for lack of interest, but because no words of mine can soften the tremendous tragedy of the sad event. He, like Lincoln, died when his services were most needed. God rest his soul, and God grant that Truman have some of the spark of genius that made the Great Man's work possible, so that he may carry it on and complete it in the same spirit as its originator intended.*

Have the Russians indeed entered Berlin, and what will the future reveal about the battles to come in the Pacific?

> *April 18, 1945*
> *...I heard from one of the enlisted men who had it from one of the radiomen, that today the Russians entered the outskirts of Berlin. That is good news indeed. The end of at least one war seems to be definitely in sight. About this one out here, the same big question in mind: Where next? And you should hear some of the speculative destinations announced with all seriousness by some of the officers and men. Some of them make me want to laugh. Others make me shudder.*

Mussolini's death, unlike Roosevelt's, seemed trivial to Lester, not fitting the crime.

> *April 29, 1945*
> *...While writing this, word has come over the radio that Mussolini has been killed. It is so anticlimatical [sic], and seems such a pale travesty of justice that the man should mercifully die, after all the unhappiness he has been responsible for.*

The end of the war in Europe brought no true celebration to the *Oxford*, for whose men the conflict would continue.

> *May 9, 1945*
>
> *. . . So peace in Europe has at last arrived. It will take a long time for us out here to realize how glad we actually feel about it. For the moment our joyfulness had the hollow ring of those who celebrate because they know they should. Thank God for it, anyway, and please God the Japs see the hopelessness of their position and succumb soon. I cannot help a mean thought. Aren't I just no damn good to say such things?*

Lester makes a prediction about the end of the Pacific war.

> *May 19, 1945*
>
> *. . .As I told you, darling, I have hopes of being home early. As a matter of fact I wouldn't be surprised if the war's end was what brought me home. It is not that I can't believe Japan cannot resist for three or four months, or even longer, but she stands to gain nothing by resistance, and an early capitulation might well serve her purpose. Now that Germany is out and she stands alone against the might of all of us, I believe that some face-saving cabinet changes will be made, and as easy a peace as possible be sought. God grant that it be soon.*

Lester's predictions turned pessimistic, however, just a week later.

> *May 26, 1945*
>
> *. . .According to all reports, the second guessers at home see war with Japan ending in a matter of three to six months. After jaunting around this Pacific for a while I am beginning to have some conception of what the distances involved really amount to and regretfully enough must say that such an estimate must be wistful thinking. It will take months merely to move the necessary men and material into position to start hostilities. After that,* quien sabe?

Does Japan surrender or not?

May 27, 1945

There is a growing opinion among the officers aboard that Japan may yet surrender (this group is divided about whether or not she will take terms or surrender unconditionally), and most of us are willing to be rather easy providing she does so. God grant that they prove right.

Japan is being pounded by U.S. bombs, which elates Lester, as it will end the war, yet his humanity extends empathy for the people being bombed.

July 17, 1945

…The news about the activities of the fleet and the B-29 raids on Japan is very interesting and encouraging. What a terrible experience it must be for those people. I am hoping now that the handwriting on the wall will be underlined by those 16-inch shells, and that the nation will sue for peace while there is something left of it. I think a month or so of such a pounding, day after day, may prove to be very salutatory on the Japanese thinking.

A couple of the ship's officers have bought Japanese officers' sabers as souvenirs, paying 100 and 125 dollars for them. They are really beautiful weapons. Supposedly they are very effective, too. Seeing them, I can understand some of the stories that have been told of their effectiveness.

The actual end of the war, V-J Day, was not mentioned in Lester's letters because he was not writing at the time. He and Shirley were together in San Francisco, their first reunion in over a year. We therefore have no written record of Lester's reactions to the use of atomic weapons on Hiroshima and Nagasaki. In later years, though, he did describe sailing into Japan in convoy, very slowly moving up the narrow channel set between two mountain ranges, and he was certain that, had the war continued, the fleet would have taken an immense pounding, with a huge loss of life, possibly his own. Therefore, he could not be neutral or philosophical on the very subject that historians, soldiers, and the average citizen have been debating ever since.

Those on the home front certainly received more frequent and more dependable news than those out on the Pacific, Shirley being no exception,

particularly as she lived in New York City and also because she was searching it out in hopes of the war ending and Lester therefore coming home.

January 15, 1945
 . . . *So many invasions on now. The Luzon invasion is like music
to my ears—another step towards ending this war.*

January 21, 1945
 . . . *I listened to the news while waiting for them, and that
cheered me up. What wonderful news, the Russians inside the Reich,
only 194 miles from Berlin, and the great news from the Philippines
so near to Manila.*

January 22, 1945
 . . . *Such wonderful, encouraging news—the Russians are today
within 6 hours by rail of Berlin, I'm beginning to hope once again.*

January 23, 1945
 . . . *The spectacular drive of the Russians on the European
front surely looks encouraging, and the closeness of the American
Forces to Manila is also a hopeful sign.*

January 25, 1945
 . . . *The war news is getting better and better nearer and nearer
to Berlin and Manila!*

January 31, 1945
 . . . *Don't be too alarmed at Tokyo Rose. The news from Europe
and the South Pacific (as you must know) is wonderful. The Germans
claim that the Russians claim that the Russians are tonight only 45
miles from Berlin. (However, they seem to be too eager to spread their
bad news. I wonder what new move they can be planning now.) Also,
the new invasion in the Philippines, and rescuing those 500 American
prisoners, is another cause for rejoicing.*
 *I am enclosing a map I just now hurriedly tore out from today's
Times showing the Russian march to Berlin. Did you ever receive
the book of war maps we sent you?*

Shirley described New York City's tribute to a fallen Franklin Roosevelt.

April 14, 1945
. . . A beautiful tribute was paid to President Roosevelt. The theater was in darkness for 5 minutes, while organ music was played. Sobbing could be heard from all sides. Then a news reel of his life was shown. They showed pictures of him at the Yalta conference— in that, he already looked like a dying man. What a tragedy for the whole world, and even more so for our people. The memorial columns of the Times were filled with hundreds of tributes to him. I only hope that Truman tries to follow his policies to the utmost. I still can't get over the shock. It was so sudden.

. . . I had the baby out today, with Vivian and Gloria. Promptly at 4 o'clock, all traffic stopped and everything was still in tribute to Pres. Roosevelt, while funeral services were being read over him in the White House. A little after 4, it began getting very dark, and a sudden, swift downpour of rain descended, which lasted for about an hour. Truly, it seemed a prophetic omen—as even the heavens were crying for the President. Even the skeptics are a little awe-stricken by this sign.

April 26, 1945
. . . . I did nothing tonight but sew and listen to the broadcasting of the Security Conference. The war news is good, but not fast enough to suit me. I hope the Russians are having their sweet revenge tonight in the streets of Berlin.

Shirley reacts to the deaths of so many of the world's leaders. Of interest are her thoughts about what the country will be like when her baby is twenty years old, hoping to raise him into a peaceful world, not foreseeing Viet Nam, which would mark his generation.

May 1, 1945
Sweetheart,
Hitler is dead! Yet I can't believe it. Or rather I don't wish to believe it. For as Ambassador Soong defined it, "Dictators die too easily these days." He seems to have escaped the final hour of

defeat of Germany and a violent death at the hand of the Russians and those he massacred. It seems like a horrible cheat of rightful justice. These past few weeks have seen the demise of so many world figures, men whose names have been familiar to me from childhood on. Roosevelt, who died mourned; Mussolini, who died ignobly and degraded; and Hitler, whose death, by whatever means it came about, died too easily. Why can't he die a death, a horrible death, for each of the 5,000,000 Jews he had massacred, and the millions of others he tortured and killed, and for all the Allied soldiers who gave their lives in a war brought about by his ruthlessness?

No, his death doesn't leave me satisfied but rather frustrated. He's escaped too easily. If I only believed in after-world retribution, how easily I could see him sizzling in Hell for all eternity. The misery he wrought in the last decade can never be undone.

The events of the last few days have been breathtaking in their rapidity. Truly, we are witnessing in this week alone, the end of a ghastly era. I pray a new one will dawn much brighter.

Berlin may fall at any hour; and the final end of the European war can be expected most any day. Churchill says by Saturday. I can scarcely be able to believe it, for I've lived with aggression and persecution and war for so long. How will peace feel? I pray it's forever. When we heard the news of Hitler's death, I held Jeff in my arms as we listened to the radio and said to him, "Darling, this is the end of a man of whom you will only read in history books; and I pray to God that this war is titled 'The Last World War' forever." Poor baby. If ever I thought I'd raise him to another hell on earth twenty years from now, I'd never be able to look him in the eye; for I'd be too ashamed of the mess I brought him into, without his permission. And I hope he has a bright future—on an equal basis with all others.

May 2, 1945
Darling,

After the death of Hitler yesterday, which seems to be pretty generally accepted today, the surrender and withdrawal of German troops from Italy is another decisive step towards the imminent Armistice.

What a joyous feeling to know that the end is almost in sight. If only the Japs would turn civilized and they are gaining nothing by holding out when they see our victorious peace in Europe.

May 3, 1945
  . . . P.S. How could I forget: at last the fall of Berlin? The war is tottering, but still it staggers on. How long, oh Lord?

New York City's reaction to war's end, and what Shirley learned from the news, crops up in the next letter.

May 7, 1945
Les darling,
  The news has come at last of the unconditional surrender of the Germans. All New York, especially along Broadway, is packed with hysterical mobs. It's not official as yet, but the radio just said that the official proclamation will be broadcast simultaneously, with the 3 powers, tomorrow morning at nine o'clock. I remember so well another broadcast on Dec. 8, 1941, which proclaimed this country to be at a state of war with the Axis powers. If only this were the final end; if only tomorrow could also be the celebration of the surrender of Japan as well.
  It's wonderful news and certainly an indication that complete victory cannot be far off, but I don't feel that all-out joyous feeling I thought I would. I'm so sorry for all the misery this war has brought, and for all the lives lost. I've seen many people crying on the streets today, those who lost their sons or sweethearts. They're bitter, and who's to blame them. Victory has come too late for them. Even Gloria, as plucky as she is, was so miserable today.
  Well, anyway, "bottoms up and drink 'er down." Here's to final peace and our own personal happiness.
  . . . The News showed the atrocity pictures of the German concentration camps. Darling, can those people be sane? Can reasoning men do those things to other men, and still remain civilized? I kept my eyes open throughout, for I never want to forget what they did. I needn't have worried about forgetting—I'll always remember. I'm

sick from those sights. Surely there's some punishment in this world big enough to exact its toll on all the Germans, for these filthy crimes they committed. The film should be compulsory for all to see, Germans and Allies alike, so that there will never again be any bestiality such as that.

Shirley's reaction to the announcement of V-E Day follows.

May 8, 1945
Les Dearest,

It's a prophetic day for all of us—victory over the Germans. I hope the peace we make will insure that victory forever. New York is quieter than everyone thought it would be, for we all realize that victory with Japan must come first before we really celebrate the end of this horrible, lousy war. Then, too, people can't forget the price of this war (not to be measured by any standards of money) in the cost of human lives or human sufferings.

Our poor Jews in Europe—their miserable plight, too, has at last been alleviated, but for at least 5,000,000 of them, Hitler's brutality has taken its toll. So it's a victory with varied emotions— supreme happiness in their defeat; a sadness or regret for what its price has been. I wish that the security conference is filled more with plans for a more lasting peace and utter subjugation of the German people than it is with bitter dissension over boundaries and futile arguments for, so it looks tonight, poor Roosevelt's dream of world security is being sadly kicked around, as evidenced by tonight's report of the San Francisco Conference.

But there is one thing God has blessed us with, and that is faith. We all have hopes for a better future and permanent peace— towards that goal we strive. I do wish that my son grows up in a world where the words "war" and "inequality of race and color" are obsolete. For what land, or gold, or "place in the sun" is worth the agonies of war?

While Lester was away, Shirley was living comfortably at home, yet the war was very much a part of her life and awareness. It was inescapable, from the news on the radio, in movie newsreels, in the newspapers and constant conversation with all who visited. It also made itself felt in more subtle ways, such as the rationing that had become just a part of the fabric of daily life, to the black-out shades that had to be pulled down at night so that no light would be emitted to guide any enemy planes that made it that far, and to the fact that nearly all the men were in some branch of the military.

The rationing did not seem to be onerous, yet Shirley frequently referred to freezing in her apartment during the winter, due to rationing of heating fuels, and she would occasionally refer to an item that was suddenly scarce due to rationing.

The young of that generation knew only war, separation, and some degree of privation at home. Mostly, they took it all in stride, in order to serve the cause in some way, reaching beyond their own wants and needs to help the country as it fought this global war.

> October 12, 1943
>   . . . It's freezing up here. I can't get used to it. You'll have to bring your rain coat with its interlining and pajamas with you.

Cigarettes were also rationed, making life very hard for smokers.

> December 3, 1944
> Darling,
>   I am frozen—this darn apartment has me shivering and chattering. Can you imagine such cold in the inferno of heat were you probably are? Texas has turned my blood to water. Skipper and I can't take these cold Northern winters any longer.
>   . . . I took my little son for a walk on my usual Sunday quest for cigarettes. That's when they get them in, and by going to a few places, I manage to get enough for the week. I only smoke about 3 or 4 packs a week, so I usually manage to get enough. How is the cigarette situation where you are?

Shirley is so cold but immediately thinks of what Lester is experiencing.

> January 9, 1945
> Sweetheart,
>   I am frozen. Oh for heat, heat. I am crying for heat. But per-

haps, you're wishing for some below zero weather. Poor darling, it must be miserably hot and uncomfortable for you.

In wartime, such mundane items as gum and cigars have become rare luxuries.

January 11, 1945
. . . I received the package of gum and cigars this morning—really, manna from heaven. We haven't seen Spearmint or Dentyne in months. Thanks loads, darling. I put aside the cigars and two cartons of cigarettes to give your folks when I see them.

Freezing, freezing, freezing. . .

January 25, 1945
. . . The room was really freezing, as only our rooms can be. In fact, it was 40° in my room. And so, struggling between the cold and weariness, I fell asleep without writing to you, for which I hope you will excuse me. And today, it hit below zero and set a record for intense cold for many years. I took Skipper out, but he refused to stay for more than a few minutes.
. . . The weather has been freezing this week — but it is still warmer outside than in our apartment. Jeffie has been sleeping in the bathrobe you sent him. It keeps him warm as toast.

February 2, 1945
. . . The room was freezing last night. . .

Even film for cameras is hard to come by.

March 24, 1945
. . . I'm enclosing 5 of the pictures that I told you we took last week. I'll send the other 5 in tomorrow's letter. They came out quite well. Now that Jeff is sitting up in his carriage, and warm weather is almost here, snapshots will be easier to take. The only problem is the scarcity of film.

. . . As are children's shoes.

> *August 23, 1945*
> *. . . we went out to buy him a pair of shoes. As long as dad had the car with him, we thought we might as well do it—since the stores are all closed on Saturdays. Well sir—your son has inherited the width of your feet, if nothing else. We went into 7 of the best baby shoe stores—and none of them had his size in—a 6 EE! We finally landed up in A&S, where we were fortunate to find the last pair they had in stock. (There's a big shortage of children's shoes.)*

So were shoes for adults.

> *November 7, 1945*
> *. . . We've been having such glorious weather lately. This afternoon I walked with Vivian and Jeff (who snoozed in comfort in his carriage), to Bedford Ave, where Vi bought a pair of shoes. They are no longer rationed.*

While Shirley was at home shivering and being deprived of so many items, Lester was on board a naval ship actually heading into battle zones. The Oxford's main purpose was to carry large numbers of troops to and from these sites, which meant that Lester was periodically exposed to the battles themselves, to some degree, along with the ever-present threat of Japanese bombers finding and strafing them.

Lester was involved in the battle at Linguyen Gulf; only later would the censor's rules allow him to mail his description to Shirley. He attempted to make light of it, in order to reassure her.

> *February 12, 1945*
> *. . .I am permitted to tell you now that the operation that I mentioned we took part in before was a landing in the Philippines, at Linguyen Gulf, on the island of Luzon, to be exact. I hate to be disappointing or unmelodramatic, but it really was a very tame affair. It was characterized chiefly by hard work on the part of the men unloading the ship. We were always well protected both in the*

air, and on the sea. As a matter of fact, we saw only three Japanese planes in the operation, and these were running like the devil. One of them got caught by our anti-aircraft fire; I saw him fall. The others I couldn't see. For the rest of it, we spent a little time in and around the Philippines and some time elsewhere, and that is all. As I say, there is really very little to be concerned about. We have very efficient surface and air escort. Of course, we have various alarms but they are mostly admonitory. Usually the planes turn out to be friendly. If not, our fighters scare them away before they can be close enough to be seen.

Mention of Lester's travels follows.

February 19, 1945
   . . . I think I can review for you again where we were. From the States we went to Finschafen, New Guinea. Then to Hollandia, New Guinea. Then down to Noumea, New Caledonia. Then to the Solomons, Guadalcanal, Tulagi, Florida, etc. From there we went to Manus. It was at Manus I met Chester. Then by a devious route we went on up to Linguyen Gulf and came back to Manus. From Manus we went to Maffin Bay, New Guinea, near which is Wake Island, and there my story of perambulation must end. That ought to about complete the tale.

This was not a drill, but a real enemy sighting.

February 25, 1945
   Churl Darling,
   . . . Suddenly the P.A. cut in. Flash red, control green. Then the general alarm gong started its monotonous clangor, and the coxswain yelled, "All hands. Routine General Quarters." There is nothing routine about this G.Q. It is the real thing this time. There are enemy planes identified in the vicinity. In all probability it is just a scouting raid, and in a few moments the all clear will sound. I'll let you know when it does, so don't worry.

Lester participated in, and later wrote about, the invasion of Okinawa.

April 5, 1945 (mailed May 2, 1945)

. . . but I want to talk to you a bit so what I've decided to do is to get you up to date tonight on the happenings to date, but not mail it until we hear from the censor that it is all right to mention our recent operations. I know I should outline what I have to say, but I'm lazy, so I'll just write about things as they come to mind and explain as necessary. OK?

I'm sort of hazy about where I left off in the journey of our travels, but I'll start with Wake Island, New Guinea. It was there we stayed and got some troops to bring up to Luzon. I'm sure I've described the bomb-torn island and the pillboxes on the beach as well as the various experiences that befell me there. At any rate we left Wake and went on up to Luzon again, stopping for a couple of days on the way up at Leyte. This trip was just a milk run. The situation at Luzon was well in hand, and we had no trouble at all. Of course there were the usual General Quarters calls morning and night; and of course unscheduled snoopers added to the multitude of G.Q.'s, but there was really nothing eventful. We left Luzon and went down to Leyte, where we stayed for quite a spell. You must have guessed we were at some place by the regularity with which you got my letters (I assume you got them, because I wrote and mailed them regularly). Our stay at Leyte was not particularly bright. During the first part of our stay there we were anchored too far out to get ashore for liberty (it meant a three-hour boat trip in rough water), and during the latter part of the stay we were alerted and weren't permitted to go ashore. That was the period of time when I kept bitching about the mail situation. And I'm sure you can easily see why. Picture the boat at anchor; not even the sensation of motion to break the monotony; the shore in sight and yet being unable to get to it; and finally what amounted to a very regular daily mail delivery service producing very recent letters for everybody on board but me. Add to that the fact that I knew that, sometime in the near future, we were due to go on another invasion (none of us knew where, but we knew it would be no fun); and you can easily see why a man would like to get all the mail he could from his beloved and lovely wife. So I know you'll excuse a lot of the uncalled-for griping on my part at that time. The delay I experienced in getting your mail also explains why I couldn't get ashore at the time to carry out Gloria's request. By the time I had received the letter we already had troops aboard and were alerted. I tried to get permission, but Dickey stymied that by refusing the request very bluntly. Of course he was within his rights (and probably right) but I had to try anyhow and I did what I could. We may still get back there, and if we do I'll still try.

At any rate we spent quite a good deal of time at Leyte. Toward the end we took troops on board, maneuvered around a bit, and bingo, one fine day we were off. Well before the troops came aboard there had been a good deal of speculation about our objective. After they came aboard we knew our objective . . . I can't say that it added to our peace of mind. But as is usually the case in the navy, once embarked on a venture there is no turning back. The weather was rough all the way up, I believe we just missed the rough part of a gale, but surprisingly enough the ship hardly rolled at all. The seas came at us mostly from just off the bow, and as a result, although there was no roll, the pitch was very pronounced. It was interesting to stand on deck and watch these big ships lift high up out of the water, and then come down again with a ponderous deliberation that served to send tons of white water in a shattered mass upon the blue solidity of the "Pacific." More often than not as the ship nosed down it would meet a swell at the very height of ascent. Then there would be white water over the bow, flooding the fo'castle. As we headed north there was a pronounced drop in temperature, which, after so long a time in the tropics, came as a pleasant surprise. It was actually coolish.

Of this phase of the trip I have told you mostly tales about our bridge games, and they were a lot of fun. But there were other happenings, too. We had our quota of alarms; but considering our heading they were surprisingly few and far between. In the meantime, frequent briefings of the officers were held in the wardrooms. None of them seemed to make the task ahead any easier. We were bringing in the assault waves, and we had the recent example of Iwo Jima fresh in mind. The obstacles as outlined appeared formidable, and the location. Well, a look at the map will make it apparent that we had cause for nervousness. Oh, I haven't told you yet. We were sup-

posed to invade and capture Okinawa. Our pay clerk issued 10 dollars' worth of Japanese yen to each of the officers. There are some around the ship yet (actually, there aren't supposed to be); but to my mind these different types of currency aren't very good souvenirs, so I haven't tried to procure any. Each day maps were broken out and probabilities and eventualities were discussed. Each day too, the convoy would engage in various drills and exercises. I was on deck one day when I noted one of the escorting destroyers turn back and slowly (almost cautiously) sidle over to a spot. Suddenly the water splashed up, and smoke came from the muzzles of its forties. At the same time over the water came the peculiar rhythmic bump, bump, bump, of the forty-mm. guns. Then as I watched, there was a tremendous column of water shooting sky high. The destroyer had located and destroyed a floating mine. Soon six or seven of the remaining destroyers were circling in their own areas and repeating the process.

That was about the most exciting event of the trip up. The night before we got there, we changed course. We knew this because now the seas were coming from directly abeam, and the ship was really rolling. That night those of the army and the beach party made their preparations to get ashore the next day. There was an atmosphere of tenseness all over the ship. As I played bridge that night, I watched one man in particular. He was a tall, dark, aquiline-looking man. With an air of knowing very well what he was doing he was cleaning and oiling his arms. As the game started he was working on a tommy gun. This took him quite a while. When he got done with that, he took his automatic, disassembled and cleaned, and assembled that. Then for quite a long time he sharpened his long, wicked-looking trench knife. What a picture it was!

In the room Ralph was making his preparations. He had to go ashore in his capacity of beach-party medical officer. His job gets him ashore at more places than I do, but frankly I don't envy him. He too had cleaned his gun, and had done what last few things there were to do.

Those of us who could had turned in early because there was an early rising schedule for the next day— April 1, L-Day. My folk's 34th wedding anniversary, April Fool's Day. Well, the only ones who were fooled were the Japs. The landing was virtually un-opposed. It was so easy as to be almost ridiculous, but actually it had terribly dangerous potentialities which never materialized, thank God. If they had, our casualty lists would have been much higher. We came in slowly to our assigned space in the area and sent in our first boats. To while away the time, Ralph and I started a game of chess. It ended in the middle, when he was called away to go ashore. By this time reports of one kind only (all favorable) had started to drift back. In the afternoon we moved in compara-tively close to shore and started unloading activities.

I had nothing to do, so I went topside to a point of vantage and watched all the activity. It was like having a ringside seat at a football game. I borrowed a pair of glasses from one of the officers and thus projected myself very close to the beach. It is impossible to describe the organized confusion that existed there, but I can al-ways say I'm glad I'm on our side. Close aboard there was a bat-tleship hurling salvos from its 14-inch rifles. On the other side but closer inshore, a destroyer would pick its target, open up, and then train its guns on some other objective. Ashore we could see the planes, all ours, come in, dive, see the bomb fall (or the puff of smoke as the rockets were released), follow its path through the air, observe the tremendous upheaval of the earth, and smoke billowing into the air above, and seconds later hear (and feel) the dull irresistible boom, which meant the explosion.

This kept up all day. The power we had there in ships and planes was simply irresistible. Nothing could stand up against it. That first day the haze from the bombardment was too thick for us to see much. At night we upped anchor and put out to sea to avoid harassment by enemy night bombers. (Coming in the next morning, our convoy shot down a Japanese plane as it tried to strafe one of the ships.)

We moved right up close this time, and in the morning I had managed to get the field glasses I had told you about. Right here in front of us was a destroyer. I watched it work for a while. Only its after turret was working. I focused on that. First there was great forcible expulsion of hot gases from the muzzle, followed almost im-mediately by a ragged ring of orange red flame. After a perceptible interval there was a loud, definite clap of the explosion of the propulsive charge. It was hard to follow and see where the shells landed, but suddenly a great cloud of white smoke arose from the hillside ahead and seconds later the earthshaking boom of the shell's explosion. And so it went throughout the day. When it wasn't a destroyer, it was a cruiser or battle wagon firing, or again our shore-based heavies, which by then had been unloaded. Whatever it was, the result was the same. The countryside was covered with craters, smoke from the various explosions was to be seen everywhere. And every so often punctuating the sentences of the artillery the dive bombers would come. All this time the work of unloading was being carried on in a very efficient manner.

The last two nights we stayed in, and I witnessed the war at night. Fires were burning everywhere and the sky was clouded with smoke. At frequent intervals both in time and space a star shell would be sent up, its brilliant dead whiteness lighting up the area over which it hung. The ships really threw it into the island at night. For a while a cruiser right behind us fired directly overhead and we heard the eerie whistling made by the passage of shells through the air. The trajectories of many of the larger shells could be followed by a red or a white line. Actually, they were pretty things to watch as they soared to their height. There was a peculiar illusion created by their path of seeming to lose height while actually they were gaining.

And there you have the general outlines of the Okinawa invasion from my point of view. Actually I had little or nothing to do with the entire affair. Even in the reception of casualties, Dickey made it plain that he didn't want me (or any of the other doctors) around. So as far as I was concerned, the whole affair was in the nature of a vacation (such vacations I wish on my worst enemies).

Ralph came ashore the night before last, and he had a few interesting things to tell us about the prisoners he had seen, and his reaction on hitting the beach, and his reaction to what may have been sniper fire. He was hit in the ass by a spent piece of shrapnel. Unfortunately, it didn't cause even a light amount of damage. Don't laugh when I say "unfortunately." The idea is that, even if he had only the slightest of injuries, he would have rated the Purple Heart and, with that to back him up, could really have made Dickey

*eat crow. But thank God he was unhurt. Indeed, we suffered no ca-
sualties on board.*

*What I have written I am sure I cannot send out—perhaps a
month from now, though it will be old enough to be sent with safety.
At any rate there's the story, and I hope you liked it.*

*Did it ever occur to you that I love you and miss you? I do.
You know that, don't you? I know you do.*

September 5, 1945
*. . . I found out tonight that I can tell you that we are at Eniwe-
tok. I can't, however, tell you where we are going, as the future movements of the ship are still restricted information. A good idea, I think.*

September 7, 1945
*. . . Yesterday was an ordinary one except for one thing. We re-
ceived an Alnav ordering us to cease zigzagging and to lift the
blackout restrictions. It was quite a sight last night to go out on
deck and see the lights from the other ships streaming cheerily across
the water—quite a difference from just the night before when all
that showed of the accompanying ships were there black silhouettes.
It was different also today to go out on the fan tail and see our
wake stretching behind us straight as an arrow. As recently as yesterday it was curving all over the ocean.*

September 14, 1945
*. . . No one knows where we are going from here, although most
people suspect Japan, and very few people give a damn about going
any place but home.*

In the Philippines.

September 17, 1945
*. . . We left Manila early in the morning, and at about 12 this
afternoon pulled into Subic Bay to discharge the naval part of our
passengers. Subic is quite a large anchorage. It is supposed to be
the place that will replace Manila as our main base in the area. To
date it is quite primitive. There is very little beach, the hills rising*

steeply out of the water. We spent the greater part of a very moist day discharging our passengers, and then this evening set special sea and anchor detail, and in the midst of a pouring rain made for open sea, and set our course for Lingayen. We have, therefore, a very pronounced roll, which doesn't make it any too easy to get around. It will be getting back to familiar territory when we get into Lingayen again. This will make our third trip up there: once on an S plus 2, once on an S plus 30, and now tomorrow again.

September 18, 1945
...Well, here we are back at Lingayen Gulf, the scene of our baptism of actual war. We are anchored close by the dock where first we discharged troops. How different the scene is today . . . and how much better! There is at least one memento of that former grim occasion. Smack in the middle of the channel leading to the anchorage rise the sticks of a sunken ship, a derelict of those more strenuous days. Our trip in and our activities on arrival were very uneventful. We came in, arrived at our proper anchorage, dropped the hook, and that was all.

The war ends, and the *Oxford* is bringing occupation troops to Japan.

September 25, 1945
...We'll be shoving off in a day or so for the coast of Japan. We will land up near the town of Nagoya. According to the newspapers, there are already over 200,000 troops in Japan. We are bringing up several thousand more. So I doubt that we will be making another trip there. I rather think that our next stop will be the States. Most probably we will stop at some island, Saipan or Guam, perhaps, to load up with troops returning to the States. Then I believe we will be decommissioned. After all, we carry too few troops to economically serve as the main means of getting the troops back. I certainly hope that it is the case anyway, because I don't think I could take another trip out here.

October 6, 1945
Churl Darling,
The minds of the higher-ups in this outfit are exceedingly ob-

scure and difficult to understand. Our orders have been changed again, so that, instead of proceeding directly to Nagoya, we are to revert back to the original plan and stay over at the small city of Wakiyama the night before, which is around a bend in the bay. Then we go on to this city near Nagoya (whose name I forget). When we get there, we may just stand by for a week before unloading troops. I can't figure it out. But I suppose it doesn't matter whether I can figure it out or not.

21

EVERYDAY LIFE AT HOME

WE MAY NOT RECOGNIZE it, but we all live our lives by routine. Otherwise, life would be chaotic. It would also overwhelm us, leaving little room for more creative endeavors. Doing the basics by habit permits everyday life to proceed unimpeded. While onboard the *Oxford,* Lester lived by a strict routine; the military is famous for structure and order. In fact, some people enlist primarily to permanently impose that structure on their lives. While not in the military, Shirley nevertheless led a very ordered life. Of course, there was Jeffrey. In the 1940s, parents tended to be more rule-bound than they are today. Each day was to be just the same as those before it. There was early morning play time; then came breakfast; the rest of her day would involve socializing, chores, or possibly a doctor's appointment. There was almost always a long afternoon walk outside with the baby in the fresh air, even in the coldest weather, and later came the social hour, when Shirley and Jeff played together. After that came his dinner, which Shirley had to prepare. There was the nightly bath, followed by bedtime. Shirley's evening would continue after Jeff was asleep. She would visit with friends, either at her own house or going out with them, often depending on child care arrangements. Her socializing would sometimes last well into the early-morning hours, when she would then slip into bed and write her nightly letter to Lester. Such was the rhythm of her days.

January 11, 1945
My darling,
*   I am healthy—the picture of a ruddy Diana. It was 5° above*

zero today, yet Jeff and I braved the elements and stayed out for 2 hours. Picture me if you can in my glamorous zero weather out-fit—boots and woolen socks, a suit and sweater, woolies down to my knees, a scarf, winter coat, kerchief on my hair, and my fur gloves. Sounds intriguing, doesn't it. I'm convinced that I am made for sunny, warm skies. And yet there is something very invigorating about it. My poor sweetheart, are you wishing, wherever you may be, for a little of this cold weather?

I accompanied Mother while she did her shopping, as she was afraid to walk without holding on to the carriage for support, for the streets are still very slippery. Skipper, too, was snug in Mickey's cast-off winter coat. Our dog's chest seems to be expanding every day. I had to buy him a new harness, as he has outgrown the old one. While waiting for Mother outside the bank, a cute little boy about 4 years old came over to pet Skipper. I warned him not to, as Skip isn't friendly to people he doesn't know. Whereupon, my little friend demanded to know, "If I tell him my name, will he be friendly?"

. . . Tonight, Mother and Dad and I went to Friedman's to get some linens and bath towels for the baby. But they have nothing left in stock. All I came out with were 2 pair of rubber pants for Jeff.

We also stopped in to pick up my hat, which I had ordered to match my new cloth coat. That is where part of your wonderful an-niversary present to me has been spent.

We get a good picture of a young mother with a baby who is experienc-ing teething for the first time.

January 14, 1945
Darling,

I'm afraid I'm not up to too much of a letter tonight, as I'm pretty thoroughly exhausted. The baby didn't feel very well today—he's teething—and he's been crying and screaming continuously. Poor little thing. It breaks my heart to see how uncomfortable he feels. Nothing shows as yet, but he'll probably get his first teeth very soon. Gloria Lang's baby got 2 teeth this week, but he's been very sick from it, running a temperature and a cold. However, Jeff has just been ir-

ritable and in pain. Your folks came over this afternoon, and I'm afraid they didn't have too pleasant a day. He screamed when he saw them (as he didn't recognize them) and was carrying on all the time they were here. I've never had a day like this— it's left me like a limp rag. My nerves are still on fire from his shrieks. I was very calm with him, but after he finally fell asleep, I sank into a chair and lit one cigarette after another. I expected the folks in the early afternoon, but as they didn't show up, I started to do my washing, while Mother soothed the baby. In the middle of it, they walked in about 4:30. They took over and stayed with the baby while I finished. About 5:30, he really started shrieking, and so I hurriedly gave him his bottle, without even bathing him or feeding him the rest of his supper. It took me an hour to get him to take even half of it-— the rest he refused. However, he wouldn't go to sleep. So finally we put him in the carriage and your dad rocked him until he finally slept. We were all so exhausted we couldn't eat, but I made coffee and we had some. It's something I'll have to get used to, for teething will affect him like that every so often. About 8:30, my folks came home from seeing Grandma Sidney at the nursing home. Gloria Siegel came by, and we all sat and talked. At 9:30 dad drove your folks to the station. They were anxious to get home as Roslyn was home alone—she was working today. (Her boyfriend is in still in Tampa, Florida, but expects to go overseas next month.) Gloria stayed another hour, and so here I am, in bed, writing to you.

Jeff is still in his carriage, in the room with me. I'm rather uneasy about him sleeping in it, but I'd hate to disturb him by changing him to his crib. Poor baby, he's all exhausted from that crying.

Darling, I'll have to turn in now, as I must catch what rest I can for he may keep me up tonight.

January 17, 1945
Darling,

Happy Anniversary, with 10 billion kisses included!

More snow today, but in the afternoon it cleared up; so I got Jeff, Skipper, and I dressed in our winter clothes, and off we trudged. I must admit it nearly broke my back, pushing that carriage (with Skipper pulling) through the slush and piled-up snow. There has been so much of it lately that no one has had a chance to clear the sidewalks. I'm afraid, darling, that I won't be very feminine by the time you come home. For with the muscles in my arms that I'm developing from pushing the carriage, I'm more than a match for Joe Louis.

January 19, 1945

. . . As uneventful days go, today was one of them. I had the baby down from 12 to 2, brought him up to feed him, and then down again and talked and walked with various other mothers till 4:30. I'm getting so tired of taking walks—why, I know every foot of pavement in the vicinity of Crown Heights, and Eastern Parkway. Never have I smelled so much fresh air, as I have this winter.

January 22, 1945
Darling,

I've been such a good girl today, I'm sure the brightness of my halo must be apparent to everyone. It's just been a day full of minor accomplishments and duties fulfilled—such a rare and noble feeling.

Another raining Monday. It has poured continuously, but I didn't mind, for as I said before, it gave me a chance to get some things done. Usually, on other nasty days, things come up that prevent me doing it, or the baby cries, or I just don't feel like it. And in the evenings, I am usually too tired or I'm going out or have company, so you can see in what dark shelf the odds and ends have been pushed and been accumulating.

At 8 o'clock this morning, after Jeff had finished his morning bottle, I stepped courageously into the freezing bathroom and washed my hair (as I haven't been to the beauty parlor lately), and then spent the next hour brushing it and setting it.

Elaine had no school today, as it is Regents week. Jeff started to wake up and cry about 9:30, so I put him in Elaine's bed with her. That Don Juan really manages to get into quite a number of feminine beds.

Making the formula occupied me for an hour and a half while Jeff slept.

In the afternoon Jeff played in his playpen, while I went house-

cleaning. Lately I have been acting on your advice, throwing out all unnecessary junk (a wonderful idea). So today I attacked our 2 medicine chests packed to the brim with medicine and cosmetics. When I got through, I must say they were more efficient and better looking chests.

After another meal and bottle at 3, and a short nap, Jeff and I played together for the rest of the afternoon, until bath and dinner time at 6. Jeff had string beans and applesauce for lunch, and for dinner had a sumptuous repast of banana and junket, cod liver oil, and his bottle.

Then off to bed, and by 7:15, I was free to eat my dinner. (Poor darling, I hope you can wait till then, till I get through with the babies. Or should you do the cooking?).

And so tonight, a very quiet evening at home, knitting and listening to the radio until now writing to you.

I hope you haven't been bored by this timetable of events in one ordinary day, but I've suddenly realized that you really don't know how I spend the day, nor even at what time our Jeff fills up his little belly.

Shirley had never learned how to cook before her marriage; Lester had to teach her.

January 27, 1945

Today, as usual, was nasty, so while Mother stayed with Jeff in the morning, I went shopping to prepare for the dinner I am going to make for your folks tomorrow. Yup, tomorrow's my debut. Now your mother and dad can see you didn't marry me only for your heart's sake but took your stomach into consideration as well.

I stayed in this afternoon, washed the clothes for the baby, then had quite a good time dancing with him.

Tonight Gloria Siegel came up to keep me company and help with the cake. Mother and Dad were too cold and tired to go out, so they retired to the living room and read.

It was such fun making it! We licked the bowls so much, that now my stomach definitely has quite a queasy feeling.

I made a very rich devil's food cake, with chocolate icing, and then (triumph of all arts!) I lettered a birthday greeting to Jeff with

orange icing, and it came out gorgeously. To top it all, I stuck half
a pink candle in the middle of it for his half year celebration.

Jeffrey's six-month birthday party.

January 28, 1945
Darling,

    Today was the day—our baby is 6 months old and I have made
a successful debut as a "real balibusta*" [Yiddish for "good house-*
keeper"] (to quote your father).

    I have been working steadily and on my feet continuously since
8 this morning, and I must admit to the reaction of healthy fatigue
right now.

    I spent this morning making the formula, feeding and taking
care of the baby, and putting up the pot roast. Then, because I was
so busy, Daddy took Jeff down for me for a couple of hours—oth-
erwise, I would never have gotten through.

    I then helped mother straighten up the house, got showered and
dressed, and began to really prepare the dinner. I made dumplings
and browned up potatoes in the roast, prepared a green salad and
the relishes, had sectioned grapefruit, and set the table with the
"company" china and silver. I expected your folks at 3:00 and I just
got all through at that time. Dad brought up Jeff (and Skipper),
and I fed him and combed his hair pretty. Mother and Dad had to
leave then, as they had a dinner appointment. Your folks and Roslyn
showed up at a quarter to four—and we passed a lovely afternoon.
Jeff was on his best behavior and (after the first few minutes of non-
recognition and crying on his part) was soon smiling and cooing at
them. Your folks were in heaven. We put him in his playpen (when
he wasn't being held or petted), and he played contentedly in it
while we talked, mainly about you and how we miss you, and prayers
for a very quick victory and your early return.

    After Jeff went to sleep, I served dinner. Thank goodness it was
all ready except to be heated up, for bathing and feeding the baby
really knocks me out, and we were all hungry and ready to eat.

    And so, modestly I must say, it was good. They really enjoyed
it, and your pop couldn't get over the fact that I can cook. To show

him how much I think of him, I even made tea (and in the tea kettle)
instead of coffee—and served it in a glass!

Then we lit the candle, and I made a prayer for Jeff (for you to
be my side for his next party) and blew it out in 1 blow! I cut the
cake, and we devoured the great masterpiece.

We sat around and talked for a while, and then I washed and
Roz wiped the dishes.

Your folks left at 10:00. It was a grand day. And so now, more
tired than I care to admit, I am ready for bed.

So sweet dreams, my dear. I dream of you every night—the
most wonderful fantasies, which someday soon will come true.

Shirley's parents often bought presents for her and for Jeff, their only
grandchild.

March 7, 1945

. . . Today's weather was fickle. Jeff and I prepared ourselves for a
long day indoors as it both rained and snowed. But lo, at 4 o'clock the
sun came marching out. My conscience wouldn't let me keep the baby
indoors, and so I bundled him up and took him outside for an hour.

. . . This evening mother and dad took me to the place where I
had ordered a suit and matching topper. I went for a fitting for it.
It is coral in color, and I think it will be very pretty. It is Dad's
anniversary gift. I'm ordering it at the same place where I got my
winter coat in East New York. From there we went to a material
place for material to cover the sea chest you sent. I'm making it
into a toy chest for Jeff. It is ideal for that purpose as it so, so sturdy,
and the toy chests they sell are like paper in comparison.

Some things never change, whether it relates to women's work or post-
war inflation.

April 10, 1945
Darling,

Speaking of this summer, our plans are yet are very indefinite.
Daddy wanted to buy or rent a cottage, but you wouldn't believe
what is going on with summer resorts, unless you were here to see it.

It's incredible. They are impossible to find, for everyone is going mad with their war riches, and are rushing into the resorts (your uncle Lou just bought a summer home in Long Beach).

Secondly, it would be no vacation for mother and me to have a bungalow. We'd have the same daily grind of housework without the conveniences of home. At least here we have a part-time maid to do the general cleaning. We thought we may go away for a few weeks to a hotel (and still may). Here, too, the prices are ridiculous. They average about $100 a week per person in most places, and try to get in anywhere. Reservations were made last summer for rooms this summer! We inquired about Grossinger's but were informed that all rooms with private baths have all been reserved since last year for this entire summer. And I don't want to bathe the baby in a public bath. Also, they won't even set their price rates till June 15th, so who knows what they will charge. People who were starving before the war are now literally walking on mink coats (the Waldorfs, for example). Somehow, I'm developing an aversion to the Catskill types who are flashing around their war money while others fight for them.

So we'll see what we will do. If we can get in anywhere, we'll probably go away for a few weeks. It's the folks treat to me. . .

Shirley tried to keep to a routine with Jeffrey, including a daily walk and an evening bath.

May 2, 1945
. . . I had a million phone calls today, when news of the end of the fighting in Italy was heard on the radio. Flo Cooper, Esther Korchin, Gert, Gloria, Daddy (at least 6 times to report on further developments), and a few others. This all held me back, and excited me so that I didn't get down with the baby until after 3. (I usually go down in the morning, and after his afternoon nap, usually about 2:30).

Socializing was a vital part of Shirley's daily life.

October 22, 1945
. . . Today was very uneventful, as it rained and I stayed in with the baby. That child never sits still for a minute. I don't

know from whom he inherits his amazing energy. The house looks as if it were struck by an atomic bomb. Nothing is safe when he is around.

And now, it is evening. Another day passed. Mother and Dad and Elaine are out, and I am alone with my miserable thoughts.

22

FAMILY

L ESTER WAS AWAY IN the Pacific, leaving his family behind but forming a new family with his friends, acquaintances and the other men aboard the *Oxford*. This has always been the case for men in the military; wartime creates a strong bond among men in constant danger, which often explains the many stories of men sacrificing themselves to save their mates.

Shirley was at home, in the midst of her family, at least the female members (the young men all being in the service). Because the electronic age, including television, was far in the future, there was less to do on one's own than there later would be. Much of life, much more than is common today, was social, and the greater part of that social life was centered on family. Even with Lester gone, Shirley's family circle had expanded to include his, most of whom lived a subway ride away.

Holidays, of course, were times for family visits, although it is striking that big parties, usually without family, so common today, are completely absent from these descriptions. More surprising, perhaps, is the amount of casual visiting that took place during the work week. Family relationships were a central part of everyday life, everyone actively involved with each other and always up to date on each other's lives.

As has always been the case, the negative aspects of living in such close proximity included family arguments, sometimes brief, sometimes lasting longer. Some families had branches that had stopped speaking to each other following an argument, causing permanent estrangements. These fractured relationships also occurred in the pseudo-families of military units, as can be seen from some of Lester's letters.

Despite this, family remains the most basic and intense of human relationships, particularly in this time and in this place.

Apparently, the couple's very first "child," Skipper, joined the family while Shirley was visiting her husband in Texas, and she took the dog home to Brooklyn with her. As she visited with his parents she finalized her living arrangements when Les would come home on leave.

> *October 12, 1943*
>   *. . . The whole family had dinner over your parent's house Sunday, and did I eat kreplach. For a change, I had to take my girdle off. Your parents are fine, and Rozzie looked very pretty. She works for the Times during the day and goes to school at night. She's crazy about Skipper, and we took a long walk together. I'm going shopping with her today, and tonight I'm sleeping over your house.*
>   *Your mother mentioned that, as she works, it wouldn't pay for us to sleep over there during the week. So we'll probably sleep there over the weekend and stay at home for the rest of the time. I guess that will work out for the best.*
>   *I'm glad that I finally came home. Mother and Dad were really glad to see me. Daddy fell in love with Skippy. I'm afraid he won't let me take him home with us.*

"Grandma Sidney" refers to Rose's mother, Tibey. Sidney is her youngest son and Rose's brother.

> *October 14, 1943*
>   *. . . Your son, the "great Skipper," is happily munching raisins beside me as I write. He's so adorable.*
>   *I went to Grandma Sydney's house last night. Sydney was there, too. He told me my derriere is spreading, so today I am beginning a diet. Alas, and Longchamps is so tempting. Daddy says even Longchamp's steak is cut down into the size of a quarter.*
>   *I'm meeting Roslyn at 1:00 today. She wants me to pick her out a dress and hat.*

I'll get some clothes next week. Daddy wants to make me a present of it, and also for the carfare home, but I don't want him to.

Shirley went back to visit Grandma Tibey and to see Frances and Milty (the latter being another of Rose's brothers—Shirley, at this point, was regularly going to the Bronx to visit Lester's family, which included his sister, Roslyn).

Sunday, Oct. 17, 1943

We saw Milt and Francis. They came in expecting to see you. Uncle thought I looked swell, and he says you're a good husband. Francy really looked very pretty.

. . . I called your mother this morning and told her. Was she thrilled at the 15-day leave. I'm going up to your house Tuesday morning—Rozzie's day off— and sleep over Tuesday night again. It's bitter cold out today and very windy. I gave everyone thrills today. I didn't know what to hold down, my hat or my dress (I'm only wearing my lynx jacket), and Skippy was pulling at the leash. So finally some man took pity on my predicament and held Skippy for me until I could repair my dignity. Me for Texas—I feel as if I'll never be warm again.

Shirley is only two years older than Roslyn yet sounds much older here. Shirley's sister, Elaine, was only fifteen years old, and she was "determined" to marry Norman.

October 19, 1943

. . . It's bitterly cold in New York. I'm up in your mother's house. I came up in the morning to be with Roslyn on her day off. We had one of our talks on "life." In the year or so since I've so talked to her, I noticed how her once static and positive ideas have gradually evolved into those of a mature person. It's really amazing to watch her thought processes change so rapidly. She's a swell girl, Les, and she thinks the world of you.

Yesterday afternoon Norman Hyman came over the house till dinnertime. I was so surprised to see him. He had an unexpected week's furlough, and then it's to be overseas duty for him. Elaine

said she's determined to marry him eventually, and mother kept
plyng him with questions as only mother can.

Once Jeffrey was born it became more difficult for Shirley to travel to
the Bronx, forcing her in-laws to trek to Brooklyn to see her, which they
often combined with a visit with Charlie's sister, Becky. Rose Korchin is
Becky's daughter. Shirley's reference to Grandma being in the hospital concerns the fact that Tibey had been placed in a nursing home because her
Parkinson's disease was progressing. Also, since Shirley and Jeffrey had moved
in with her parents, there was no room for Rose to have her mother live with
them, a fact that haunted Rose for years afterward.

> *November 19, 1944*
> *Sweetheart,*
>
> *After I finished writing to you last night, your folks surprised*
> *me with a visit. I was awfully glad to see them, as they haven't*
> *been down in quite a long while, and they rescued me from my usual*
> *Saturday night doldrums.*
>
> *They couldn't get over the baby, how adorable he looks. Of*
> *course he was sleeping, but they gazed at him in raptures. Mom*
> *brought him down a little bunny, which she had saved for him. I*
> *gave them copies of the pictures which I had sent you (they finally*
> *sent me the reorders after more than a month). We talked of this*
> *and that, and it all came back to how much we all miss you and*
> *love you, and how wonderful it will be when we are all together*
> *again. Rozzie is having a hectic and gay week with Harold. He*
> *took her out last night to a hotel for dinner and dancing. The folks*
> *left at 10:00, as they wanted to see Becky. Also, the upstairs Rose*
> *Korchin had a heart attack (she's convalescing in a royal manner*
> *now), and they wanted to visit her, too.*
>
> *…Mother's brother Sammie was over, and they kept him*
> *mighty amused. Wonder of all wonders — Sammy is finally deciding*
> *to get married. Now that Grandma is in the hospital and he is*
> *alone, he has come to the great decision that, at forty years of age,*
> *it is time he had a wife. He has started taking out Miss Silverman*
> *(Daddy's secretary) and a few other girls. Who knows but that the*
> *bachelor might yet relent? Rhoda, in her usual sprightly way, was*

digging up all her unmarried relatives for him to go out with, and assured him that, nice boy that he is, there is no reason for him not to get married, etc., etc.

Shirley helps Roslyn decide between two suitors.

November 26, 1944

. . . Roslyn came over in the afternoon. She brought Jeff an adorable little knitted suit, for which I voiced my sincere appreciation. It was bitter cold, so we took a short walk and we came up to the house half-frozen. Especially Roz—you know how cold she gets. I made hot chocolate, and then we played with Jeff for a while. He decided his lungs needed exercise, and so whenever he saw we weren't paying him enough attention, he practiced yelling. In between screams, Roz and I talked about various things, most important of which is her perplexing love life. She still isn't sure whether or not she loves Harold, even though she's getting involved with him to the extent that he is sending war bonds home in both their names, which certainly means something. He is now stationed in Tampa, Florida, undergoing operation training, after which he most probably will ship out. And Leon still writes to her from France. Poor girl, it is true that she has scarcely had time to really know either of them.

Roz left about 5—she had an appointment. Then Dad came home.

The domestic scene that follows revolves around Elaine, Shirley's sixteen-year-old sister, who had been nicknamed "Ewee" and who had been baking cookies for her new boyfriend, Spinny.

December 2, 1944

. . . While I was feeding him, your mother dropped in to visit. She had to be in Brooklyn to get some papers signed by the Spectors and came over here. Jeff didn't know her at first and started to howl. He's pretty wary of unfamiliar faces. Finally she won him over and had him smiling again, and had a grand time giving him the bottle. I asked her to stay for dinner and spend some time with

me tonight. She agreed, and called up Pop to see if he wouldn't come down, too. He was too tired, but she stayed anyway. We had dinner and sat around and talked for a while. Elaine came home early, as she didn't feel well, and she and Phyllis decided to bake cookies to send to Spinny, who is in England. The 2 kids didn't know much about it, so in the end, it was Mom who was showing them what to do, while I rolled the dough out for them. It was lots of fun, and we all enjoyed it, even though we were soon splashed with flour. Ewee seems to be quite serious about Spinny and was determined to send him cookies to show him she can bake. (He should only know how she can bake!).

Surprisingly enough, the cookies turned out to be quite good. After tasting one, Mom went home, as it was already 12:00 o'clock.

The next letter reveals that Grandma Tibey's condition had deteriorated a great deal.

December 3, 1944

. . . Mother and Dad visited Grandma this afternoon in the hospital. They are still trying to get her out of Kings County, to go into a private nursing home. But it seems, because she attempted to take her own life, they won't let her go as yet. Perhaps in a few weeks—for there is nothing wrong with her mentally, it's just the state law. She is still very depressed and has no will to live. You can imagine how badly it makes Mother feel.

Next, Roslyn is allowed to visit Harold in Florida.

February 4, 1945

. . . Today, Roslyn came over. She is finally going to go to Florida to see Harold before he goes overseas. No one was more surprised than I when she said your father finally decided to let her go.

I guess this is the real thing. It has taken her a long time, but after all, their knowledge of one another has mostly been by mail, and she wanted to be absolutely certain. So I guess that, after the war, Roslyn shall be Mrs. Harold Cohan, if everything turns out, as I hope it will.

She plans to leave this coming Saturday and stay for a week. She came down to borrow some luggage, and I loaned her two valises. We had a pleasant afternoon outside with the baby, and she stayed until a little while ago.

March 15, 1945
. . .We had a swell time with the folks. That serving tray I bought them was delivered on time, and mom made good use out of it. It really is a beautiful tray, all hand painted, and they were very pleased with it. Mom made such a good meal—borscht, pickled fish, blintzes, and homemade cookies. We toasted them for their anniversary, and then offered a fervent prayer for your return—soon. I fed Jeff his supper, and then your dad put him to sleep in Roslyn's old doll carriage. He just fits in it. We all talked and schmoozed the time away and really enjoyed it. Jerry Green was there, too. That kid is quite a ladies' man. You should see the way he makes up to me!

March 17, 1945
Sweetheart,
I'm writing to you in a house suddenly gone mad with confusion and the hustle bustle of a party. Mother is having a gathering for Frances for her second anniversary. Poor girl, neither for her first or second anniversary has Milton been here with her. Milt is in Marseilles, France. She'll be here soon, and will spend the night.

Roslyn is now back from Florida and seeing Harold, and now is sad to part from him as he begins his army duty in Europe. She may take a puppy from Shirley, one of a litter sired by Skipper.

March 25, 1945
. . .Today we went up to your folks for dinner and to celebrate their anniversary. It is a week early, but your father won't be home next Sunday.
We just got home a little while ago at 11:00 clock. Poor Jeff had to be awakened from sleep 3 times, but now finally he is fast asleep in his own crib.

> . . . *Tonight, the woman who owns that black cocker spaniel from 881 Washington Ave. called me up to inform me that her dog is finally in heat, and to arrange a mating for Skipper with her. She wants to see Skipper's papers, so I'll show them to her tomorrow. We haven't agreed on any terms yet, but I can have a puppy if I want one. I don't know where, as yet, the mating will take place. But I expect in a veterinary hospital.*
>
> *I called up your folks tonight but completely forgot to ask Roz whether she still wants a puppy. She was so excited and downcast. She had just come back from seeing Harold off at the train. His 5-day extension furlough was over tonight, and from here, he'll probably go overseas, unless he's lucky. She's taking it very emotionally. It took her a long time to make up her mind, but now that she's fallen in love, she's fallen intensely—as she does everything. I understand she called me last night to have Harold speak to me, but I was out. So I haven't yet met him. From her description of him, he seems to be all that she wants. He's young in years but old otherwise, as she is—so they make a good pair.*

Shirley again describes Grandma Tibey, to whom she refers as Grandma Sidney.

> *April 29, 1945*
>
> *We went to visit Grandma Sidney for a little while. I wither up and age a few years every time I visit that place. Grandma is about the same. She talks of wanting to undergo an operation to curb the Parkinson disease—stop the shaking, at any rate. But it's an operation involving the brain, pretty dangerous and not successful at all times. She doesn't have any desire to go on living the way she is and is willing to undertake the chances of the operation. It's enough to break your heart. Poor Mother—she feels it so terribly.*

Lester's Aunt Dora becomes quite ill. She is Lester's mother's sister.

> *May 3, 1945*
>
> . . . *I heard tonight from your dad that your Aunt Dora has been taken very sick. She's had a hemorrhage yesterday—from her*

lung—and blood has been flowing almost continuously from her mouth. She has 3 nurses in attendance, and her doctors expect it to turn into pneumonia. Your dad said that, when she was a child, she had pus on a lung, and it collapsed. After all these years, it has taken its toll. I'll keep you in touch with how she is.

May 9, 1945
    . . . I also spoke to your folks and Roz tonight. Everything is fine at home. Your Aunt Dora is getting much better. The folks haven't heard from you in a week, but I assured them you were fine, and read them all the news. Roz tells me she spoke to Barney Korchin the other day—he was at Aunt Becky's house when she called her up. He told her that he is going to go to the Pacific, probably Hawaii, and will look you up.

Mother's Day, a day for visiting relatives, included both of Shirley's grandmothers, Tibey in the nursing home and Frunka at the home of her daughter, Rose. Lillian, Rose's daughter and therefore Shirley's first cousin, was also a close life-long friend of Shirley's. David was Lillian's first husband; George was Rose's husband.

May 13, 1945
    . . . Today was Mother's Day, and therefore visiting my grandmas was in order. We went first to Grandma Sidney, and Jeff made that desolate place ring with giggles. He was the delight of all the patients and nurses. From there we went on to my Aunt Rose, where Grandma Frunka was spending the day. I gave Jeff his supper there and put him to bed in Lillian's baby's carriage. Their Neil is blond and blue-eyed, too, but there the resemblance ends. In coloring, he resembles David, but in looks he seems to take after Uncle George, unfortunately. We sat and talked until 9, and then we brought Grandma home and got back at almost 10. I hate to disturb the baby's schedule that way, but once in a great while an occasion does arise. He seems none the worse for it—as a matter of fact, when I put him to bed a few minutes ago, he was buoyant and full of fun, while I am lying here, a dead duck.

Roslyn decided to get a puppy.

June 24, 1945

I was supposed to go to the movies tonight with Gloria and her folks (to the Kameo Roof Garden—I haven't been there in years)—but Elaine didn't get home until after Flo went and my folks were in N.Y. When she did finally come home, Roz's mom and I went to call for the puppy.

Roz was still trembly and afraid and ready to back out, but she was finally convinced when she saw the puppy. It's so adorable—really the best in the litter. And better than both Skipper and its mother. She has long ears and a wide nose, and is as frisky and cunning as can be. Roz was given all instructions, and she took her home by subway wrapped in a diaper! Even your mother admitted she's a beautiful dog. Mrs. Adelson gave Roz all the papers to fill out for the registration, and all it will cost will be $4. How I hated to part with that puppy. If I had my way, and the room for it, I would have taken it home. Darling, we really are a pair from God! The two slap-happiest people in the world—thank goodness we were joined together. No one else could have stood us.

The following letter marks the anniversary of Shirley's parents. Grandma Tibey became quite ill.

June 25, 1945
Darling,

Today is Mother and Dad's anniversary—23 years. I sent them a lovely bouquet of roses and baby's breath in our name. It looks so beautiful on the piano. We're going to go out this Saturday night to celebrate—Mother made reservations at the Persian Room of the Savoy Plaza—to hear Hildegarde, which should be fun.

Mother's mother was taken sick over the weekend. She has heat prostration—her sweat glands don't function, one of the results of the Parkinson's disease. Dr. Vogel has been there every day, and now she seems to be pulling out of the danger. I don't know how that woman yet lives, for she's merely a skeleton. In her case, death would be welcome, and yet it doesn't come.

July 1, 1945

   . . . Today the two of us sat across the street with Jeff, while waiting for the folks. Then we went to see Grandma. As usual, because of the heat, she was ill again. A special nurse was there. If possible, she looked worse than ever. That darn home depresses me terribly. If that's an answer to the end of life, and the sacrifices of parents, well, then, life can't be worth very much.

Even July 4 was a reason to visit family.

July 4, 1945

   . . . Today being a holiday, I'm hardly aware of that fact any longer—Daddy was home, and we went visiting with Jeff. We picked up Daddy's mother, and then went over to visit Grandma Sidney. She had a lot of company today—relatives from the Bronx. We stayed there for a while and then went down to Coney Island to see Aunt Kitty. I gave Jeff his supper there (you should see the paraphernalia I travel with), and then put him to sleep in my cousin Eleanor's daughter's crib. While he slept we all ate and sat around talking. Aunt Kitty's son is convalescing in Australia now, from malarial fever. She's quite worried about him. We stayed till about 9 o'clock (Jeff woke up then—he must have known it wasn't his own crib). And so here we are, back home. It's been a pretty exhausting day. It always is, to go visiting with the baby. But at least it's a change of scene for me.

Harold comes home on leave, and he and Rozzie are supposed to visit.

July 14, 1945
Sweetheart,

   This has been a very dull Saturday. Rozzie called up this morning to let me know that Harold had come home last night for a 30-day furlough, and that they expected to be down to see us this afternoon. Jeffie and I hung around the house, all dressed up in our nicest clothes, to make a perfect impression on our future relative. However, they never showed up. When I called up at 5 o'clock to find out what had happened, Roz informed me that Harold had made different plans. For some reason or other, I'm always in a slough of despondency on Saturdays, and I thought they would keep me company and help cheer me up a little, as I've been all alone.

August 28, 1945
> *...The great Spinny arrived home today. Elaine hasn't eaten a meal in a week from nervousness, and also from a desire to please. I believe that she's a bit disappointed in him. She built up a picture in her mind of him as being a man, but he's still a baby.*

Shirley asks Lester not to tell Uncle Sidney about the grave condition of his mother, Tibey.

August 29, 1945
Darling,
> *The folks went away today for a much needed rest in the country. They're at Grossinger's—Mother's favorite place. How I wish I could join them.*
> *...Darling, if you get to Manila, which is very probable, you'll be able to look Sidney up. I'm enclosing his address in this letter. It will make mother feel good to know that you saw him. However, don't mention the fact that Grandma is in the nursing home or is so critically ill. The boys still think she's at home and her condition is about the same. You can see, by reading the letter, that he thinks she's still well enough to go to the beach.*

Elaine and Spinny continue their story.

August 29, 1945
> *.... Elaine wasn't seeing Spinny tonight, and so she stayed in for me. She's quite disappointed in him, for he still likes to hang out with his mob on the street corners instead of seeking secluded dates with her. I gave her quite a lecture on her love life tonight, for she's quite disgusted and taking it much too seriously. I pointed out to her that she shouldn't expect him to be much different, for*

he is so young and irresponsible, for all of his 21 years and being
overseas. She now quite realistically agrees that he isn't really what
she wants, but in the meantime she is infatuated with him! Quite
a gal. She really has some sense beneath that babyish exterior.

Plans concerning both sisters appear in the next letters.

October 5, 1945
 . . . At any rate, Elaine as you know is graduating this term,
and hopes to go away, out of town, to college. She hoped for Cornell,
but they wrote back today that they are not having a February se-
mester. It's pretty difficult these days getting in to a good college.
Even with her high average, she'll need luck or pull, or both. How-
ever, in case we don't get anything by the time you get home, we
would be able to stay here without too much inconvenience to the
folks as long as Elaine won't be here.
 Roslyn told me that she expects to get married as soon as you
come home. So be prepared for a hosanna [blessed event], my friend.

October 22, 1945
 . . . Harold, Roz's fiancé, is discharged and will be home to-
morrow or the next day. Your mom says that Roslyn is simply walking
on air. She said that they were at Becky's yesterday, but they didn't
think I'd be home, so they didn't call or come here. The whole family
was there, for Rose and Elliot came home for a week with their baby.
(I seem to be considered as pretty much of an outsider in your fam-
ily.)
 Leo Korchin finally came home today. He called Esther but
wasn't able to see her for a couple of days. Then he will be dis-
charged, and home for good.

Further on Rozzie and Harold:

October 24, 1945
 . . . Your mother called me up this morning and invited me for
dinner tonight. Harold was to be there, and she was making all my
favorite things. It's pretty hard for me to leave the house early

enough to get there in time for dinner; but I promised her I would.

. . .Harold and Roz sat in our places at the table and looked starry-eyed at each other. It made me feel so-o-o miserable, as I sat in Rozzie's old chair, alone at the table.

Harold is planning to enter Columbia for the spring term. He has three more years to go! Your folks have the determined idea that you are going to go to medical school when you return.

The family hid the severity of Tibey's illness from Sidney, allowing him to accept an education position, a harbinger of jobs to come, as he spent a lifetime devoted to that field.

November 6, 1945

. . .We received a cablegram from Manila this morning! Mother was so excited that she couldn't even hear the message as it was being telephoned to her. It was from Sidney. He has been offered a civilian education position in Tokyo, at $3,725 for a contract of nine months. He wanted to know whether Grandma's condition permitted him to take it. Mother wired him back to accept. He doesn't know where Grandma is, or how bad her condition is. There's no point in his being tied down to her, as he'd have to be, and watch her suffer. As it is, he'd have to wait months for a ship to come home anyway. This will be a wonderful break for him, and I think it will entitle him to a better job when he comes home (as he dislikes teaching). Milton writes that he will probably be home by Christmas, anyway.

23

JEFFREY NEIL

L ESTER COULD NOT WAIT to go home. He lived and dreamed it. How did Shirley spend her days? Her free time, he already knew, was filled with friends and relatives, going to the movies or seeing the occasional play in Manhattan. But what about those hours when she was not free? What was she doing then?

Shirley was also a married woman with an infant son, and though it happened almost seventy years ago, some things never change. She spent her time caring for a baby, which has always been a full-time job. So most of her time, and a good portion of the letters, involved the rhythms of Jeffrey's day. Les had gone to sea before Jeff was born. It fell to Shirley to keep the first-time father up to date on his son's development. She spoke of his behavior and his disposition, but she most often shared the small details of his every moment.

The day began very early in the morning; those hours were often a time to play in bed before getting up to start the day, and Jeff was blessed with a generally happy disposition. He was not grumpy when he awoke, but smiled and laughed. Breakfast came soon afterward—a bottle of milk or, later, food. Diaper-changing needed to be done several times, and Jeffrey took a nap or two each day, allowing Shirley time to catch up with bill paying, sewing, or her own grooming. She described the luxury of taking a shower, washing and fixing her hair.

Each day, regardless of the outside temperature, she took the baby out in his carriage for a walk in Prospect Park, which was right across the street, or up toward the Brooklyn Museum, or just around the neighborhood. Sometimes they went by themselves, but often they were joined by her friends. Only rain or snow kept them inside.

Jeffrey's good nature was a source of pride to his mother, and the baby's pleasant temperament was always noticed by friends or even complete strangers. Only occasionally would he become fussy, as all infants do when they are tired, teething, or sick. Shirley wrote worried letters to Les describing the condition and the poor child's suffering. Generally, though, Jeff was healthy and in good spirits.

Shirley liked to describe Jeffrey's laugh and what seemed to make him laugh, and how much he liked to play. She admitted to Lester, but not to others, her conviction that Jeffrey was a much better, brighter, and well-behaved baby than the others, and she had support for this claim. She also told him about all the compliments that Jeffrey got. Sometimes, she commented as well on his high level of activity.

Every afternoon around 5:00 was designated play time—devoted solely to amusing Jeffrey—a time of quiet bonding. Sometimes, Sam and Rose joined in, and everyone had a great time making the baby laugh.

Jeff brought Shirley great happiness but also kept her quite busy, and he served to distract her, at least for some periods of time, from missing Les. He was the focus of her days.

She tried to capture Jeffrey's little moments for Lester, hoping that he could somehow get to know his son in this way.

> *October 13, 1944*
> *. . . Jeffrey Neil asked me to send his daddy a great big kiss for him. He really is a happy little fellow—he breaks into a wide grin at the slightest opportunity. Now he is at the stage of staring in fascination at his hands. However, right now he is staring at them in frustration, for I have them tied inside his drawstring nightgown, and he can't get at them to suck his thumb, as he so loves to do. His distraught cries finally brought me to his rescue, and I untied him, so now he's free to mutilate himself as he pleases. Aren't I soft hearted?*
> *Your son is also possessed of a most militaristic attitude. His favorite position in his crib is to lie with his fist clenched in a most threatening attitude, daring anyone to fight him. We call him now "the boxer."*

Shirley certainly earned points for tolerating the cold for the sake of her baby.

> *December 1, 1944*
> *. . . It was bitter cold today for a change. I had the baby out and stayed out until my ears and toes were numb. What a healthy lass I'm turning out to be. Jeff's cheeks and mine were the color of apples, but what a racket that kid has. He lies snug and warm in his carriage, while valiant mama and Skipper trudge wearily and frostbitten through the streets.*

Part of the day's routine was a social hour.

> *December 3, 1944*
> *. . . After that, Jeff miraculously fell asleep (he doesn't believe much in sleeping during the day), and so I was able to sit on Eastern Parkway for half an hour, until he woke. It was really too cold to sit still any longer, anyway. I came home about 4:30, and put Jeff in his playpen for his "social hour," where he began to industriously pull on his gymnasium. It's such fun to watch him swat it around vigorously. He's a strong little brute. Thus were we engaged in "socializing."*

Shirley tries to capture Jeffrey's spirit.

> *January 9, 1945*
> *. . . It was bitter cold, but Mother took the baby out. When I came home, his little cheeks were pink, and he was so beautiful. He is a darling baby, even more than we dreamed of. But beside his adorable looks, he is a bandit. There is a devil in his eyes. He's full of spirit and life and giggles. His greatest delight these days is to twist my nose and entangle his fingers in my hair when I bend over him, and then giggle happily as I kiss his fat little neck. We have so much fun together. He's 5½ months now and rapidly advancing to a precocious stage. He understands more, and croons to himself, and plays industriously with his rattle. And you should see him squeal and kick up his legs in an ecstasy of delight, when he sees me coming to play with him (a real chip off the old block). Sweetheart, I don't mean to make you lonesome when*

I write to you of these things. It's just I want you to know how he is getting along, and how rapidly he is growing. I'd give everything in the world to have you see him. It's a damn shame and so unfair, all that you're missing. But, my sweetheart, we'll make it all up to you when you come home, I promise you that.

The descriptions of feeding Jeff his spinach, and his decision to refuse the bottle, seem timeless.

January 10, 1945
. . . Nothing of undue importance happened today except that I nearly froze to death wheeling our precious baby around. I had him out (and Skipper, too, who is threatening to move back to Corpus if this weather continues), from 12 to 2, and then brought him up to feed him. I gave him strained spinach for the first time. He succeeded in getting it everywhere but in his mouth. He was splashed from head to toe with that nauseating color by the time I managed to finally get 2 teaspoons in him. He's a pretty good eater; takes to his new vegetables with a surprising lack of fuss. But just this week, he has evidently decided that he is too big a man to take a bottle of milk any longer, and so now he will graciously take half of it, and will play around and drive me frantic while I try to get him to take the other half. He thinks he can disarm me by flirting outrageously and being coy, but I am indifferent to his charms (although it's hard to keep from laughing at some of the antics he employs to get out of drinking his milk.
Today, the milk battle lasted for an hour, at the end of which I was fit for the old folk's home.
. . . Jeffie and I did the Samba and the Rumba in his Social hour this evening, and then my little man went to sleep.

The early morning hours.

January 20, 1945
Darling,
I couldn't hold out any longer. I took a man to bed with me, but it was in the morning (and who has the energy to participate

then), and the other offender is a guy by the name of Jeffrey Neil. Ever hear of him? He's quite famous for his conquests of feminine hearts.

Daddy came in the room (everyone comes in my room —it's now called the "Grand Central Station terminus") and saw the little blond head (that so amazingly resembles yours) on the pillow beside mine. But I'm afraid Jeff was more interested in his new surroundings than he was in the gal beside him, for he scarcely gave me a glance.

Jeff's first teeth:

February 23, 1945
Darling,

I am so proud, I could burst! This morning, as I was feeding Jeff his cereal, the spoon made a clackety-clack noise against something in his mouth. Suspecting what it might be, I could hardly wait for him to swallow. Then I investigated—and there sure enough were the tops of 2 shy little teeth popping up in the bottom front gum. I called Mother and Dad in, and we all took turns marveling (like idiots) at the only 2 baby teeth in the world. Jeff looked pleased with himself, and lay there with a smug expression on the cherubic countenance.

I suppose it is about the right age for him to get them, but I could hardly wait to see them. And now that he has them, I am desolate. It seems I must say goodbye to my baby-boy; for today he is a man-child.

I'm still futilely sterilizing. Why I do it, I don't know. For Jeff puts everything he can find in his mouth. And today, the funniest thing occurred. I was in the kitchen making the formula, and I left Jeff in his playpen in the dining room. All of a sudden, I heard the heartiest chuckles and giggles coming from that direction. Running in to see what was causing it, what did I see but Skipper, with his head thrust between the bars, placidly licking the baby's face. And Jeff loved it!

Therefore, I ask you, why must I still sterilize?

Jeff seems more active than other babies.

March 24, 1945

. . . Do you like that button that our son has instead of a nose? He's really an adorable baby, but what a devil! He's always afraid he'll miss something, and so sleep, for him, during the day, is out of the question. Those hawk eyes of his are too busy darting here and there, to have any time for sleep and rest.

It's not been hard raising him, for he is so sweet at all times. But it is worth it, for his devilishness; he is so adorable, I practically eat him up. He already has quite a personality of his own, whereas the other neighborhood babies of his age still lie quietly in their carriages. This one is never still for a moment. He's very unhappy in his carriage, for he doesn't have the room to roll and kick about as he prefers. He's quite cranky in the street when the carriage is still. But as soon as I start walking with him he's as contented as a lamb. So I have been walking all winter. But really it's no joke, and I'd like to break him of that habit. As soon as I go into a store and leave him outside, he starts screaming, and a million women rush over to rock him and sympathize with the poor baby, and cast baleful glances at this heartless momma. So it's no use. I just hope he'll grow out of it. Well, the mommas of all geniuses had their tribulations!

But in the house, in his playpen, he's a doll. There, with all the room he needs, he rolls and creeps and plays with his rattles to his heart's content, always giggling and smiling and following me about with his eyes.

March 26, 1945

. . . Oh! I almost forgot the most important thing. Our son said "da-da" today, and has chattered incessantly with it all day. Isn't he wonderful?

Jeff reaches another milestone, leaving Shirley saddened.

April 27, 1945
Darling,

I want to tell you that our baby for the first time stood firmly on his own two feet today while clasping the top of the crib for support. Also, from a sitting position, he somehow dexterously managed to twist around and lean on his knees while holding on to the crib. He looked so adorable, all smiles and independence. Now I feel that he's really left my arms. I love him, darling. We can really be proud of him. Tonight, I tickled him in his ribs, and he came out with such an unexpectedly low, hearty chuckle, that I just had to laugh with him. And how he giggles at Skipper!

Jeff has teething problems, but an infant's moods are labile.

August 25, 1945
Les darling,

. . . About 9:30, Jeff woke up screaming, and continued to do so, off and on, until 4 A.M. this morning. Needless to say, I'm a wreck. I thought I'd be able to write to you before I went to bed as I usually do, but he never even gave me the chance. Poor baby, it's heartbreaking to see how miserable he was. He kept his whole fist in his mouth. I gave him an aspirin, rubbed some whiskey on his gums, and finally in desperation, some paregoric (for it's supposed to be harmful if it's used often). Do you know of anything at all that would have a soothing effect, and yet wouldn't be injurious to use?

At four in the morning, out of sheer weariness, he finally fell asleep, and so did I.

You'd think he'd know better, but there he was at 7:30, bright and chipper, demanding breakfast. I've been in a semi-stupor all day as a result.

. . . Your mother and sister came over, and we spent a very nice afternoon together. Jeff showed off all his new tricks, and he does possess some pips. He strides along with giant steps in his new shoes, holding on with one hand to me. Every once in a while, he bursts out with "Oh, God," which he must have heard someone say. It's a riot to hear. When we ask him where Daddy's picture is, he unerr-ingly points to it, and kisses it when we bring him close to it. He holds up his feet, so we can play "this little piggy" on his toes, which he adores. And he mimics all our words and expressions in a general way. Also, he now claps his hands, and blows kisses enchantingly. All this in the few weeks since I've been away. I'm amazed at the

change in him.

Thank goodness he was his old sunny self again this afternoon and so we really had an enjoyable time with him.

Lester, so far away, is trying to get to know Jeff. He is full of questions about the newborn.

August 19, 1944
...I know that yesterday was to have been Jeff's first day out-side. How did he take his first excursion into the great big world? Was he google-eyed with wonder or did he just keep on sleeping? And speaking of sleeping, how is that 2 o'clock feeding coming on? Is he keeping everyone awake at night? I hope that no one is spoil-ing him. You know how I feel about little brats.

Lester is overcome by emotion from a description.

September 26, 1944
...I love your description of the baby. When you tell me about how he laughs and follow you around with his eyes, my throat chokes up. Oh, how I want this war over, to be back with my family once more. Every day away from you is a day torn from my life. It is worthless, meaningless.

He acts just as any proud father would act.

October 19, 1944
Churl Darling,
The pictures came today in one envelope, and in another were two letters from you. To be very corny, it was indeed a red-letter day. The pictures are tremendous. I love them. I've done nothing but sit and look at them. Then as the officers pass but I grab them, like any doting daddy, and say, "Say, how'd you like to see some pic-tured of my son?" Not one has had guts enough to interfere by say-ing no, so I show them off, making admiring comments over their shoulders, such as, "Look at the size of him, will ya, and only two months old. Able to hold his head up already. Isn't he a terrific

kid? How do you like that smile of my wife's. Isn't that worth about a million and a half at a conservative estimate?" I'm becoming a real new-father pest; but I have to let the others see how proud I am of my wife and son. Darling, have pictures like that taken often—hey [are] marvelous, and the baby changes so rapidly now that I need them to keep up with him.

A Happy Birthday wish segues into a heartfelt question.

January 28, 1945
Churl Darling,

You might wish Jeff a happy birthday for me, give him a little hug, and explain to him that his dad would like to be with him, but due to the pressure of urgent business is detained elsewhere for the time being. How can the Government ever repay me for the time away from my wife and son? I miss you both so keenly that it cuts. I try not to think of the long interval that probably still remains, although I am really more fortunate in that respect than many of the other men on board. The dental department rotates its men more frequently than some of the others.

24

IN SICKNESS AND IN HEALTH

S HIRLEY, ONLY TWENTY-ONE OR twenty-two years old at the time, had more than her share of medical problems. Most were dental, which was particularly ironic. But she also developed other mild illnesses and colds, complained of fatigue, and had repeated problems with a bad back. As she later learned, these early medical issues, except for the dental problems, were likely related to other, as yet-unknown medical conditions.

Shirley discovered, in the next letter, that mothers are not allowed to get sick. She had a case of the old-fashioned grippe.

> October 13, 1944
> Darling,
>
> I was unable to write yesterday, for I very stupidly came down with the grippe. I say stupidly, for, with a small baby, I can't afford to get sick. However, God was very good, for it only lasted one day, and today I'm feeling much better.
>
> I woke up yesterday feeling very sluggish, with every bone in my body aching, and burning up. My temperature was almost 102, so mother took the baby down for me in the afternoon. At night, I started to feel really low-down, so mother called the doctor. (Really, I must get just a tiny bit sick more often; it's the only time now that a man looks at me with interest — even if he is an old fossil who gets paid to do so.)
>
> My temperature was 102½, so I was made to stay in bed and

take pills every 4 hours to break the fever. I perspired all night, and this morning it was miraculously gone. I just feel a little shaky but all better. Formulas, bathing the baby, and taking care of the baby still go on, no matter whether I get sick or not, and I simply can't get sick any more.

Shirley does not allude to the reason why she doesn't wear high heels.

November 18, 1944
. . . We went to a shoe store there—"Betty Berks" (across the street from your relative's) store. They sell sample shoes, and I thought I could get a pair of low-heeled dress shoes. It breaks my heart not to be able to wear high-heeled shoes any more. What good are my legs?

Is it possible that Shirley's lack of energy relates to her problems wearing high heels? The doctor's diagnosis seems woefully inadequate in hindsight.

November 24, 1944
. . . He also told me that I have "War Nerves." Imagine, placid me having War Nerves. He said that I miss you very much, and that I am lonesome and unhappy without you, and that I feel tied down and would like to have a gay time, which the baby and circumstances don't allow. I agreed it was all true, and he said that is why I take refuge in fatigue and sleep—that I don't like to wake up and face the fact that you aren't with me. It's all true in a way but preposterous. I'm fairly happy, and thank God for the baby, he makes my days fly by—but it is true. I am very lonely without you. But there's nothing else I can do but grin and bear it.
He gave me some vitamin pills to pep me up and to raise my blood pressure, which is a little low. Alas, he said that I have no gland trouble, but to cut down my salt and fluid intake. And that was that.
Did I gain anything by going?—I don't know.

And why would Shirley's back hurt so much?

January 15, 1945

. . . It left me with a backache—I haven't had many of them lately, but tonight I had a pip. After I got through sponge bathing and feeding the baby, I was even too tired to eat dinner. Darling, why did you ever marry such a female 4-F? What in the world would I ever do with a house to clean and meals to cook? I think I'll train Jeff.

With her regular dentist in the navy, Shirley had to go to see a substitute, and she required a good deal of work, considering how young she was.

January 23, 1945

. . . I went on my usual weekly traipse to Phil Levin today, and as usual he accomplished very little —merely put a permanent filling in one tooth to replace the temporary one. I have yet to get done: 1 more filling, 2 more permanent fillings to replace the temporary ones, and my bridge. I suppose that means I'll be seeing him for the rest of the year. I offered to pay him for the work so far, but he very nicely refused. He said I could settle up with him at the end. I hope your patients pay as they come. He gave me an idea of the expense in a dentist's office—he just bought a new light for his dental outfit which cost $75. Boy, oh boy.

February 4, 1945

. . . I foolishly walked with Gloria yesterday to Sutter's—pushing the baby carriage. She had to call for pies there, as her future in-laws were coming over to dinner. Last night showed the result of that walk on me, for my back pained me considerably. Lately, it hasn't only been hurting me in the place where it usually does (at the base of the spine), but now, I seem to have sprained or done something to the upper part. Oy, what an old kvetch I'm turning out to be.

April 24, 1945

. . . I went to Phil Levin for a change today. He drilled away almost all of the tooth in front of the bridge, in order to put a full crown on it (the one that's almost exposed). Fortunately, it can be saved. He didn't give me an injection today. Ain't I a real brave girl? But did it hurt—and my gum is so sore where he had to drill

all around the tooth, under the surface. Next week he'll prepare the tooth in back of the bridge for a ¾ crown. He says after that it will take about 4 or 5 more visits to complete the bridge. Does it always take that long? He's finished all my other cavities, though.

25
DISCHARGE HOPES
AND DREAMS

A CAREER OFTEN FOLLOWS the path of an arc. The novice struggles to acquire skills and gain confidence. Then he is in charge and fulfilled by his accomplishments. Eventually, that is replaced by the growing sense that he has performed these same tasks endless times before.

In retrospect, Les's career as a naval dentist was brief but emotionally intense. First came the uncertainties when he joined the crew; then he developed the sense of professional competence and mastery of military protocol. He even accepted the interminable loneliness with a certain resignation. But in time came a readiness to have it all over and done with. All of this occurred in less than a year and half, so that the shape of this arc was steep and narrow, but an arc it surely was.

We see the earliest signs of this final stage in the spring of 1945, as he initially begins to mention an eventual, albeit still hypothetical, return home. But by that summer, there is a definite change of mood in Lester's letters, as well as in the information that he is sending to Shirley. Whereas, up to that point, all talk of coming home had been theoretical and emotional, a sad refrain of yearning, his conversation begins to be fact-based about returning home. Suddenly, many letters contain long passages detailing naval regulations about discharge, including the number of months of sea duty required, what constituted that sea duty, when that count of months started, etc. There were two problems, however. One was that the navy, at that point in the war, was changing its regulations; the other was the constant rumors about these changes floating about the ship. Nobody knew what might be true, and each new bit of information was discussed, debated, written home about, and ruminated upon. All this is reflected in Lester's letters to Shirley, with its inevitable emotional surges or deflations.

Discussions among the men, and letters to Shirley, reflect an exquisite parsing of naval language. What exactly did the navy mean by its use of certain terms? What exactly was the current definition of needed points and how to earn them? Did those months in dry dock, before the ship was launched, count toward those points? Everyone thought that they had the latest answers, although at least some of it was mere rumor, untethered to actual fact. Compounding this for Lester was news from Shirley, and his relatives, friends, and fellow officers, about other naval men who had already returned home. The circumstances of each of these rotations home were endlessly discussed and held up to compare with their own situations. There did not appear to be a single set of rules that was universally applicable and generally known. Lester, like his fellows, had had enough of their separations and of their coping mechanisms. By then, they just wanted to go home, or at least to know when they would.

At one point, they learned that the ship was scheduled to sail back to California, but, lacking the necessary number of points, they would have to continue to serve and remain aboard when it returned to the Pacific. His goal was to leave the ship permanently when it docked Stateside, though he did not know if it was possible.

Even in the closing weeks rumors were rife, with little clarity. In reality, he was close to achieving his wish, but he did not know it. When it finally became clear to him that his return home was indeed possible, a commanding officer had to take several steps to allow this to actually occur, including a request for his replacement and an approval of Lester's transfer off the ship. But that officer would not directly answer Lester's queries, leaving him in painful uncertainty. He was left to deduce the answer, and only in the final week or so did he have any certain knowledge that the end of his service was near. He was finally able to write to Shirley, "This will be my last letter to you."

Lester swings between the fanciful and the practical as he starts to consider life after the navy.

> Undated—probably March 1945
>   . . . I kept day-dreaming all day today about my orders coming
> in, of how I'd get back to the States, and where to request the next
> duty. Incidentally, that isn't fanciful. I wish you would let me know

your preference, because they may grant my request, and I'd like to go where you would like it. I was thinking you might like to visit California; but taken by and large, I believe the best thing to do is to stay in or around New York, if possible. Perhaps some air station on the Island, Mitchell Field, for instance. What think you?

This is the first of many ruminations on when his date of service is thought to have begun, and the number of points required.

March 17, 1945
...Amongst other things the chaplain and I discussed last night was the question of whether or not the bureau will count our tour of duty as starting with the commissioning of the ship (September 11) or with the date on the orders ordering us to report to duty. That is the great unsolved question. My orders to report to F.S.N.Y. in connection with the Oxford were dated May 17. I reported to FSNY July 20. If either of those dates is the one to be considered, I will be home a great deal earlier than otherwise, provided, of course, that everything else goes well. And that rests in the hands of God.

A rumor. . .

April 24, 1945
. . .Well, my sweetest wife, I think that is about enough for tonight. I'll answer the rest of your letters tomorrow night. Oh yes, there was something I wanted to tell you about. Butch told us today that he had a letter from a friend of his who is in a position to know, and he claims that the official tour of sea duty for a medical officer has been cut from 18 months to 12 months. If that is true, it means that certainly I ought to be home by September, and possibly before; but don't count on anything until I get a flimsy. Let's just exist from day till day until then. Goodnight sweetheart.

August 24, 1945
. . .All of us are eagerly awaiting the announcement of some new system for speeding up discharges. That's the only thing that matters right now.

Lester's coping skills are starting to fray.

> *August 25, 1945*
> *Churl Darling,*
>   *At sea again, and here we go slipping into the old routine, only now it is a little harder to stay calm and philosophical about all of this because frankly, more than ever, I want off, not so much out (I'll take my turn for that, but off, so that I can spend the time waiting for it with you).*
>   *... Before we left I got off a letter to the dental personnel officer telling him that I'd like my next duty at the Brooklyn Naval Hospital or the Floyd Bennett Naval Air Station. Dr. Golden wrote a similar letter to his chief. We'll see what happens now.*

Coping was wearing down.

> *September 4, 1945*
>   *... Al-navs are coming in frequently now, dealing with such subjects as how to treat the Japanese, and the desirability of staying on in the regular navy. They are really painting a glowing picture of life in the peacetime navy, but most of us aren't having any. We just want out. Along that line, Ralph was just in for a little bull session on the desirability of staying in. We talked back and forth and reached the same conclusion as always: that, while there was much to be said for the desirability of staying in, there were enough disadvantages to offset any advantages. Ralph has adopted a policy of watchful waiting. For me, it's out, and soon, I hope.*

And the points required for discharge kept changing.

> *September 11, 1945*
>   *... The big topic of conversation of course is the new and revised point system. Of course you know that as things stand now I have 42 points. That leaves seven points to make up, which should take nine months of sea duty. The whole thing is ridiculous, though. Very few people can qualify under the present system, and they are bound to grade the requirements sharply downward, very soon. There is a*

tremendous amount of resentment about the way the whole thing was handled. This is especially true of the Medical Corps, where the minimum requirement, instead of being 49 points, is 60 points. Almost no one can qualify under that heading. My immediate hope is to get relieved soon and to get shore duty in the New York area. If that were the case I wouldn't mind staying in for a few extra months while we surveyed the situation and decided at our leisure where to locate, and where to settle.   It seems logical to me that the official tour of duty should be much curtailed under the present system inasmuch as there are a great many younger dental officers and older ones who have had no sea or foreign service. If they are not sent out now, they probably never will get any. That would be rather unfair. So I think they may send them out soon. After all, now that the ships aren't blacked out, and are cruising under peacetime conditions, life at sea isn't bad. Another possibility is that they may decommission the ship prior to turning her over to the Merchant Marine. In the latter case I would either get shore orders or a discharge. At any rate I am hoping for a change soon. And I'm really hoping.

September 12, 1945

   . . . As usual, that talk is still running on points, or the possibility of getting orders. As things stand now I have about 42 points. That means I lack 7 points of the critical score for discharge, which will take about nine months of overseas duty to make up. However, my tour of sea duty should end, at the worst, in six months, and I confidently expect to be relieved well before that time. Even should that not be the case, it is very likely that the ship will be recalled for the use of the maritime service sometime in the immediate future, which of course would mean that the entire crew would get off. I expect that what will probably happen is that we will make one trip to Japan and then pick up troops, either there or some place else out here, and return to the States. The entire procedure should take about two months. Within that time it is probable that the points system will be changed, so that the critical score will be lowered sufficiently to include my group. Or possibly two or three of those alternatives may take place at the same time. At any event I

*believe that I am on the way to shore duty or discharge. If things
break right I may be home in time to celebrate our wedding anniversary with you, or earlier than that. Wouldn't that be wonderful?*

*As I keep saying, however, it isn't out that I want so badly right
now, it is off. I wouldn't mind getting duty in the New York area
for a few months before getting discharged. I could use the time to
look around and make up our minds exactly where we wanted to
open, and to locate.*

Here, Lester is about one month from discharge and is as yet unaware
of it.

October 9, 1945
*. . . I still can tell you nothing of our future movements for the
very simple reason that we do not know of them. Our troops are on
board and are likely to stay here for another week. After that, who
knows? The States and discharge, I hope. It will heartbreaking to
go back to the States and then have to come out here on another
trip. I can't even stand the thought of it.*

October 10, 1945
*. . . A news flash tonight announced that the navy had reduced
the critical point score for medical officers from 60 to 50. If that
is true, Dr. Golden will qualify. I hope that, by the time he gets off,
I'll be able to go with him.*

In reality, Lester was drawing ever nearer to his reunion with Shirley,
yet here he was doubtful about even seeing her at Christmas.

October 18, 1945
*. . . There have been some rumors of a reduction in the critical
point score for discharge. I hope they are accurate. At the present
time I have 42 and ¾ points. On November 11, I should have
43½ points, which is within ½ point of the rumored 44. We
should be in the States by that time. I have hopes that the ship
will be decommissioned. It would be heartbreaking to have to go*

*back to the States and then come out here when I am within ½
point of enough for discharge; but that would be the navy way of
doing things. Even if I have enough points, there is a little joker
in the set-up that permits them to keep me for 120 days after I
have the critical score. However, let's keep our fingers crossed. I
have hopes of being home by Christmas, not very high hopes, but
there exists that possibility.*

October 19, 1945
*. . . On December 11, I will have 44¼ points. The whole thing
hinges on when we get back to the States, how long we are due to
stay in the States, whether we are due to make another trip out here
or be decommissioned, and finally whether they will provide a relief
for me, if necessary, or hold me for the 90 days that the law allows
them to. At any event darling, keep your fingers crossed, and I may
be home for Christmas.*

Lester finally begins to sense that this is possibly his last trip.

October 23, 1945
Churl Darling,
*Of course the burning question is if and when I'm getting off
the ship, and after that out of the navy. I don't want you to get too
excited about it lest something unforeseen arise and delay my getting
off the ship. It does look, however, as if this is to be my last trip.
There is an Alnav which states that personnel who will reach the
critical score in 60 days are not to be shipped out of the States. We
will probably be in the States the latter part of November or the
early part of December. If we decommission, points or no points, I
won't be coming out here again, so I sincerely hope that that is what
does happen   . . . I will fall within the category of those who will
reach the critical score within 60 days and, as such, should not be
allowed to leave the States. There is another part to the Alnav which
states that, if a man is required to fill a particular position, he may
be held for a period of not exceeding 90 days. It is emphasized that
this is only in case of necessity, not to suit the convenience of the
commanding officer. What I have done, and a few of the other of-*

*ficers that qualify have done likewise, is to notify the skipper that
we will have the critical score at such a date. It is now his responsibility to secure a relief for those of us who need one. I will probably
need a relief, but it should be very easy to get one for there are many
dental officers who have had no sea duty.*

Now Lester had to obtain the permission of his captain, which was not
as easy as it should have been.

October 29, 1945

*. . . This afternoon I got to thinking about getting off the ship
when we got back and decided that my status needed a little clarifi-
cation. I went up to speak to the skipper about it. It seems that there
has been a new complement authorized by the bureau for APAs and
nobody knows what it is (because we haven't received any mail). I
asked the captain if, in view of the fact that by the time we reached
San Francisco (or whatever port we are going to make) I'd be eligible
under that 60-day provision, he wouldn't write and ask for a relief
for me, or, if he didn't consider me essential, of course that wouldn't
be necessary. He answered as follows: (a) That there was a new complement in the mail, and he would and could do nothing until he
had seen it and got the facts of the situation; (b) that if the complement authorized a dentist, he would consider a dentist essential, and
that if it didn't authorize a dentist, I would get off; (c) that even if
the complement authorized a dentist he would act very promptly to
secure a relief for me as soon as we hit the port so that I could get off.
I tried to get him to write for a relief anyway, but he wouldn't, but he
practically promised me that he'd get me one as soon as the situation
clarified. He told me further that he had heard from the Flag that
this ship was definitely slated for disposition, and that meant decom-
missioning, perhaps after one or two trips more, but again (which is
my earnest hope). The situation isn't bad at all, because that paragraph of the Alnav which he interprets as meaning "essential" actually
says that the man should be retained "only in case of urgent military
necessity," and I scarcely think that the dentist is urgent military necessity, and if I don't have a relief in quick order I'll report to the Pacific Coast headquarters in Frisco, directly for orders.*

Lester's very last letter follows. He is still at sea, but the next time any letters can be mailed, he will be back in this country.

November 7, 1945
Churl Darling,

This will, in all probability, be the last letter you will receive from me before speaking to me on the telephone. We leave tomorrow afternoon for the States. I went to see the skipper yesterday morning to find out his opinion on my essentiality, and to urge him to write for a relief for me. He insisted once more that, if the new complement mentioned a dental officer, he would consider me essential. I reminded him of the new Alnav and its definition of essential men, but he stuck to his guns. Then I suggested again that he write for a relief for me. He was very reluctant, and I left with no definite assurance that he would do so, but an hour later I met the ship's secretary in the ward-room and he told me that the captain had directed him to write asking for a relief for me. In the afternoon yesterday the rough draft of the letter had been approved by the skipper, so that the request has left the ship in today's mail, or if it has been held up will leave tomorrow morning. So I gained the most important part of my request. The only trouble is that 15 days (the length of our trip back is cutting things a bit too fine to suit me). But I expect that the worst that will happen is that I won't be able to leave the ship the same time as the other officers, but a day or so later.

We received our orders from the port director this morning. We are to load tomorrow morning and get underway for the West Coast tomorrow afternoon. We will travel by the great circle route, passing close to Japan and the Aleutians, the trip to take 16 actual days, 15 calendar days; the difference being caused by our crossing the date line.

. . . In the afternoon one of the men of the first lieutenant's office informed me that my stool was all crated, and that the box for my magazines and books was all ready. I had them brought to my office. They had built a very large box for the books. And there was a great deal of room left after I fitted the books and magazines into it. Indeed, there was so much room that I was able to pack all of the souvenirs into it as well as the books. That makes one less pack-

age for handling. So you can see that I'm really acting as if I'm going to get off this time. Incidentally, I'm taking a great kidding from the other crew members and officers as being an "essential" man.

    Wish us God speed, and in a matter of days I should be in your arms again. Incidentally, suppose when I get started from the Coast I call you, and tell you I can't leave until a day or so before I actually can. You can arrange for a room in a hotel for the right time, and send me a telegram en route (or let me know in advance). Then when I get in I'll go right to the hotel to meet you. We'll spend the first day or so together. Then I can meet Jeff and the folks. How does that sound? Or do you have a better idea? And now, darling, your understandably impatient husband bids you a fond Goodnight.

During these same several months, Shirley had also been evaluating Les's chances of discharge and imagining their life after the navy. These next letters coincide with the writing of Lester's letters, but are from her perspective.

May 8, 1945

    . . . Darling, let's go away together, as soon as you come home, for at least a couple of weeks. I want to leave the baby at home in charge of a nurse and Mother (for she wouldn't be able to handle him alone). I'd love him to be with us, but there's plenty of time for that later. I know you understand—even if the folks don't—what being alone with you will mean. We need and deserve a second honeymoon, and following a schedule for Jeff won't let me have much time to donate and give myself to you as I want to.

    And darling, there's one more thing I want you to do for me. Start hinting subtly to your folks—I can take care of mine—that you want to meet me and stay with Jeff and me alone for the first day and night, that is, if you want to. For I don't want to be constrained and hampered in front of others as I greet you for the first time, or watch you greet Jeff in front of others. They will be sacred moments to me, and they deserve to be sacred to the 3 of us alone. I may be premature in urging you to do this, but it may take a great deal of tact and explaining on your part, so that your folks won't be hurt but will understand and approve as I want them to. (Just thinking of being with you is starting me off on a wonderful dream, again, which I've just pulled out of.)

Then Shirley hears of a better way to orchestrate Lester's homecoming.

May 10, 1945

*. . . By the way, Esther gave me a better idea than the one I wrote
you about previously concerning your homecoming. Here's what they're
going to do.When Leo gets in. he's going to check in at a hotel and call
Esther to tell her he's in. She's going to leave the baby at home, not telling
anyone that she knows of Leo's arrival. She'll spend that day and night
with him; the next day, he'll go home to make his son's acquaintance
without any commotion. Later that day, he's going to call his folks and
tell them that he just got in. In that way, they won't be hurt by not knowing that he preferred to spend the first day with his wife, and so everyone
will be happy.*

*I think it's an excellent idea, don't you? No explaining, no apologies
for time spent with me, and no crowd to spoil your homecoming and to
make the baby all upset and confused. Tell me what you think of it.*

Just as, earlier in the war, Shirley had been surrounded by men in service,
those men are all coming home—all except Lester.

August 25, 1945

*. . . And now, ladies and gentlemen, let's go to press: Churl's
journal or news of the day.*

*1) Al Sobel has been discharged from the navy and will be
home Monday. (He's been in service for 5 years.)*

*2) Spinny's ship is supposed to be in New York today—for a
30-day furlough. Elaine is all smiles.*

*3) Sidney Cooper is home and discharged. From them comes
only a hint of apartment for us. Flo and Sid may live with Flo's
mother in New Jersey (in a home they've just bought), so that Sid
will be nearer to his factory. She promised to hold her apartment
for me if she does decide to move out. It's 4 rooms, in Jackson
Heights (only 15 min. from Times Sq.), beautiful, large, sunny rooms
in a brand-new house, and for $80. In Brooklyn, the equivalent
rents for $100 and up. What do you think? Should I take it, if I
can? It's the only one I've heard of, and it does put us on the island,
where I'd like to be. The cheapest rent we could get anywhere, in a*

*decent house, is about $75 and up. This sounds quite good—if
she decides to move. Tell me what you think.*

*4) Aaron is still home and expects to be discharged any day,
as he has enough points. As he only reports to the naval hospital
every few days for injections, he has already opened up a law office
in Manhattan. Besides which, he is planning to enter as a silent
partner with an uncle of Rhoda's in a refrigeration business to give
them a steady income. Not bad, eh!*

5) Leo Korchin now doesn't expect to be home before Christmas.

*And so, Les, with oceans of love, I remain your N.Y. correspon-
dent, Churl Halbreich; and I wish to say that all these discharges are
turning me green—but our day will soon come. Goodnight, darling.
All my love. I'm going to bed with some wonderful memories.*

Churl

Shirley has no idea how close Lester is to his discharge.

October 17, 1945
Darling,

*Hip, hip, hooray! The navy has finally come through with
their lowered discharge points. It's still not as fast as the Army—
it's not fast enough to suit me—but at least you should be eligible
for discharge by January 1st. I called up 90 Church Street today
and found out that the points accumulate month by month, and so
you should have almost 44 points by New Year's. As you'll only need
43 by then, you should be out. Praise to the Lord! I hope, though,
that you'll be home before that. I'm sending along the clipping relating to it, from tonight's World Telegram.*

Lester is now definitely on his way home to her, yet Shirley remains unaware of this. However, this is her last letter that she wrote to Lester.

November 5, 1945

*. . . God only knows what goes on in that great mind of the navy's.
Why on earth are you sitting around doing nothing, when ships are
so desperately needed—and you could be on your way home?*

26

MID-WAR RENDEZVOUS

THE PROSPECT OF A reunion certainly does wonders for the lonely heart. As it approaches, everything seems to get better and easier to bear. Yet the clock seems to slow down too, as a reminder that there is still time to serve in the sentence.

This was the case for Les and Shirley in the summer of 1945, after a full year of separation. Lester's ship, having made its rounds throughout the Pacific, was eventually ordered back home for repairs. As is true in all large organizations, the rumors precede the facts, so that Les had hints of this possibility long before it was made official. There was just a slight problem, however, even in returning to the United States. The ship's home port was on the West Coast, while Shirley lived on the East Coast, a trifle of 3,000 miles in the days before air travel became routine, and when the military often displaced civilian passengers. In addition, there were difficulties of communication. Les, onboard ship, had no access to regular or reliable postal service which, even under the best of circumstances, took at least a week to deliver a letter across that distance. The constraints of censorship were still very much in place, which prevented a direct discussion of such basics as where, when or for how long the ship would be in port. This instead had to be sent through a code, one that had not been previously arranged, so it had to be easy enough to be understood.

Luckily for all concerned, the official announcement of this stopover was given with enough time for Les to write more than once. Shirley received these letters with enough warning to be able to make the arrangements to cross the country by train. She went with another young wife, after her parents had assured her that they would take care of Jeffrey. At some point in her long journey, Shirley was actually aboard a plane when the intercom announced the Japanese surrender, and the pilot decided to celebrate by flying loop-de-loops. Shirley never forgot those heart-stopping moments of abject terror, retelling the story many times over the years of celebrating victory over Japan by flying upside down.

The reunion eventually took place, which is marked by a three-week gap in the correspondence. The letters resumed once their rendezvous ended and normal life picked up again.

For that is the downside of those breathtaking moments—they always come to an end. All the eagerness and anticipation, all the joy, is followed by a profound sadness after the parting. Each had somehow adapted to the loneliness, but now the pain was even worse than before, like opening a fresh wound. They had to return to their lonely lives with no end in sight.

Lester chose a parenthetical remark and underlining to alert Shirley to a subtext. Later in his letter, he was more direct.

July 9, 1945

Darling, I suggest that instead of going to the mountains for your vacation this year, you come to San Francisco. I know it is a long trip, but it will be very worthwhile, if you understand me (and I'm sure you do). I don't know what the transportation system is now (it must be very crowded going to the West now), and I don't know if conditions at home will permit your taking such a trip. I suppose you would have to leave the baby at home, it would be silly, I guess, to take him across the continent even by plane. If you do decide to come, be in San Francisco by August 5th. If you come, and do get a room at a hotel (get a nice one), do as I suggest now. Ralph has an aunt living in the city. There is always someone in the house. So, after you get settled in your hotel, get in touch with them at the address and phone number given below. Then, if and when we do make port, I will call there the first thing to find out where you are. And once I find out, watch out, you San Francisco traffic!

Lester ran into his friend, Al Sobel, who asked if his wife could travel with Shirley.

July 10, 1945
. . . I decided about four o'clock that, as long as we were alongside a dock, I would take a stroll for myself. I had barely reached the outside of the dock limits when whom should I see but Al Sobel. We exchanged greetings, and he asked me to ask you to get in touch with his wife and ask her to accompany you on your journey rather than go by her lonesome. It was a lot of fun meeting Al. We have bumped into each other in the unlikeliest places, and may do so again. At any rate, it was good to talk over old times with him and anticipate new ones. I hadn't anticipated a long walk, but I walked with Al to the navy landing, and took a boat to the ship from there.

More coded messages, this time to tell Shirley to come earlier.

July 11, 1945
. . . I have only time for a quick note today, and I'd like to get it off before we get underway. Ralph had a letter from his aunt in today's mail that mentioned their intention to leave the city earlier than usual this year. In view of this fact you will have to make your trip out there even earlier than you had planned. I think that if you get there about the 26th or 27th of July it will give you about enough time to spend with them.

Shirley reacts with just a "slight" bit of happiness upon getting Lester's letter telling her of his imminent arrival in San Francisco.

July 16, 1945
Darling,
"Oh joy, or rapture unforeseen,
The clouded skies are now serene."
Heavenly bliss, can it really be so?
I received your letter of July 9th this morning, telling me to come to San Francisco by August 5th. Believe me, darling, rain or

*shine, mud or slime, Churl will get to Frisco! Mother and Dad are
still away in the country, so they don't know as yet of my plans. It's
a good thing they are having this vacation now, for they'll need the
added strength. From your descriptions of the port you're in, I can
surmise that it is Manila.*

*I'll do what you suggest about wiring for reservations at the
Chancellor Hotel, and I'll also get in touch with Ralph's aunt when
I arrive.*

*God, I can scarcely believe it. In less than 3 weeks, I'll be in
your arms, after this long vacuum of time, since you've been away.*

*Let me see if I can now write a little more coherently and tell
you what has been happening at home (however, after receiving your
letter today, nothing seems to have any importance beside the fact
that I will be seeing you soon).*

Shirley does not immediately understand the meaning of Lester's coded
messages, especially as he had been changing the code. She details some of
her efforts to make this trip happen.

July 17, 1945
Darling,

*I received 3 letters from you this afternoon, and I must admit,
darling, they have left me in a state of confused uncertainty. They
are dated July 10, 11, and a short note of the 11th, also.*

*In the first 2 letters you tell me to come to Frisco earlier than
the 5th, but to come on the 2nd or 3rd of August instead. You said
that I should come earlier, so that Ralph's aunt, who is leaving town,
could show me around. If they are leaving town earlier, how could
I get in touch with you through them? And of course, time is very
essential to me. I can't afford to leave the baby with mother or a
nurse longer than necessary. Then in your 3rd letter, which was a
short note, you suggested that I even come out a week earlier, so
that I could sightsee with them, but then what would I do all by
myself after they leave until you arrive on the 5th? After puzzling
this out for a while, I came to the conclusion that that was just your
way of letting me know that you unexpectedly found out that the
ship will arrive a week earlier. This means that I will have to leave*

this Monday (if by train). I don't mind at all—that is, if I can get all reservations in this short notice. Just to make sure, I sent a night wire to Ralph's aunt, checking if she really would be leaving earlier and explaining the situation to them.

I called up Al Sobel's parents to get in touch with Jeannette, his wife, as you had suggested. She is away for the summer in Sharon, Mass; but they gave me her phone number so that I could call her. I called her immediately but had to wait an hour till the lines were cleared. The little I saw of her that day at the Sobels' house, she had seemed like a very sweet girl. I finally spoke to her, and she was so excited, for she hadn't received any recent mail from Al and didn't know that he intended to come in. She said immediately that she would go with me, which was wonderful news for me. Then we had to get busy making arrangements. We hung up, and I sent the night letter off to Ralph's aunt to make sure that our getting there a week earlier wouldn't be a wild goose chase. She also thought that to be a good idea to check up on it. Then I sent a telegram to the Chancellor Hotel, asking for two rooms for a week beginning July 26. In the meantime, she was to call the airport and find out if we could make reservations for the 24th or 25th of July. She called back and said it couldn't be done as there was an immense waiting list ahead of us. I told her I would get in touch with Esther's sister, Pearl, to see if she could get us plane seats. And she said she would call the airport again, and we'd both also try to get train reservations (which is also practically impossible). She promised to call me tomorrow morning, after we had gotten some information on the subject.

After this, about 11:00 o'clock, my folks got back from the country. As I predicted, they said it would be all right, but they don't like the idea of my going by plane at all! (As a matter of fact, I wouldn't mind too much if we weren't able to get reservations by plane—I'm awfully afraid of them. I confess this to you alone, so please don't laugh at my fears.) However, Jeannette flew out to Frisco last year to see Al, and she made a wonderful trip in 16 hours without even being put off. But today, with all the traffic to the Pacific, I fear we're going to find it most difficult either way.

This one trip required a huge amount of arranging and effort. It illustrates some of the difficulties that communication in the 1940s presented, but that they accepted as standard.

July 18, 1945
Les Dear,

I spent all day today making preparations and trying for reservations for Jeannette and myself, and changing the time of our going to a week later, almost the original date.

For I received your letter of July 10th today (I believe you wrote it on the 11th but made a mistake in typing the date) in which you told me to disregard the note you had written me earlier telling me to come out on the 26th of July. Instead, you now write to come out of the 2nd or 3rd of August. Whew! I don't know whether I'm coming or going or circling around. At any rate, as soon as I got this latest letter, I telegraphed the Chancellor Hotel, telling them to disregard my previous telegrams, and to now reserve two rooms for the week beginning Aug. 2nd instead. (I still haven't received any confirmation from them regarding my first telegram anyway.) I called Pearl next, but she told me she would be unable to get me plane seats, as her contact with the airport had been drafted recently. Then I called up a few baby nurses that had been recommended to me, but they were all too busy to be able to come at that time. At noon, Jeannette Sobel called up, and I informed her of our change of plans for a week-later departure, and told her about what I had accomplished so far. She promised to call the airport and ask now for reservations for July 31 or Aug. 1 while I would try to get train reservations just in case, and send more hotel reservation telegrams (our calls and wires alone are a fortune). (By the way, is all this detail boring you?)

In the afternoon, I got my father and my uncle Arthur busy working to get me train seats. (It's a good thing we'll leave in July, for after Aug. 1, no civilians will be allowed any berths to the coast.) As it is now, we can only reserve berths 5 days in advance. Then we could probably get to Chicago, but from there the Gov't. has taken over all Pullmans, and we would have to wait around until they release the few they do. It's a terrible risk, but the thought of possibly standing in a coach from here to Frisco is killing.

> *Then I called Jeannette, and she informed me of one point in our favor, however. She'd called up TWA and been able to get us 2 seats for July 31, leaving at 10:00 P.M. We'll get official confirmation tomorrow. However, these seats are only to Kansas City, from there we have to wait for seats on any available plane, or take the train (coach) from there to Frisco.*

> *And so there rests of our plans for tonight. At least we'll get as far as Kansas City. All this mass of details and restrictions, when all I would love to do would be to fly to you on my magic carpet. I'm pretty much worn out from all the excitement and the continuous shifting of plans.*

Unfortunately, all good things must end, and Shirley is now on her way home after the two-week rendezvous with Les in San Francisco. She is quite sad, but she manages to maintain her habit of description for Lester.

> *August 20, 1945*
> *Darling,*

> *As you can see from my writing, I'm having a hard time trying to make this at all legible. The train is lumping along in its own merry way, oblivious of the fact that I want to write. There's no desk in the club car, and no ink or stationary. I'm writing this now, with a borrowed pen. When we get to Salt Lake City, I'll try to buy a bottle of ink, and mail this off to you.*

> *Yesterday's trip up to Los Angeles was uneventful, except for my miserable feeling of desolation at leaving you. Darling, I'm so lonesome for you already, how can I possibly bear a separation of months?*

> *I went straight to Helen's house yesterday and spent the afternoon with her. We went for a ride up in the hills, and I finally saw the Hollywood bowl, also the outsides of a few movie studios. Helen drove me to the station in plenty of time to catch my train. I left my hat in her car, but it doesn't matter as I was going to get rid of it anyway.*

> *So here it is, another day. You must be in San Francisco by now, sweets. I wish that I could be with you. It would be my rotten luck*

to have the ship stay there for weeks, during which time we could have been together. But I hope, at least, that you will be able to come home on leave, if the ship is in Frisco for any length of time.

It's you I'm so crazy about. I love you so very much, sweetheart. Thank you for these two lovely weeks and for being as marvelous as you are.

I'll close now, dear. I'll try to write every day, even if you won't be able to read this horrible writing.

All my love to you.

August 21, 1945
Darling,

The longest part of the trip is now over—just another day and night, and I'll be home. However, I have hardly any of the enthusiasm at the prospect of journey's end that I had on the trip out to the coast. You've made that my home—isn't that supposed to be where the heart is? Only the thought of Jeff is making me at all eager to get back.

Darling, in this vast country of ours, what luck I had in meeting you. It was a kindly fate, or chance, whichever way you look at it.

These past two weeks occupied me for fully an hour. They were so wonderful. In a way, they were a closing episode to our carefree marriage. It will be most improbable that we will be together like that again, unhampered by children or the office. But it would be lovely, if we could slip away like that, once in a while, by ourselves. So let's drink a toast, to the mad Halbreichs, long may they reign insane—and absurdly happy.

Sweets, this motion of the train is really getting impossible. Now, I can scarcely make out my own writing.

So goodnight, my darling. I wish I could be with you. And I keep hoping, as ridiculous as it may be, that when you call me Thursday evening, you'll be able to tell me you received your orders—and will be home soon. Is it too much to hope for? Like the fool I am —and always will—hope for the seemingly impossible.

I love you, and even more than that!

27

DREAMS OF THE FUTURE

IN THE MIDDLE OF his time at sea, Lester was adapting to bachelor life and attempting to control his emotional reactions to it, while working his normal hours in the dental clinic, and performing his other duties. This took all of his time and energy, and he did not allow himself the luxury of looking ahead to life after the war. Thinking along those lines might have been more painful than comforting. As a result, he never discussed the future in his early letters.

This defensive strategy began to fail, however, in the last months of Les's time at sea, as the prospect of going home emerged as a real possibility. Lester's guardedness seemed to drop as his enthusiasm grew, and his thoughts raced along different paths. Suddenly, he was bursting with ideas about what to do after the navy; they kept bubbling out of him.

One minute Les was writing to Shirley about how wonderful it would be to move to a small town in upstate New York. He would enumerate the reasons why country life was superior to life in Brooklyn or Manhattan, as they had been planning. They could build a guest house to allow their parents to visit regularly, he argued, hoping to sweep aside Shirley's main objection before she even voiced it.

In another letter Les discussed traveling to Europe for awhile before settling down. Other letters would find him proposing that they spend time in South America, with Lester working there as a dentist, or maybe working in Manhattan rather than Brooklyn, or Brooklyn rather than Manhattan, or an entirely different location altogether, such as California. Shirley must have been confused by this cascade of ideas, and she must have wondered what had happened to her staid, responsible husband.

As fate would later dictate, none of these romantic post-war idylls came to pass. But that is almost beside the point. In these free-flowing and exuberant thoughts, Les's depression was evaporating. Believing that he could actually be home soon, he allowed his imagination free rein. These letters are a delight to read.

Les's first thoughts about his post-naval life, many months before it actually happened, remained vague, but his impulse was to live close to home. He did, however, want an initial period of time to be alone with Shirley before reuniting with the rest of the family.

> *January 17, 1945*
> *...I am thinking of our plans when I get back, in a nebulous sort of way. I understand that the bureau may listen to one's request for a location when returning from overseas. I thought that Floyd Bennett would be a good billet. How about you? Frankly, I am not particularly interested in travel and believe that, if they will let us stay close to home, we will be best off. I am decided on one thing, though. I want to meet you first away from the rest of the family, and with you spend two weeks, at least, before returning home. My thoughts run to a vacation at Banff or Mexico City; but my heart is set on nothing but a period of time with you alone and only you.*

Lester's thoughts quickly develop and range all over New York State. Beyond the issue of which New York City locality to choose, Lester suddenly suggests living in an upstate city, backing it up with facts and adding the added possibility of buying a farm. Some of Lester's happiest college memories had been of summers spent working on farms around Cornell, so that this dream did not appear out of the blue.

> *January 25, 1945*
> *... Have you been thinking at all about our post-war plans? Where shall we go? What shall we do? Shall we stay in Manhattan, Brooklyn? Shall I practice in the city, and should we move out on the Island, or Queens, or the other suburbs? Or shall we, do you*

think, move altogether to some smaller community, Buffalo, or Albany for instance? Shall we endeavor, do you think, to try to get a small bit of acreage with a house on it? What do you want to do? What do you want to save for? Do you have any possible locations selected if we stay in the city? If we should decide to get out, where would you prefer to go? I think of those things often, and I know they are hard to write about and will not be what we decide to do. But we might at least make some tentative plans. The question of staying in New York or moving out of it is one that has been plaguing me for a long time now. There is much to be said on both sides, of course. The one thing about New York that mitigates against it is the expense of living there. Rent expense and food expense are much higher than they are in a smaller community, and it seems that the fees and resulting income are not proportionately high. In other words, you work harder for less money. I have been playing with this idea for a long time. It is probably very impractical, and of course out here there are no figures to back me up; but you might talk it over with your dad, and my dad, and see what they think of it, and I'd like you to elaborate on it, too. How would it be, do you think, to be located in some metropolis like Rochester, Buffalo, Albany, Troy? We could afford a house from the beginning (and I think we both prefer to live in a house rather than an apartment), if we had enough money at the beginning, or if not we could save it later. We could buy ourselves a small farm, say 25 or 35 acres, or less. We could plan to live on that farm summers, at least, and eventually possibly build there for permanent residence. This is what I base the thought on. After this war, there is going to be an intensification of already existing competition in New York. Add to that the inevitable disturbing factor of reconversion and the task of discharging some millions of men back to civilian life, plus the recollection of what happened in the last war (after, I mean), the depression of the early twenties, and the inflation that followed on its heels; and I think that we may safely anticipate a similar period. I realize that the powers that be are planning to ease the shock, but that I believe is the best they can do—"ease the shock," not eliminate it. A depression or bad times are always worst in a place like New York. Inflation or deflation are both countered best from a small farm. I

suggest the places I did because I know them to be small but sufficiently large, clean, and progressive communities. I believe that, in
a place like that, a man would have as good an opportunity as in
NewYork. Consider also the advantages. Let us compare it with a
Manhattan practice. Rent for a good location in Manhattan is
bound to be at least 85 to 100 dollars for the office. That doesn't
include the rent for the home. For that sum you could get either
one of the finest locations available in one of these other places, or
else pay the rent of both home and office. I believe, too, that for Jeff
it would be better to live in such a small community rather New
York (although I am not altogether sure about that), especially if
he had this small farm to spend some time at.

Of course, living in NewYork City has many advantages; but I
believe that with transport as cheap and efficient as it will be after
the war, those advantages will be almost as easily available to out-
of-towners. Indeed for those who come in for a couple of weeks a
year, they may be more easily obtained. You know what I mean by
that.

Let us consider the idea of the farm. I do not suggest that we
live on the farm, although that is within the realm of possibility.
The country in many regions of New York State is good farming
country. I suggest that we should or could buy say twenty-five acres
or fifty acres of good land and arrange to farm it on shares. That
is, have a farmer work it for us and take his payment out of the income it produces. If we lived nearby, I'm sure we could save much
money on meat, butter, eggs, and other foodstuffs, particularly with
the advent of new cold storage and refrigeration. We might also put
up, or have on it already, a good enough building to act as a summer
cottage. We could spend some time there summers. I know that it
would be invaluable for Jeff to have some of that experience as his
background. We wouldn't even have to make money on the farm. If
we broke even on it, or even lost a little on it, it would still pay for
us to have it as a refuge in time of emergency. And no one can pre-
dict when such a time will arrive. There is more to it than that, of
course. For instance, consider this. Both our parents are not getting
younger. I know your dad's ideas about a farm, and I know my
folks', but I can't vouch for Rosie. Assuming she would not be dis-

*agreeable, however, can you see how they, too, could spend their sum-
mers there? It might even be that your dad or my dad, or both,
might want to get out of the city altogether. I don't say that they
would, or should, become farmers, but there is no reason why they
shouldn't become supervisors, and then there is every chance for the
place to pay. At any rate, my darling, that is how I've been thinking
in my sketchy way. What do you think about it?*

Good night for now my darling. Write soon.

Lester dreams about having a house built.

February 5, 1945

*. . . Miller acts as an engineer on board, but his real interest is
in architecture. He seems to be talented and to have some good
ideas. I think I mentioned to you that I saw the plans he is working
on for his own house in California. He has something very elaborate
and spacious in mind calling for a swimming pool and needing
about four acres of ground to set off. The house really is a beauty,
and I admired it very much. I am after him to draw a set of plans,
on a more modest scale, for us. He promised that, if he had enough
time this voyage, he would work on something for me. So come on,
send me your ideas of your future home. Tell me what style you prefer and how you'd like it built, etc., and maybe we will have a dream
house someday. It is fun to think about and will be even more so if
we have something real to exercise our imagination on.*

Lester soon saw his idea of life in upstate New York as a fantasy and concentrated on buying a house somewhere in the New York City area.

February 8, 1945

*. . . I am thinking that if, when I get back ashore, the navy
does give me duty in the New York area, it will probably be very
practical for us to buy an inexpensive (ha, ha) home. And along
those lines I let my imagination run free. I say "buy" because,
doubtless at the conclusion of this war (as at the end of the last),
there is bound to be a housing shortage. Rents are expensive (and
will be more so later, when everyone will be looking for homes).*

*By owning our own home, we will not only be making a great sav-
ing on rent, but at the end of a period of time, for the same outlay
of money that even a moderate-priced apartment would have cost,
we will own our house. Our first house needn't be the one to end
all houses, but it can be a good comfortable place to stay and
weather the post-war storm. In about ten years we will be able to
think of building our dream house. The house that will incorpo-
rate in itself exactly what we want. At that time such a plan will
be very feasible, while for immediate post-war realization the plan
is visionary. (Visionary too, I am sure, is my little idyll about life
in a small upstate town . . . but one can't help thinking about
such things.) I would appreciate your ideas, and your dad's, and
my dad's, on such subjects. I know your father has ideas. If he
will put them down on paper in a letter to me, I would be glad to
discuss them with him, for instance, as a modifier for the desirability of that idea. I note that, in the Sunday Times, the City of
New York and the Metropolitan Life Insurance Company are buying blocks of land along the East River to construct low- and mid-
dle-cost housing units on, such units to rent for something like
14 dollars a room. How do they, and you, think that affects the
desirability of owning your own home? My dad, I know, is not
too convinced about the desirability of owning your own home
because of his sad experience in Montgomery Street, but exactly
why I do not know, and it is true too that that house was a two-
family job (I have a one-family house in mind) and it was bought
in the years soon after the end of the last war, in the boom years
to be exact (exactly what I am trying to avoid now).*

*If I should be fortunate enough to get duty in the New York
area (and I have hunch that I might), I toy with the idea of buying
on Long Island in one of the more prosperous communities and living there. That time could be used to get known. After all, it is possible to combine a midtown practice with a dash of local practice,
particularly at first.*

*If the idea sounds good to you, you people in your drives (are
you still driving?) might note possible desirable locations, or spots.
I do not suggest buying yet (although even that might not be bad).
I am not sure who to write to (your dad would know or could find*

out) to find out the direction of population and community trends in the New York Area. I believe I shall write to SS White and Ritter, and also to the City of New York Chamber of Commerce, perhaps to the Port Authority, for statistics and information. You might map it from your end.

As far as financing the deal is concerned: We have and will have some money, but I don't believe we would have to touch it. The Federal Gov't will guarantee loans of a sufficient amount for us to swing the deal, and if New York follows New Jersey (which is likely), she too will back us up. As for furniture: It will probably get a lot worse before it gets better. By judicious and conservative buying, we can probably do very nicely and fairly economically for ourselves. Does all this sound like prattle to you? Are you laughing at me? I hope not, for I am very serious. Unfortunately, all the foregoing is based on ideas. I haven't the vaguest ideas of prices and no way to find out soon but I shall.

And that, my darling wife, brings us up to today, a day nearer home. A day when these thin schemes of mine and yours can be turned into reality; and above all, a day when we two shall be one more together again.

Lester is soon asking Shirley whether, besides New York City, she might like to live in California.

April 2, 1945

. . . At routine G.Q. I spoke with Dr. True about the lovely thought of orders home. He, too, says that on returning from overseas I am likely to get a duty I prefer as to location (at least to the extent of getting it in the naval district). He says it is possible to get almost anything you want by dropping in on the department while in Washington. I don't know whether or not it is that good, but in the event that they do grant me my choice, I want to be prepared for them. What would you prefer? Do you want to stay in New York, or do you want to see some other part of the country? I'm not sure what is best. From out here it seems that Metropolitan New York (or one of the hospitals out on Long Island) is the best bet. I don't believe the housing shortage is as acute in New York as it is

elsewhere in the country. There is no place like New York for things to do and places to go. We wouldn't need a car. We would be with the folks again. Besides New York I had considered duty at the naval lighter-than-air school at Lakehurst New Jersey. After that, some-place around San Diego or Los Angeles, CA (one of the airfields). I had also thought of requesting duty at a naval College (Cornell, etc.). So write and tell me what you want and why.

Shirley had written to Lester about a plan his cousins had to open a fancy Park Avenue practice that could include him.

May 1, 1945

  ...About that practice deal, very few friends will do anything about establishing anyone in practice. I'm not counting on that at all. What I am counting on, I hope, is the ability to inspire in my future patients the same degree of confidence I have inspired in the personnel aboard this ship, both officers and men. If I can carry this over to a civil practice, I'm sure we'll have nothing to worry about. I say this, not to boast, but I have never been the subject of such fulsome praise from so many different people. Some of the men have gone out of their way to see that the good word about me has been spread. It is the one thing I am very proud of. So far as Eliot and Leo are concerned, the idea sounds very lovely, but the end of the war is still not here, and I cannot easily see how anyone can foretell conditions at that time. I would be more impressed with the idea if Ellie had a Park Avenue practice to go back to. Unfortu-nately, he doesn't. It will be a case of two, instead of one, trying to break into the neighborhood. Just idly thinking along those lines leads me to doubt the advisability of a practice of that nature. I think that it would tend to throw one into too close contact with people who have essentially a false set of values. Thus, while it might (and it is by no means certain it would) lead to a more luxurious sort of life, I think the luxuries are all too likely to be paid for by a sacrifice of familial happiness. Nothing is worth that. I want enough money to give us the necessities and the essentials to a gra-cious and pleasant life. More money than that is likely to be a li-ability in the long run. First in life I want to live happily with you

my darling, and with our children. Nothing must interfere with that. I love you and miss you so.

Ambitious plans for their reunion began to take on some concrete reality. Lester and Shirley both hoped for some time alone before being surrounded by family:

May 12, 1945

. . . Churl darling, I want you to take that current favorite dream of yours and work on it and plan for it so that when it does become a reality we will have a beautiful week or two together alone before we have to come back to the world of everyday. Suppose we delegate the authority for our post-war honeymoon planning to you. You decide the place (and its alternatives, depending on the season), what clothes you will need, estimate the expenses, earmark a small amount regularly for it. Then, when that magic day does finally arrive, all you will have to do when I call you when I hit the States is tell me where to meet you. We'll have our time alone together, and then we can return to the others. I want you to plan everything exactly as you want it. How does that sound? Then, instead of a merely nebulous dream we will have a happy reality.

June 20, 1945

. . . Darling, your idea coincides exactly with mine in the matter of this homecoming. I think, too, that my folks will understand that I want to meet you alone first. The idea, as described in your later letter, is a good one, though. What they don't know won't hurt them. It probably is best to do something like that. And I've said before that we should take two weeks together somewhere. That part of it, I leave to you. We shall go and do whatever you like. I don't care what it is as long as we are together. After that, I'll be better prepared to go home to people, and to meet my son. Let's do it that way, darling. When I get to the coast I can phone you, let you know when I'll get to New York. We can tell the folks it will be a few days later. In the meantime you can get a room at a hotel, and I can go directly to the hotel, stay with you for a few days, then call the folks,

spend a day with them, then run off with you. How does that sound?
You elaborate on that idea will you sweetheart.

With time on his hands, Lester's post-war thoughts began to wander far.

July 15, 1945
. . . I've had another brainstorm, but one you might want to
think over for post-war usage. It revolves around the scholarship
features of the G.I. bill of rights. You know you get tuition paid,
and 75 bucks a month for living expenses if you are married. I will
probably take a refresher course in dentistry, but I have been playing
with the idea of enrolling at some foreign university, say the Sor-
bonne, Edinburgh, Heidelberg, Mexico, who knows, and using the
75 bucks as expense money. The immediate post-war period may
well be our last opportunity for any extensive globe-trotting, similar
to the time when you get out of college and you say, "Well, before
settling down, I'm going to get a job on a steamer and see the world."
God knows, I've had a bellyful of ocean travel, but it would be fun
after this is over to go traveling en famille, in Europe or Mexico,
or South America. Everything will be in a terrible state of flux im-
mediately after the end of the war, and it may well be the wisest
thing to do. At any rate, it is a nice idea to play with, don't you
think?

As his discharge crept closer, Lester's dreams were turned toward everyday reality.

September 5, 1945
. . .What I am writing now to say is about the chance for the
apartment of Flo's. I think that, if you like it and are satisfied, you
ought to take it. I was going to suggest that you look around now.
I have been reading about how scarce apartments are in New York,
and I say take what you can. We really do need a place to live in
now. I suppose four rooms is more than we need (or is it?) At any
rate, I say take it.

Post-war real estate issues intruded as well.

October 3, 1945

. . . I read another one of those articles about the housing situation in a Colliers yesterday. It is a hell of a situation, and the worst part of it seems to be that it will last about 10 years. In the meantime, you and I and people like us are going to take a hell of a shellacking. Prices for buying and building seem to be up 20 to 40%, and rents of course are correspondingly high. The best advice seems to be not to buy or build now. But it is just as difficult to rent, and a family has to live somewhere, don't they? How does the problem appear to you on the home front? From this far away it doesn't look very good.

Lester still had dreams, and they turned south—far south.

October 9, 1945

. . . Ralph and I were talking of the housing problem again the other night. How about giving me a summary of what it is like in N.Y. right now. What prospects have we of getting a place when the time comes? Do you think that it will pay to buy or build now in spite of the higher costs, in view of the tremendously high rents that seem to prevail?

I was speaking to Mr. Cunningham the other night. He is one of our passenger naval officers, who will be in charge of the telegraphic censorship in the Nagoya area. Before the war he spent quite some time in Buenos Aires, and quite innocently (he anticipated any question) he mentioned the large incomes earned by some dentists he knew there, and, he was careful to add, with a proportionately small expenditure of time and energy. I can't help toying with the idea of going there myself to see if all of these stories of Rio de Janeiro or the other South American cities are true. If there was a definitely favorable exchange, I think it might do to spend a few months there investigating the situation. It certainly wouldn't be lost time, because it would be an interesting trip (indeed, if the exchange values were favorable, we might even save a good deal of money by staying there for a while). How does that proposal sound to you? Wild and harebrained, I suppose. Well, these long days on board ship probably makes much nonsense seem sensible. But give it some thought and let me know your opinion.

Lester nevertheless continued to defend this latest idea.

October 14, 1945

... *Darling, do you mind my talking about the South American idea? I know it's silly, but at the same time it may not be so silly. You know that, under the educational provisions of the GI Bill, I could arrange to take courses at a university there (which the gov't would pay for) and, as a married man, get paid 80 dollars a month. Whether I took courses actually or not would matter very little. The eighty dollars would pay for our rent at a rather nice place and the services of a maid or two. There is at least this much to be said for the idea. If we ever plan to take a trip like that (for the sake of the trip alone), this will probably be our last opportunity before I am trammeled with the ties of an established practice and whatever other responsibilities the approaching years will bring. It is true too that there is a terrific amount of inflation in the States, especially N.Y., right now. I am not such a fool as to believe that inflation doesn't exist down there too, but I do believe that it is relatively less and now that the war is over will decrease much faster than it will at home. And if that is so the cost of such a trip would be less than it is ever again likely to be. Not only that, by my working there for a time, as I could do either in dentistry or some other connection, we would probably even be able to save a respectable amount of money. Frankly, I am rather intrigued with the idea. After all, places like Rio de Janeiro, Buenos Aires, or Montevideo are as cosmopolitan as any city in the world. I know that I am at all times prone to go to extremes in my enthusiasms, and I know you know it, but even allowing for that I still think the idea is a good one. At any rate, I think I'll write to my dental association for information as to licensing requirements, and to the state department for more detailed information, while in the meantime, if I get enough energy, I'll break out Ralph's Spanish books and review a little. If you are interested in it, you might conduct inquiries on your own. If not ... not. At any rate let me know your considered opinion.*

Lester began to calculate the cost of setting up his dental office, too—

even with navy discounts.

> *October 26, 1945*
> *... Today was field day, and as usual I had no patients. But I put in a very busy day, nevertheless. About ten o'clock this morning, I was looking through the Dental supply catalog when it occurred to me that it might be a good idea to estimate the cost of setting up an office based on the prices given in the navy supply catalog. These prices are much lower than those offered to the average dentist, but it's possible that I will be able to procure many of the items through the surplus commodities board.*

> *October 27, 1945*
> *When one of my patients failed to show up, I brought an adding machine into the office, and we added up the items that we listed yesterday. The total comes to $2,632.00. Of course, as I said last night, it isn't an accurate reflection of what we will spend because I already have much of the material listed, and some of it is super-fluous. On the other hand, the prices quoted are almost invariably much cheaper than those quoted to the individual dentist, and the figure doesn't include some other items such as waiting room fur-niture, laboratory bench, and so forth. If I'm able to buy from the navy, it will certainly pay to do so, especially on the few big items such as chair, cabinet, unit, and x-ray. I'm sending a copy of the requisition for your interest.*

Shirley, though she was not on board the ship, was also having many thoughts about their life after Lester's discharge. She did not respond en-thusiastically to Lester's idea of living upstate and having a farm, nor did she like the idea of their parents under the same roof with them.

> *February 8, 1945*
> *... Speaking of post war plans, I, too, have been doing quite a bit of dreaming. And I too am as undecided. A small town vs. New York shall be the question. But you and I know our roots are too firmly embedded in this city to ever be able to move too far away. All you say about the fierce competition there will be here, I know*

is true. I thought perhaps we could live in a suburb of New York, and practice in the city, and (or) in the suburbs. Frankly, darling, having a farm run by someone else is a lovely but expensive dream. Perhaps someday, but not too rustic, please! I never did fancy canning and preserving. As to the two families getting together in one farm—well!

But it is nice to dream and plan. I'm so eager for our life together, however vague its practical aspects are. I just know that we can build it just as beautifully, no matter where we may eventually settle. A few good friends, a comfortable existence, the ways and means to get to the theater and out occasionally—all these will make our home, no matter where it may be. And you—you will make my life.

You know, darling, speaking of buying a farm and settling somewhere upstate, you remember Phil Levin had that idea. However, now, he has decided to stay where he is. (He says the daughter of the mayor of the town where he was planning on settling warned him there is too much anti-Semitism there, and too small a Jewish population to support him. This, too, must be taken into consideration.)

It's an interesting topic; I'd like to discuss it more with you.

Shirley's last letters to Lester often focused on the difficult post-war real-estate market.

October 5, 1945

. . .Yes, my sweet, we are still homeless, but definitely. New York has the worst housing crisis in its history, and in this shortage I am trying vainly for an apartment. I have spoken to the superintendents of practically all the houses around here (the customary procedure is to offer them gelt [money] for an apartment, which I have done, but to no avail. The folks wouldn't let me take Flo's apartment and live so far away with the baby, and no phone. (For their foresight, I am most grateful.) As it has turned out, Flo has decided to keep the apartment anyway instead of moving to Jersey with her mother. The only way to get a place is by sheer luck, by knowing someone who is moving out and subletting, or by pull. People simply aren't

moving, for they've no place to move to. They expect it to be this way for the next year, at least. All I can do is keep my fingers crossed and pray. I have a couple of leads, and that is all. They most probably won't work out.

October 17, 1945

. . .We're still very much homeless. I was told to call up the Hotel Commodore, Officer's Headquarters, for help. However, I was told that they have no prospects for months to come; in fact they are sending out desperate appeals for apartments through the newspapers, and various channels, but they've had scarcely any luck. I can't wait to get in my own apartment—hope by some miracle we can get one anywhere.

Shirley and Lester's dreams diverged when it came to living in foreign lands, despite the real estate problems.

October 29, 1945

. . .About South America, darling, I'd go with you anywhere. However, I don't think that the Southern Americas are quite the paradise they've been pictured to be, at least not at the present. There's a lot of internal fighting going on down there, and prices are not that low—we could never live there on $80 a month with a child. And we now have Jeff to consider, whether or not he would thrive in a new climate. It's not the two of us anymore, sweets, carefree and irresponsible—we have a baby to think of. The thought of a trip to the Latin countries fascinates me, but could it be in the realm of a possibility to us? I don't think so. The sooner you start your practice, the better. Do you agree or not? We'll talk about it when you come home.

28

EPILOGUE

A LL THINGS COME TO an end, and eventually so did both theatres of World War II, the European in May 1945, and the Pacific a few months later, in August. The great American armed forces, which had so rapidly built up in size to fight that multi-front war, now had to disgorge its fighting men back to the civilian lives of which they had so long dreamed. This did not happen overnight, of course, nor on the exact date of the war's end. For those overseas, obligations of service continued, in some cases for several more months, until they met the requirements for discharge from their branch of service. Indeed, the military had ongoing needs for men to fill post-war occupation and pacification duties. It was a complex time of competing expectations, for going home and of remaining in, that gave rise to frustrations on both sides, as the servicemen and military authorities slowly figured it out.

This was true for Lester, as we have just seen. Soon after V-E Day he began his calculations about when he might expect his discharge, although the United States was still very much at war with Japan. Yet, even after V-J Day in August, he remained on active duty. The *Oxford* returned from its refit in California, sailing to various Pacific islands until finally steaming into Tokyo Bay itself. Lester was not eligible for discharge until November of that year, as the *Oxford* made another trip back to California, three months after the war's end.

Lester and Shirley's letters abruptly end at that point; once they were no longer separated they had no further need to communicate by mail. We have no record of how they each felt about their reunion; we can only rely on our own imaginations, inspired by what we have come to know of this young couple during their trying time apart.

Beyond the obvious—making up for lost time—Les began to get to know his son, with Shirley's help. While Jeffrey was only fifteen months old when his father returned home, Lester later came to believe that this early deprivation had taken a major toll on Jeff and on how his life unfolded.

There was a severe housing shortage as the war ended, just as they had feared, due to the thousands of military men being discharged and attempting to set up homes. Shirley had written about the difficulty of finding an apartment for the two of them. In fact, they continued to live with her parents until they finally found their own small place in Brooklyn a year or two later. Finally, Les was able to begin his long-delayed professional life, opening a practice on Eastern Parkway in Brooklyn, and the young family prospered through the remainder of the 1940s. Their only regret was the absence of more children, but Shirley had been told years before that a severely tipped uterus would prevent any pregnancy at all. By giving birth to Jeffrey, she had already defied those odds.

As the 1940s were drawing to a close, Lester and Shirley moved into a large apartment complex in Manhattan named for New York's first English governor, Peter Stuyvesant. They lived in Stuyvesant Town while Lester commuted to his Brooklyn practice.

The spring of 1949 brought a major surprise; Shirley discovered that she was pregnant, defying the odds for a second time. She gave birth to their daughter, Terri Beth, the following winter, on February 24, 1950. The family now included a newborn as well as a boy in kindergarten, who was almost six years old.

Shortly thereafter, war again entered their lives in the form of the Korean Conflict. Lester had remained in the naval reserve, which he had joined during his days in the Cornell naval ROTC. His early call to duty for World War II had been both expected and desired; he would have volunteered had he not already been in the reserves.

But nobody anticipated a second call to duty. By then, Lester was thirty-three years old and the father of two young children with a thriving dental practice. The navy only called up six dentists at this time. They also sent Les only to Boston. He wondered why the navy could not have called up a younger dentist, possibly one already living near Boston, rather than him.

The one positive aspect of this time was that being stationed on the East Coast allowed Les to come home each weekend to see his family.

After this second service in the military, Shirley had had enough and insisted that he resign from the reserves, even though he was just a few years short of the twenty years that would have brought them the benefits of a naval retirement. So Shirley and Les suffered through the obligations of service in the naval reserves without reaping any of the rewards. He left the navy with the rank of lieutenant commander.

Two years after Terri's birth, the family left Brooklyn and Manhattan for the suburbs in northeastern Queens. They bought their first house and converted the garage into Lester's office. The area was being built up for the post-war boom of young families, and there were two very large developments of garden apartments that promised a source of new patients for Lester's practice.

And these new patients came, enabling the practice to grow quite well. He hired a receptionist who worked for him for many years, and his practice expanded into the neighboring towns as well. Les later said that the one irritating aspect of his practice was his ongoing difficulty in collecting the fees that his patients owed him, but he took classes over the years to try to learn better management skills.

Shirley defied the conception odds a third time when she gave birth to a second son, David Martin, on July 24, 1958, although the six- and nine-year differences between the children do attest to her difficulty in conceiving. By this time, Jeffrey was fourteen, and Terri was turning nine.

Overall, the years following World War II through the late 1960s were very stable and happy ones for the family. Les and Shirley had a solid marriage, they made many friends, the practice did sufficiently well, their own parents remained in good health, and their children grew up in a warm and nurturing home.

There was one shadow that marred these years, however. In 1952, about two years after Terri's birth, Shirley had undergone tests for some neurological complaints and was diagnosed with multiple sclerosis (MS). The doctors had informed Lester of the diagnosis, but they had agreed to keep this from Shirley, continuing this protective secret-keeping for many years. Five years later, when Shirley was pregnant with David, her doctor had even considered and applied for a medical abortion due to the dangerous effects of pregnancy for MS patients, although that never came to pass (and the reason was never explained to Shirley).

Since pregnancy does worsen the symptoms of MS, often one to two years later, the date of the original diagnosis, 1952, was significant, as Shirley had given birth to Terri two years before. Also significant were Shirley's symptoms after Jeffrey was born: her fatigue, her back pain, and her difficulty wearing high-heeled shoes. Her physician had diagnosed "war nerves" at the time, but they were probably early signs of the disease that the pregnancy had worsened.

After David's birth, Lester had a family room added to the house so that Shirley could have a changing table and playroom for the baby on the main floor, eliminating the need to use the stairs all day, which would physically tire her and is not advised for people with MS.

By 1961 and the celebration of their twentieth anniversary, Shirley had learned that she had MS. She could no longer wear high-heeled shoes at all and so wore flats to that party. At that time, it was the only observable manifestation of the disease.

Les and Shirley were willing to try many treatments for MS, but at that time there were not many known treatment options. In 1964 Shirley went into the hospital for three weeks of spinal injections and treatments in a hyperbaric oxygen chamber, to no avail. Les began a regimen of body-building exercises to increase his strength, as he thought that he would one day be caring for a disabled wife. Throughout this time, the children were not told of their mother's MS, and life was kept as normal as possible.

Shirley's form of MS did not relapse and remit, as is more common. She was able to maintain good functioning for many years. Thus, Les and Shirley's first twenty-six years of marriage were generally productive and happy ones, except for their war separation and the MS diagnosis. However, on June 1, 1967 that all changed quite dramatically and tragically.

Early that morning the telephone rang. It was Jeff's wife, Judy (Jeffrey had graduated from high school in 1961 and entered Cornell's School of Industrial and Labor Relations, where he met Judy. They married upon graduation, in June 1965, and Jeff entered law school at New York University). Judy reported that Jeff had had an accident. Lester immediately left for their apartment to help, and Shirley called Judy to tell her this, but the phone was answered by a policeman, who told her, "I'm sorry, ma'am. Your son is dead." That ended their normal world.

The immediate cause of death was strangulation from hanging and the death was ruled a suicide, but that had never seemed right to those who knew Jeff, since there were no warning signs. It remained an unresolved question until years later, when Terri learned about autoerotic asphyxiation, which seemed to best explain the circumstances.

The funeral was held the next day, according to Jewish law, with hundreds of people in attendance and also during the period of Jewish mourning known as *shiva*.

Jeffrey's death occurred as Terri was about to graduate from high school and then start college in the fall. On her first weekend home, she learned that her mother could not get out of bed, and that in fact she had MS. Shirley did recover and walk again, but the death of her son was a catastrophic emotional stressor that exacerbated her disease in that very dramatic manner.

David, then age nine, was felt to be too young to understand what was happening and did not attend the funeral. The rest of his childhood, unlike that of his older siblings, was spent with parents who were grieving the loss of their older son and whose mother now became progressively more handicapped.

Les's dental practice suffered during this time and eventually fell apart. He continued to work, but no longer primarily at his office next to the house. He had to find work elsewhere and opened various offices in different parts of Brooklyn, Queens, and Nassau as he continued to try to earn a living. He eventually retired in 1982, at age sixty-five.

Slowly, after Jeff's death, Shirley and Lester began to recover their equilibrium. They were still the parents of two other children, one of whom was young and living at home. They resumed their social and family lives and, once past the initial trauma, carried on. Once Lester retired, they sold the house in Queens and moved to a retirement community in central New Jersey, near Terri, where they lived for the next seven years.

David had graduated from high school in 1976 and from college in 1980, going on to law school right after that, graduating in 1983. He had first worked in Washington, DC, and then in San Francisco, where he soon met his first wife, Rebecca, and they married in 1989. They had three children, Emily, born in 1991; Eli, born in 1994; and Bailey, who came in with the new millennium, in January 2000. The marriage ended in divorce a few years later, and David has since remarried.

Lester's father, Charles, passed away in 1974, at about age ninety; his mother, Esther, living on until 1982, to about the same age. After Charlie's death, Les and his sister, Roslyn, moved their mother into an apartment much closer to them, just a few miles from Les and Shirley. It was from that apartment that Essie hitchhiked, with a jar of chicken soup under her arm, to Les and Shirley's house to take care of her grandson, David, when she discovered that he was home, alone and sick, and this happened while she herself was still convalescing from a broken hip.

Sam and Rose died within a few months of each other, in 1987, at the ages of ninety-one and eighty-six, respectively. It can surely be said that Lester and Shirley came from long-lived stock.

Despite recovering from the initial trauma of Jeffrey's death, the 1970s saw the slow domination of the MS over Shirley's and Lester's lives as she began to inexorably lose functions. What had been held at bay for so long began to win out. The first to go was walking, but in increments and over time. Shirley fought it and even tried to deny it, but her MS was by then relentless. She reacted, at first, by trying to walk less, but then, admitting that she needed assistance, she would hold onto Les, and then graduated to a cane. Eventually, though, came the walker, the wheelchair, the motorized scooter. She bravely kept up her life, however, trying to do as much as possible.

As Shirley's lower limbs lost function, so too did her arms and hands. Objects became harder to hold and routine tasks became harder to accomplish, and more and more had to be done for her. Eventually, by the early 1990s, she reached the point where most things had to be done for her. Even some of her internal organs betrayed her, so that, in her last years, Shirley became a quadriplegic who required constant and total care. Les provided it by himself for as long as he could, but in time it became too difficult for him, and he eventually was forced to bring in help. He never once considered moving Shirley out of the house, and he drastically limited his own time away from home in order to be there for her.

Shirley bore these unrelenting losses with dignity and even humor, becoming, in the process, a hero to her daughter. While others might idealize movie stars or athletes, Terri always saw her mother as the person whom she most admired.

In 1990 Shirley and Lester sold their home in the retirement community, which had never worked out as well as they had hoped, since Shirley's handicaps had kept them from meeting and making many friends. They had managed to make a few, whom they valued greatly, but they had never been able to fully participate in the social life of the community. The only positive aspect of living there was the ability to see their daughter frequently, but that had never been an authentic substitute for friends their own age. Eventually, they moved back to Queens, into an apartment that was close to their original house. This move returned them to their long-term friends and their relatives, all of whom lived in that vicinity. They wanted to see them regularly and to renew those lifelong ties.

Within a few years of their return, though, Shirley was no longer able to enjoy its benefits, as her MS continued to progress, finally attacking her brain and depriving her of reasoning skills and short-term memory, and then even long-term memory. She sometimes could not even recognize her son or daughter during this last, painful stage, although she always was able to recognize her beloved Lester.

Shirley quietly passed away on July 12, 1995, at the age of seventy-two, but she lingered until Terri was able to reach her bedside, and though she was no longer conscious, her blood pressure spiked when Terri took her hand and spoke to her in a nonverbal hello—and goodbye.

After Shirley's death, Les made the decision to move to California to live with David and his family in Los Angeles. However, after about a year, he decided to return to his familiar life in Queens, having discovered that he could not live through his children, no matter how much he loved them. He would be better off with friends his own age, especially those whom he had known for so many decades. Once back in his apartment in Queens, Les dated a woman, but she passed away a year later. He then began to see another woman, Adele, whom he grew very close to, who also lived in his building. He discovered that he was actually happy and living a life free of care-taking responsibilities.

But decades of heavy smoking caught up with Lester just at the start of the millennium, which saw the birth of his third grandchild, Bailey, but which also brought a deep, bloody, persistent cough. In June, the doctors had diagnosed Stage 4 lung cancer, and gave him another twelve to eighteen months to live, but he died just four months later, on October 25, 2000, at the age of eighty-three. He had been planning to spend the coming winter in Florida with Adele, but that was not to be.

Shirley and Lester are buried side by side, along with their first-born son and Lester's parents, in a cemetery in Queens. True to his unique literary skills, Lester had not been satisfied with the typical inscription for Shirley's headstone and had written his own message, imparting just a hint of the depth of his own emotions. Five years later, his daughter attempted to do the same for him.

Lester had written for Shirley, his wife of fifty-three and a half years:

BELOVED WIFE, MOTHER, AND GRANDMOTHER
A gentle woman, with a core of steel,
Who bore her afflictions with grace.
May God grant you the peace you so richly deserve.
April 14, 1923–July 12, 1995
You are in our hearts forever.

Terri wrote on Lester's headstone:

A THOUGHTFUL, MORAL, AND COMPASSIONATE MAN
He had the love of his family, the affection of friends,
And children proud of their father's example.
May God grant eternal peace
For his kind heart and generous nature.

April 7, 1917–October 25, 2000

This was their story.

CPSIA information can be obtained at www.ICGtesting.com
Printed in the USA
BVOW021137010413

316874BV00009B/21/P